MW00914237

ZAGAT®

Washington, DC Baltimore Restaurants
2008

LOCAL EDITORS
Olga Boikess and Marty Katz

STAFF EDITORS
Shelley Gallagher with Donna Marino Wilkins

Published and distributed by
Zagat Survey, LLC
4 Columbus Circle
New York, NY 10019
T: 212.977.6000
E: washbalt@zagat.com
www.zagat.com

ACKNOWLEDGMENTS

We thank Charlie Adler, Chuck Alexander, American Institute of Wine and Food-DC Chapter, Bernice August, Baltimore Foodies, Richard K. Bank, Greg Bland, Mary Ann Brownlow, Capital Alumni Network, Karen Cathey, Jean and Gary Cohen, Lori Edwards, Elaine Eff, Heidi Elswick, Bill, Lorraine and Megan Fitzsimmons, Gail Forman, Alexandra Greeley, Melissa Harris, Henry "Hoppy" Hopkins III, Stuart Jacobs, Barbara Johnson, Michael Karlan, Danny Katz, John Lawrence, Les Dames d'Escoffier-DC, Judy Levenson, Bob Madigan, Natalie Mertes, Nycci Nellis, Jo-Ann Neuhaus, Rebecca Penovich, Catherine Piez, Professionals in the City-DC, Christina Rocha, Dave Sarfaty, Trish Schweers, Donna Shirdon, Steven Shukow and Tastedc.com, with special thanks to Jodi Lannen Brady and Holly Bass for their editorial work, as well as the following members of our staff: Josh Rogers (assistant editor), Rachel McConlogue (assistant editor), Sean Beachell, Maryanne Bertollo, Deirdre Bush, Sandy Cheng, Reni Chin, Larry Cohn, Alison Flick, Jeff Freier, Caroline Hatchett, Roy Jacob, Natalie Lebert, Mike Liao, Dave Makulec, Chris Miragliotta, Andre Pilette, Becky Ruthenburg, Carla Spartos, Kilolo Strobert, Liz Borod Wright, Sharon Yates and Kyle Zolner.

The reviews published in this guide are based on public opinion surveys, with numerical ratings reflecting the average scores given by all survey participants who voted on each establishment and text based on direct quotes from, or fair paraphrasings of, participants' comments. Phone numbers, addresses and other factual information were correct to the best of our knowledge when published in this guide; any subsequent changes may not be reflected.

© 2007 Zagat Survey, LLC
ISBN-13: 978-1-57006-880-5
ISBN-10: 1-57006-880-1
Printed in the
United States of America

Contents

Ratings & Symbols

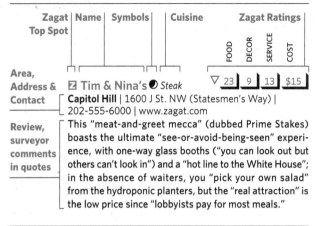

	Zagat Top Spot	Name	Symbols	Cuisine	Zagat Ratings			
					FOOD	DECOR	SERVICE	COST

Area, Address & Contact

☒ **Tim & Nina's** ◕ *Steak*   ▽ 23 | 9 | 13 | $15

Capitol Hill | 1600 J St. NW (Statesmen's Way) | 202-555-6000 | www.zagat.com

Review, surveyor comments in quotes

This "meat-and-greet mecca" (dubbed Prime Stakes) boasts the ultimate "see-or-avoid-being-seen" experience, with one-way glass booths ("you can look out but others can't look in") and a "hot line to the White House"; in the absence of waiters, you "pick your own salad" from the hydroponic planters, but the "real attraction" is the low price since "lobbyists pay for most meals."

Ratings   **Food, Decor** and **Service** are rated on a scale of 0 to 30.

0 – 9   poor to fair

10 – 15   fair to good

16 – 19   good to very good

20 – 25   very good to excellent

26 – 30   extraordinary to perfection

▽   low response | less reliable

Cost reflects our surveyors' average estimate of the price of a dinner with one drink and tip and is a benchmark only. Lunch is usually 25% less.

For **newcomers** or survey **write-ins** listed without ratings, the price range is indicated as follows:

I $25 and below

M $26 to $40

E $41 to $65

VE $66 or more

Symbols   ☒   Zagat Top Spot (highest ratings, popularity and importance)

◕   serves after 11 PM

Ⓢ   closed on Sunday

Ⓜ   closed on Monday

⌿   no credit cards accepted

About This Survey

 This **2008 Washington, DC/Baltimore Restaurants Survey** is an update reflecting significant developments since our last Survey was published. It covers 1,143 restaurants in the Washington, DC/Baltimore area, including 113 important additions. We've also indicated new addresses, phone numbers, chef changes and other major alterations.

WHO PARTICIPATED: Input from 6,714 avid diners forms the basis for the ratings and reviews in this guide (their comments are shown in quotation marks within the reviews). Collectively they bring roughly 1.04 million annual meals worth of experience to this Survey. We sincerely thank each of these participants – this book is really "theirs."

HELPFUL LISTS: Whether you're looking for a celebratory meal, a hot scene or a bargain bite, our lists can help you find exactly the right place. See Washington, DC's, and Baltimore's Most Popular, respectively (pages 9 and 189), Key Newcomers (pages 7 and 189), Top Ratings (pages 10–16 and pages 190–194) and Best Buys (pages 16 and 194). We've also provided 72 handy indexes (pages 151–186 and pages 251–267).

OUR EDITORS: Special thanks go to our local editors for this update, Olga Boikess, a Washington lawyer and avid diner who has edited this Survey since 1987, and Marty Katz, a Baltimore writer, photographer and barbecue researcher who has worked with us since 1995.

ABOUT ZAGAT: This marks our 28th year reporting on the shared experiences of consumers like you. What started in 1979 as a hobby involving 200 of our friends has come a long way. Today we have over 300,000 surveyors and now cover dining, entertaining, golf, hotels, movies, music, nightlife, resorts, shopping, spas, theater and tourist attractions worldwide.

SHARE YOUR OPINION: We invite you to join any of our upcoming surveys – just register at **zagat.com,** where you can rate and review establishments year-round. Each participant will receive a free copy of the resulting guide when published.

AVAILABILITY: Zagat guides are available in all major bookstores, by subscription at **zagat.com** and for use on a wide range of mobile devices via **Zagat To Go.**

FEEDBACK: There is always room for improvement, thus we invite your comments and suggestions about any aspect of our performance. Just contact us at washbalt@zagat.com.

New York, NY
July 25, 2007

Nina and Tim Zagat

What's New

DINING DEMOCRACY: DC's top toques are applying their talents in more affordable settings. In burgeoning Downtown, nationally acclaimed chefs Michel Richard (Citronelle) and Robert Wiedmaier (Marcel's) have, respectively, opened the French-American bistro Central and the Belgian-accented Brasserie Beck, both of which feature top-flight cuisine in relaxed but stylish environs. Likewise, veteran Cathal Armstrong (Eve) has debuted two populist places in Old Town Alexandria: an Irish fish-fry shop called Eamonn's – A Dublin Chipper, and Majestic, a down-home American. And rising culinary star Barton Seaver is showcasing sustainable seafood and local produce at Hook, his New American date-night destination in Georgetown.

FROM AFRICA TO THE ANDES: International chefs are keeping DC ahead of the culinary curve. At Alexandria's Farrah Olivia, owner Morou Ouattara weaves influences from his native Ivory Coast into the New American cooking, while several other spots are proving Peruvian's the next hot cuisine. Examples include Las Canteras in Adams Morgan and La Limeña in Rockville. In fall 2007, restaurateur Mauricio Fraga-Rosenfeld will bring the Latin trend to Arlington with Yaku, a newcomer proffering Peruvian-Chinese (Chifa) fare.

BALTIMORE AND BEYOND: Although Baltimore lost its beloved Hampton's, new eateries are filling the void. Chef-owner Galen Sampson has opened Dogwood, an earthy New American in Hampden, where the retro-cool Rocket to Venus has also lifted off with its Eclectic eats. The stylishly redone Pazza Luna, offering Italian fare, and the exotic Nasu Blanca, with its mix of Japanese and Spanish cuisines, have landed in Locust Point, while Canton now counts Jack's Bistro, a modern Eclectic, among its assets. Annapolis additions include Kyma and Osteria 177, serving Med and American-Italian fare, respectively, while the Tidewater Inn in Easton is luring more than just locals with Local, its New American dining room.

CLEARING THE AIR: Following in the footsteps of DC and nearby Montgomery and Prince George's counties, the state of Maryland will require all bars and restaurants to be no-smoking by February 1, 2008. Since 64% of our surveyors say they'd dine out more if venues were smoke-free and only 2% say they'd eat out less, the newly affected eateries should find the ban a boon.

CHECK, PLEASE: The average cost of a meal in DC ($34.69) and Baltimore ($33.20) is roughly on par with the U.S. average of $33.28, but that isn't dissuading diners, 82% of whom say they are eating out the same as or more than they did a few years ago.

Washington, DC
Baltimore, MD
July 25, 2007

Olga Boikess
Marty Katz

Washington, DC's Key Newcomers

Our take on the most notable new arrivals of the past year. For a full list, see the Additions index on page 170.

Bastille	Food Matters
Bebo Trattoria	Hook
BLT Steak	Il Mulino
Brasserie Beck	La Limeña
Café du Parc	Las Canteras
Café Panache	Liberty Tavern
Cava	Majestic
Central Michel Richard	Mio
Chima	Overwood
Comet Ping Pong	Oyamel
Eamonn's	PS 7's
Famoso	Ray's The Classics
Farrah Olivia	Vapiano

In the year to come, casually chic eateries from leading restaurateurs will continue to redefine DC's culinary scene. Examples include Haidar Karoum's **Proof,** a wine-centric New American in the Penn Quarter that's slated to debut at press time, and **Hudson,** Greggory Hill's loungey New American remake of the West End's David Greggory. Also opening in fall 2007 is an as-yet-unnamed New American bistro from local heavy-hitter Ris Lacoste (ex 1789).

Neighborhood options are also proliferating. **Kemble Park Tavern,** a seasonal American, will pop up in the Palisades, while gentrifying locales will see a spate of new eateries. Among them are **Logan @ The Heights,** a Latin-accented American in Columbia Heights, **Bouche Bistro,** an Eclectic wine bar in the U Street Corridor, and **Veranda,** a Mediterranean in Shaw near the new Convention Center.

The favorable demographics that have drawn national and global chains like **Chima** and **Vapiano** to DC will attract a cornucopia of contenders in the coming year. A Penn Quarter outlet of the NYC-based **Chop't Creative Salad** will arrive on the scene in summer 2007, as will a Georgetown branch of the Belgian bakery-cafe, **Le Pain Quotidien,** and a Reston link of the Italian-esque **Il Fornaio.** Local successes will not be outdone, however: Bethesda's **Rock Creek** and Glover Park's **Sushi-Ko** are debuting doppelgängers in Chevy Chase, while a clone of Bethesda's **Olazzo** will arrive in Silver Spring.

On a more upscale note, the capital's luxury hotels are continuing to court celebrity talent. Last year, the Willard InterContinental tapped consulting chef Antoine Westermann for its double-decker French bistro, **Café du Parc.** And adding some luster this fall is Eric Ripert (NYC's Le Bernardin), who will help the Ritz-Carlton open **West End,** a bistro named after the hotel's neighborhood.

Washington, DC's Most Popular

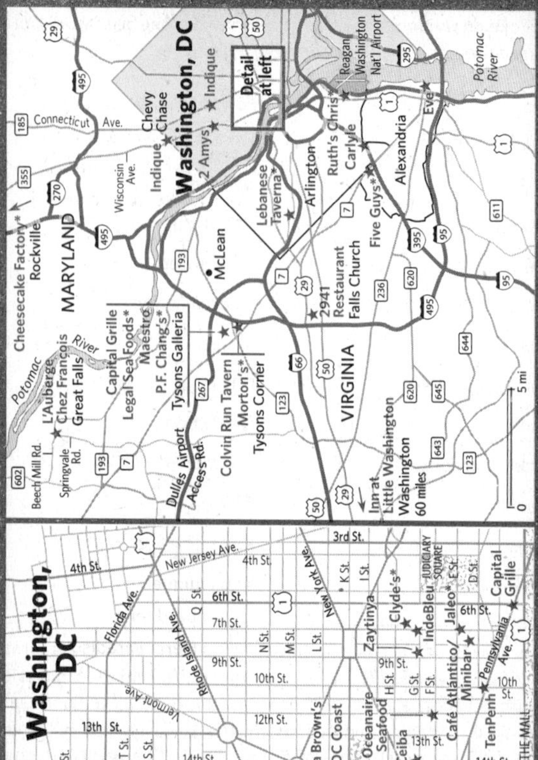

Washington, DC's Most Popular

Each surveyor has been asked to name his or her five favorite places. This list reflects their choices.

1. Kinkead's
2. Citronelle
3. Jaleo
4. Zaytinya
5. TenPenh
6. Inn at Little Washington
7. L'Auberge Chez François
8. 1789
9. 2941 Restaurant
10. Clyde's
11. Ruth's Chris
12. Prime Rib
13. McCormick & Schmick's
14. Lebanese Taverna
15. 2 Amys
16. Ceiba
17. DC Coast
18. Old Ebbitt Grill
19. Capital Grille
20. Morton's Steak*
21. Colvin Run Tavern
22. Legal Sea Foods
23. Oceanaire Seafood
24. Cheesecake Factory
25. Vidalia
26. Maestro
27. Cashion's Eat Place
28. Café Atlántico/Minibar
29. Carlyle
30. Nora
31. Eve
32. Five Guys
33. Obelisk
34. Georgia Brown's
35. IndeBleu
36. Indique*
37. Tabard Inn
38. Pizzeria Paradiso
39. Lauriol Plaza
40. P.F. Chang's

It's obvious that many of the above restaurants are among the Washington, DC, area's most expensive, but if popularity were calibrated to price, we suspect that a number of other restaurants would join the above ranks. Given the fact that both our surveyors and readers love to discover dining bargains, we have added a list of 80 Best Buys on page 16. These are restaurants that give real quality at extremely reasonable prices.

* Indicates a tie with restaurant above

Top Food Ratings

Ratings are to the left of names. Lists exclude places with low votes, unless indicated by a ▽.

29	Inn at Little Washington		Vidalia
28	Makoto		BlackSalt
	Maestro		Komi
	Citronelle		Rabieng
	Marcel's		Rasika
27	Eve		Persimmon
	2941 Restaurant		1789
	Ray's The Steaks	25	Colvin Run Tavern
	L'Auberge Chez François		L'Auberge Provençale
	Obelisk		Corduroy
	Gerard's Place		Ritz, Grill (Pent. City)
	Le Paradou		El Pollo Rico
	Prime Rib		Il Pizzico
	Seasons		Nora*
26	CityZen		Sushi Taro
	Kinkead's		Peking Gourmet
	Palena		Bangkok54
	Tosca		2 Amys
	Thai Square		Café 15
	La Bergerie		Asia Nora

BY CUISINE

AMERICAN (NEW)
29	Inn at Little Washington
27	Eve
	2941 Restaurant
	Seasons
26	CityZen

AMERICAN (TRAD.)
24	Colorado Kitchen
23	Tuscarora Mill
	Artie's
22	Ashby Inn
20	Old Ebbitt Grill

CHINESE
25	Peking Gourmet
24	Hollywood East Cafe
23	Mark's Duck House
22	Full Kee (DC)
	A&J

FRENCH
27	L'Auberge Chez François
26	La Bergerie
25	L'Auberge Provençale
24	Jean-Michel
	Le Mistral

FRENCH (BISTRO)
24	Bistrot Lepic
23	Montmartre
22	Le Refuge
	Petits Plats
	Café Bonaparte

FRENCH (NEW)
28	Citronelle
27	Gerard's Place
	Le Paradou
25	Café 15
24	Bis

HAMBURGERS
25	Morton's Steak
24	Five Guys
23	Matchbox
20	Old Ebbitt Grill
18	Ted's Montana Grill

INDIAN
26	Rasika
25	Bombay Club
24	Indique
	Passage to India
23	Heritage India

ITALIAN
- 28 Maestro
- 27 Obelisk
- 26 Tosca
- 25 Il Pizzico
- 24 Pasta Mia

JAPANESE
- 28 Makoto
- 25 Sushi Taro
- Kaz Sushi Bistro
- 24 Sushi-Ko
- Tachibana

MEDITERRANEAN
- 25 Zaytinya
- 22 Olives
- Brasserie Monte Carlo
- 21 Tavira
- Café Olé

MEXICAN
- 23 El Mariachi
- 22 Guajillo
- Samantha's
- 20 Taqueria el Poblano
- Rosa Mexicano

MIDDLE EASTERN
- 23 Panjshir
- 22 Kazan
- Lebanese Taverna
- Neyla
- Moby Dick

NUEVO LATINO
- 25 Café Atlántico/Minibar
- 24 Ceiba
- 23 Ceviche
- 20 Café Salsa
- 19 Merkado Kitchen

PAN-ASIAN
- 25 Asia Nora
- 24 TenPenh
- 21 Raku
- 20 Spices
- 19 Cafe Asia

PIZZA
- 25 2 Amys
- 24 Pasta Plus
- Pizzeria Paradiso
- 23 Matchbox
- 22 Coppi's Organic

SEAFOOD
- 26 Kinkead's
- BlackSalt
- 25 Pesce
- 24 Oceanaire Seafood
- DC Coast

SOUTH AMERICAN
- 25 El Pollo Rico
- 24 Crisp & Juicy
- 23 Fogo de Chão
- 20 Grill from Ipanema
- El Chalan

SOUTHERN
- 26 Vidalia
- 23 Morrison-Clark Inn
- Del Merei Grille
- Georgia Brown's
- Acadiana

SOUTHWESTERN/TEX-MEX
- 22 Guajillo
- Sweetwater Tavern
- Mi Rancho
- 19 Uncle Julio's
- 18 Cactus Cantina

SPANISH
- 24 Taberna/Alabardero
- 23 Sol de España
- Jaleo
- 21 Mar de Plata▽
- 18 Andalucia

STEAKHOUSE
- 27 Ray's The Steaks
- Prime Rib
- 25 Capital Grille
- Morton's Steak
- 24 Ruth's Chris

THAI
- 26 Thai Square
- Rabieng
- 25 Bangkok54
- 23 Duangrat's
- Regent, The

VIETNAMESE
- 23 Pho 75
- Huong Que
- 22 Minh's
- Taste of Saigon
- 21 Green Papaya

BY SPECIAL FEATURE

BREAKFAST

27 Seasons
24 Bis
Bread Line
23 Willard Room
Johnny's Half Shell

BRUNCH

27 Seasons
26 Rabieng
25 L'Auberge Provençale
Ritz, Grill (Pent. City)
Cashion's Eat Place

CHEF'S TABLE

28 Citronelle
27 2941 Restaurant
26 Tosca
BlackSalt
23 IndeBleu

CHILD-FRIENDLY

25 Bangkok54
24 Hollywood East Cafe
22 Minerva
20 Argia's
19 P.F. Chang's

DINING ALONE

28 Marcel's
26 Kinkead's
Palena
25 2 Amys
Cashion's Eat Place

HOTEL DINING

29 Inn at Little Washington
28 Maestro
(Ritz-Carlton Tysons Corner)
Citronelle
(Latham Hotel)
27 Seasons
(Four Seasons)
26 CityZen
(Mandarin Oriental)

MEET FOR A DRINK

28 Citronelle
Marcel's
26 CityZen
Vidalia
Rasika

POWER SCENES

29 Inn at Little Washington
28 Maestro
Citronelle
Marcel's
27 Eve

PRIVATE ROOMS

28 Maestro
Citronelle
Marcel's
27 2941 Restaurant
Le Paradou

SMALL PLATES/TAPAS

25 Zaytinya
24 Indique
Taberna/Alabardero
23 Heritage India
Sake Club

TRENDY

27 Eve
26 Komi
Rasika
25 Zaytinya
23 Johnny's Half Shell

WORTH A TRIP

29 Inn at Little Washington
Washington, VA
27 Foti's∇
Culpeper, VA
25 L'Auberge Provençale
Boyce, VA
22 Ashby Inn
Paris, VA
20 Rail Stop
The Plains, VA

BY LOCATION

ADAMS MORGAN

25 Cashion's Eat Place
24 Pasta Mia
23 Little Fountain Cafe
21 Meskerem
La Fourchette

BETHESDA

26 Persimmon
25 Morton's Steak
24 Ruth's Chris
Grapeseed
Passage to India

CAPITOL HILL

- 24 Bis
- 23 Charlie Palmer Steak
- Montmartre
- Johnny's Half Shell
- 22 Park Cafe

CLARENDON

- 23 Pho 75
- 22 Tandoori Nights
- Tallula
- Delhi Club
- 21 Faccia Luna Trattoria

CRYSTAL CITY

- 25 Morton's Steak
- 24 Ruth's Chris
- 23 Jaleo
- 21 McCormick & Schmick's
- 20 Legal Sea Foods

DOWNTOWN

- 27 Gerard's Place
- 25 Corduroy
- Café 15
- 24 TenPenh
- Ceiba

DUPONT CIRCLE

- 27 Obelisk
- 26 Komi
- 25 Nora
- Sushi Taro
- Pesce

FALLS CHURCH

- 27 2941 Restaurant
- 26 Rabieng
- 25 Peking Gourmet
- 24 Crisp & Juicy
- 23 Duangrat's

GEORGETOWN/ GLOVER PARK

- 28 Citronelle
- 27 Seasons
- 26 1789
- 25 Morton's Steak
- 24 Sushi-Ko

GOLDEN TRIANGLE

- 27 Prime Rib
- 26 Vidalia
- 25 Equinox
- Bombay Club
- Morton's Steak

OLD TOWN ALEXANDRIA

- 27 Eve
- 26 La Bergerie
- 24 Five Guys
- 22 Le Refuge
- Landini Bros.

PENN QUARTER

- 27 Le Paradou
- 26 Tosca
- Rasika
- 25 Café Atlántico/Minibar
- Capital Grille

TYSONS CORNER

- 28 Maestro
- 25 Colvin Run Tavern
- Capital Grille
- Morton's Steak
- 24 Fleming's Steak

U STREET CORRIDOR

- 23 Dukem
- Crème
- 22 Al Crostino
- Coppi's Organic
- 21 Ben's Chili Bowl

WEST END

- 28 Marcel's
- 25 Asia Nora
- 21 Circle Bistro
- 17 Agua Ardiente

WOODLEY/ CLEVELAND PARK

- 26 Palena
- 25 2 Amys
- 24 Indique
- 23 Sake Club
- 22 Lebanese Taverna

Top Decor Ratings

Ratings are to the left of names.

__28__ Inn at Little Washington
2941 Restaurant

__27__ Willard Room
Mie N Yu
Maestro

__26__ CityZen
L'Auberge Chez François
Fahrenheit & Degrees
Rasika
Oya
L'Auberge Provençale

__25__ Ritz, Grill (Pent. City)
IndeBleu
Sake Club
Lightfoot
Seasons
Zola
1789
Zaytinya
Café MoZU

Bombay Club
Citronelle
Ceviche
Le Paradou

__24__ Prime Rib
Zengo
Charlie Palmer Steak
Marcel's
Viridian
Taberna/Alabardero
Tabaq Bistro
Eve
TenPenh
Capital Grille
Ceiba
La Ferme
Ashby Inn
Café 15

__23__ Tandoori Nights
Colvin Run Tavern

OUTDOORS

Addie's
Café du Parc
Cafe Milano
L'Auberge Chez François
Lauriol Plaza

Old Angler's Inn
Sequoia
701
Straits of Malaya
Zaytinya

ROMANCE

Asia Nora
Firefly
IndeBleu
Inn at Little Washington
Little Fountain Cafe

Neyla
Palena
Rasika
Tabard Inn
Two Quail

ROOMS

Blue Duck Tavern
Brasserie Beck
CityZen
Clyde's
Comet Ping Pong
Fogo de Chão
Maestro

Oya
Rasika
Taberna/Alabardero
2941 Restaurant
Viridian
Zaytinya
Zola

VIEWS

Ashby Inn
Café MoZU
Indigo Landing
Old Angler's Inn
Ruth's Chris

Seasons
Sequoia
701
Tabaq Bistro
2941 Restaurant

subscribe to zagat.com

Top Service Ratings

Ratings are to the left of names.

28 | Inn at Little Washington
Maestro

27 | Seasons
L'Auberge Chez François
Marcel's
Makoto

26 | Ritz, Grill (Pent. City)
Citronelle
L'Auberge Provençale
Prime Rib

25 | 2941 Restaurant
Obelisk
Bombay Club
Eve
Tosca
1789
Willard Room
La Bergerie
CityZen
Fogo de Chão

24 | Le Paradou
Nora
Café 15
Gerard's Place
Capital Grille
Komi
Colvin Run Tavern
Vidalia
Kinkead's
Sol de España
Mark and Orlando's

23 | Palm
Morton's Steak
Morrison-Clark Inn
Le Mistral
Ruth's Chris
Rasika
Taberna/Alabardero
Tavira
Asia Nora

Best Buys

In order of Bang for the Buck rating.

1. Five Guys
2. Ben's Chili Bowl
3. California Tortilla
4. El Pollo Rico
5. Pho 75
6. Bread Line
7. Crisp & Juicy
8. Florida Ave. Grill
9. Urban BBQ
10. Au Bon Pain
11. C.F. Folks
12. Pollo Campero
13. Tryst
14. Bob & Edith's Diner
15. Moby Dick
16. Hard Times Cafe
17. Teaism
18. Amma Vegetarian
19. A&J
20. Sakoontra
21. Chinatown Express
22. Bob's Noodle
23. Rocklands
24. Udupi Palace
25. Negril
26. Fu Shing Cafe
27. Diner, The
28. Bangkok54
29. Busboys & Poets
30. Chutzpah
31. Taqueria el Poblano
32. Parkway Deli
33. Dukem
34. Cassatt's
35. Jaipur
36. Open City
37. Luna Grill & Diner
38. Vegetable Garden
39. La Madeleine
40. French Qtr./Louisiana

OTHER GOOD VALUES

Bob's 88 Shabu Shabu
Bombay Bistro
Café Bonaparte
Caribbean Feast
Delhi Club
Domku
Etete
Food Matters
Full Kee (DC)
Huong Viet
India Palace
Irene's Pupusas
Joe's Noodle House
Kabob Palace
La Limeña
Mai Thai
Mandalay
Mark's Kitchen
Matchbox
Minerva

Minh's
Mitsitam
My Bakery & Café
Myung Dong
Nirvana
Palena
Pasta Mia
Pizzeria Paradiso
Rabieng
Ray's The Steaks
Regent, The
SBC Café
Skewers/Luna
Sweet Ginger
Taipei Tokyo
Taqueria Tres Reyes
Thai Square
2 Amys
Vegetate
Yuan Fu

WASHINGTON, DC
RESTAURANT
DIRECTORY

	FOOD	DECOR	SERVICE	COST

A&J ⊄ Chinese

| | 22 | 8 | 13 | $15 |

Rockville | Woodmont Station | 1319C Rockville Pike (Wootton Pkwy.), MD | 301-251-7878

Annandale | 4316B Markham St. (Little River Tpke.), VA | 703-813-8181

"Try anything for $3–$4" at this Rockville/Annandale duo "always packed with homesick Chinese" looking for "fiery" hot garlic dishes, "amazing potstickers" and "cheap and delicious dim sum"; just beware: the fare outshines the "spare surroundings" of these "cafes hidden" in "tacky strip malls", and "you get better service if you speak Chinese."

Acadiana Cajun/Creole

| | 23 | 21 | 22 | $49 |

Mt. Vernon Square/New Convention Center | 901 New York Ave. NW (9th St.) | 202-408-8848 | www.acadianarestaurant.com

Jeff Tunks & Co. (Ceiba, DC Coast, TenPenh) "capture the spirit of Louisiana" at their latest "hit" across from the new Convention Center; a "wonderful reinterpretation" of Cajun and New Orleans cuisine is served in a "sophisticated" modern setting enlivened by "sparkle" chandeliers, fanciful alligator statues and "gracious service"; notwithstanding some quibbles about "impersonal", "already-seen decor" and "not exactly authentic" fare, "everyone, including the staff" seem "happy to be there."

Addie's American

| | 23 | 16 | 20 | $41 |

Rockville | 11120 Rockville Pike (Edson Ln.), MD | 301-881-0081 | www.blackrestaurantgroup.com

"Not your typical restaurant", this "warm" Rockville Pike New American (from the owners of Black's, BlackSalt and Black Market) sits in a "little yellow house" across from the White Flint Mall with two small, brightly colored, "whimsical" dining rooms boasting "bizarre decor"; the "skillful", "imaginative" cooking here "never disappoints", but the "noise level" and "long waits" may, so it's best to reserve in advance and head to the outside patio.

Afghan Afghan

| | ▽ 20 | 9 | 18 | $22 |

Alexandria | 2700 Jefferson Davis Hwy. (Raymond Ave.), VA | 703-548-0022

"The only thing bland is the name" (and the decor) at Alexandria's Afghan kitchen, which gets "packed on the weekends" when the "expat population gathers for parties"; there's an "authentic" menu full of "scintillating tastes" including "super" kebabs, and "attentive, kind" service that makes up for the shortcomings – namely, a "dumpy", "crazy" "cavernous" "barn" of a dining room.

Agraria American

| | – | – | – | E |

Georgetown | Washington Harbour | 3000 K St. NW (30th St.) | 202-298-0003 | www.agrariarestaurant.com

Get back to the land without leaving the city at this elegantly rustic New American in Georgetown's Washington Harbour that showcases ingredients from family farmers who are part-owners; design firm Adamstein & Demetriou used earthy materials (stone walls, bamboo-backed booths) to set an urbane scene, with multiple fire-

	FOOD	DECOR	SERVICE	COST

places, patio seating and several private dining rooms; N.B. there's an inviting marble-topped bar for sipping trendy cocktails.

Agrodolce *Italian* — 22 | 17 | 19 | $31

Germantown | Milestone Shopping Ctr. | 21030J Frederick Ave. (Father Hurley Blvd.), MD | 301-528-6150 | www.agrodolce.tv

Expect "interesting" Italian including "delish" wood-oven pizza, "pastas that can't be beat" and an "extensive wine list", all at "moderate prices", at this Germantown "oasis in a strip mall"; the "staff makes customers its top priority", but the "crowded, noisy" setting can feel "claustrophobic", so it's a good thing there's a "beautiful courtyard."

Agua Ardiente ☒Ⓜ *Nuevo Latino* — 17 | 19 | 14 | $34

West End | 1250 24th St. NW (bet. M & N Sts.) | 202-833-8500 | www.agua-ardiente.com

"Latino tapas" go "trendy nouvelle" at this "sexy" Nuevo Latino West End "gem" where the "vibe is more club than restaurant" (dark-red walls, pillar candles) and the "hot nightlife" draws crowds; too bad service is "lacking" and "caters more to drinkers than diners", because food lovers laud the "awesome arepas", ceviche and other vittles.

A La Lucia *Italian* — 22 | 16 | 19 | $38

Alexandria | 315 Madison St. (bet. Fairfax & Royal Sts.), VA | 703-836-5123 | www.alalucia.com

The "terrific", "authentic hearty" fare at this "charming" Italian in Old Town Alexandria makes "regulars" of "local celebrities James Carville and Mary Matalin" as well as plenty of others who fill this "always busy spot" to dig into "amazing pastas" and "desserts that will make you cry"; loyalists love the "great" owner, Michael Nayeri (a "Galileo refugee"), but a few find fault with the "sketchy service" and bemoan how "tough" it is to get a reservation despite the additon of a "cozier" back dining area and wine bar.

Al Crostino *Italian* — 22 | 19 | 23 | $38

U Street Corridor | 1324 U St. NW (bet. 13th & 14th Sts.) | 202-797-0523 | www.alcrostino.com

With an "unexpectedly extensive" lineup of "truly special specials", servers who "know their menu" and "bartenders who know their vino", this "hip" U Street Italian bistro and wine bar (a "casual" spin-off of Dupont Circle's Al Tiramisu) is a "welcome" spot to experience "fresh and fun flavors"; the owners, the Diotaiuti brothers, "know how to make you feel right at home" in the "intimate" (read: "crowded") quarters.

Al Tiramisu *Italian* — 23 | 18 | 21 | $46

Dupont Circle | 2014 P St. NW (bet. 20th & 21st Sts.) | 202-467-4466 | www.altiramisu.com

A cozy "nook" off Dupont Circle, "where you can speak Italian as well as eat and drink it", this "cozy and pleasantly noisy" spot from the brothers behind Al Crostino treats you like "family", while you "sit next to famous people"; a "quality cellar" and "inventive" dishes ("the polenta was whipped into a creamy cloud" and the namesake dessert is "spectacular") impress most, but "watch out for the prices" on specials – the "printed menu is much cheaper though more ordinary"; N.B. reservations required for dinner.

Amada Amante *Italian*

20 | 21 | 20 | $42

Rockville | 9755 Traville Gateway Dr. (Shady Grove Rd.), MD | 301-217-5900 | www.amadaamante.com

"Off the beaten path", this "glitzy" Rockville Italian is ideal for "a romantic dinner or quiet business meeting"; the "ever-changing menu" and service draw mixed responses however: admirers praise the "city-quality" dishes, while faultfinders fret over the "minimally informed staff" and "standard" fare; all notice the "downtown-DC prices."

Amici Miei *Italian*

20 | 17 | 19 | $38

Potomac | 1093 Seven Locks Rd. (Montrose Rd.), MD | 301-545-0966 | www.amicimieiristorante.com

A neighborhood eatery that manages to bring Italy to a suburban shopping center, this Potomac bistro with "standout dishes" and "delicious" homemade pastas, plus a "surprisingly good wine list for Montgomery County", attracts admirers; though most appreciate the "gracious hosts" who "kibbitz about home", a few fault the "perfunctory" service and "ho-hum" fare.

Amma Vegetarian Kitchen *Indian*

22 | 9 | 17 | $15

Georgetown | 3291 M St. NW (bet. Potomac & 33rd Sts.) | 202-625-6625
Vienna | 344A Maple Ave. E. (bet. Beulah Rd. & Park St.), VA | 703-938-5328

"You won't regret trying" the "daggone good" dosas, "yummy" mango lassis and other South Indian veggie fare at this "Georgetown walk-up" and its "unpretentious" self-serve Vienna sister; while vegetarians and other "characters" praise the quick and "cheap home cooking" that's "like eating at your grandmother's – if she were Indian", this "bare-bones" duo is "not recommended for date night" since the "decor is almost nonexistent."

Amsterdam Falafelshop ◐✇ *Mideastern*

– | – | – | I

Adams Morgan | 2425 18th St. NW (Belmont Rd.) | 202-234-1969 | www.falafelshop.com

At this tiny Adams Morgan storefront, late-night revelers line up for garlicky, falafel-filled pitas that can be loaded up with pureed eggplant, pickled cabbage and other spicy salads from the complimentary toppings bar and then paired with a side of Dutch-style fries doused in mayonnaise; N.B. it doesn't accept credit and is open through the wee hours (till 4 AM on Friday and Saturday nights).

Andalucia *Spanish*

18 | 14 | 18 | $33

Rockville | 12300 Wilkins Ave. (Parklawn Dr.), MD | 301-770-1880 | www.tasteandalucia.com

"Break out the map to find" this family-run Spanish suburbanite "tucked into an industrial area" in Rockville, where the "homestyle" paella and "good old-fashioned service", plus "great live" flamenco on Thursdays, draw patrons; but "disappointed" cynics scoff at the "weird atmosphere" that's "like your aunt's living room."

	FOOD	DECOR	SERVICE	COST

Ardeo *American*

21 | 20 | 20 | $43

Cleveland Park | 3311 Connecticut Ave. NW (bet. Macomb & Ordway Sts.) | 202-244-6750 | www.ardeorestaurant.com

Expect "sophisticated" fare that's "upscale without being intimidating" at this Cleveland Park New American boasting art deco rooms with "wonderful ambiance", a "caring staff" and a "delightful brunch" frequented by the "media elite"; just remember to "turn up the hearing aid" if you're "banished" to the noisier upstairs, or try tapas at their next-door wine bar; N.B. the post-Survey arrival of chef Trent Conry (from sister restaurant 701) has kept the kitchen on an even keel.

Argia's *Italian*

20 | 17 | 19 | $32

Falls Church | 124 N. Washington St. (bet. Broad St. & Park Ave.), VA | 703-534-1033 | www.argias.com

"A welcome change to corporate chains in the 'burbs", this Falls Church "neighborhood" trattoria scores points for its Italian "family-style plates for sharing", outdoor patio and "attentive but not overbearing" service; it's "way too noisy" shout some, but others find it perfect for a "quick bite before going to the State Theatre" next door.

Artie's *American*

23 | 19 | 22 | $31

Fairfax | 3260 Old Lee Hwy. (south of Fairfax Circle), VA | 703-273-7600 | www.greatamericanrestaurants.com

"You'll never have a bad meal" at this Fairfax "fail-safe" where the "friendly" staff does "anything to make a guest happy" including serving "consistently good" Traditional American fare (try hickory-smoked Black Angus rib-eye) in "portions fit for an elephant"; "make sure to call ahead" to avoid a "long wait" for one of the green-paneled booths in the "classy", "nautical" dining room – or snag a stool in the bar, "a popular watering hole" for the "young and perky."

Arucola *Italian*

18 | 14 | 16 | $34

Upper NW | 5534 Connecticut Ave. NW (bet. McKinley & Morrison Sts.) | 202-244-1555 | www.arucola.com

The jury's out on whether this "wildly popular" "neighborhood hangout" draws crowds for "good brick-oven pizza" and Italian "dishes that go beyond the checkered-tablecloth and sauce-and-pasta standards" or because of "nonexistent competition" in the "wilds of upper Connecticut Avenue"; you can avoid the "rat race" that occurs here after movies at nearby Avalon Theatre ("babbling children" at "tables a little on top of each other") by heading to the "relaxing" patio.

Ashby Inn, The ⛛Ⓜ *American*

22 | 24 | 22 | $54

Paris | The Ashby Inn | 692 Federal St. (Rte. 17), VA | 540-592-3900 | www.ashbyinn.com

Take a "wonderful ride to the country" and "spend an evening in Paris under the stars" or enjoy a "great value" alfresco Sunday brunch at this Traditional American set in a "high-end" inn in "upper-crust" hunt country Virginia; although it changed hands in 2005, the "warm, rustic" feel and mountain views remain the same.

Asia Bistro *Pan-Asian*

▽ 19 | 18 | 18 | $24

Arlington | Pentagon Row | 1301 S. Joyce St. (Army Navy Dr.), VA | 703-413-2002 | www.asiabistropentagonrow.com

Zen Bistro & Wine Bar *Pan-Asian*

NEW **Arlington** | Pentagon Row | 1301 S. Joyce St. (Army Navy Dr.), VA | 703-413-8887 | www.zen-bistro.com

Pentagon Row shopaholics break for "good, cheap sushi" and an "interesting mix" of Chinese, Thai, Malaysian and Japanese dishes at this "cafeteria-esque" Pan-Asian in Arlington; "funky" touches, including tabletop bonsai, add some life to the "dimly lit", earth-toned space, and on big game days, sports fans cheer the bar's 50-inch TV; N.B. its new next-door offshoot, Zen Bistro & Wine Bar, offers Pan-Asian tapas and international wines in loungey environs.

☑ Asia Nora ☒ *Pan-Asian*

25 | 22 | 23 | $53

West End | 2213 M St. NW (bet. 22nd & 23rd Sts.) | 202-797-4860 | www.noras.com

"Dark exotic surroundings provide a romantic setting for succulent organic Pan-Asian" at Nora Pouillon's West End subterranean where dishes of "amazing colors, textures and tastes" are "stylishly presented" by "very attentive" servers in "schnazzy" ("pajama"-like) garb; though "disappointed" trendsters say some of the "excitement has moved on", most are stimulated enough by the "first-rate" fare.

Au Bon Pain *Bakery*

16 | 10 | 12 | $11

Capitol Hill | 800 N. Capitol St. NW (H St.) | 202-789-1397 ☒
Penn Quarter | 601 Indiana Ave. NW (6th St.) | 202-638-8060
Downtown | 1001 Pennsylvania Ave. NW (10th St.) | 202-393-8809
Downtown | 1299 Pennsylvania Ave. NW (bet. 11th & 12th Sts.) | 202-783-9601
Downtown | 1401 I St. NW (bet. 14th & 15th Sts.) | 202-842-2467 ☒
Downtown | 700 13th St. NW (G St.) | 202-639-0846 ☒
World Bank | 1701 Pennsylvania Ave. NW (bet. 17th & 18th Sts.) | 202-887-9331 ☒
Golden Triangle | 1801 L St. NW (18th St.) | 202-296-8696
Golden Triangle | 1850 K St. NW (19th St.) | 202-887-9721 ☒
Arlington | Fashion Centre at Pentagon City | 1100 S. Hayes St. (Army Navy Dr.), VA | 703-415-0973
www.aubonpain.com
Additional locations throughout the DC area

"Grab coffee and a muffin on the way to work" or "a quick sandwich and soup" "on the run" at these bakery chain links that double as "better-than-average breakfast bistros" and "Downtown lunch staples"; "erratic" "high-school cafeteria" service prompts some to redub it – "oh, the pain" – but "afternoon bake sales" with "discounted" croissants and pastries sweeten the deal.

Austin Grill *Tex-Mex*

16 | 15 | 16 | $22

Penn Quarter | 750 E St. NW (bet. 7th & 8th Sts.) | 202-393-3776
Bethesda | 7278 Woodmont Ave. (Elm St.), MD | 301-656-1366
Silver Spring | 919 Ellsworth Dr. (Georgia Ave.), MD | 240-247-8969 ●
Alexandria | 801 King St. (Columbus St.), VA | 703-684-8969

(continued)

Austin Grill

Springfield | 8430A Old Keene Mill Rd. (Rolling Rd.), VA | 703-644-3111

www.austingrill.com

"Chat up" the "friendly" staff as you "get your Tex-Mex fix" at these Lone Star State "clones" that attract a "young margarita crowd" to the bar and "ex-hip power mommies" and their pint-sized posses to "noisy" dining rooms that are decked out in "funky" (or "tacky") Austin "junkyard" best; "passable" "nouvelle Mexican" fare leaves some yawning, but "addictive bottomless" chips and salsa earn it a "yee haw!"

Azucar *Pan-Latin*

▽ 26 | 19 | 24 | $28

Silver Spring | Layhill Ctr. | 14418 Layhill Rd. (Bel Pre Rd.), MD | 301-438-3293

"Tucked away in a Silver Spring strip mall", this tidy Pan-Latin, brightened with bold colors and small potted plants, is "starting to be discovered" by Anglos for its "surprise entrees and mean margaritas"; the "large menu" of "reasonably priced" "authentic" Central and South American dishes, including ceviche that "sparkles" and the "best" mole around, keeps it "mobbed" with locals, especially on weekend nights when Latin musicians perform.

Bamian *Afghan*

- | - | - | I

Falls Church | 5634 Leesburg Pike (Rock Springs Ave.), VA | 703-820-7880 | www.bamianrestaurant.com

The frosted glass doors of this Falls Church Afghan lead to a stunning surprise: a large dining hall where affordable, traditional fare is served amid ornate woodwork, crisp linens and an impressive chandelier; well-designed for weddings, banquets and special events featuring live music, it has rapidly become an Afghan community center as well as a place to have a meal that tastes like home.

Banana Café &
Piano Bar *Cuban/Puerto Rican*

18 | 17 | 15 | $25

Capitol Hill | 500 Eighth St. SE (E St.) | 202-543-5906 | www.bananacafedc.com

"Consistently great" mojitos and authentic Cuban and Puerto Rican fare ("try the ropa vieja – the best-dressed old clothes in town") keep fans "going back" to this "colorful" Capitol Hiller where "three-star, tour-resort decor" and a "raucous" gay-friendly piano bar create a "lively" atmosphere; even if the "eclectic" food "often sounds better than it is" ("as though the menu were written by Hemingway, but cooked by my Aunt Sarah") and "your waiter may go missing", you'll still have a "fun" time.

NEW Banana Leaves *Pan-Asian*

- | - | - | I

Dupont Circle | 2020 Florida Ave. NW (Connecticut Ave.) | 202-986-1333 | www.mybananaleaves.com

An appealing redo of a bi-level townhouse above Dupont Circle, this Pan-Asian features a crimson-walled bar/lounge on the first floor (with low seats nestled into a bay window) and a soothing moss-green dining room upstairs; the budget-friendly menu of sushi, noodle bowls and more is available in both areas.

⚡ Bangkok54 *Thai*

| 25 | 23 | 23 | $25 |

Arlington | 2919 Columbia Pike (Walter Reed Dr.), VA | 703-521-4070 | www.bangkok54restaurant.com

"East meets chic" at the area's "best Thai", a "very welcoming" family-run "gem" where "romantic lighting", "museumlike" artifacts and "gracious" servers belie its Arlington strip-mall setting; it's "like eating at a Bangkok market" given the variety of "invigorating flavors" in the "above-and-beyond-fantastic", "low-priced" fare from chef Endoo Tonkphontong – but when the menu says "spicy, it means it"; N.B. a summer 2007 expansion will add some 80 seats.

Bangkok Joe's *Thai*

| 20 | 23 | 20 | $31 |

Georgetown | Washington Harbour | 3000 K St. NW (Thomas Jefferson St.) | 202-333-4422 | www.bangkokjoes.com

It's all "sleek and beautiful" at this art deco Washington Harbour Thai where you can "start off the night" sipping "fabulous", "unique" saketinis, then "make a meal" of the dumpling bar or nosh on "reasonably priced", "noodlelicious" entrees; the "cool and happening" Georgetown vibe (great "people-watching") makes up for "hit-or-miss" service and food that's a little "too stylish."

Bardeo Wine Bar & Cafe *American*

| 21 | 21 | 22 | $35 |

Cleveland Park | 3311 Connecticut Ave. NW (bet. Macomb & Ordway Sts.) | 202-244-6550 | www.bardeo.com

A "classy" Cleveland Parker with a "fabulous atmosphere", this New American wine bar is a "delightful" spot to "taste trendy new" vintages (by the glass, half-bottle and in flights) with a "luscious" cheese plate, or to share "exciting" small dishes perfect for a "light dinner"; its "knowledgeable" staff "is great at choosing" a bottle "to suit your tastes", but budget-watchers warn that all those "small portions" "can really run up the bill."

Bar Pilar ◑ *American*

| 16 | 19 | 17 | $21 |

Logan Circle | 1833 14th St. NW (bet. S & T Sts.) | 202-265-1751 | www.barpilar.com

Interesting, affordable New American small plates with beer and wine pairings, along with soccer on the screen, make this "homey (but still hip)" saloon above Logan Circle "a great place to hang out before a show at the Black Cat"; partyers acknowledge that part of the "fun" is being "jammed next to someone" in the "dark", "narrow" room decorated with "Hemingway-themed" memorabilia; N.B. post-Survey chef and menu changes may outdate the Food rating.

NEW Bastille Ⓜ *French*

| - | - | - | M |

Alexandria | 1201 N. Royal St. (3rd St.), VA | 703-519-3776 | www.bastillerestaurant.com

Charming rusticity transports diners to provincial France at this wine bar and bistro tucked away in Old Town Alexandria; the menu, however, reflects the recent Parisian revolution in Gallic fare, as chef-owners Christophe Poteaux and Michelle Garbee (both from the late Aquarelle) reinvigorate the classics with Med flavors like cardamom, fennel, harissa and lemon confit; N.B. there's also a secluded outdoor patio.

Bazin's on Church 🅼 *American* — | — | — | E

Vienna | 111 Church St. NW (Center St.), VA | 703-255-7212 | www.bazinsonchurch.com

Chef-owner Patrick Bazin (ex Occidental) brings fine dining to Vienna, a prosperous town short on upscale eateries, in the form of this stylishly rustic New American; area bec fins can dig into zesty dishes highlighting seasonal ingredients at a marble wine bar or in one of the brick-and-mahogany dining rooms.

🆕 Beacon Bar & Grill *American* — | — | — | M

Scott Circle | Beacon Hotel | 1615 Rhode Island Ave. NW (Massachusetts Ave.) | 202-872-1126 | www.beaconhotelwdc.com

This New American near Scott Circle has ample bar space, shareable plates and plenty of nightly food and drink specials to facilitate get-togethers with friends; a $35 Saturday night prix fixe deal (three courses, each paired with a different wine) could be the start of a romantic evening out, while a post-meal cocktail in the seasonal rooftop lounge should be an interesting conclusion.

🆕 Bebo Trattoria *Italian* — | — | — | M

Arlington | 2250B Crystal Dr. (23rd St. S.), VA | 703-412-5076 | www.robertodonna.com

With DC's Galileo closed for renovations, chef-owner Roberto Donna (along with his culinary crew and a custom-made wood-burning oven for pizza and panini) has set up shop in Arlington's Crystal City with this midpriced Italian located in the airy, orange-hued space that Oyamel once occupied; also making the trip are a full menu of trattoria favorites and a chic bar scene; N.B. there's a four-course, family-style brunch on Sundays.

Belga Café *Belgian* 21 | 19 | 17 | $38

Capitol Hill | 514 Eighth St. SE (bet. E & G Sts.) | 202-544-0100 | www.belgacafe.com

While you "can't get better than a big pot of mussels, a creamy beer" and the "fabulous frites" at this Capitol Hill Belgian bistro, its "refined" versions of "delicious" "difficult-to-pronounce" Northern European specialties are "worthy of multiple visits" too; if you can manage to get a table, an "excellent selection" of "rare" brews is delivered with "European charm" (or "haughtiness") in "candlelit", though "cramped" and "noisy", Barracks Row quarters – but sometimes keeping service prompt becomes a "losing battle."

Benjarong *Thai* 22 | 18 | 20 | $25

Rockville | Wintergreen Plaza | 885 Rockville Pike (Edmonston Dr.), MD | 301-424-5533 | www.benjarongthairestaurant.com

"A cut above" the "chains in the area", this Rockville "class act" "never fails" with "consistently good" Thai (like the "soft-shell crabs that will knock you out" and "mango and sticky rice to die for") delivered "fast" in "serene" surroundings; though it's "authentic", don't worry about the heat – the "spice range" suits everyone from "wimps to superheroes."

Ben's Chili Bowl ●⋢ *Diner*   21 | 13 | 17 | $10

U Street Corridor | 1213 U St. NW (bet. 12th & 13th Sts.) | 202-667-0909 | www.benschilibowl.com

"Line up with everybody from Dupont hipsters to cabdrivers" to "the mayor" (past and present) at this "legendary" U Street "perfect dive" for "stand-up-and-slap-your-mama" eats; the "friendly, not too chatty" staff delivers "giant" half-smokes [spicy hot dogs] and "chili-and-cheese fries that are not on the USDA food plan" – but this is one "late-night DC" "greasefest" "worth the year of your life it might cost you"; P.S. it "caters to vegetarians" too.

NEW Bezu M *Asian Fusion*   – | – | – | M

Potomac | Potomac Promenade Shopping Ctr. | 9812 Falls Rd. (River Rd.), MD | 301-299-3000 | www.bezurestaurant.com

A chic oasis in a suburban Potomac shopping center, this French-influenced Asian fusion addition offers a midpriced menu that focuses on seafood enlivened with Pacific Rim flavors; an onyx bar, an elegant lounge and a chef's table situated beneath a bamboo chandelier are all sophisticated touches.

Bis *French*   24 | 22 | 22 | $51

Capitol Hill | Hotel George | 15 E St. NW (bet. New Jersey Ave. & N. Capitol St.) | 202-661-2700 | www.bistrobis.com

"All the cosmos align" at this "minimalist" Capitol Hill New French bistro with "subdued lighting, plenty of Olympians lobbying Congress" and an "inventive, comforting" menu that includes a "fabulous frisée salad and a primo wine list"; then there's the "happening" bar, "fun and efficient service" and the anticipation that "you never know who you'll see" during any given "power lunch" or "pricey" dinner.

Bistro D'Oc *French*   20 | 17 | 20 | $36

Downtown | 518 10th St. NW (bet. E & F Sts.) | 202-393-5444 | www.bistrodoc.com

"Escape" on "a lovely trip to the Languedoc" at this "oasis in a vast wasteland of buildings" in Downtown DC, where "hearty French classics" via chef-owner Bernard Grenier are served "without the stereotypical service" in a "rumpled", "quaint" bistro setting (colorful "painted walls, wood floors"); plus, it's a "convenient dinner stop" before or after shows at Ford's or E Street's Landmark theaters; P.S. the Thai specialties are "a treat."

Bistro Français ● *French*   19 | 17 | 18 | $36

Georgetown | 3128 M St. NW (bet. 31st St. & Wisconsin Ave.) | 202-338-3830 | www.bistrofrancaisdc.com

"A late-night haven", this "cozy" "Georgetown institution" serves "quintessential French bistro fare" (try the roast chicken and pommes frites) until 3 AM; the "*très*-Euro atmosphere" has quite a "Parisian feel", complete with "aloof", "disappearing waiters" and "crowded" tables, but at 30-plus years, its "longevity attests to its excellence."

	FOOD	DECOR	SERVICE	COST

Bistro 123 *French*
FOOD 19 | **DECOR** 16 | **SERVICE** 18 | **COST** $42

McLean | Tysons Corner Ctr. | 1961 Chain Bridge Rd. (International Dr.), VA | 703-288-1369 | www.bistro123.com

Skip the mall food court and go for frogs' legs at a "real restaurant" in Tysons Corner serving "consistent" French fare in digs too large for a true "bistro atmosphere" (its former Vienna location was "cozier"); "jolly and fun" chef Raoul Jean-Richard still reigns in the kitchen, while his wife oversees the "gracious" dining room, but naysayers dis the "sometimes stretched" service and the "uninspired" eats.

Bistrot du Coin *French*
19 | 18 | 13 | $33

Dupont Circle | 1738 Connecticut Ave. NW (Florida Ave.) | 202-234-6969 | www.bistrotducoin.com

"The sideshow never stops" at this "bustling" and "noisy" Dupont Circle "hot spot" favored by "see-and-be-seen" "young professionals" ordering a "solid selection of French country fare" like "*magnifique*" mussels and "*fantastique*" frites; sure, there's "genuine, rude service to match" and it gets "excessively loud" in the "lofty" space on weekends, but most consider this "party" a "great start for a night out."

Bistrot Lafayette Ⓢ *French*
21 | 17 | 21 | $42

Alexandria | 1118 King St. (bet. Fayette & Henry Sts.), VA | 703-548-2525 | www.bistrotlafayette.com

Enjoy "unfussy" French "comfort" fare at this "romantic hole-in-the-wall" in Old Town Alexandria, where chef-owner Keo Koumtakous prepares classics like steak tartar and escargots in garlic butter; there's "warm" service in a dining room that sports walls covered in old French art deco magazines ("like eating at the home of a Parisian friend"), and if you go on Mondays, the wine is half-price.

Bistrot Lepic & Wine Bar *French*
24 | 19 | 20 | $48

Georgetown | 1736 Wisconsin Ave. NW (S St.) | 202-333-0111 | www.bistrotlepic.com

Georgetown's gentry rubs elbows with the French Embassy crowd at this "quiet" neighborhood "Parisian bistro", a "tiny storefront" where the "cassoulet is terrific", the "pig's feet rock" and you're "cramped up all cozy with your neighbors"; upstairs, the wine bar/lounge feels like a "secret" that's "perfect" for dates, while a private party room sports 500 bottles of vino on the walls; the only negative is the staff's sometimes "poor attitude."

Black Market Bistro *American*
24 | 19 | 21 | $37

Garrett Park | Penn Pl. | 4600 Waverly Ave. (Strathmore Ave.), MD | 301-933-3000 | www.blackmarketrestaurant.com

"Another hit from the Blacks" (Addie's, Black's Bar & Kitchen, BlackSalt), this New American serves "creative, well-plated" seafood, steaks and pizza in a "charming" former post office building "next to the tracks" in Garrett Park ("the train whistle is not too distracting"); "Pottery Barn" decor and two fireplaces add to the "quaint" "country charm", and critics who carp about "long lines" will be pleased to know that it now accepts limited reservations; N.B. there's an outdoor porch plus an on-site retail market.

	FOOD	DECOR	SERVICE	COST

☑ BlackSalt Ⓜ *American/Seafood*

| 26 | 20 | 21 | $53 |

Palisades | 4883 MacArthur Blvd. NW (U St.) | 202-342-9101 | www.blacksaltrestaurant.com

The Black restaurant family's latest "winner", a fin-fare-focused New American in the Palisades, earns praise for "sophisticated and assured" creations that "explode with taste", along with a wine list of "exceptionally well-valued gems"; if you can't snag a table in the "minimalist", "noisy" dining room or the unreserved cafe, go for a "drink at the great bar", down a couple of the "freshest" oysters you've ever tasted and then pick up some "pristine" fish to cook at home.

Black's Bar & Kitchen *American*

| 23 | – | 20 | $43 |

Bethesda | 7750 Woodmont Ave. (bet. Cheltenham Dr. & Old Georgetown Rd.), MD | 301-652-5525 | www.blacksbarandkitchen.com

Recently reopened after a floor-to-ceiling renovation, this New American from the family behind Addie's, Black Market and BlackSalt is Bethesda's "go-to place" for "terrific seafood", a "fantastic raw bar" and "plenty of choices for meat eaters"; the setting now offers lots of light, a red-tiled open kitchen, glass bifold doors and a black pebble patio with reflecting pool; N.B. the menu was expanded to include small plates plus meat and game prepared on a hardwood grill.

NEW BLT Steak Ⓢ *Steak*

| – | – | – | E |

Golden Triangle | 1625 I St. NW (bet. 16th & 17th Sts.) | 202-689-8999 | www.bltsteak.com

Strategically positioned near the White House in Golden Triangle, this NYC-bred, French-accented New American steakhouse from chef Laurent Tourondel lures power types with luxe trappings, a raw bar and a state-of-the-art audio/visual–equipped private event space; there's also a long bar for networking and booths for privacy.

Blue Duck Tavern *American*

| ▽ 26 | 25 | 21 | $63 |

West End | Park Hyatt Hotel | 1201 24th St. NW (M St.) | 202-419-6755 | www.parkwashington.hyatt.com

Every "outstandingly original" dish is "a winner" declare early fans of this "wonderful" Park Hyatt Hotel restaurant that showcases regional New American cuisine crafted by chef Brian McBride (ex Melrose); the "chic" Tony Chi–designed space boasts a "stunning" open kitchen with a cobalt-blue, state-of-the-art, wood-burning Molteni range, but the "slow" service leaves a few diners "cold."

Bob & Edith's Diner ❶ *Diner*

| 16 | 9 | 16 | $13 |

Arlington | 2310 Columbia Pike (Wayne St.), VA | 703-920-6103
Arlington | 4707 Columbia Pike (bet. S. Buchanan & S. Wakefield Sts.), VA | 703-920-4700
www.bobandedithsdiner.com

"Cure a hangover" with "breakfast food at any hour" at this pair of 24/7 "mom-and-pop" "true greasy spoons" in Arlington that "get crowded with hipsters", "clubbers, drag queens and night-shift workers" at 4 AM; there's "brisk, responsive service", but "don't expect anything fancy" or healthy from these "throwback" diners – their menu neglects "anyone on a diet."

Bobby Van's Steakhouse Steak

| 20 | 18 | 20 | $54 |

Downtown | 809 15th St. NW (bet. H & I Sts.) | 202-589-0060 | www.bobbyvans.com

The "K Street lobbying crowd" "brings corporate cards" to dine on "prime" porterhouse at this "quintessential" Downtown chophouse where "solid" cuts, an "old clubby atmosphere", a "hopping" happy hour and an "everyone-knows-your-name" crowd draw more than meat eaters; but the unimpressed say it's "just another steakhouse" and "there are certainly better"; N.B. Bobby Van's Grill, a casual off-shoot, opened near the Convention Center post-Survey.

NEW Bob's 88 Shabu Shabu ● Japanese

| – | – | – | I |

Rockville | 316 N. Washington St. (bet. Beall Ave. & Martins Ln.), MD | 301-294-5888

Foodies are buzzing about this authentic North Rockville Japanese that shares the same disregard for decor as its parent, Bob's Noodle, across the street; the tables, equipped with sunken burners, are set up for cook-it-yourself shabu-shabu, but less adventurous types can always order sushi instead.

Bob's Noodle ⊅ Taiwanese

| 22 | 9 | 17 | $16 |

Rockville | 305 N. Washington St. (W. Jefferson St.), MD | 301-315-6668

"Please don't tell anyone how good this place is" plead admirers addicted to the oodles of "ridiculously cheap" noodles that headline at this "authentic Taiwanese" in North Rockville, where "it's all about the food" (surely, it "ain't about the decor"); "native Chinese" and other regulars know to order the more "adventurous" soups and stir-fries, but newcomers can ask for "friendly" Bob's "help in navigating the menu" and "translating the specials" posted in Mandarin.

Bombay Indian

| ▽ 24 | 15 | 18 | $24 |

Silver Spring | White Oak Shopping Ctr. | 11229 New Hampshire Ave. (Lockwood Dr.), MD | 301-593-7222

"Mango lassi worth the clogged arteries" and other "succulent Indian" choices ("try the chicken tikka masala") at this Silver Spring "gem" almost make it "worthwhile to live in the suburbs"; sure, the decor "isn't exactly lovely", but "seniors and families" appreciate "service that's not rushed" and portions generous "enough to take home leftovers."

Bombay Bistro Indian

| 23 | 12 | 20 | $23 |

Rockville | Bell's Corner | 98 W. Montgomery Ave. (Adams St.), MD | 301-762-8798

Fairfax | 3570 Chain Bridge Rd. (Lee Hwy.), VA | 703-359-5810
www.bombaybistro.com

"Who cares what the place looks like" when "top-notch" Indian comes "bargain"-priced and with "no pretension"?; this family-friendly Rockville/Fairfax duo offers an "exceptional" lunch buffet including "outstanding chicken tikka" and "tandoori delights", plus sit-down dinners that are "equally tasty" – just remember to "order

	FOOD	DECOR	SERVICE	COST

two glasses of water" to prepare for "heat" that "can overwhelm even the most devoted curry lovers."

Bombay Club *Indian* 　　　25 | 25 | 25 | $45

Golden Triangle | 815 Connecticut Ave. NW (H St.) | 202-659-3727 | www.bombayclubdc.com

In a "beautiful" British Colonial officers club setting, this Golden Triangle powerhouse "right near the White House" sets the "gold standard for elegant Indian food" and "exquisite service"; at "well-spaced" tables "shrouded by palm fronds", politicians, media folks and dealmakers "talk in confidence" over "wonderful" "well-balanced" fare, while mere mortals simply soak up the "pure comfort"; P.S. it's "ever-so-romantic with piano music at dinner."

Bombay Palace *Indian* 　　　23 | 20 | 22 | $36

Golden Triangle | 2020 K St. NW (bet. 20th & 21st Sts.) | 202-331-4200

"Grace and style abound" at this "luxe Indian spot" in Golden Triangle with "traditional" tandoori "standards", "delicious veggie fare" and "no lack of flavor" at the "dangerously good" weekend lunch buffet; though the "bright" dining space strikes some as too "clinical" for the "zesty" fare, and penny-pinchers scoff it's "overpriced", most find it a "solid" "friendly" choice.

Bombay Tandoor *Indian* 　　▽ 20 | 16 | 16 | $24

Vienna | 8603 Westwood Center Dr. (Leesburg Pike), VA | 703-734-2202 | www.bombaytandoor.com

An "underappreciated sleeper" "hidden" in a Tysons Corner office building, this "scrumptious" Indian impresses with an "extensive" lunch buffet, popular tandoori dishes like chicken tikka and traditional offerings such as bhindi masala (okra) – all "a little spicier" than those of its "watered down" competitors; the "minimal decor is "uninspiring", but expats are only coming here for the food; N.B. check out the sitar performances on Thursdays from 7–10 PM.

Boulevard Woodgrill *American* 　　19 | 17 | 17 | $27

Arlington | 2901 Wilson Blvd. (Fillmore St.), VA | 703-875-9663 | www.boulevardwoodgrill.com

"Booming" Clarendon's answer to "simple", "reliable" American "comfort food" (meatloaf, mac 'n' cheese, "grilled stuff") fits that Arlington locale "like a comfortable glove"; it's great for "lunch with the girls" – and their babies – or for "brunch with the in-laws", since it "never surprises, but doesn't disappoint either"; the "hipster decor" – "heavy chrome and mirrors" – may be "a bit too '80s" and the service just "ok", but the "hopping" happy-hour bar scene equals "yuppie heaven."

NEW Brasserie Beck ⊠ *Belgian/French* 　- | - | - | M

Downtown | JBG Bldg. | 1101 K St. NW (11th St.) | 202-408-1717 | www.beckdc.com

Inspired by vintage railroad stations and his North European culinary roots, chef-owner Robert Wiedmaier's Downtown French-Belgian brasserie is done up in dark wood, white tiles and lots of mirrors; a trendy, casual alternative to sibling Marcel's, it offers a mid-priced menu of steamed mussels (in multiple preparations) and hearty stews; N.B. patrons can wash it all down with some 50 wines under $50.

Brasserie Monte Carlo *French/Mediterranean*

22 17 20 $45

Bethesda | 7929 Norfolk Ave. (Cordell Ave.), MD | 301-656-9225 | www.bethesdarestaurant.com

Discovering this "intimate", "underappreciated" French-Med brasserie is like "finding a hidden corner of Provence in Bethesda" where a "limited" menu of "delicious", "homey" bistro fare is served in a "small", "charming" space; with "welcoming" chef-owner Sonny Abraham ("he's a doll") at the reins, you'll have a "romantic evening."

Bread Line ☒ *Bakery*

24 10 15 $13

World Bank | 1751 Pennsylvania Ave. NW (bet. 17th & 18th Sts.) | 202-822-8900

"Absolutely the best" "bread-based lunch" in town keeps this "wonderful" weekday-only bakery/cafe, "just steps from the White House", jammed; luckily, the "long lines move quickly", and loyalists, including the WH press corps, are "rewarded with the freshest, most flavorful sandwiches" on "terrific, crunchy" artesian bread (it "bites back"), "inventive" soups, "amazing salads" and "don't-miss" fries "worth every penny"; N.B. sit outside in nice weather.

B. Smith's *Southern*

19 21 19 $41

Capitol Hill | Union Station | 50 Massachusetts Ave. NE (Columbus Circle) | 202-289-6188 | www.bsmith.com

Union Station's "gorgeous" "old presidential" reception room, featuring 30-ft. ceilings, white marble floors and Ionic columns, is the "lovely" setting for the Capitol Hill branch of this former model/"celebrity owner's" national chain serving "dressed-up Southern comfort fare"; while some cheer the "elevated soul food", especially at the "absolutely delicious" jazz brunch, others are irked by "lackadaisical" service and insist the eats "should be rated on heaviness."

Buca di Beppo *Italian*

15 17 17 $26

Dupont Circle | 1825 Connecticut Ave. NW (Florida Ave.) | 202-232-8466
Gaithersburg | 122 Kentlands Blvd. (Great Seneca Hwy.), MD | 301-947-7346
www.bucadibeppo.com

Dupont and Gaithersburg iterations of this "campy, cheesy" kid-friendly Italian chain prove "fun, fun, fun for large parties" due to "ginormous" "family-style" portions that "feed a herd of garlic lovers"; but naysayers knock the "noisy", "kitschy", "garish" rooms at this "red-sauce" "tourist pit", asking do "people like this place"?

Buck's Fishing & Camping Ⓜ *American*

20 19 16 $45

Upper NW | 5031 Connecticut Ave. NW (Nebraska Ave.) | 202-364-0777

At her "cozy" Upper Northwest "neighborhood dining and watering hole", Carole Greenwood turns out "innovative", "deliciously simple" New American "home cooking", while co-owner James Alefantis presides over its "relaxed, atmospheric bar" and the "New Agey campsite" of a space (wooden tables, flour sacks lining bench seats); the no-reservations policy means it's usually "packed to the gills on weekend nights" with unhappy campers facing "long waits" or "sitting next to strangers" at the communal table.

NEW Buona Sera M *Italian* | - | - | - | M |

Bethesda | 8003 Norfolk Ave. (bet. Auburn & Del Ray Aves.), MD | 301-652-1400 | www.buonaseramd.com

A former local favorite, Buon Giorno, has been reborn in the same Bethesda corner digs that were spiffed up for its short-lived replacement, Saffron; loyalists returning for its traditional, midpriced Italian fare should note that a new blue awning marks the spot.

Burma *Burmese* | 21 | 8 | 17 | $20 |

Chinatown | 740 Sixth St. NW (bet. G & H Sts.) | 202-638-1280

The "killer" stairs you need to climb to get to this "no-frills", "friendly" family-run Burmese "sleeper" "tucked away on the second floor" of a building near the Verizon Center in Chinatown will seem like a small obstacle after you've tried the "authentic" "tasty combinations" served here; the "green tea leaf salad is a must", but it's best to "take a bunch of friends" and "share several" dishes since "you can't beat the food for the price."

Busara *Thai* | 20 | 18 | 18 | $27 |

Glover Park | 2340 Wisconsin Ave. NW (Calvert St.) | 202-337-2340

Reston | Reston Town Ctr. | 11964 Market St. (Discovery St.), VA | 703-435-4188

McLean | 8142 Watson St. (International Dr.), VA | 703-356-2288 www.busara.com

Named for their "attractive", "if formulaic", black lacquer and blue topaz neon designs, this Thai trio "strives for the familiar rather than the fantastic", turning out "surprisingly good" versions of pad king and honey-roasted duck; Glover Park's "enchanting" garden is a "delight", "noisy" Reston is ideal for "families" and "large groups" and Tysons Corner offers "an interesting alternative to the power lunch"; only purists pan the operation as a "lowbrow suburban McThai."

Busboys & Poets ● *American/Eclectic* | 18 | 23 | 17 | $21 |

U Street Corridor | 2021 14th St. NW (V St.) | 202-387-7638 | www.busboysandpoets.com

"Everyone is welcome" at this "high-energy", "socially conscious" U Street "lounge/restaurant/bookstore/community space" that serves the "right mix" of "decently priced" American-Eclectic "comfort food and trendy dishes" ranging from catfish and collard greens to peanut-butter-and-banana panini in a "vast", WiFi'd room that's "perfect for a latte and your laptop"; there's "always something going on" in the back performance space, so even though there are often "long waits for tables" (and for the "staff to show up"), there's "lots to look at"; N.B. look for an Arlington offshoot in late 2007.

	FOOD	DECOR	SERVICE	COST

Butterfield 9 *American* — 22 | 23 | 21 | $51

Downtown | 600 14th St. NW (bet. F & G Sts.) | 202-289-8810 |
www.butterfield9.com

"Swanky" "contemporary" styling, "movie star" lighting and a "calm
pace" may make this Downtown New American prime for hosting
"older parents", but it's also got enough of a "wow factor" in its
"mildly adventurous" cooking, "beautiful people", "pretentious
staff" and "quite expensive" tabs that it's great for a "business meeting" or "romantic" outing as well; wallet-watchers recommend the
$25 prix fixe lunch or the pre- and post-theater menus.

NEW Buzz ● *Coffeehouse* — - | - | - | I

Alexandria | 901 Slaters Ln. (Portner Rd.), VA | 703-600-2899 |
www.buzzonslaters.com

The newly minted neighborhood near Potomac Yards is treating this
industrial-chic, WiFi-equipped Alexandria coffeehouse, dessert
lounge and bakery as an unofficial community center, with folks
stopping by for coffee klatches and after-dinner treats; plus, a recently added wine bar serves vino, cocktails and other fancy drinks.

Cactus Cantina *Tex-Mex* — 18 | 15 | 16 | $24

Cleveland Park | 3300 Wisconsin Ave. NW (Macomb St.) | 202-686-7222 |
www.cactuscantina.com

A "fun" "circuslike atmosphere" and "reasonable prices" make this
"kid-friendly" Cleveland Park Tex-Mex a place that "everyone in the
city loves"– from "families to the happy-hour set to empty nesters";
foodies may eschew the "mass production" fare, but less fussy
friends keep "coming back" to wash down those "to-die-for" fajitas,
"great guac" and "perfect" chips from the "mesmerizing" tortilla-
making machine with "intoxicating" "swirled margaritas."

Cafe Asia *Pan-Asian* — 19 | 16 | 15 | $25

Golden Triangle | 1720 I St. (17th St.) | 202-659-2696
Rosslyn | 1550 Wilson Blvd. (N. Pierce St.), VA | 703-741-0870
www.cafeasia.com

"Ultrathin" staffers serve Pan-Asian that "covers all bases" "from safe
to adventurous" at this pair of "swanky" "cafeterias", where "$1 sushi"
and "cheap sake" keep "happy-hour" "hipsters" "coming back";
"funky", "ultramodern" digs and a "clubby" atmosphere in Rosslyn
draw diverse "twentysomethings", but some feel Golden Triangle
could "take some lessons" from its VA sibling and "lighten" things up.

Z Café Atlántico/Minibar *Nuevo Latino* — 25 | 22 | 22 | $49

Penn Quarter | 405 Eighth St. NW (bet. D & E Sts.) | 202-393-0812 |
www.cafeatlantico.com

"Phenomenal" mojitos and "mouthwatering" guacamole made tableside kick start a "mini-vacation" on this Penn Quarterite's "three
levels of Caribbean fun"; its Nuevo Latino kitchen "makes cutting-
edge food deliciously edible", while "terrific" pre-theater and weekend
Latin dim sum keep it "affordable"; at its six-seat, reservations-only
Minibar – a $120-per-person "carnival" of "art and chemistry" – "dar-
ing types" test their "bravado" on 30-plus bite-size "creations."

Café Bonaparte *French*

22 | 21 | 19 | $25

Georgetown | 1522 Wisconsin Ave. NW (bet. P & Volta Sts.) |
202-333-8830 | www.cafebonaparte.com

An "endearing" Georgetown treasure, this "cozy" cafe with a "Left
Bank-y atmosphere" (and "trademark shortage of space") serves up
"fabulous crêpes", omelets, soups, pastries, "classic" French bistro
fare like coq au vin, plus a "fabulous selection of coffee"; the "bar is
great for after-work cocktails" or a "quick pick-me-up" following a
day of nearby shopping.

Café Citron 🗷 *Pan-Latin*

17 | 17 | 16 | $25

Dupont Circle | 1343 Connecticut Ave. NW (Dupont Circle) |
202-530-8844 | www.cafecitrondc.com

"Indulge your inner diva while the DJ spins some salsa" at this Pan-
Latin "haven" that libertine Duponters "love"; "pleasant" *lomo sal-
tado,* "energizing" appetizers, "great happy-hour specials" and
"pitchers of mojitos" compensate for a "noisy", "cramped" space
that turns into a "fabulous" nightclub after dinner, complete with
"booty-shaking" "beautiful" people "looking to score."

Cafe Deluxe *American*

18 | 16 | 18 | $28

Upper NW | 3228 Wisconsin Ave. NW (Macomb St.) |
202-686-2233
Bethesda | 4910 Elm St. (Woodmont Ave.), MD | 301-656-3131
McLean | 1800 International Dr. (Greensboro Dr.), VA |
703-761-0600
www.cafedeluxe.com

"Simple meals" that "young and old" "actually enjoy" ("upscale"
meatloaf and prosciutto pizza) are the reason this trio of American
bistros never seem to be "anything but full" ("enjoy the bar" while
you "wait and wait"); critics contend they're "slightly dull" and "im-
possibly loud", but tell that to the "neighborhood families" who "always leave happy" after enjoying "reliable" if "not deluxe" fare.

Cafe Divan *Turkish*

20 | 16 | 18 | $29

Glover Park | 1834 Wisconsin Ave. NW (34th St.) | 202-338-1747 |
www.cafedivan.com

"Praise" goes to chef-owner Cavit Ozturk for outfitting this "lovely"
"if a bit diminutive" Glover Park Turkish with "lots of glass" for "window views" on both sides, and then serving "fabulous" whole roast
lamb from a wood-fired rotisserie oven, along with "excellent" veggie options like smoked eggplant and "freshly baked bread"; reas-
sured regulars report it's "always a good sign" when you see "many
native Turks" eating the "authentic" "reasonably priced" fare.

NEW Café du Parc *French*

- | - | - | M

Downtown | Willard InterContinental Washington |
1401 Pennsylvania Ave. NW (bet. 14th & 15th Sts.) |
202-942-7000 | www.cafeduparc.com

The White House is just a bonbon's toss away from the Willard
InterContinental's handsome double-decker French bistro, where
the menus were designed by one of France's top toques, consulting

chef Antoine Westermann; its cafe tables, overlooking Pennsylvania Avenue's Pershing Park, are an ideal perch for people-watching.

☑ Café 15 *French*

| 25 | 24 | 24 | $71 |

Downtown | Sofitel Lafayette Sq. | 806 15th St. NW (H St.) | 202-737-8800 | www.sofitel.com

You'll find "elegance personified" at this "very European" yet "modern" Downtown hotel dining room where "outstanding" New French fare "of the highest caliber" is served to "corporate movers and shakers" by a "cordial" staff; those who find it a bit "stuffy" for a casual dinner say it's "best for lunch" or for a "divine breakfast", but if you fancy an evening "tasting menu with wine pairings", this one is "not to be missed"; N.B. terrace seating adds appeal.

Cafe Japoné ● *Asian Fusion*

| 17 | 12 | 16 | $33 |

Dupont Circle | 2032 P St. NW (21st St.) | 202-223-1573

Climb the stairs at this dual-purpose "neighborhood standard" near Dupont Circle for "fresh and tasty" raw-fish creations in a "divey" space where you can "watch them roll your sushi right in front of you", then listen to live jazz or join the "drunk college students singing karaoke" in the "rocking" bar; in stark contrast, downstairs you'll find an "all-white ice" "grotto" design at Japoné Restaurant, where Japanese-French fusion is served in "chic" fashion.

Cafe Milano ● *Italian*

| 20 | 19 | 18 | $54 |

Georgetown | 3251 Prospect St. NW (bet. Potomac St. & Wisconsin Ave.) | 202-333-6183 | www.cafemilano.net

Every night is "like a fabulous dinner party with A-list guests" ("the VP, George Clooney") at this Georgetown Italian, but on Thursday nights "the gorgeous girls hang out", creating eye candy as "delectable" as the fare and a "scene so alive" you feel like you're "in the know"; but C-listers say if the "snooty" staff doesn't know you, you'll be so "far from the action" you'll feel like you're "eating on the floor of the Chicago Mercantile Exchange."

Café Mileto *Italian*

| 17 | 13 | 16 | $24 |

Germantown | Cloppers Mill Village Ctr. | 18056 Mateny Rd. (Great Seneca Hwy.), MD | 301-515-9370 | www.cafemileto.com

"Far better than any of the nearby chains", this Germantown "strip-mall" Italian proves a "dependable family-friendly staple" that offers fare "a notch above the usual"; the "plastic tablecloths" and "attitude"-heavy staff won't impress, but "fresh" pasta and "terrific" wood-fired pizza will, plus the entrees are priced "well within most budgets" (especially the "excellent" "bargain" lunch buffet).

Café Monti ☒ *Austrian/Italian*

| 22 | 3 | 11 | $20 |

Alexandria | 3250 Duke St. (S. Quaker Ln.), VA | 703-370-3632 | www.cafemonti.com

"Top-notch" schnitzel and "terrific" pasta make it "worth putting up with the crummy decor" ("worse than McDonald's") and "garage ambiance" of this Alexandria diner – a "peculiar and charming cross between a fast-food franchise and a European cafe"; it's "best for

	FOOD	DECOR	SERVICE	COST

takeout", but you can "order at the counter", "find your own seat" and wait for "excellent" Austrian-Italian dishes and "wonderful desserts" to be "delivered to your table."

☑ Café MoZU *American*

| 22 | 25 | 21 | $60 |

SW | Mandarin Oriental | 1330 Maryland Ave. SW (bet. 12th & 14th Sts.) | 202-787-6868 | www.mandarinoriental.com

The "beautiful, bright and airy" Tony Chi–designed interior with "delightful water views" is the highlight of this Asian-influenced New American in the Mandarin Oriental, which offers a "nice quiet escape" for business or a "ladies' lunch date" "just steps from the Mall"; while most praise the "very flavorful and light" fare, including "creative" sushi, a few say the staff may not be "up to [the] standards" of such a lofty hotel.

Café Olé *Mediterranean*

| 21 | 13 | 18 | $25 |

Upper NW | 4000 Wisconsin Ave. NW (Upton St.) | 202-244-1330 | www.cafeoledc.com

Offering a "winning" "contemporary twist on Mediterranean meze" and "interesting" wines by the glass, this "friendly" "unadorned" tapas spot in Upper NW's Tenleytown is a "great" place for "grazing on small plates" "before or after a movie next door"; do yourself a favor, though, and go "during warmer months" when the "relaxing terrace" helps you "avoid the crowded indoor scene."

NEW Café Panache Ⓜ *American*

| - | - | - | M |

Ashburn | 43135 Broadlands Center Plaza (Broadlands Blvd.), VA | 703-723-1424 | www.cafepanache.net

This polished New American cafe brings a hint of sophistication to suburban Ashburn with its gleaming bar, flattering lighting and beckoning outdoor plaza; the midpriced entrees work for business or romance, while the children's menu signals that eating here can also be a family affair.

Café Saint-Ex *Eclectic*

| 19 | 19 | 17 | $29 |

Logan Circle | 1847 14th St. NW (T St.) | 202-265-7839 | www.saint-ex.com

A "laid-back atmosphere that can make just about anyone feel cool" ("artists" with "black-framed glasses" and "yuppies" with "popped collars" alike) defines this "cozy" art deco–inspired Logan Circle "watering hole"; a "see-and-be-seen" sidewalk patio, "reliably good" seasonal Eclectic fare and a staff that "knows its beer" (as well as its wine) explains the "mob" scene, while downstairs in its "cavernous belly", DJs spin "late-night" tunes.

Café Salsa *Nuevo Latino*

| 20 | 17 | 19 | $28 |

Alexandria | 808 King St. (bet. Alfred & Columbus Sts.), VA | 703-684-4100 | www.cafesalsarestaurant.com

Find "fanciful food, fantastic mojitos and fun folk" at this bi-level "great date place" in Old Town Alexandria where you can "learn how to shake it salsa style" during Tuesday night dance lessons; the service is "friendly but clumsy" say some, but the "to-die-for" plantain chips and other Nuevo Latino appetizers "excel" – especially when they're half-price during "the best happy hour in town"; P.S. save room for the "mmmm" tres leches cake.

Café Spice *Indian*

▽ 18 | 20 | 17 | $26

Gaithersburg | Rio Entertainment Ctr. | 9811 Washingtonian Blvd. (Sam Eig Hwy.), MD | 301-330-6611 | www.cafespice.com

In brilliantly hued, "chic, upscale" surroundings overlooking a man-made lake in a popular Gaithersburg mall, this NYC import serves "well-made" Indian "adapted for the American palate" ("not too spicy"); the "nicely decorated" stainless-steel bar/lounge and an open kitchen offer pre- and post-movie diversions, but sticklers who find the fare "lacking" snipe that it tastes like it was "cooked by someone born in Indiana", not India.

Cafe Taj *Indian*

19 | 15 | 19 | $30

McLean | 1379 Beverly Rd. (Old Dominion Dr.), VA | 703-827-0444 | www.mycafetaj.com

"Cheerful and attentive servers enhance the experience" at this "quiet" "neighborhood" Indian in a McLean mini-mall, where the "decor is nothing special" and the dishes are lightly "spiced" as if for novice tongues (though they'll also "accommodate any preference"); a few say "quality varies", but most agree the lunch buffet is an "unbeatable bargain", so look for the "winning" butter chicken with a sauce "so good" you'll "make a soup out of it."

California Tortilla *Tex-Mex*

18 | 11 | 17 | $10

Chinatown | 728 Seventh St. NW (bet. F & H Sts.) | 202-638-2233
Bethesda | 4862 Cordell Ave. (Woodmont Ave.), MD | 301-654-8226
Germantown | 19847-O Century Blvd. (Pinnacle Dr.), MD | 301-540-7717
Olney | Olney Village Ctr. | 18101 Village Center Dr.
(Olney Sandy Spring Rd.), MD | 301-570-2522
Potomac | Cabin John Shopping Ctr. | 7727 Tuckerman Ln.
(Seven Locks Rd.), MD | 301-765-3600
College Park | 7419 Baltimore Ave. (Knox Rd.), MD | 301-927-8500
Rockville | Rockville Town Ctr. | 199 E. Montgomery Ave. (Courthouse Sq.), MD | 301-610-6500
Silver Spring | Burnt Mills Shopping Ctr. | 10721 Columbia Pike/
Colesville Rd. (Hillwood Dr.), MD | 301-593-3955
Arlington | 2057 Wilson Blvd. (bet. Courthouse Rd. & Rhodes St.), VA | 703-243-4151
Fairfax | Fair Lakes Promenade Shopping Ctr. | 12239 Fair Lakes Pkwy.
(Pender Creek Circle), VA | 703-278-0007
www.californiatortilla.com
Additional locations throughout the DC area

At this "kooky", "fast and friendly" homegrown regional chain, "spunky cashiers" ring up "gourmet burritos" "as big as your head" that "beat the pants off any other fast food" and are quite the "deal for the dinero"; the rest of the "reasonably healthy" Tex-Mex menu includes the "largest hot sauce collection this side of the Rio Grande", "creative and filling salads", fajitas, quesadillas and a "great selection of vegetarian options"; "unlimited soda" and "frequent specials" make it kid-friendly and a "teenage favorite", plus you can sign up for their "hilarious" e-newsletter.

☑ Capital Grille, The Steak
25 | 24 | 24 | $58

Penn Quarter | 601 Pennsylvania Ave. NW (6th St.) | 202-737-6200

McLean | 1861 International Dr. (Leesburg Pike), VA | 703-448-3900

www.thecapitalgrille.com

These "masculine, clubby" steakhouses with "character" and "superb service" serve "amazing porterhouse" and other "brilliant" cuts, backed by the "best martinis" and a "huge wine selection"; the DC branch draws "power brokers" and a "who's who in Congress", but the bill at any of them is "easier to swallow if you're on an expense account"; "between the cigar smoke and the beef you'll take a year off your life, but it's worth it."

Capri Italian
21 | 17 | 20 | $44

McLean | Giant Shopping Ctr. | 6825K Redmond Dr. (Old Dominion Dr.), VA | 703-288-4601 | www.restaurantcapri.com

Nicky di Chiara is the "heart and soul" of his family's McLean Italian – a "great neighborhood spot" that serves "Supreme Court Justices, real estate tycoons and suburban families" "expertly grilled and filleted" fish, "homemade" pastas and special dishes for the kids in sunny surroundings; some say the service is "inconsistent", but you can expect the "warmest reception" when the "owners are present."

Caribbean Breeze Pan-Latin
17 | 21 | 17 | $29

Arlington | 4100 N. Fairfax Dr. (Randolph St.), VA | 703-812-7997 | www.caribbeanbreezeva.com

"Trade winds blow into the Ballston corridor" at this "Little Havana in Yuppyville", an offshoot of Café Salsa that "turns into a salsa club" on Wednesday, Friday and Saturday nights; though the "eclectic crowd" in the "glassed-in" space may notice the "spotty service" and Pan-Latin fare that "sometimes comes up short on flavor", it's more focused on the mojitos.

Caribbean Feast ☒ Jamaican
▽ 21 | 7 | 15 | $15

Rockville | 823 Hungerford Dr. (Mannakee St.), MD | 301-315-2668

"Hey mon", "if you like spicy island" fare, this Rockville "lunch spot" is "your place" for "generous servings" of Jamaican "homestyle cooking" that will "stick to your ribs"; "counter service", "cafeteria seating" and "uninspired decor" make the "authentic" jerk chicken and other vittles "best as takeout."

☑ Carlyle American
24 | 22 | 22 | $36

Arlington | 4000 S. 28th St. (Quincy St.), VA | 703-931-0777 | www.greatamericanrestaurants.com

"All things considered", this Shirlington New American is possibly the Arlington area's "best" "high-end" venue for "all occasions"; the "interesting, not too challenging" menu of "to-die-for" dishes is "priced for frequent visits" and served by "quick and polite" youngsters in "casually elegant" surroundings, and there's an "energetic bar" as well; but take advantage of the "call-ahead seating" plan to "keep the waits down" since no reservations are accepted.

NEW Casa Oaxaca *Mexican*
— | — | — | I

Adams Morgan | 2106 18th St. NW (California St.) | 202-387-2272 | www.oaxacaindc.com

From the owners of Guajillo in Arlington, this charming bi-level Adams Morgan cantina showcases southern Mexico's flavorful cuisine in a budget-friendly menu that features the namesake region's seven traditional moles; the rustic setting's dark-red walls are enlivened by colorful handicrafts, mirrors and cowhide.

☑ Cashion's Eat Place M *American*
25 | 21 | 22 | $46

Adams Morgan | 1819 Columbia Rd. NW (bet. Biltmore St. & Mintwood Pl.) | 202-797-1819 | www.cashionseatplace.com

"Exquisitely talented" chef Ann Cashion gives a "down-home" (Southern) spin to the "amazingly creative" "ever-changing" seasonal menu at her "vibrant" Adams Morgan New American, where a "seashell"-shaped room with high ceilings and a "sophisticated" staff contribute to "the best date place in town", plus they whip up one of the tastiest Sunday brunches "you'll ever hope to find"; P.S. there's "people-watching" at the sidewalk tables.

Cassatt's *New Zealand*
20 | 13 | 16 | $18

Arlington | 4536 Lee Hwy. (Wolcomb Ln.), VA | 703-527-3330 | www.cassatts.com

An art gallery, coffeehouse, wine bar and short-order grill all rolled into one, this "casual" "popular" Kiwi kitchen takes its inspiration from the New Zealand cafes favored by it owners; best for "great breakfasts" washed down with "fabulous" coffee that "leaves Starbucks in the dust" or for a "soup/salad/sandwich lunch", it's "frequented mostly by nearby North Arlington families."

Caucus Room, The ⑤ *American*
21 | 22 | 22 | $61

Penn Quarter | 401 Ninth St. NW (D St.) | 202-393-1300 | www.thecaucusroom.com

Lined with mahogany and "power brokers" doing business over "excellent" cuts of beef, "crisp" salads and "outstanding" wines, this "expense-account" Penn Quarter New American steakhouse is "preferred by DC's young professionals", who see "romantic" as well as business possibilities in its clubby booths and "dark", "inviting" bar; though some say it's "stuffy" and "bland", others dig the "discreet" service at this "epicenter of power in Washington."

NEW Cava *Greek*
— | — | — | M

Rockville | 9713 Traville Gateway Dr. (Shady Grove Rd.), MD | 301-309-9090 | www.cavamezze.com

It's a family affair at this Rockville meze mecca where the owners enlisted their fathers to build the bar and tables, and then hung vintage black-and-white photos of their relatives on the walls; the small-plates-only menu selections are based on heirloom Greek recipes and are dished up in portions generous enough that even the grandmas would approve.

	FOOD	DECOR	SERVICE	COST

NEW Cee Fine Thai Dining *Thai* — | — | — | M

Fairfax | 9901 Fairfax Blvd. ... y. (Rebel Run), VA | 703-293-9898 |
www.ceefinethaidining.co...

Offering an extensive, ... ced roster of over 90 multiregional
dishes and eclectic desse...s, this stylish Fairfax Thai accents its
modern setting (textured burnt-orange walls, dark polished wood)
with traditional Asian artifacts; its mod bar has meet-for-a-drink potential, and there's even a stone-walled patio for dining alfresco.

Z Ceiba Ⓢ *Nuevo Latino* — 24 | 24 | 22 | $48

Downtown | 701 14th St. NW (G St.) | 202-393-3983 |
www.ceibarestaurant.com

With "wonderful" South and Central American–inspired dishes "bursting with complex flavors" and presented in "beautiful" Downtown
digs, this "happening" Nuevo Latino is as "great for an anyday meal"
as a "business lunch" or a "special occasion"; so start with a "mean
caipirinha", move onto the "must-have" ceviche sampler, then get
an "amazing" crispy whole fish before enjoying the "best part" –
complimentary "caramel popcorn brought with the bill."

**NEW Central Michel
Richard Ⓢ** *American/French* — | — | — | E

Penn Quarter | 1001 Pennsylvania Ave. NW (11th St.) | 202-626-0015 |
www.centralmichelrichard.com

Named for its strategic Penn Quarter location between the Capitol and
the White House, this oh-so-contemporary New American–French
bistro from culinary star Michel Richard (Citronelle) exudes California
glamour – think buttery leather banquettes, glass-enclosed wine
displays and blond wood trappings; plus, its polished granite bar
hosts one of the buzziest after-work scenes in town.

Centro Italian Grill *Italian* 21 | 19 | 19 | $44

Bethesda | 4838 Bethesda Ave. (bet. Arlington Rd. & Woodmont Ave.),
MD | 301-951-1988 | www.centroitalian.com

It's "nice to be seen" in the "happening", "stylish", gold-toned
dining room of this "NY-type Italian" in the "heart of Bethesda's
Restaurant Row", where the service is "low-key" and the "signature
thick spaghetti" and "wonderful fish" get raves; those diners who
dismiss it as a "too noisy" "wannabe" may be swayed by a post-
Survey chef change.

Cesco *Italian* 23 | 16 | 20 | $46

Bethesda | 4871 Cordell Ave. (Norfolk Ave.), MD |
301-654-8333

A Tuscan "off-the-beaten path" "gem", this "terrific" Bethesda trattoria dishes up native born chef-owner Francesco Ricchi's "wonderful Northern Italian soul food", including osso buco and pappardelle
with duck sauce; there's a "friendly staff" that's "always willing to
adjust the menu", but the "average setting" that "could use a face-
lift" and "inconsistent fare" ("superb when it's on", "middling" when
it isn't) mar the experience; N.B. Ricchi is also spending time at his
other restaurant, D'Acqua.

	FOOD	DECOR	SERVICE	COST

Ceviche *Nuevo Latino* | 23 | 25 | 22 | $33 |

Silver Spring | 921J Ellsworth Dr. (bet. Fenton St. & Georgia Ave.), MD | 301-608-0081 | www.latinconcepts.com

"Unexpectedly chic" among "otherwise cookie-cutter" restaurants, this "cool", "casual" Nuevo Latino in the "new Downtown Silver Spring" wins acclaim for a "hip", "airy" dining room, "friendly service" and the "to-die-for" "eponymous dish"; occasional "live music adds to the ambiance" of this "great date place", even if it "gets a little loud sometimes"; N.B. a Glover Park location is expected to open soon.

C.F. Folks ☒ *Eclectic* | 23 | 7 | 19 | $14 |

Golden Triangle | 1225 19th St. NW (bet. M & N Sts.) | 202-293-0162 | www.cffolksrestaurant.com

"Greasy spoon" looks belie "gourmet delights" at this "folksy" Golden Triangle lunch-only counter south of Dupont, where you can sample "a different country every day" from the Eclectic daily special menu; nearby office workers look past the "brassy" service to find an "oasis of value", especially for crab cakes; P.S. "you can sit outside" too.

Charlie Palmer Steak *Steak* | 23 | 24 | 22 | $62 |

Capitol Hill | 101 Constitution Ave. NW (bet. 1st St. & Louisiana Ave.) | 202-547-8100 | www.charliepalmer.com

"Bring your Gucci wallet and wear your Manolos" to this "sexy", "star-studded" Capitol Hill hot spot where "movers and shakers" dine on "excellent" New American chophouse fare (the "seafood is just as good as the steak") backed by "first-class" wines; the "gorgeous ultramodern setting" with a "view of the Capitol Dome" is a "welcome change" from the "usual" meat palace "stodginess", and if you want to be even more casual "try the bar service."

☑ Cheesecake Factory ❶ *American* | 18 | 17 | 17 | $27 |

Upper NW | Chevy Chase Pavilion | 5345 Wisconsin Ave. NW (Military Rd.) | 202-364-0500
Rockville | White Flint Mall | 11301 Rockville Pike (Nicholson Ln.), MD | 301-770-0999
Arlington | The Market Common Clarendon | 2900 N. Wilson Blvd. (Clarendon Blvd.), VA | 703-294-9966
McLean | Tysons Galleria | 1796 International Dr. (Westpark Dr.), VA | 703-506-9311
www.thecheesecakefactory.com

"Go hungry" to these "touristy" yet "reliable" "Disneyland"-like Americans known for "obscene portions" and "divinely decadent cheesecake bliss" brought to table by a "well-trained staff"; "encyclopedic menus" mean there's "something for everyone" – and everyone seems to be here, judging by the "very long wait"; if you're in a mall setting, "put your name on the list and shop for an hour."

Chef Geoff's *American* | 18 | 16 | 18 | $34 |

Downtown | 1301 Pennsylvania Ave. NW (bet. E & F Sts.) | 202-464-4461
Upper NW | 3201 New Mexico Ave. NW (Nebraska Ave.) | 202-237-7800
www.chefgeoff.com

"Chic and comforting at the same time", this pair of New Americans puts a "thoughtful modern spin" on "standard pub fare" while "leav-

FOOD | DECOR | SERVICE | COST

ing some cash in your pocket"; Downtown delivers a "huge happy-hour scene" and a "great stop before a show" at nearby Warner Theatre, while Upper NW (with its "kid-friendly" dining room, "charming terrace" and "bustling" bar) provides "a perfect fall-back location" for families and collegiates; you can enjoy a "fantastic live jazz brunch on Sundays" at both.

Chesapeake Chicken & Rockin' Ribs BBQ

– | – | – | I

NEW Bethesda | 7007 Wisconsin Ave. (bet. Leland & Walsh Sts.), MD | 301-656-7634 | www.chesapeakechicken.com
See review in the Baltimore Directory.

Chez Mama-San Ⓜ Japanese

▽ 21 | 21 | 20 | $37

Georgetown | 1039 33rd St. NW (M St.) | 202-333-3888
"Don't expect sushi" at this "oasis in Georgetown" – but count on an "excellent presentation" of "homey Japanese" (meatloaf, pork cutlets, "miso soup to die for") in a "beautiful space" with jade-green silk cushions, exposed bricks and classic music that makes you feel "just like" you're dining in Japan, "complete with tables of Japanese businessmen"; eating here is definitely a "relaxing" experience, "particularly if you don't mind leisurely service."

Chi-Cha Lounge ● S American

16 | 20 | 14 | $26

U Street Corridor | 1624 U St. NW (bet. 16th & 17th Sts.) | 202-234-8400 | www.latinconcepts.com
"The scene is young and the air is thick" at this "glam place" "best for drinks", a "round of hookah" and "lounging on comfy couches with the U Street hipster crowd"; though "more of a hangout than a restaurant", "surprisingly good" "South American finger food" means "you don't have to sip sangria on an empty stomach", and even the "overpriced" smokes and "spotty service" can't kill the "electric chill."

NEW Chima Brazilian/Steak

– | – | – | E

Vienna | 8010 Towers Crescent Dr. (Leesburg Pike), VA | 703-639-3080 | www.chima.cc
Tysons Corner's latest business-class steakhouse is a glossy Brazilian churrascaria, where an all-you-can-eat meat parade is bolstered by a hot-and-cold buffet of salads and sides, an extensive wall of wines and over-the-top desserts; accessorized with native arts and crafts, its glamorous quarters feature a spacious bar area.

China Garden Chinese

19 | 11 | 13 | $22

Rosslyn | Twin Towers | 1100 Wilson Blvd. (Arlington Rd.), VA | 703-525-5317 | www.chinagardenva.com
"Tourists from China come by the busload" to this "authentic" Cantonese in Rosslyn, so be sure to "go early" for weekend dim sum that "rivals the best in NYC and San Francisco"; the rest of the week, a "varied menu" "exceeds standard Chinese fare" without "breaking the bank", but critics carp it's "gone downhill", with "frantic" service ("the coming and going of service carts bumps up your blood pressure") and a setting that's equally dim.

	FOOD	DECOR	SERVICE	COST

China Star *Chinese* ▽ 20 | 8 | 13 | $20

Fairfax | Fair City Mall | 9600G Main St. (Pickett Rd.), VA | 703-323-8822 | www.chinastarfood.com

At this "real deal" Szechuan in Fairfax, "don't bother to order from the conventional Americanized" offerings – instead "get the Chinese menu with chef's specialties" including "fiery" dishes ideal for those who "really want to sweat"; the "seedy strip-mall" setting and service are less than stellar, but the "inexpensive", "generous portions" shine.

Chinatown Express *Chinese* 22 | 6 | 14 | $14

Chinatown | 746 Sixth St. NW (H St.) | 202-638-0424

"Passersby watch handmade noodles being stretched" at this Chinatown "hole-in-the-wall" where "in-the-know" diners come for "cheap, fast" soup dumplings ("a must"), BBQ ("the way to go") and "huge bowls of homemade fresh noodles" "for only $5"; there's "iffy service" and a "dive atmosphere" that prompt some to say it's "better for takeout", but others focus on the generous fare, warning "if you go away hungry, it's your own fault."

Ching Ching Cha Ⓜ *Tearoom* ▽ 19 | 24 | 25 | $18

Georgetown | 1063 Wisconsin Ave. NW (M St.) | 202-333-8288

The air is "perfumed" with dozens of "delicious teas" at this "peaceful" tearoom in Georgetown that's "only a stone's throw from Starbucks, but worlds away in uniqueness"; the Chinese ritual ceremony is "expertly performed and explained" in a "meditative" traditional-style setting that includes "low tables with floor mats", and there are also "delicate" light dishes to accompany the wide variety of "wonderful" infusions.

Chopsticks *Japanese* ▽ 19 | 11 | 16 | $26

Georgetown | 1073 Wisconsin Ave. NW (M St.) | 202-338-6161

"Surprisingly affordable for Georgetown", this "cozy", "quiet" Japanese rolls out "well-spiced" sushi in "a tiny space without much flair" yet "authentically Tokyo" in its "simplicity of decor"; "the quality of the fish" is "outstanding", the "soft-shell crabs are consistently delicious" and the "fried tofu is light and spicy", so "if you can get seated, it's an excellent experience."

Chutzpah *Deli* 19 | 10 | 16 | $16

Fairfax | 12214 Fairfax Towne Ctr. (Monument Dr.), VA | 703-385-8883

NEW **Vienna** | 8100 Boone Blvd. (Aline Ave.), VA | 703-556-3354

www.chutzpahdeli.com

"It ain't New Yawk" – "you still have to go 200 miles north for the real thing" – but this Fairfax deli facsimile (and its new Tysons Corner twin) "gets the dishes right", especially the corned beef, "piled high to the sky" on rye, "authentic egg creams", "chicken soup for the soul" and other "traditional goodies"; fortunately, "you're not there for the decor", and as for service, well, as expats say, "if you ask for a kasha knish, they'd answer 'gesundheit.'"

	FOOD	DECOR	SERVICE	COST

NEW Circa ◐ *American*
| | - | - | - | M |

Dupont Circle | 1601 Connecticut Ave. NW (Q St.) | 202-667-1601 | www.circacafes.com

Located in the prime Dupont Circle space vacated by WrapWorks, this midpriced New American is a coffee shop in the morning, a wine bar in the evening and a casual eatery in between; decorated with polished wood and racks of wine bottles, it offers a cosmopolitan setting for snacking on pizzas and other small plates.

Circle Bistro *American*
| | 21 | 18 | 17 | $44 |

West End | One Washington Circle Hotel | 1 Washington Circle NW (New Hampshire Ave.) | 202-293-5390 | www.thecirclehotel.com

A "cozy, romantic" New American "find" within "walking distance" of the Kennedy Center, this "minimalist" West End space may have that hotel feel, but it's "pleasant" enough for brunch, a "quiet" power breakfast or an "artfully prepared" (though a few say ultimately "forgettable") dinner; others say "head for" the "warm", "friendly" bar with fireplace, instead, and get a bite off the "nice, varied mini-menu."

Z Citronelle *French*
| | 28 | 25 | 26 | $88 |

(aka Michel Richard's Citronelle)

Georgetown | Latham Hotel | 3000 M St. NW (30th St.) | 202-625-2150 | www.citronelledc.com

Georgetown's "Washington monument" for "visiting dignitaries" is chef-owner Michel Richard's "extraordinary" New French, where "sterling ingredients, a sure hand and a dollop of whimsy" (try the "breakfast" dessert, a "masterwork of trompe l'oeil") make it "the best DC has to offer"; get a table near the see-in kitchen to watch the "fun", then relax in the "lovely" modern space and be "spoiled" by an "impeccable" staff; P.S. the lofty prices match the "high caliber", but both the bar/lounge and terrace offer a more casual menu.

City Lights of China *Chinese*
| | 18 | 11 | 16 | $23 |

Dupont Circle | 1731 Connecticut Ave. NW (bet. R & S Sts.) | 202-265-6688
Bethesda | 4820 Bethesda Ave. (Woodmont Ave.), MD | 301-913-9501
www.citylightsofchina.com

"Crispy, dry shredded beef made in heaven" and "large portions" of many other "delicious" favorites keep regulars returning to these Chinese eateries that are both "wallet- and waistline-friendly"; the "bright" Dupont Circle spot is "always packed and worth the wait", but the Bethesda outpost boasts more "beautiful" decor; still, sticklers snap that this "staple" is "past its sell-by date" and the service is all about "moving you in and moving you out."

Z CityZen 🅢🅜 *American*
| | 26 | 26 | 25 | $100 |

SW | Mandarin Oriental | 1330 Maryland Ave. SW (bet. 12th & 14th Sts.) | 202-787-6006 | www.cityzenrestaurant.com

For "New York chic" in a "government town" head to this New American "extravaganza" in the "plush" Mandarin Oriental in SW; its "sleek" look, with an open kitchen, a wall of flames in the bar and lots of steel, leather and wood, suits the "fashionable" enthusiasts

	FOOD	DECOR	SERVICE	COST

of its "glorious" tasting menus, "attractive wine list" and "creative" details like the "fantastic mini–Parker House rolls"; add in a "personable" staff and you might want to remember this "flawless operation" "for birthdays and anniversaries."

☑ Clyde's ● *American* | 18 | 21 | 19 | $30

Chinatown | Gallery Pl. | 707 Seventh St. NW (bet. F & H Sts.) | 202-349-3700

Georgetown | Georgetown Park Mall | 3236 M St. NW (bet. Prospect St. & Wisconsin Ave.) | 202-333-9180

Chevy Chase | 5441 Wisconsin Ave. (Western Ave.), MD | 301-951-9600

Rockville | 2 Preserve Pkwy. (bet. Tower Oaks Blvd. & Wootton Pkwy.), MD | 301-294-0200

Alexandria | Mark Ctr. | 1700 N. Beauregard St. (Seminary Rd.), VA | 703-820-8300

Reston | Reston Town Ctr. | 11905 Market St. (Reston Pkwy.), VA | 703-787-6601

Vienna | Tysons Corner Ctr. | 8332 Leesburg Pike (Westpark Dr.), VA | 703-734-1901

NEW Broadlands | Willow Creek Farm | 42920 Broadlands Blvd. (Croson Ln.), VA | 571-209-1200
www.clydes.com

While this "original" American "dining saloon" has "created a vast legion of copycats", it remains a "staple" that's "always good, year after year" (it's the Most Popular restaurant in the Baltimore Survey); with "fresh" oysters, "delicious" crab cakes, "the best" burgers and other "bar food, par excellence" served in a "brash" setting amid "nostalgic decor", it's "reliably good"; P.S. the two newest branches – a "gorgeous" Victorian "sight to see" at Gallery Place and a tavern complex in Broadlands, VA – are "great for just hanging out."

Coastal Flats *Seafood* | 22 | 20 | 22 | $29

Fairfax | Fairfax Corner | 11901 Grand Commons Ave. (Monument Dr.), VA | 571-522-6300

McLean | Tysons Corner Ctr. | 1961 Chain Bridge Rd. (International Dr.), VA | 703-356-1440
www.greatamericanrestaurants.com

"Entirely New England" lobster rolls, gumbo that "takes you to old New Orleans" and decor that suggests an "escape to Key West" make these Fairfax and Tysons Corner seafooders "a welcome addition to any topographical map"; from the Great American chain (Carlyle, Sweetwater Tavern, etc.), it "keeps up with its sister restaurants" thanks to an "eager staff" that "knows how to make the team service approach work", but "crabby" critics cringe over waiting "up to three hours" to sit in "one big" "loud" room.

Coeur de Lion *American* | ▽ 23 | 26 | 25 | $59

Mt. Vernon Square/New Convention Center | Henley Park Hotel | 926 Massachusetts Ave. NW (10th St.) | 202-414-0500 | www.henleypark.com

At this "hidden gem in the Henley Park Hotel" near the Convention Center, the New American fare is served in a "delightful Edwardian" dining room (complete with fireplace and glass ceiling) that's "one of the most romantic settings in DC"; you can expect "solid" dishes, plus a "nice jazz bar" with a dance floor.

Colorado Kitchen Ⓜ American | 24 | 15 | 15 | $28 |

Upper NW | 5515 Colorado Ave. NW (Kennedy St.) | 202-545-8280

"Traditions are tweaked" at Gillian Clark's Upper NW "kitschy" "neighborhood haunt", where the "indefatigable" chef turns "familiar" American "home cooking" into something "totally new", turning out the "best meatloaf", mac 'n' cheese and warm doughnuts, along with "fabulous" brunch favorites like shrimp and grits; while fans tolerate her "no substitutions" rule in order to "fill their bellies with loving food", many wish the "rude" staff was more loving; N.B. closed Mondays and Tuesdays.

Ⓩ Colvin Run Tavern American | 25 | 23 | 24 | $61 |

Vienna | Fairfax Sq. | 8045 Leesburg Pike (Gallows Rd.), VA | 703-356-9500 | www.kinkead.com

"Bring on the beef cart" is the mantra at Bob Kinkead's New American "class act" in Tysons Corner, where a "hearty menu" featuring meats "carved tableside" is served in four uniquely "elegant", regionally themed rooms by folks who "know their craft"; hailed as "good for dates or deals" by "dressy" heavy-hitters, this "civil world of dining" stuck in "mall-land" is "well worth the price of admission."

NEW Comet Ping Pong Ⓜ Pizza | - | - | - | I |

Upper NW | 5037 Connecticut Ave. NW (Nebraska St.) | 202-364-0404

At this Upper NW pie parlor that's just a dough toss away from their Buck's Fishing & Camping restaurant, owners Carole Greenwood and James Alefantis serve up crisp-crusted pizzas and market-fresh salads on mini Ping-Pong tables (there are larger ones in the back for playing a match); the skylit retro-Americana setting is crafted from salvaged artifacts, with a bathroom that's a must-see.

Comus Inn Ⓜ American | ▽ 20 | 22 | 19 | $58 |

Dickerson | 23900 Old Hundred Rd. (Comus Rd.), MD | 301-349-5100 | www.thecomusinn.com

The "elegant setting in the shadow of Sugarloaf Mountain" makes this "romantic" New American in "rural" Montgomery County "the perfect date or getaway", especially on Saturday nights when there's live piano music; the à la carte New Orleans–style menu takes advantage of "Maryland's agricultural bounty", but naysayers who find "just ok" service say "it's hard to justify the price"; N.B. open Wednesday–Sunday.

Coppi's Organic Italian | 22 | 19 | 20 | $28 |

U Street Corridor | 1414 U St. NW (bet. 14th & 15th Sts.) | 202-319-7773 | www.coppisorganic.com

Fans "savor every bite" of the organic "inventive" Ligurian specials and "yummy" "creative" pizzas cooked in a wood-fired oven that's the open kitchen's "centerpiece" at this "friendly" U Street eatery – a "cozy, hip" spot that pays "homage" to the home country's bicy-

FOOD | DECOR | SERVICE | COST

cling history with related "paraphernalia throughout"; while some snipe the prices are "hefty" for a pie-parlor setting, this "better than average Italian" nonetheless has sweet tooths cycling "back for the Nutella calzone."

☑ Corduroy ⊠ American

25 | 16 | 23 | $48

Downtown | Sheraton Four Points Downtown | 1201 K St. NW, 2nd fl. (12th St.) | 202-589-0699 | www.corduroydc.com

"The word is getting out" on this New American "gem", "hidden" on the second floor of a "business hotel" not far from the Convention Center, where chef-owner Tom Power "makes magic" with "the best local produce" (the food "will be on your mind for days"), the "deep wine list" is "one of the most fairly priced in town" and the "staff is enthusiastic"; it's only the decor that some consider "lame."

Crème American

23 | 21 | 20 | $33

U Street Corridor | 1322 U St. NW (13th St.) | 202-234-1884

Dishing up "down-home dishes with a new flair" in the "trendy U Street Corridor", this "stylish" New American "neighborhood joint" with "eager service" makes pork and beans "chic", and draws raves for its "most inspired" mushrooms; the "diverse crowd" at its "long" "black bar" or in the dining room can "pair chicken soup with a martini" or test-drive the "infamous $9 Kobe hot dog" – but they'd better "go early", since it doesn't take reservations.

Crisp & Juicy Peruvian

24 | 4 | 13 | $11

Rockville | Sunshine Sq. | 1331G Rockville Pike (Congressional Ln.), MD | 301-251-8833

Silver Spring | Leisure World Plaza | 3800 International Dr. (Georgia Ave.), MD | 301-598-3333

Arlington | 4540 Lee Hwy. (Woodstock St.), VA | 703-243-4222 ⊟

Falls Church | 913 W. Broad St. (Rte. 17), VA | 703-241-9091

"How do you say 'yum' in Spanish?" – the "mouthwatering" rotisserie chicken at these suburban "lunch counters" "lives up to its name", proving that "Peruvians know something about *pollo*"; while the birds "can't be beat", some say that "it's really all about" the "addictive" sauces and "crunchy" fried yuca on the side; since there's "barely a place to perch", try takeout instead.

Crystal Thai Thai

23 | 16 | 19 | $25

Arlington | Arlington Forest Shopping Ctr. | 4819 Arlington Blvd. (Park Dr.), VA | 703-522-1311 | www.crystalthai.com

"Masked in a local strip mall", this "high-class" Arlington Thai demonstrates "a crystal clear understanding" of what's "pleasing to the palate" – its signature crispy whole fish and "wonderful" soft-shell crabs for starters; it's "not near anything" and the "decor is not as pleasant as the menu", but the "staff remembers regulars."

Cuba de Ayer ⓜ Cuban

▽ 19 | 12 | 16 | $23

Burtonsville | 15446 Old Columbia Pike (Athey Rd.), MD | 301-476-9622

"Once you find" this "great" "strip joint" you're certain to "come back" for "generous portions" of "tasty" "home-cooked Cuban" that's "worth the trip" to Burtonsville; the cubano sandwiches are "good" as are the "greasy" yuca fries, but "don't miss the 'old rags'" (ropa vieja).

Cubano's *Cuban*

| 21 | 17 | 19 | $29 |

Silver Spring | 1201 Fidler Ln. (Georgia Ave.), MD | 301-563-4020

Amigos say "*sí, sí*" to the "homestyle Cuban classics" at this "Little Havana in the *corazón* of Silver Spring" that "may not look like much" from the outside but features "fabulous paintings" hung on "vibrantly colorful walls" indoors; some say the service is "genuine", others "slow", but it's a "good-value choice", especially when you can "sit on the deck in warm weather" and sip "killer" mojitos.

Curry Club 🅼 *Indian*

▽ | 24 | 21 | 23 | $34 |

Glover Park | 1734 Wisconsin Ave. NW (R St.) | 202-625-9090 | www.curryclub.net

Fans find a nice "surprise" at this Glover Park curry house where Indian recipes get a "fresh and delicious" "British spin" with "just the right level" of heat for "American palates", along with "excellent wines chosen to complement the spicy meal"; the owners create a "relaxing" vibe in the second-floor space where customers feel so "regal sitting against silk cushions" that they "want to hang out all night"; downstairs there's a take-out counter and small lounge.

NEW D'Acqua ◐ *Italian/Seafood*

| - | - | - | E |

Penn Quarter | 801 Pennsylvania Ave. NW (bet. 7th & 9th Sts.) | 202-783-7717 | www.ristorantedacqua.com

Veteran chef-owners Francesco Ricchi (Cesco) and Enzo Febbraro (ex Filomena) are behind this glamorous seafood-focused Modern Italian in the Penn Quarter, where diners can select their fish from a marketlike display and have it oven-roasted, grilled or salt-crusted and baked; the late-night nibbles and Tuscan gold-and-blue decor are also likely bait for a lounge scene.

Da Domenico 🆉 *Italian*

| 21 | 16 | 22 | $43 |

McLean | 1992 Chain Bridge Rd. (Leesburg Pike), VA | 703-790-9000 | www.da-domenico.com

Flash "back to old-fashioned style and service" at this Tysons Corner "institution" known for "classic" Italian – and the "occasional operatic outburst" from the owner's brother (who mixes "romantic" arias and "originals, often about the Redskins or other local newsmakers"); expect to fondly "remember the experience more than the menu" that "lacks bang" or the "dark, outdated" "*Godfather*-like" decor.

Dahlia *American*

| 21 | 11 | 16 | $42 |

Upper NW | Spring Valley Shopping Ctr. | 4849 Massachusetts Ave. NW (49th St.) | 202-364-1004

Chef-owner David Scribner, a "veteran" of two trendy eateries (Felix and Smith Point), is "feeding ladies who lunch" at his "serious" New American in Upper NW's Spring Valley; with more than a few "stars on the menu" – the fish and "pizzas are a must" – many hail it as a "much needed" option, but the "snoozy" saloon decor and "spotty service" take it down a notch.

	FOOD	DECOR	SERVICE	COST

David Craig Bethesda *American* ▽ 25 | 17 | 25 | $51

Bethesda | 4924 St. Elmo Ave. (Norfolk Ave.), MD | 301-657-2484 | www.dcbethesda.com

Big-city chef David Craig brings a taste of DC to Bethesda with this "spare" New American; the menu, with such "outstanding" selections as "spectacular" squash ravioli and a "scrumptious chocolate bread pudding", "makes for tough choices", but the "friendly" service can help with that; aesthetes admit, however, if you're not "watching the chef at work" through the room's windowed back area, there's "little atmosphere."

D.C. Boathouse *American* 14 | 16 | 17 | $28

Palisades | 5441 MacArthur Blvd. (Cathedral Ave.) | 202-362-2628

While the food "won't win any awards", there's "a little something for everyone on the menu" at this "comfy neighborhood" American (with Greek additions) in the Palisades, where boating and college memorabilia decorate the walls and ceiling; there's the "bonus of knowing most people there", especially when you're sitting in the *Cheers* bar, only better", but some deem this one just "ok, if you're in the mood for burgers and lots of kids."

Z DC Coast ⚡ *American* 24 | 23 | 22 | $51

Downtown | Tower Bldg. | 1401 K St. NW (14th St.) | 202-216-5988 | www.dccoast.com

What makes this Downtown New American a "surefire winner" is its yin-yang blend of contrasts: the "outstanding" cooking, focused on "wonderful fish", is both "adventurous and comforting", its "delightful deco" look is "both classic and modern" and it serves a "great power lunch without the stuffiness"; although the "space is acoustically challenged" ("upstairs is quieter and has a view"), many find the buzz "energizing" especially at the "cocktail hour scene."

Dean & DeLuca *Eclectic* 21 | 14 | 15 | $21

Georgetown | 3276 M St. NW (33rd St.) | 202-342-2500 | www.deananddeluca.com

"A little bit of Manhattan" in Georgetown, this "cramped" "Bergdorf Goodman of foods" woos "self-styled foodies" with an "amazing selection" of Eclectic "gourmet treats" and wine; after "great grazing" in the "open marketplace", enjoy some "people-watching" on the "sunny enclosed patio" before shopping for "meticulously prepared" items – it's an "excellent place to pick up a quick dinner to take home"; but some believe the service "has to improve."

Delhi Club *Indian* 22 | 11 | 19 | $21

Arlington | 1135 N. Highland St. (Clarendon Blvd.), VA | 703-527-5666 | www.delhiclub.com

Clarendon's "best table service Indian" curries favor with Arlingtonians via "pungent but not overwhelming" spicing – though the "vindaloo will keep you reaching for water to quench the flames"; "great vegetarian options compete with or surpass" the "solid, if unremarkable" meat dishes, but the "cramped" dining room is "a bit on the drab side" and "service is so prompt you almost feel rushed."

	FOOD	DECOR	SERVICE	COST

Delhi Dhaba *Indian* — 17 | 10 | 15 | $20

Upper NW | 4455 Connecticut Ave. NW (Yuma St.) | 202-537-1008
Bethesda | 7236 Woodmont Ave. (Elm St.), MD | 301-718-0008
Arlington | 2424 Wilson Blvd. (Barton St.), VA | 703-524-0008
www.delhidhaba.com

"Don't be fooled by the cafeteria style" of this "cheerfully cheap" Indian trio; despite "no-frills" settings with "funky Indian music videos", fans "return and return" for "pungent" tikka masala, "yummy" butter chicken and "first-rate" breads; it's too bad "prices went up" and "portions went down" according to snappish surveyors who find "nothing special" about these "steam-table" buffets.

Del Merei Grille *American* — 23 | 18 | 22 | $35

Alexandria | 3106 Mt. Vernon Ave. (Kennedy St.), VA | 703-739-4335 |
www.delmereigrille.com

"Frickles" (fried pickle chips) are "a must" at this "star" in Alexandria's Del Ray area, where the New American comes "with a down-home" Southern twist; the "hospitality and good grub" more than "make up for" any "lack in appearance" ("think strip mall"), so "choose your meat, choose your sauce and choose your sides" at this "fresh take on the neighborhood grill" and let the "energetic, youthful" staff "welcome one and all."

Diner, The ❶ *Diner* — 18 | 15 | 17 | $18

Adams Morgan | 2453 18th St. NW (bet. Belmont & Columbia Rds.) |
202-232-8800

Even though "there's nothing fancy" about this Adams Morgan "hot spot", "something can be said for $5 eggs and fresh coffee at 3 AM on a Tuesday"; with a "cool retro vibe" that "seamlessly combines chili dogs and martinis", this "staple" "appeals to an eclectic mix of patrons" "at all hours", but if you're hungering for the "fantastic" weekend brunch that gets "overstuffed with hungover hipsters", start waiting in line now.

Dino *Italian* — 19 | 18 | 18 | $38

Cleveland Park | 3435 Connecticut Ave. NW (bet. Macomb & Ordway Sts.) | 202-686-2966 | www.dino-dc.com

Cleveland Parkers "love the concept" – Tuscan- and Venetian-inspired "big and little plates, informality and good wine" – at this corner spot with wraparound windows that's become a "home away from home"; "wonderful" cheeses, "inviting" Italian tapas and "well-priced" vino meet most expectations, but a few find "kinks", including "less impressive" full entrees and a "disorganized" staff.

Dish + Drinks *American* — 19 | 15 | 19 | $43

Foggy Bottom | The River Inn | 924 25th St. NW (bet. I & K Sts.) |
202-338-8707 | www.dishdc.com

Kennedy Center patrons "never want to tell people about" this dining "secret": a "tiny" hotel enclave in Foggy Bottom serving "reliable" New American "comfort food" "within walking distance" of their theater seats; a post-Survey chef change has Peggy Thompson (ex Morrison-Clark Inn) putting her own spin on the menu, but so far there's been little change in the "spotty" service or the "minimal decor – only that Willam Wegman triptych."

District ChopHouse & Brewery *Steak* | 20 | 18 | 19 | $37 |

Penn Quarter | 509 Seventh St. NW (bet. E & F Sts.) | 202-347-3434 | www.districtchophouse.com

"Even the salads feel masculine (grilled lettuce anyone?)" at this "testosterone-y" Penn Quarter "institution" where "size does matter" – especially when it comes to steak; "a bit old-fashioned, but in a good way", this "upscale brewpub in a former bank building" has "high ceilings" and "1940s decor" that evokes "an old money supper club", plus the staff knows how to get you "fed and out the door in plenty of time" for tip-off at the Verizon Center; P.S. escape the "noisy bar" by heading upstairs to "play some pool."

Divino *Argentinean* | 20 | 19 | 16 | $36 |

Bethesda | 7345B Wisconsin Ave. (Montgomery Ave.), MD | 240-497-0300 | www.divinolounge.com

If the "crowded bar" in the front of this Bethesda "hot spot" suggests this is "not a place you would think to have dinner", you'll be "pleasantly surprised at the quality of the tapas" and the Argentinean grilled meats and seafood served in the rear (if not the "unpredictable service"); still, those who "come for the bar" and the "fun" tango class on Wednesday nights "don't have much to say about the fare"; N.B. a DC branch is set to debut in 2007.

NEW **Dock at** | – | – | – | M |
Lansdowne *American/Seafood*

Lansdowne | Lansdowne Town Ctr. | 19286 Promenade Dr. (Belmont Ridge Rd.), VA | 571-333-4747 | www.thedockatlansdowne.com

Though docked in the new Lansdowne Town Center, this polished seafooder evokes ocean breezes, serving affordable fresh fish and American classics beneath billowy sails; the relaxed yet sophisticated surroundings come complete with an outdoor patio and bar.

Dogfish Head Alehouse ❶ *Pub Food* | 17 | 15 | 15 | $21 |

Gaithersburg | 800 W. Diamond Ave. (west of Quince Orchard Rd.), MD | 301-963-4847 | www.dogfishheadalehouse.com

"Outstanding microbrews" from its Rehoboth Beach brewery are this Gaithersburg pub's biggest draw, since the "ordinary fare", sprawling "TGI Fridays"-like setting (made a bit more "homey with lots of dark wood") and "very young and inexperienced" crew aren't particular highlights; so go just to enjoy the "exceptional" small-batch suds and then "call a cab"; N.B. a Falls Church offshoot is in the works.

Dolce Vita *Italian* | 22 | 14 | 18 | $29 |

Fairfax | 10824 Lee Hwy. (Main St.), VA | 703-385-1530 | www.dolcevitafairfax.com

"A fine taste of Italy on Lee Highway", this "friendly", "family-run" Fairfax Italian isn't "just some local pizza joint"; "honest" "old-world" cooking (osso buco, chicken Marsala, grilled calamari) draws "crowds" to the "loud", "cramped" dining room "hidden" in a "tiny" suburban strip mall; at night, a "roving guitar player" is either "annoying and loud" or a "wild" "gas"; P.S. its next-door deli is a "great place to get panini" for lunch.

Domku Bar & Café Ⓜ *E Euro./Scandinavian* ▽ 26 21 17 $27
Petworth | 821 Upshur St. NW (bet. 8th St. & Georgia Ave.) | 202-722-7475
"Unique" describes this Baltic "gem" in the "changing Petworth neighborhood" in Upper Northwest serving "excellent", "made-from-scratch" Eastern European and Scandinavian fare (it's "not always what you think") along with the "best martinis" and unusual house-seeped aquavits in a "shabby-chic" lounge and bar/cafe; a real "hidden gem", "it's a great place to spend an evening" in an atmosphere "akin to New York's [Greenwich] Village."

Duangrat's *Thai* 23 18 19 $31
Falls Church | 5875 Leesburg Pike (Glen Forest Dr.), VA | 703-820-5775 | www.duangrats.com
This "reliable" Falls Church Thai serves "beautifully presented food" and an "amazing" weekend dim sum brunch in a "classy" if "tired" space; though "its popularity" "may be its undoing" since the "slow service" and "noisy", "crowded conditions" "ruin the experience" for some, the dance demos on Saturday nights are a nice reason to visit; P.S. "try their sister restaurant, Rabieng", a "lower-priced" option.

Dukem ◗ *Ethiopian* 23 12 16 $19
U Street Corridor | 1114-1118 U St. NW (12th St.) | 202-667-8735 | www.dukemrestaurant.com
"Ask the cabbies" to recommend the "best Ethiopian in the city" and they'll steer you to this "adventurous" U Street staple for "dirt-cheap and delicious" fare "with a kick", which is scooped up with "stretchy", "spongy" injera bread; "once a hidden gem" (to non-natives), this "no-frills" spot with nightly live music is "now generating long lines and worthwhile waits", as is its equally "fabulous" off-shoot in Baltimore's Mt. Vernon area; P.S. try the "traditional" coffee ceremony on Sunday afternoons.

DuPont Grille *American* 19 19 19 $36
Dupont Circle | Jurys Washington Hotel | 1500 New Hampshire Ave. NW (19th St.) | 202-939-9596 | www.dupontgrille.com
See and be seen through "all glass walls" in this New American "overlooking Dupont Circle" with "panels that open in good weather to transform" the room into an "outdoor experience"; while fans say the "inventive food" is "a surprise for a restaurant in an Irish hotel", critics contend the "creative" ingredients can sometimes result in "weird food combos" and the service can be "uneven"; P.S. a post-Survey chef change may fulfill diners' hopes that it "kicks it up a notch."

NEW **Eamonn's –** - - - I
A Dublin Chipper/PX *Irish*
Alexandria | 728 King St. (Washington St.), VA | 703-299-8384 | www.eamonnsdublinchipper.com
Cathal and Meshelle Armstrong (Eve, Majestic) bring Dublin to Old Town Alexandria via this dark-wood Gaelic fast-food establishment

offering fish 'n' chips, battered burgers and Irish beer; when the blue light outside an unmarked door on Columbus Street is on, tipplers can buzz for entry to the upstairs PX, a speakeasy-themed lounge.

Eat First ● Chinese

| 22 | 6 | 15 | $19 |

Chinatown | 609 H St. NW (6th St.) | 202-289-1703

"No ambiance, no atmosphere – no problem" because the food at this "spartan" "standard" with "no-nonsense service" in Chinatown is "cheap and fabulous", especially if you "stick to the Chinese menu" ("not for the faint of heart") posted on "sheets of paper taped to the wall"; in contrast, the "Americanized" choices get dissed as "Chinese for those who long for Chung King" – but that still works for others who just want a quick "bite before a game."

El Chalan ● Peruvian

| 20 | 13 | 17 | $27 |

Foggy Bottom | 1924 I St. NW (20th St.) | 202-293-2765 | www.elchalanrestaurant.com

Climb "down a few steps off Pennsylvania Avenue" into the Foggy Bottom "office jungle" to find this "friendly" "upscale Peruvian" in a "funky underground space"; it may be "cramped and cacophonous", but it "doesn't disappoint" with "hearty" Andean dishes and "traditional" pisco sours; midday, "it can be busier than the lunchroom at the nearby World Bank" since most of the employees seem to be here.

Elephant & Castle ● Pub Food

| 13 | 15 | 15 | $25 |

Downtown | 1201 Pennsylvania Ave. NW (12th St.) | 202-347-7707 | www.elephantcastle.com

"Blimey, we're in London – minus the smoke, British accents and ancient-ness"; "when you're in the mood for a pint", or for "affordable dining after the museums" on the Mall, this Downtown facsimile that attracts "office happy-hour" visits is handy for its "great" brew "selections on tap", even if the "grub" is, at best, "fair"; however, pub purists proclaim "there isn't much difference" between this "wannabe" and the TGI Friday's it replaced except that the "tchotchkes on the walls are British."

Elevation Burger ⊠ Hamburgers

| ▽ 21 | 13 | 19 | $8 |

Falls Church | 442 S. Washington St. (Annandale Rd.), VA | 703-237-4343 | www.elevationburger.com

"They keep it simple" at this "promising", "friendly" Falls Church self-serve burger joint that racks up "healthy" points with "wonderful fries" cooked in olive oil, "tasty Kobe beef burgers", "decadent" milkshakes and a 'Half the Guilt' option that "turns super-sizing on its head" by combining a veggie and a meat patty; still, down-to-earth critics don't buy its organic "commitment", calling it "overhyped"; P.S. "come late if you hate kids."

Eleventh Street ● American

| ▽ - | 16 | 16 | $24 |

Arlington | 1041 N. Highland St. (Washington Blvd.), VA | 703-351-1311 | www.eleventhstreetlounge.com

Where "twenty- and thirtysomethings come to see and be seen during happy hour" in Arlington's Clarendon area, this "loungey bar"

	FOOD	DECOR	SERVICE	COST

now has cheese and charcuterie plates as well as New American mini-entrees courtesy of chef Antonio Burrell (ex Viridian); it's "kind of noisy and small", but it's also "cute", colorful and "nicely out of place" in this gentrifying locale; P.S. its "great martinis" are half-price on Thursdays from 4–8 PM.

El Gavilan *Salvadoran* ▽ 23 | 13 | 20 | $21

Silver Spring | 8805 Flower Ave. (Hartwell Rd.), MD | 301-587-4197
This lively Silver Spring cantina dishes up "authentic" Salvadoran fare like "good pupusas" (pork- and cheese-filled tortillas) and the "best skirt steak in town" among other "varied" options; the "comfortable" "neighborhood" setting and reasonable prices make it "nice for families", and live Central American music on weekend nights adds some atmosphere.

El Golfo *S American* ▽ 21 | 13 | 20 | $22

Silver Spring | 8739 Flower Ave. (Piney Branch Rd.), MD | 301-608-2122
"The whole staff knows you" at this "great little find" "off the beaten track" in Silver Spring, where the "responsive" service means there are "no waits" for "flavorful" South American fare that includes "outstanding corn tamales" and "one of the best tres leches cakes"; better yet, this "family-friendly" spot "fills you up without unduly affecting the pocketbook"; P.S. "don't leave without" trying the flan – "no excuses."

Ella's Wood Fired Pizza *Pizza* 19 | 12 | 18 | $22

Penn Quarter | 901 F St. NW (entrance on 9th St., bet. F & G Sts.) | 202-638-3434 | www.ellaspizza.com
"Crispy Neapolitan-style" pies are the "stars of the show" at this Penn Quarter bistro that's "loved" for "loading on" "imaginative" toppings like roasted garlic puree with wild mushrooms; the "comfortable", "great-for-kids" "joint" near the Verizon Center is perfect for a "quick dinner before a game", and the "great happy-hour specials" make it a "fun" affordable "meeting place for young professionals" who try to grab a slice of "free pizza at the bar" before "the vultures swoop in."

NEW El Limeño *Mexican/Salvadoran* - | - | - | I

Petworth | 201 Upshur St. NW (2nd St.) | 202-829-5551
White tablecloths and colorful art dress up this wallet-friendly Latin located in Petworth, overlooking the Soldiers' Home; it serves home-style Mexican and Salvadoran cuisine in an atmosphere suited to both a casual meal or a low-key celebration, with a bar at the back of the dining room that's handy for small gatherings.

El Manantial *Italian/Spanish* ▽ 21 | 18 | 24 | $37

Reston | Toll Oaks Village Ctr. | 12050A North Shore Dr. (Wiehle Ave.), VA | 703-742-6466 | www.elmanantialrestaurant.com
"The key to this Reston gem is the service", from the owner to the "enthusiastic" servers who "consider anything that's less than a perfect" presentation a source of "shame for generations"; though "a little expensive for a neighborhood" eatery in a "modest strip mall",

the Iberian, Italian and French fare and the "extensive wine selection" inspire "return" trips "again and again."

El Mariachi *Mexican* | 23 | 13 | 21 | $24 |

Rockville | 765C Rockville Pike (Wootton Pkwy.), MD | 301-738-7177
With white tablecloths and "fabulous" seafood, this Rockville Mexican is "not your typical taco joint"; yes, you can still get fajitas and enchiladas, but these dishes score extra for their atypical "authenticity", as does the "fantastic" white sangria; the "frequently swamped" and "tight"-spaced dining room accounts for the low decor score, but "reasonable prices" more than make up for "long" "waits on weekend nights."

☒ El Pollo Rico ⌫ *Peruvian* | 25 | 4 | 15 | $10 |

Wheaton | 2541 Ennalls Ave. (Veirs Mill Rd.), MD | 301-942-4419
Arlington | 932 N. Kenmore St. (Fairfax Dr.), VA | 703-522-3220
"Finger-licking" spit-roasted, spicy cluckers that are "cheap and tasty" explain why the "granddaddy of Peruvian chicken joints" "feeds more people than the Red Cross" from its Wheaton and Arlington quarters; the "factory atmosphere" and "lines out the door" spell "takeout" for most, but the choice is simple – these "incredibly flavorful" pullets with "delicious" sauces are virtually "the only things on the menu", so "just say quarter, half or whole"; N.B. cash-only with an ATM on-site.

El Tapatio's *Mexican* | - | - | - | I |

Bladensburg | 4309 Kenilworth Ave. (Tilden Rd.), MD | 301-403-8882
Possibly the "best of the taquerias" in Bladensburg's "Little Mexico", this "friendly", "family-owned" spot serves the "classic comfort food" of its owners' native Guadalajara, including barbecued goat and *caldo de mariscos* (shellfish soup) in "simple" yet festive surroundings (purple walls, red tables); multilingual loyalists sum it up as a "great value" in any language.

NEW Emilio's *Italian* | - | - | - | M |

Lansdowne | Lansdowne Town Ctr. | 19308 Promenade Dr. (Belmont Ridge Rd.), VA | 571-333-3350
At this Lansdowne Town Center palazzo, extensive brickwork, tiles and Romanesque statuary set the stage for wood-fired pizzas and other hearty, midpriced Italian fare; colorful blown-glass fixtures illuminate the bar area, which features high-topped tables for sipping wine and nibbling antipasti while still keeping an eye on what's happening in the open kitchen.

Equinox *American* | 25 | 20 | 23 | $63 |

Golden Triangle | 818 Connecticut Ave. NW (bet. H & I Sts.) | 202-331-8118 | www.equinoxrestaurant.com
Todd and Ellen Gray's "wonderful" Golden Triangle New American near the Oval Office rings "superb" to its many fans who fawn over the "highly innovative" tasting menus full of "exquisite delights" and "local flavors" paired with "tastefully chosen" wines (there are à la carte selections as well); the service is "attentive without being in-

trusive", and even if a few faultfinders want an "update" of the "subdued" decor, others find it amenable for "quiet" conversation.

Etete ● Ethiopian

▽ 21 | 15 | 17 | $23

U Street Corridor | 1942 Ninth St. NW (T St.) | 202-232-7600

The "most upscale looking" of the Ethiopian restaurants "clustered" on this U Street area block offers a "thrilling trip to the Horn of Africa" with "helpful" hospitality and "authentic" "delicious" food; its "intimate" "trendy" setting works well "for a date" or "for those made timid" by unfamiliar food and no utensils, since diners use the "flavorful" injera bread as wraps to scoop up the spicy "tasty" fare.

Etrusco ⃞ Italian

20 | 20 | 19 | $46

Dupont Circle | 1606 20th St. NW (bet. Connecticut Ave. & Q St.) | 202-667-0047

"Lovely and oft-overlooked", this Dupont Circle Northern Italian with "well-prepared" fish (often flown in from Italy), "outstanding pasta" and a "warm" setting is often a "first choice for hosting out-of-town guests", "family reunions" and dates; most patrons feel like they've "escaped" from the hectic city when they have a meal in its white-walled "enoteca-style" room, so even if trendsters snip that "simplicity can be boring", the majority finds a "hidden gem."

Evening Star Cafe American

22 | 17 | 19 | $34

Alexandria | 2000 Mt. Vernon Ave. (Howell Ave.), VA | 703-549-5051 | www.eveningstarcafe.net

The New American "pride" of Alexandria's Del Ray area pairs "high-style" fare with a "beyond extensive" 1,000-plus wine selection (from an attached shop) in "cool-without-trying" digs that include a "funky" diner-esque dining room and bar, plus a "comfy lounge with live music" upstairs; it "caters to all palates and budgets", so it's "crowded" and "service suffers" – but that just adds to its "small-town feel."

⃞ Eve, Restaurant ⃞ American (aka Eve)

27 | 24 | 25 | $71

Alexandria | 110 S. Pitt St. (bet. King & Prince Sts.), VA | 703-706-0450 | www.restauranteve.com

"Save the superlatives" for this Old Town Alexandria New American "foodie paradise", where Irish-born chef-owner Cathal Armstrong's "creative insights into flavors" transform "interesting ingredients" (tripe as well as foie gras) into "mind-blowing" meals with "memorable" matches of wine; "knowledgeable" staffers "treat you like VIPs", and you can choose among its "romantic bistro", "happening bar" or tasting room where the "beautiful dance of waiters" is "worth every penny"; since "none of the many faces of Eve disappoint", she's a "tough" reservation.

Extra Virgin Italian

17 | 19 | 15 | $42

Arlington | 4053 S. 28th St. (bet. S. Quincy & S. Randolph Sts.), VA | 703-998-8474 | www.extravirginva.com

"Like the new girl in school", this "modern" Italian south of Arlington in Shirlington "gets your attention" with "excellent presentation" and "exceedingly pretty" looks; but the "too sexy" entrees are "a little disappointing", and the [often] "clueless" service and "hefty" price tag leave the less-smitten sighing it's "a little full of itself" and, not surprisingly, "needs time to improve."

Faccia Luna Trattoria *Pizza*   21 | 14 | 18 | $22

Alexandria | 823 S. Washington St. (bet. Green & Jefferson Sts.), VA | 703-838-5998
Arlington | 2909 Wilson Blvd. (Fillmore St.), VA | 703-276-3099
www.faccialuna.com

"When the moon hits your eye" "stop by" for a "wood-fired" pizza pie and find *amore* at this "first-date-worthy" trattoria that's perfect for "yuppie couples"; "crispy thin-crust" creations, "friendly" service and a "classy" yet "casual" setting also make these Old Town Alexandria and Arlington "standards" "great for a family outing" – just not on "buzzing" weekend nights when "waits can be long."

Fadó Irish Pub *Pub Food*   16 | 19 | 16 | $22

Chinatown | 808 Seventh St. NW (bet. H & I Sts.) | 202-789-0066 | www.fadoirishpub.com

"Disney does Ireland" at this Chinatown chainster, a "McDublin" bar with "attractive", though "a bit clichéd", themed dining rooms (library, cottage, store and lounge) and "basic", "unremarkable" pub fare; go for a "classic pint" of Guinness and some "Irish football on the telly" or have "tons of fun" in the "lively" scene that occurs after a game at the nearby Verizon Center; P.S. trivia fans "go on Mondays for quiz night."

☑ Fahrenheit & Degrees *American*   22 | 26 | 23 | $53

Georgetown | Ritz-Carlton Georgetown | 3100 South St. NW (bet. K & M Sts.) | 202-912-4110 | www.ritzcarlton.com

Do some "star spotting while waiting for the valet" at the "cool" Ritz-Carlton Georgetown, where the "expensive" New American fare is "expertly prepared" and delivered in a "stunning", "intimate, candlelit" setting, drawing "an embassy crowd and the classier breed of lobbyist"; meanwhile, Degrees, its "romantic" lower-level bar/lounge, is so "elegant" that it makes would-be sippers feel they're "not hip enough."

NEW Famoso Ⓢ *Italian*   - | - | - | E

Chevy Chase | The Collection at Chevy Chase | 5471 Wisconsin Ave. (Wisconsin Circle), MD | 301-986-8785 | www.famosorestaurant.com

At this second-story Northern Italian in The Collection at Chevy Chase, the kitchen is overseen by chef Gabriele Paganelli from the Emilia-Romagna region in Italy (and from the Romagna Mia restaurant in Toronto); the softly lit space is ripe for a scene, with a granite-and-marble bar and an elegant, settee-strewn lounge.

NEW Farrah Olivia Ⓜ *American*   - | - | - | E

Alexandria | 600 Franklin St. (S. Washington St.), VA | 703-778-2233 | www.farraholiviarestaurant.com

This elegant Old Town Alexandria destination provides a white-tablecloth setting for distinctive New American cuisine that features

	FOOD	DECOR	SERVICE	COST

influences from France and from chef-owner Morou Ouattara's native Ivory Coast; coconut-shell rings that hang from the ceiling enliven the sophisticated, neutral-toned room.

Faryab ⓜ Afghan

| 22 | 13 | 19 | $29 |

Bethesda | 4917 Cordell Ave. (bet. Norfolk Ave. & Old Georgetown Rd.), MD | 301-951-3484

The "drab decor" of this "bargain" Bethesda Afghan "doesn't do justice" to "unabashedly good" pumpkin stew, "juicy" lamb kebabs, "standout" "vegetable combinations" and the pastalike aushakl; "low-key" service is either "efficient" or makes you "feel like you're standing in line at Kabul airport", but a slice of "rich" ("though not cloying") baklava sweetens the deal.

Felix ⓩ American

| 18 | 19 | 18 | $40 |

Adams Morgan | 2406 18th St. NW (bet. Belmont & Columbia Rds.) | 202-483-3549 | www.thefelix.com

With a "sleek" South Beach Florida vibe, "tasty" New American fare and a "superb" martini menu poured by "hottie bartenders", this "cool" restaurant/club in Adams Morgan is "still a fun place to stop into", even if a couple of taste arbiters slam its 1980s *Miami Vice* look" and "humdrum" eats; "wonderful live entertainment", Sunday night flicks and HBO bring it up a notch, while the next-door Spy Lounge offers mood lighting, a sexy loft and DJs several nights a week.

15 ria American

| 19 | 19 | 18 | $44 |

Scott Circle | Doubletree Hotel | 1515 Rhode Island Ave. NW (Scott Circle) | 202-742-0015 | www.15ria.com

A hotel restaurant that's "just hip enough", this Scott Circle New American wins some points for a "broad and interesting menu", "appetizers that shine" and "outstanding" drinks in the "cute bar"; but "despite its best intentions", the "service is spotty" and it still "feels like you're sitting in a hotel lobby" unless you head to the "outdoor patio with better seating"; N.B. the kitchen has settled in after several chef changes.

Filomena Ristorante Italian

| 22 | 19 | 20 | $40 |

Georgetown | 1063 Wisconsin Ave. NW (M St.) | 202-338-8800 | www.filomena.com

"Go to be seen not heard" at this Georgetown Italian where "disturbingly huge portions" of "fresh" "homemade" pasta (kneaded by the "Italian grandmothers in the front window" and smothered in sauce "just like nonna's gravy") are dished out in "bustling, jubilant" digs often "crammed" with seasonal decor; it's all "tacky in a lovable way", though some find it so "touristy" you'll feel like a visitor "even if you're a local."

Finemondo ⓩ Italian

| 18 | 19 | 17 | $34 |

Downtown | 1319 F St. NW (bet. 13th & 14th Sts.) | 202-737-3100 | www.finemondo.com

You're "somewhere much warmer and more relaxed than Downtown DC" when you come to this "rustic" business district Italian from restaurateur Savino Recine (Primi Piatti); a "cozy lounge" is perfect for sipping wine in winter, and on warm days "they open the front windows" as you dine on "delicious" whole fish and "excellent" gnocchi; however, foes find the "inconsistent" fare "not very innovative" and the service "inattentive", insisting there's "far better Italian out there for the price."

Finn & Porter *Seafood/Steak*   17 | 19 | 18 | $41

Downtown | 900 10th St. NW (New York Ave.) | 202-719-1600
Alexandria | Hilton Alexandria | 5000 Seminary Rd. (Quaker Ln.), VA | 703-379-2346
www.finnandporter.com

These "tastefully done" steak and seafood eateries in Downtown DC and Alexandria are a "cut above" most hotel dining with a "good menu selection", including sushi, and "terrific" bars; the Virginia location's glass-enclosed wine room boasts more than 1,000 bottles, and DC's soaring space, near the Convention Center, has a water wall and huge floor-to-ceiling windows; but the finicky find "uptown decor, uptown prices, dockside service" and point to "much better" competition that swims in the same waters.

Fiore di Luna Ⓜ *Italian*   22 | 22 | 20 | $55

Great Falls | Seneca Sq. | 1025 Seneca Rd. (Georgetown Pike), VA | 703-444-4060 | www.fiorediluna.com

Great Falls' "strip-mall" "secret" caters to tony locals with "delicious" Northern Italian fare (try the three-, five- or seven-course tasting menus) and an "impressive wine selection" in a "chic" setting with lots of polished wood and an outdoor patio; but critics cite "small portions", "variable" service and meals that are "a tad expensive if you enjoy vino" as evidence that the "results don't quite meet its ambitions"; N.B. a limited bar menu is also available.

Firefly *American*   21 | 23 | 20 | $42

Dupont Circle | 1310 New Hampshire Ave. NW (bet. N & 20th Sts.) | 202-861-1310 | www.firefly-dc.com

"Magical" touches like the glittery faux "tree in the dining room" with hanging lanterns and the check delivered "in a bell jar" (used for catching fireflies) lend this Dupont Circle bistro a *Midsummer Night's Dream* vibe that's "equally matched" by its New American cuisine; plus, despite tables so "close together" you can "check out what everyone is having" and a somewhat "posturing" staff, it's an "inviting" place for a date; N.B. new chef Daniel Bortnick (ex Poste) is adding his own seasonal sensibility to the menu.

⚡ Five Guys *Hamburgers*   24 | 8 | 15 | $9

Chinatown | 808 H St. NW (bet. 8th & 9th Sts.) | 202-393-2900
Georgetown | 1335 Wisconsin Ave. NW (Dumbarton St.) | 202-337-0400
Mt. Vernon Square/New Convention Center | 2301 Georgia Ave. (Bryant St.) | 202-986-2235
Alexandria | 107 N. Fayette St. (King St.), VA | 703-549-7991 ⊘
Alexandria | 4626 King St. (Beauregard St.), VA | 703-671-1606 ⊘

(continued)

(continued)

Five Guys

Alexandria | 7622 Richmond Hwy. (Fordson Rd.), VA | 703-717-0090 ☞

Herndon | Fox Mill Ctr. | 2521 John Milton Dr. (Fox Mill Rd.), VA | 703-860-9100 ☞

Springfield | 6541 Backlick Rd. (Old Keene Mill Rd.), VA | 703-913-1337 ☞

Manassas | Manassas Corner | 9221 Sudley Rd. (Centerville Rd.), VA | 703-368-8080

Woodbridge | Marumsco Plaza | 14001 Jefferson Davis Hwy. (Longview Dr.), VA | 703-492-8882

www.fiveguys.com

Additional locations throughout the DC area

"Believe the hype" about this local chain's "bag-soaking fresh-cut fries" and "juiciest, messiest burgers ever" – they're a "heart attack in the sac" but a "gut-busting delight" that's a sure "hangover" cure as well; voted the Top Bang for the Buck in both the DC and Baltimore Surveys, these "no-frills" spots "never disappoint, except for the lines", and they are "expanding exponentially", "breeding addicts" around the Beltway and in Baltimore and Annapolis even faster than they can flip 'em; P.S. "wussy" fare like veggie or grilled cheese is also served.

Fleming's Prime Steakhouse & Wine Bar *Steak*

24 | 22 | 23 | $54

McLean | 1960A Chain Bridge Rd. (International Dr.), VA | 703-442-8384 | www.flemingssteakhouse.com

With "great" chops, the "best tuna mignon" and "outstanding wines", this "absolute dream steakhouse" duo in Tysons Corner and Baltimore's Inner Harbor gives the "big names" a "run for their money" and has a "flair for casual dining" that appeals to "young professionals"; though contrarians cringe over "bad" acoustics and "uneven" meals (quipping the service was "rare", while the "meat was overdone"), these beef-busters are in the minority.

Florida Ave. Grill Ⓜ *Diner*

21 | 10 | 20 | $14

U Street Corridor | 1100 Florida Ave. NW (11th St.) | 202-265-1586

"The Capitol's capital of soul food", this "DC landmark", a U Street Corridor "old-school diner" "lined with photos of famous African-Americans", offers "super-cheap" Southern "comfort food" like "grits", "half-smokes, cornbread, hash browns and down-home breakfast treats" "with a lot of flavor and even more fat"; so join "all of the local churchgoers in their Sunday best" for weekend brunch "served with a side of sweetness" by an "awesome staff."

Flying Fish *Seafood*

19 | 17 | 15 | $35

Alexandria | 815 King St. (Alfred St.), VA | 703-600-3474 | www.flyingfishdc.com

This "fun", "hip" sushi spot in Old Town Alexandria has "excellent crab cakes" and other seafood, plus Asian-accented dishes, "gigunda martinis", "yummy saketinis" and "even better people-watching"; unfortunately, the "only thing flying are the fish" since service is deemed "slow at best" – you might have better luck if you "sit at the sushi bar" and watch the "chefs do their stuff."

Fogo de Chão *Brazilian/Steak*
23 | 21 | 25 | $54

Downtown | 1101 Pennsylvania Ave. NW (11th St.) | 202-347-4668 | www.fogodechao.com

Head to this "gluttonously wonderful" Downtown Brazilian steak-house for an "endless procession" of gauchos slicing "mouthwater-ing" meats tableside ("all you can eat and then some") plus an "extensive" antipasto and salad bar and "constantly replenished" sides, all for a fixed price; "your stomach may be fuller than your wallet", but carnivores judge it "worth the splurge"; P.S. it's good for groups as "there's no question how to divide the bill."

Fontina Grille *Italian*
17 | 16 | 17 | $29

Rockville | King Farm Village Ctr. | 801 Pleasant Dr. (bet. King Farm & Redland Blvds.), MD | 301-947-5400 | www.fontinagrille.com

"Traditional Italian without checkered tablecloths", this "pleas-ant" Rockville "hangout" is a "reliable choice to bring guests" for "decent pizza", "wonderful" risotto dishes and a "good-value lunch buffet"; but despite the "family-oriented large portions", less simpatico sorts say the service "has a lot to improve on" and the fare's pretty "ordinary."

NEW Food Matters M *American*
– | – | – | M

Alexandria | Cameron Station | 4906 Brenman Park Dr. (Somerville St.), VA | 703-461-3663 | www.foodmattersva.com

Co-owners Christy and Tom Przystawik (ex Café Atlántico) prove that food matters at their New American cafe, wine bar and gour-met market in Alexandria's newly minted Cameron Station neigh-borhood; within the vast, sun-drenched modern-industrial space, there's a 15-seat room that serves regular communal dinners de-signed to spotlight locally sourced ingredients.

Fortune *Chinese*
19 | 10 | 13 | $22

Falls Church | Seven Corner Ctr. | 6249 Arlington Blvd. (Patrick Henry Dr.), VA | 703-538-3333

If you skip the "mediocre regular Chinese menu", you can improve your fortune by ordering the "deluxe dim sum" that's served every day at this Falls Church restaurant known for "reasonable" prices, solid "variety and quality" and "an ongoing stream of carts" filled with "authentic" dishes including "duck, fish and crab delicacies"; most find it's "great for larger crowds", despite "poor ambiance" and lackluster service.

Foti's ⊠M *American*
▽ 27 | 23 | 23 | $68

Culpeper | 219 E. Davis St. (East St.), VA | 540-829-8400 | www.fotisrestaurant.com

Chef Frank Maragos and hostess-wife Sue Maragos (both ex The Inn at Little Washington) have put Culpeper, VA, on the foodie map, serving "excellent" New American with "inventive" Med flourishes in their brick-walled, "candlelit" storefront in this picturesque Piedmont River Valley town; while some make it their "dress-up anniversary or birthday dinner choice", a few ask whether "instant fame may have overwhelmed" this fledgling – but given the owners' "experience", it will likely remain a "winner."

Franklin's *Pub Food* ▽ 17 | 19 | 18 | $21

Hyattsville | 5123 Baltimore Ave. (Gallatin St.), MD | 301-927-2740 | www.franklinsbrewery.com

"Stick with the standard" Traditional American pub fare and "you can't go wrong" at this "lively" "cheerily decorated neighborhood favorite" in "up-and-coming" Hyattsville; hopsheads "taste the love" in the "great" "craft beers" "brewed on-site", while the young and old alike "wander through the old-fashioned general store" annex proffering candy, wine, beer, stationery, "gag gifts" and "eclectic" "hard-to-find" items.

NEW French Hound, The ⑤Ⓜ *French* - | - | - | M

Middleburg | 101 S. Madison St. (Federal St.), VA | 540-687-3018 | www.thefrenchhound.com

The Federal-period Middleburg townhouse most recently occupied by Aster is now done up in French provincial style to complement this venture's unpretentious Gallic bistro menu; its engaging chef/co-owner, John-Gustin Birkitt, honed his whisk in Napa Valley's Bouchon and, along with wife Marny, worked as a private chef in Provence – a pedigree that draws tony locals and countryside day-trippers alike.

Full Kee ●⇨ *Chinese* 22 | 6 | 14 | $17

Chinatown | 509 H St. NW (bet. 5th & 6th Sts.) | 202-371-2233

Surveyors assure "you will survive the ambiance" ("hanging ducks") at this quintessential Chinatown cash-only "hole-in-the-wall" and be rewarded with "incomparable" Hong Kong–style dumpling soup, "fresh" seafood, stir-fried chives that are a "special treat" and other "options that scream authenticity, such as pig entrails and jellyfish"; its best to "stick to the menu in Chinese" or the "specials posted on the wall" – if you can get the "indifferent" "waiters to translate", that is; N.B. the same-named Falls Church eatery is under separate ownership.

Full Kee ● *Chinese* 22 | 12 | 14 | $19

Falls Church | 5830 Columbia Pike (Leesburg Pike), VA | 703-575-8232

"If you plan to order chop suey, don't take up the table space" at this Falls Church "haven for night owls", where "lovers of true Chinese" look past a "spare", "utilitarian setting" and "curt" service to the "incredible selection" of "affordable" and "authentic Cantonese and Hong Kong" dishes ("get a steaming bowl of shrimp dumplings for only $5"); service may leave something to be desired, but the "prevalence of Asian diners" could explain the staff's "problem with English"; N.B. the Chinatown eatery of the same name is under separate ownership.

	FOOD	DECOR	SERVICE	COST

Full Key ● *Chinese* ▽ 20 | 7 | 11 | $18

Wheaton | Wheaton Manor Shopping Ctr. | 2227 University Blvd. W. (Georgia Ave.), MD | 301-933-8388

You can find some of the "finest seafood and authentic greens" as well as the "best roast pork and duck around" at this Hong Kong-style noodle and dumpling shop in Wheaton, but frustrated eaters who ask for something that "looks good at the other tables" say the staff often "brings you something else"; still, if service or "ambiance is not a concern", and your budget is, this "low-cost" option is the "place to go."

Fu Shing Cafe *Chinese* 18 | 12 | 15 | $16

Gaithersburg | 576 N. Frederick Ave. (Lakeforest Blvd.), MD | 301-330-8484

"Especially delicious" salt-and-pepper scallops and "unusual chicken won tons" are among the "surprisingly tasty" highlights at this "cafeteria-style" "hole-in-the-wall" Gaithersburg Chinese that draws "an overwhelmingly Asian clientele" (Sinophiles can find "unique items" by "ordering off the Chinese menu"); now that the better-appointed Rockville location has closed, many regulars just pick up the "cheap and fast" food to go.

Gallery Ⓜ *Pan-Latin* - | - | - | M

Silver Spring | Blair Mill Arts Ctr. | 1115 East-West Hwy. (Blair Mill Rd.), MD | 301-589-2555 | www.gallerysilverspring.com

Located in Silver Spring's Blair Mill Arts Center, this spacious gallery, restaurant and lounge provides a post–industrial-chic backdrop for art lovers, with ottomans and sofas arranged conversationally, soft lighting and a short Latin menu that encourages sharing (including upbeat takes on ceviche); outdoor dining and private party facilities are likely to prove popular.

⊠ Georgia Brown's *Southern* 23 | 21 | 21 | $42

Downtown | 950 15th St. NW (bet. I & K Sts.) | 202-393-4499 | www.gbrowns.com

"Stick-to-your-ribs" "Southern comfort food" goes "upscale" at this "classy" (if "noisy") Downtown "dining institution" near the White House, where the service is "excellent" and the "satisfying" fare includes "divine" shrimp and grits, "addictive" fried green tomatoes and "delicious" fried chicken livers; just "expect to put on five pounds", especially at the "decadent Sunday jazz brunch" where you can "fill up" on the "limitless buffet" and then "box up" the entree "to take home for dinner."

Geranio *Italian* 21 | 20 | 21 | $42

Alexandria | 722 King St. (bet. Columbus & Washington Sts.), VA | 703-548-0088 | www.geranio.net

"Delicious" lobster risotto, a "cozy fire" and "warm" hospitality help make this "intimate" Old Town Alexandria Italian "wonderful for celebrations"; some "don't know why it's not talked about more" with such "serious food", but it could be the "high-ticket price" or the atmosphere that's almost "too quiet for whispering sweet nothings";

P.S. discounts on orders placed before 7 PM and after 9:30 PM will have you "smiling when the bill comes."

❷ Gerard's Place 🅱 *French*   27 | 21 | 24 | $75

Downtown | 915 15th St. NW (bet. I & K Sts.) | 202-737-4445 | www.gerardsplacedc.net

Although co-owner Gerard Panguad is no longer cooking at this Downtown New French "hideaway", he's still consulting on the menu and helping to train post-Survey chef addition Jonathan Thompson (ex Bradley Ogden in Las Vegas); the five-course tasting menu and à la carte dinner selections seem "expensive" to some, but the eatery also offers a "more affordable" three-course lunch menu ($29.50); still, critics say it could use "a little collagen" to "liven up" the atmosphere.

Good Fortune ➊ *Chinese*   21 | 10 | 15 | $21

Wheaton | 2646 University Blvd. W. (bet. Georgia Ave. & Veirs Mill Rd.), MD | 301-929-8818

This "Costco-size" Wheaton Chinese may be "dim sum paradise" ("sometimes the number of carts at your table is overwhelming"), but don't overlook a "wide range" of "gourmet-level" Cantonese entrees including steamed whole fish "fresh out of the tank"; even the "shabby" decor and "grumpy" service don't distract from "authentic food" at "reasonable prices."

Grapeseed *American*   24 | 18 | 22 | $49

Bethesda | 4865 Cordell Ave. (Norfolk Ave.), MD | 301-986-9592 | www.grapeseedbistro.com

Surveyors recommend you "go for a wine lesson" at this Bethesda New American that "creates dishes inspired by the vintages it pairs with them"; the "patient" staff will "take you through the menu", but "stick with the small plates and half-glasses" advise regulars who maintain that "noisy", "cramped" quarters and sometimes "shocking" bills are their "only complaints."

Green Field Churrascaria *Brazilian*   19 | 14 | 17 | $33

Rockville | 1801 Rockville Pike (Twin Brook Pkwy.), MD | 301-881-3397 | www.greenfieldchurrascaria.com

Be sure to "fast before" "feasting" at Rockville's "all-you-can-eat" Brazilian BBQ where a "large" salad bar and buffet set the stage for the "main attraction" – "meat, meat and more meat"; indulge "until you pop and then take one more bite" of the "great variety and selection" of "grilled stuff" "delivered to your table impaled on a sword"; those "picky on taste" quibble that it's just "quantity over quality", but more optimistic "folks with big appetites" do nothing but swear by the "carnivorous fun."

Green Papaya *Vietnamese*   21 | 21 | 17 | $31

Bethesda | 4922 Elm St. (Arlington Rd.), MD | 301-654-8986

"A shimmering waterfall", "slow-turning bamboo fans and soft lights" "set the mood" for "serene" "Zen"-like dining in this "upscale" Vietnamese "only a few steps away from the maddening crowd of other Bethesda" eateries; look past "snooty" service to enjoy "absolutely delicious" caramel pork loin, "wonderful" soft-shell crabs and "excellent" noodle dishes.

Greystone Grill *American*

| 20 | 20 | 19 | $41 |

NEW **Rockville** | Rockville Town Ctr. | 33 Maryland Ave. (Courthouse Sq.), MD | 240-430-4739 | www.greystonegrill.com
See review in the Baltimore Directory.

Grille, The *American*

∇ | 25 | 24 | 25 | $63 |

Alexandria | Morrison House | 116 S. Alfred St. (bet. King & Prince Sts.), VA | 703-838-8000 | www.morrisonhouse.com

The "attention is placed on you" at this "very intimate" Old Town Alexandria hotel eatery thanks to "some of the best service around" – "efficient, quiet and unobtrusive"; while some say its New American fare is "not the most imaginative", others laud the "fantastic Sunday brunch" and the "stately but not stuffy" atmosphere that makes it "delightful" for business or a special-occasion meal; N.B. check out the live piano music Thursday–Saturday.

Grillfish *Seafood*

| 18 | 16 | 17 | $34 |

Golden Triangle | 1200 New Hampshire Ave. NW (M St.) | 202-331-7310 | www.grillfishdc.com

"Nothing overshadows" the "fintastic", "simply prepared" entrees at this "hip", "reasonably priced" Golden Triangle seafood "standby" that's a "great happy-hour" spot despite the "nothing fancy" approach to fare and decor; but seasoned sorts are "not impressed with the unimaginative fish" and are further annoyed that the "noisy room" means they can't "hear anything" their companions have to say.

Grill from Ipanema *Brazilian*

| 20 | 16 | 18 | $34 |

Adams Morgan | 1858 Columbia Rd. NW (bet. Belmont Rd. & 18th St.) | 202-986-0757 | www.thegrillfromipanema.com

Step inside this "sexy" Adams Morgan Brazilian where there's so much Portuguese "floating around the room" from the "super-friendly" staff that "you could be in Rio"; though the "cramped quarters and lively crowd aren't for the faint of heart", fans keep "coming back" for *feijoada* (a traditional bean dish), "spicy" seafood stew and "wonderful", "real" caipirinhas – in fact, "downing several" will leave you sighing "aaaah."

Guajillo *Mexican*

| 22 | 15 | 17 | $25 |

Arlington | 1727 Wilson Blvd. (bet. N. Quinn & N. Rhodes Sts.), VA | 703-807-0840 | www.guajillogrill.com

Meals "get off to a great start" at this "colorful" Arlington cantina near the Courthouse metro: "fresh chips", "homemade salsa" and a "few rounds" of "top-shelf" margaritas "to help the spicy food go down"; "outstanding chicken mole", the "best fish tacos north of the border" and other "true Mexican" (and Tex-Mex) dishes follow, so "trust your waiters' opinion" and you'll find "authentic" choices; "lively" crowds pour into the "cramped" bar for an "excellent" tequila selection and pint-sized drinks.

	FOOD	DECOR	SERVICE	COST

Gua-Rapo ● *Nuevo Latino* | 17 | 20 | 13 | $27 |

Arlington | 2039 Wilson Blvd. (Courthouse Rd.), VA | 703-528-6500 | www.latinconcepts.com

Set in a "funky warehouse" space that "echoes" ones found in Manhattan's TriBeCa and Greenwich Village, this tapas-style Nuevo Latino in Arlington's Courthouse serves up "monster" arepas and "snazzy" drinks to young revelers smoking shishas, enjoying "live music" Thursday–Saturday and "impressing" their dates; an over-30 crowd dismisses food that's "all about appearances" and staffers who act "like you're putting them out by ordering", but hipsters shrug "you're paying for the scene."

NEW Guardado's Ⓜ *Pan-Latin/Spanish* | – | – | – | I |

Bethesda | 4918 Del Ray Ave. (Norfolk Ave.), MD | 301-986-4920 | www.guardadosnico.com

Though Latin *antojitos* and Spanish tapas – those small servings packed with flavor – rule the menu at this off-the-beaten-path cantina from chef-owner Nicolas Jose Guardado (ex Jaleo), those Bethesdans with heartier appetites can opt instead for paella, steaks, chops or seafood entrees; meanwhile, both the simple, white-walled dining area and the convivial bar are suitable choices for relaxing with friends.

Haad Thai *Thai* | 19 | 13 | 17 | $22 |

Downtown | 1100 New York Ave. NW (bet. 11th & 12th Sts.) | 202-682-1111

"Crammed at lunch, empty on the weekends", this Downtown Thai provides "office folk" with an "inexpensive", "quick", "well-seasoned" lunch in a tropical setting (albeit with "background music that sounds like it's from the Thai version of *American Idol*"); there's "nothing innovative" here, but "better-than-average" menu "standards" and quick "to-go" options make it "dependable."

Haandi *Indian* | 23 | 15 | 20 | $27 |

Bethesda | 4904 Fairmont Ave. (Old Georgetown Rd.), MD | 301-718-0121
Falls Church | Falls Plaza Shopping Ctr. | 1222 W. Broad St. (Leesburg Pike), VA | 703-533-3501
www.haandi.com

Loyalists "get stuck on favorites" at these Northern Indian "standbys" in Bethesda and Falls Church, where everything from the "delicately spiced dishes" to "powerfully hot vindaloos" "dances on the palate"; they're "not much to look at", and harsher critics call them "predictable" and "pedestrian", but "accommodating" and "attentive" service, "excellent vegetarian fare" and a "bargain lunch buffet" keep folks "coming back for years."

Hakuba *Japanese* | ▽ 23 | 17 | 21 | $29 |

Gaithersburg | Kentlands Market Sq. | 706 Center Point Way (Market St.), MD | 301-947-1283

Enjoy "relaxed" dining "with Downtown DC–quality food" at this Gaithersburg Japanese serving traditional tempura as well as what some call the "best sushi in the 'burbs"; the "contemporary" dining room may come across as "stark and cold", but you'll warm up to the "entertaining" chef-owner ("sit at the sushi bar for the full experience") who "always yells 'see you tomorrow' when you leave."

Hama Sushi   *Japanese*   21 | 17 | 19 | $29

Herndon | Village Center at Dulles | 2415 Centreville Rd. (Sunrise Valley Dr.), VA | 703-713-0088 | www.hama-sushi.com

Obi   *Japanese*

Reston | Reston Town Ctr. | 1771 Library St. (bet. Freedom Dr. & Market St.), VA | 703-766-7874 | www.obisushi.com

Perhaps there's "nothing very unique" about this "cramped" strip-mall Japanese in Herndon – just "good" "fresh" "tuna, salmon, yellowtail" and other sushi; though it strikes some as a "little on the pricey side", it's "worth it" to "splurge on specials" posted on "a frequently changing blackboard"; P.S. owner Yong Son also has a share in Obi, a "welcome" option in the Reston Town Center serving "solid" Japanese "favorites" in a "dramatic venue."

Hank's Oyster Bar   *Seafood*   23 | 18 | 21 | $36

Dupont Circle | 1624 Q St. NW (bet. 16th & 17th Sts.) | 202-462-4265 | www.hanksdc.com

"Neighborhood charm" oozes from Jamie Leeds' tiny "pearl" of a seafood eatery in the Dupont Circle area, where an "upbeat" crew "knowledgeably guides diners through the daily offerings" of "delectable" oysters, "amazing lobster rolls", "fried clams how they're supposed to be" and other "wonderful" fresh fish; the "party atmosphere" in the "narrow" "retro" room and the sidewalk cafe "makes for a fun evening, but not a quiet dinner", so "arrive early" since they don't take reservations, and expect some local "flavor."

Hard Times Cafe   *American*   19 | 13 | 17 | $15

Bethesda | 4920 Del Ray Ave. (Old Georgetown Rd.), MD | 301-951-3300

Germantown | 13032 Middlebrook Rd. (Century Blvd.), MD | 240-686-0150 ◑

College Park | 4738 Cherry Hill Rd. (Baltimore Ave.), MD | 301-474-8880

Rockville | Woodley Gardens | 1117 Nelson St. (Montgomery Ave.), MD | 301-294-9720

Alexandria | 1404 King St. (West St.), VA | 703-837-0050

Arlington | 3028 Wilson Blvd. (Highland St.), VA | 703-528-2233 ◑

Herndon | Kmart Shopping Ctr. | 428 Elden St. (bet. Herndon Pkwy. & Van Buren St.), VA | 703-318-8941 ◑

Springfield | Springfield Plaza | 6362 Springfield Plaza (Commerce St.), VA | 703-913-5600 ◑

Woodbridge | 14389 Potomac Festival Plaza (Gideon Dr.), VA | 703-492-2950

www.hardtimes.com

You might want to "take a Mylanta before" you go to one of these "family-friendly" "Taj Mahals of chili houses" serving four styles of bean-laden stew "that have just enough heat" (Texas, Cincinnati, Terlingua Red and vegetarian), plus Traditional American fixings like "great" cornbread, "not-to-be-missed" beer-battered onion rings, sweet tea, boardwalk fries, "homemade root beer" that's "to die for" and "mouthwatering" Frito chili pie; with "Patsy Cline on the jukebox" and "a happy hour that would make a cowboy tear up", addicts say, despite this chain's name, "life is good."

Harry's Tap Room *Seafood/Steak*

21 | 22 | 18 | $35

Arlington | Marketplace Commons | 2800 Clarendon Blvd. (N. Fillmore St.), VA | 703-778-7788 | www.harrystaproom.com

This "modern" "handsome" Clarendon "hot spot" with a bar that "looks like Frank Sinatra's Palm Springs living room" draws "sophisticated" Arlington first-daters plus "couples and singles in their 20s, 30s and 40s" for "excellent" steamed mussels, twin petite filets, "well-thought-out" wines by the glass and "friendly bartenders" that make a "great martini"; it's "more economical" than other steakhouses and has an "amazing" weekend brunch, but despite its name, this is one "taproom with very few taps."

Hee Been *Korean*

▽ 21 | 16 | 18 | $26

Alexandria | 6231 Little River Tpke. (Beauregard St.), VA | 703-941-3737

An "eastern pearl in a rough setting" in Alexandria, this Korean BBQ with a "grill at your table" serves "pure" "traditional" dishes like hot pot casseroles and bibimbop (vegetables and/or meat over rice); its "amazing" lunch buffet offers a range of ever-changing surprises – "sometimes you'll be treated to escargot in a cream sauce", other times snapper or sushi – but the "highlight is its diverse and unusual selection of *panchan* (side dishes)"; a "lovely" "blond wood" setting, though, strikes some as "overblown" and "lacking character."

Heritage India *Indian*

23 | 20 | 19 | $36

Dupont Circle | 1337 Connecticut Ave. NW (bet. Dupont Circle & N St.) | 202-331-1414

Glover Park | 2400 Wisconsin Ave. NW (Calvert St.) | 202-333-3120

"Fit for a raja" rave regulars of this Glover Park venue that turns out "innovative, spicy" dishes "as exciting as any first-rate Indian in London" and "as sumptuous as its surroundings"; though some feel "doted on" by the staff, others call them "clueless" – but either way you "pay for" this "high-class" spot; P.S. the Dupont branch offers an "imaginative" happy hour featuring "knock-your-socks-off" street food and tapas at the bar for half-price.

Hinode *Japanese*

20 | 15 | 19 | $25

Bethesda | 4914 Hampden Ln. (Arlington Rd.), MD | 301-654-0908

Rockville | 134 Congressional Ln. (bet. Jefferson St. & Rockville Pike), MD | 301-816-2190

"Best known for an all-you-can-eat lunch buffet" that's an "outstanding" "bargain", this Japanese duo in Montgomery County delivers "reliable", "Western-friendly" sushi and tempura in "kid-friendly" digs where the "staff remembers regulars and makes you feel at home"; the Rockville location even "has a tatami room" "where you get to sit on the floor."

Hollywood East Cafe ◑ *Chinese*

24 | 12 | 19 | $22

Wheaton | 2312 Price Ave. (Elkin St.), MD | 301-942-8282

	FOOD	DECOR	SERVICE	COST

(continued)

Hollywood East Cafe

Wheaton | 2621 University Blvd. W. (Veirs Mill Rd.), MD | 240-290-9988
www.hollywoodeastcafe.com

One in a pair of Wheaton Hong Kong–style Chinese spots, the "homey" if "dingy" Price Avenue "original" "always" provides "a satisfying adventure" via "authentic", "inventive" fare and a staff you can turn to "for help to avoid dishes skewed for Western palates"; the "spiffier" University Boulevard location is a "dressed-up version" of the "old" "favorite" with the added appeal of "outstanding" weekend dim sum – "plentiful carts" bear 60-plus selections.

NEW Hook *American*

– | – | – | M

Georgetown | 3241 M St. NW (bet. 33rd St. & Wisconsin Ave.) |
202-625-4488 | www.hookdc.com

Rising star chef Barton Seaver, formerly of Café Saint-Ex, has moored this midpriced New American in Cilantro's old Georgetown berth; a cerulean blue space with chrome and dark-wood accents sets the stage for a menu focused on sustainable seafood and local produce, while eye-candy perched along the roomy bar is yet another lure.

Hunan Dynasty *Chinese*

– | – | – | I

Capitol Hill | 215 Pennsylvania Ave. SE (bet. C St. & Independence Ave.) |
202-546-6161 | www.hunandynastydc.com

With a prime location on Capitol Hill, private party rooms and $5.95 weekday lunch specials, this second-story Chinese is drawing lawmakers and their staffers; an old-fashioned dining room is the setting for an extensive, multiregional menu that also includes sushi.

Hunan Lion *Chinese*

21 | 18 | 19 | $26

Vienna | 2070 Chain Bridge Rd. (Old Courthouse Rd.), VA | 703-734-9828

"Ridiculously busy during the lunch hour", this Tysons Corner Chinese wins "applause" for "unusual" Hunan and Mandarin selections and "quiet" evening dining; but style-conscious sorts say the space, which is "showing age" after nearly 25 years, reminds them of "a dowager all dressed up at the dance"; P.S. "get the takeout" instead.

Hunter's Head Tavern *British*

∇ 20 | 24 | 17 | $33

Upperville | 9048 John Mosby Hwy./Rte. 50, VA | 540-592-9020

It's "cozy" by the fireplace in winter and there's a "great courtyard" in summer at this historic tavern (circa 1750) that's "as British as you can get" in Upperville; "authentic" pub grub (bangers and mash, fish 'n' chips) plus "great burgers" incorporate ingredients "from a nearby organic farm", but the "strange" ordering format ("place all orders at the bar, then a server delivers") may take some getting used to.

Huong Que *Vietnamese*
(aka Four Sisters)

23 | 13 | 21 | $23

Falls Church | Eden Ctr. | 6769 Wilson Blvd. (bet. Arlington & Roosevelt Blvds.), VA | 703-538-6717

"Trust the sisters' recommendations" at their "first-class" Falls Church Vietnamese where a "stunning fresh flower arrangement" at

FOOD DECOR SERVICE COST

the entrance presages their "authentic, flavorful", "affordable" fare; the "charming" staff (often including one of the four sibling owners) "helps you navigate the massive menu" in a large room that's "great for big groups or families"; P.S. its setting in a "bustling" Asian shopping center makes you feel "like you're in Saigon."

Huong Viet ☕ *Vietnamese* ▽ 23 | 8 | 18 | $20

Falls Church | Eden Ctr. | 6785 Wilson Blvd. (bet. Arlington & Roosevelt Blvds.), VA | 703-538-7110

Although it may not look like much, this modest Eden Center diner is "always filled with the many Vietnamese and Westerners who love the soup" and the variety of "authentic" selections – "amazing grilled beef, excellent lemongrass chicken" and caramel fish that could just be the "best dish" here; the "staff's English isn't the best, but they make up for it in personality and friendliness."

NEW Il Mulino Ⓢ *Italian* - | - | - | E

Downtown | 1110 Vermont Ave. NW (L St.) | 202-293-1001 | www.ilmulino.com

Old-world elegance pervades this Downtown dining room where tuxedoed waiters dramatically plate the rich Italian delicacies that have earned its NYC counterpart top Survey ratings year after year; *abbondanza* (the tradition of abundance) is celebrated with complimentary antipasti, as well as free grappa at the end of the meal.

Ⓩ Il Pizzico Ⓢ *Italian* 25 | 17 | 21 | $35

Rockville | Suburban Park | 15209 Frederick Rd. (Gude Dr.), MD | 301-309-0610 | www.ilpizzico.com

"Pasta doesn't get any better" than at this "unbelievable" Rockville trattoria fawn "appreciative" fans who "never expected" to find such a "delicious Italian" in an "ancient strip plaza"; those who appreciate the "value" and "low-key ambiance" of Sicilian native chef Enzo Livia's "true gem" say their only lament is that a lack of "reservations can mean long waits", "especially on weekends."

Il Radicchio *Italian* 18 | 11 | 16 | $23

Arlington | 1801 Clarendon Blvd. (Rhodes St.), VA | 703-276-2627

"Pay for the pasta sauces, no charge for the pasta" is the theme at this "bargain" Italian, a "mix-and-match heaven" in a "small hole-in-the-wall" Arlington Courthouse space that also dishes out "Milano-style thin-crust pizza"; some enjoy the "simple decor" and love "sitting outside when weather permits", but others find the "run-down" digs "outdated" and the "all-you-can-eat" fare a bit "uninventive."

Ⓩ IndeBleu *Indian* 23 | 25 | 21 | $62

Penn Quarter | 707 G St. NW (bet. 7th & 8th Sts.) | 202-333-2538 | www.bleu.com

"Swanky hipsters" say this "ultrachic" Penn Quarter spot "does Washington proud" courtesy of chef Vikram Garg's French-infused Indian food; the "distinctive, special" cuisine, "choreographed" service and "glamorous" space – including a "sleek, sexy" "sybarite's heaven" of a bar/lounge and a "light and airy" dining room with a chef's table that "merry-go-rounds into the kitchen" – make the clientele feel "like A-listers"; N.B. new menus will feature lower prices and more accessible fare.

India Palace *Indian*

▽ 23 | 16 | 21 | $24

Germantown | Fox Chapel Shopping Ctr. | 19743 Frederick Rd. (Gunners Branch Rd.), MD | 301-540-3000 | www.aaoji.com

"A great variety" of "delicious Indian classics" with "complex flavors" "never disappoints" at this Germantown shopping-center eatery, where the "friendly" service is "excellent, efficient and unobtrusive" and the "succulent" tandoori dishes come "hot and spicy – just as they should be"; too bad the same can't be said of the "cold" and "barren" space; N.B. try its lunch buffets for $8.95 on weekdays and $9.95 on weekends.

Indigo Landing *American*

- | - | - | E

Alexandria | 1 Marina Dr. (George Washington Memorial Pkwy.), VA | 703-548-0001 | www.indigolanding.com

This posh regional New American mines coastal South Carolina's rich culinary traditions in a picturesque, naturalistic setting overlooking the Potomac River in Alexandria; the nautically themed dining room offers sweeping views of DC, as well as a menu that mixes down-home and luxury ingredients (as in its signature shrimp and grits with bacon, leeks, oysters and mushrooms); there's also a bar/lounge and a 100-seat veranda for balmy nights.

☑ Indique *Indian*

24 | 22 | 21 | $34

Cleveland Park | 3512-14 Connecticut Ave. NW (bet. Ordway & Porter Sts.) | 202-244-6600

Chevy Chase | 2 Wisconsin Circle (Western Ave.), MD | 301-656-4822
www.indique.com

"Check your expectations at the door" of this "exotic" Cleveland Park Indian where a "contemporary spin" on traditional dishes makes "believers" of the curry-cautious, while impressing "in-laws from India"; an "intimate" (some say "crowded"), "romantic, but still happening" room and "reasonable prices" make it a "great date spot"; N.B. its Chevy Chase sibling opened post-Survey and focuses on tapas and innovative elixirs.

☑ Inn at Little Washington *American*

29 | 28 | 28 | $141

Washington | The Inn at Little Washington | 309 Middle St. (Warren Ave.), VA | 540-675-3800 |
www.theinnatlittlewashington.com

"Heaven on earth" is found in the VA countryside at this "romantic" "mecca of fine dining" that scores a triple: a No. 1 rating for Food, Decor and Service; its loyalists find a "gourmand's paradise" that features the "best" New American cuisine, a setting that's a "treat for the eyes" and "choreographed" "masterful service" that makes you "feel coddled from the moment" you pull in; everything from the "exquisite" amuse-bouche to the "hilarious" "cow-shaped mooing cheese cart" "exceeds expectations" – but, of course, "perfection doesn't come cheap"; N.B. try to get a room for the night.

	FOOD	DECOR	SERVICE	COST

Irene's Pupusas *Central American*

| | - | - | - | I |

Hyattsville | 2218 University Blvd. E. (Riggs Rd.), MD | 301-431-1550

Silver Spring | 2408 University Blvd. W. (Georgia Ave.), MD | 301-933-4800

Wheaton | 11300 Georgia Ave. (University Blvd. W.), MD | 301-933-2118 ●

Expats and bargain-seekers alike head to this trio of Central American roadhouses in suburban Maryland for Salvadoran pupusas (stuffed corn tortillas) along with homestyle Honduran specialties, most notably beef and seafood soups; a lively atmosphere – Latin music on the jukebox, sports on the plasma screens – helps to compensate for the simple surroundings.

i Ricchi ⊠ *Italian*

| | 23 | 21 | 22 | $58 |

Dupont Circle | 1220 19th St. NW (bet. M & N Sts.) | 202-835-0459 | www.iricchi.net

With "delicious" dishes, "wonderful service" and a "cozy atmosphere", this "bustling" "expense-account" Italian near Dupont Circle prompts "multiple trips" back; the "terrific" grilled meats (homemade sausages, marinated pork chops), pastas and soups "bring the true taste of Tuscany" to DC; but "if you're not a regular", "you get the feeling that you're lucky to be eating here" say some who are further bothered by decor that's a little too "Olive Garden for such a swanky place."

Irish Inn at Glen Echo *Irish*

| | 17 | 19 | 19 | $40 |

Glen Echo | 6119 Tulane Ave. (MacArthur Blvd.), MD | 301-229-6600 | www.irishinnglenecho.com

"Coziness and charm count for a lot" at this "little country house" in a "sylvan" Glen Echo setting "right next to a national park", where "superb", "friendly" service and "small" "private" rooms that "allow for conversation" make for "gracious dining"; an Irish dinner menu that "just misses" may be "overpriced for what it delivers", so "casual" diners turn instead to the "comfortable" pub for lighter "home runs" ("hurrah for the shepherd's pie!") and "fun" live music on Sunday and Monday nights.

Islander Caribbean Ⓜ *Caribbean*

| | ▽ 20 | 10 | 16 | $24 |

U Street Corridor | 1201 U St. NW (12th St.) | 202-234-4971

Ok, so the decor is "super cheesy" and the mounted TV "does nothing to improve the ambiance" at this "homey" U Street "joint", but it's "long been a local favorite" for Caribbean "jerk chicken as hot as the islands" that's "prepared by natives and it shows"; if you're rushed, "just forget about it", because the "friendly" staff provides "true island service (i.e. in no hurry)."

Jackie's *American*

| | 20 | 23 | 19 | $35 |

Silver Spring | 8081 Georgia Ave. (entrance on Sligo St.), MD | 301-565-9700 | www.jackiesrestaurant.com

"Hands down the hippest spot in Silver Spring", this "garage converted into a bustling bistro" "surprises" first-timers with its "cool vibe" and "funky" "factory-chic" looks; though the frugal find fault with "small overpriced portions", a "lively crowd" appreciates American "comfort food with a zing" like "mini-Elvis burgers" and daily specials (fried chicken, meatloaf) that round out the "interesting menu."

NEW Jack's Restaurant & Bar American | – | – | – | M |

Dupont Circle | 1527 17th St. NW (bet. Church & Q Sts.) | 202-332-6767 | www.jacksdc.net

Chef-owner Herbert Kerschbaumer's Swiss-German heritage inspires the New American–Continental cuisine at this Dupont Circle bistro, which also serves more casual fare like burgers and salads; a long bar dominates the cozy interior.

Jaipur Indian | 23 | 20 | 20 | $24 |

Fairfax | 9401 Lee Hwy. (Circle Woods Dr.), VA | 703-766-1111 | www.jaipurcuisine.com

You "won't regret your trip" to this "jewel of North Indian cuisine" that's "surprisingly good considering its location" "tucked in the bottom of a high-rise apartment complex" in Fairfax; enjoy a "romantic dinner for two" in "lovely" (if "very pink") rooms "filled with Indian art" and attended by "particularly accommodating" staffers, or else go for the "ridiculously delicious and cheap lunch buffet."

☑ Jaleo Spanish | 23 | 20 | 19 | $33 |

Penn Quarter | 480 Seventh St. NW (E St.) | 202-628-7949 ●
Bethesda | 7271 Woodmont Ave. (Elm St.), MD | 301-913-0003
Arlington | 2250A Crystal Dr. (23rd St. S.), VA | 703-413-8181
www.jaleo.com

Invite your amigos to "nibble the evening away" on "tantalizing", "imaginative" yet "authentic" Spanish tapas with "never-ending sangria to wash it all down" at this trio of "crowd-pleasers"; they're a "loud", "chaotic" "fiesta", especially if there's flamenco dancing, and they're among the "few places where 'small plate' does not equal 'large bill'"; P.S. beware of "long waits", as they take only a limited number of reservations.

Jean-Michel French | 24 | 18 | 22 | $49 |

Bethesda | Wildwood Shopping Ctr. | 10223 Old Georgetown Rd. (Democracy Blvd.), MD | 301-564-4910

The "refined" French fare, including "outstanding" soufflés, at this "traditional", "often forgotten" Bethesda "gem" proves both that "suburban seniors still have good taste" and "elegant" eateries can be found in strip-mall settings; the eponymous owner-host, a "perfect gentleman", oversees guests in the "quiet" dining room, so even if "the crowd is not what you'd call young and hip", the overall experience is as "steady as ever."

Jerry's Seafood Seafood | ▽ 24 | 11 | 19 | $42 |

Seabrook | 9364 Lanham Severn Rd. (¾ mi. east of Rte. 495, exit 20A), MD | 301-577-0333

In the "middle of nowhere" in Prince Georges County, you'll find one of the "best seafood" houses in the area, where the signature crab bomb is "bursting with sweet succulent meat" and "everything from

	FOOD	DECOR	SERVICE	COST

the salad dressing to the stewed tomatoes tastes wonderful"; sure, this "old-time" "family-run" Seabrook spot is "pure camp", but the patrons are a "powerhouse" of local notables so there's often a "wait."

Joe's Noodle House *Chinese*　　22 | 6 | 14 | $17

Rockville | 1488C Rockville Pike (Twinbrook Pkwy.), MD | 301-881-5518 | www.joesnoodlehouse.com

"Adventurous" diners can "throw a dart at the menu" to come up with something to "savor" at this "small mall storefront" in Rockville, where the "cheap and quick" Szechuan meals are "ordered at the counter" then delivered to your table; the "friendly staff could be a little more attentive", but the "treats", from stir-fried snow peas to chicken gizzards, come "without all the grease"; P.S. "watch the heat 'cause when they say it's hot, it is *hot.*"

Johnny's Half Shell 🗷 *American/Seafood*　23 | – | 20 | $39

Capitol Hill | 400 N. Capitol St. NW (D St.) | 202-737-0400 | www.johnnyshalfshell.net

Having shucked its "cramped" Dupont Circle digs in favor of a spacious Capitol Hill setting, this "terrific" New American seafood bistro – now serving steaks in addition to "Gulf classics" – evokes a San Francisco oyster house with its tiled floor, marble-topped bar and wood-and-etched-glass booths; there's a see-and-be-seen terrace too, and you can expect the same "hospitable" staff; N.B. its new take-out taqueria serves up breakfast, inexpensive tacos and daily specials.

Juniper *American*　　▽ 19 | 22 | 20 | $52

West End | Fairmont Hotel | 2401 M St. NW (24th St.) | 202-457-5020 | www.fairmont.com

"Oh, what a way to start the day" say early-risers of the seasonal Mid-Atlantic fare dished up from breakfast onward at this New American "jewel in the West End" that's well-located for business meals; plus, the "redecorated" hotel dining space features stately columns, large mirrors and French doors that open to a "wonderful" outdoor garden.

Kabob Palace
Family Restaurant ● *Mideastern*　▽ 25 | 6 | 12 | $13

Arlington | 2333 S. Eads St. (23rd St.), VA | 703-979-3000 | www.mykabobpalace.com

"One serving will feed you for days" at this "simple", "friendly" "hole-in-the-wall" in Arlington's Crystal City that's favored by "all the cabbies and limo drivers" for "out-of-this-world" kebabs and other "authentic Pakistani" and "earthy Afghan" fare; a "great place for a quick meal" or, better yet, for "takeout", it's open until midnight daily.

Kam Po *Chinese/Peruvian*　　– | – | – | I

Falls Church | 5884 Leesburg Pike (Washington Dr.), VA | 703-578-4017

This Falls Church restaurant is no ordinary strip-mall eatery, as evidenced by its inexpensive fare: a melding of Peruvian standards and ceviche, plus a traditional Chinese menu that reflects Peru's Sino-Cantonese heritage; as you might expect, the simple beige-and-plum-toned interior draws a crowd of Latin expats.

	FOOD	DECOR	SERVICE	COST

NEW Kansai Sushi *Japanese*

	-	-	-	M

Vienna | 128 Maple Ave. W. (Park St.), VA | 703-319-1300

Situated on Vienna's main drag, this modest, traditional Japanese prepares classic sushi, sashimi and *chirashi* (raw fish and other ingredients scattered over rice) as well as noodle dishes, tempura and grilled meats; it also creates Americanized rolls that earn it kudos with kids, and customers can choose to eat at the sushi bar, in a small dining room or do carryout.

Kazan ⑤ *Turkish*

	· 22	17	22	$37

McLean | Chain Bridge Corner Shopping Ctr. | 6813 Redmond Dr. (Chain Bridge Rd.), VA | 703-734-1960

"Charming owner-host Zeynel Uzun keeps an eye on things" at his "cozy hometown Turkish" eatery in McLean, and thanks to his "amazing memory for names and faces", he offers a "great welcome each time"; the "wonderful" Middle Eastern menu features "delicious" signature doner kebab, hummus and dolma, plus almond orange baklava that's the "perfect finish"; though the decor is merely "acceptable", the outdoor terrace is a "pleasant" alternative.

Kaz Sushi Bistro ⑤ *Japanese*

	25	17	20	$39

World Bank | 1915 I St. NW (bet. 19th & 20th Sts.) | 202-530-5500 | www.kazsushi.com

Kaz Okochi "does wonderful things with raw fish" at his "appealing" bistro near the World Bank, where he "breaks out of the sushi mold" with "unique freestyle Japanese dishes" and "snazzy" "low-priced daily bento specials" that artfully "blend East and West"; so step into his "minimalist" dining room and "let him take you" and the diplomats around you "on a sumptuous culinary journey."

☑ Kinkead's *Seafood*

	26	21	24	$59

Foggy Bottom | 2000 Pennsylvania Ave. NW (I St.) | 202-296-7700 | www.kinkead.com

"The perfect catch" for "seafood-inside-the-Beltway power dining", Bob Kinkead's Foggy Bottom "classic", rated the DC Survey's Most Popular, "easily holds its own with newer pretenders to the throne", serving "glistening" fin fare "inventively prepared" in "classy" quarters filled with "celebs and politicos"; it has a "can't-miss location" – a "short walk from the White House" and an "easy trip" to the Kennedy Center – and while the service is generally "meticulous", it's probably "best enjoyed in the company of a VIP."

Kolumbia, Restaurant ⑤ *American*

	18	17	18	$50

Golden Triangle | 1801 K St. NW (18th St.) | 202-331-5551 | www.restaurantkolumbia.com

Chef Jamie Stachowski and his sommelier wife, Carolyn, are the "dynamic duo" powering this "eclectic" New American in Golden Triangle, where there's "always a surprise on the menu" to complement a "solid" wine list; the "long narrow bar" hosts an "upscale happy hour", and there are "ultra-discreet booths" in which to "meet a hip business associate for lunch" or for an "intimate" dinner, even though sticklers say the staff is "unpolished" and the decor needs a "spruce up."

	FOOD	DECOR	SERVICE	COST

⚡ Komi 🖻 M *American* — 26 | 18 | 24 | $53

Dupont Circle | 1509 17th St. NW (P St.) | 202-332-9200

"So much talent in such a small place" is the story at this Dupont Circle New American where "talented" chef-owner Johnny Monis "thrills" with "fresh combinations" and "surprising ingredients" and his crew "explains each dish with such fervor that you want to try" them all; the "stylish" spot also offers a "bargain" weeknight fixed-price menu format with à la carte choices; P.S. don't skip the cheese course that offers "the stinky, the ripe and the crumbly."

Konami *Japanese* — 22 | 18 | 19 | $28

Vienna | 8221 Leesburg Pike (Chain Bridge Rd.), VA | 703-821-3400 | www.konamirestaurant.com

"An oasis of calm amid Tysons Corner's legendary traffic jams", this Japanese boasts a "shockingly serene" and "charming" "outdoor patio with a fountain and mini-garden"; they "don't try to be too inventive" here, but you can enjoy "affordable" sushi that's so "fresh" it "practically wriggles" along with an "excellent variety of bento boxes" and other options, so it's "a good place to take a co-worker who will only eat 'safe' food."

Kotobuki M *Japanese* — ▽ 24 | 7 | 18 | $25

Palisades | 4822 MacArthur Blvd. NW (U St.) | 202-625-9080

Chef-owner Hasao Abe creates "fine sushi" "without pretension", focusing on a "pared-down selection" of "super" sashimi and *kama-meshi* (a traditional rice and vegetable pot) in this "small, basic" dining space "tucked away in the Palisades"; if you can look past the "spare" decor in the "tiny, cramped" room, you'll rave over the "bargain" dollar-a-piece happy hour that some say is the "best" raw-fish value in the city.

Kramerbooks & Afterwords Cafe ● *American* — 17 | 13 | 15 | $22

Dupont Circle | 1517 Connecticut Ave. NW (bet. Dupont Circle & Q St.) | 202-387-1462 | www.kramers.com

"You might get picked up by any gender" while you "digest a book along with your dinner" at this "mercurial" Dupont Circle "scene" that's become a "neighborhood institution"; a late-night "meeting space for politicos and artists alike" (it's open 24 hours on Fridays and Saturdays) but full at all times with "literate loiterers" pretending to read while "people browsing", it offers an American menu that some call "dull" and others say is "rescued by brunch"; if you have "hunger pains after a night of carousing", however, the "nothing fancy" dishes will do just fine.

⚡ La Bergerie *French* — 26 | 22 | 25 | $55

Alexandria | 218 N. Lee St. (bet. Cameron & Queen Sts.), VA | 703-683-1007 | www.labergerie.com

"*C'est magnifique*" declare devotees of this "charming" Old Town Alexandria boîte serving "classic" French fare in a "splendid" setting with "fresh flowers and cozy banquettes" that's perfect for a "long romantic lunch"; it's "worth every penny of the bankroll you'll need" –

| | FOOD | DECOR | SERVICE | COST |

from the "amazing Caesar salad, prepared tableside" to the "must-order" quenelles to the "best dessert soufflé in town", all served by a "solicitous staff"; P.S. don't miss the "bargain" prix fixe lunch.

La Chaumiere ⑧ French

| 24 | 21 | 22 | $48 |

Georgetown | 2813 M St. NW (bet. 28th & 29th Sts.) | 202-338-1784 | www.lachaumieredc.com

For those who love "true French fare without all the fusion", this Georgetown "treasure" is a "real jewel", turning out the "best quenelles", cassoulet and soufflé Grand Marnier in "welcoming", though a bit "cramped", quarters (there's a "blazing midroom fire" for "cozy" winter dining); "you will see famous people nearly any night", but no matter who you are the "staff treats you like family"; P.S. the budget-minded say "you don't have to mortgage your house to hold a large party" here.

La Côte d'Or Café Ⓜ French

| 21 | 19 | 20 | $46 |

Arlington | 2201 N. Westmoreland St. (Lee Hwy.), VA | 703-538-3033 | www.lacotedorcafe.com

"Like France – but nearer", this Gallic enterprise on an Arlington "commercial strip" boasts two "charming" separate entities – one focusing on "classical" French fine dining and the adjacent Bistro des Celestins around the corner, serving up cafe fare "done very well"; most love these "great" options for a "casual" meal or a "special occasion" (either works for a "quiet romantic dinner"), but a few are ticked at the "tiny" "overpriced portions."

Lafayette Room American

| ▽ 24 | 26 | 25 | $79 |

Golden Triangle | The Hay-Adams | 800 16th St. NW (H St.) | 202-638-6600 | www.hayadams.com

Have the "quintessential, elegant" DC experience at a table overlooking the White House "with politicos all around" in this classically "beautiful" space in The Hay-Adams hotel; it's not just the "terrific location" and "outstanding notables-watching" that win votes, but the "truly fine" New American fare and "first-rate service" as well; so go ahead and splurge for those "special occasions and holiday meals"; N.B. no dinner on Saturdays or Sundays.

La Ferme French

| 22 | 24 | 21 | $51 |

Chevy Chase | 7101 Brookville Rd. (bet. Taylor & Thornapple Sts.), MD | 301-986-5255 | www.lafermerestaurant.com

You'll "return to another era" at this bit of the "French countryside" in a "historic Maryland suburban setting" "geared toward the older set", where a "deft hand in the kitchen" prepares "delicious" fare just like "a bistro in Paris"; the old Chevy Chase farmhouse looks a "little retro" to modernists, but the staff "bends over backwards for private parties" so there may be "no place better for grandma's birthday."

La Fourchette French

| 21 | 18 | 18 | $36 |

Adams Morgan | 2429 18th St. NW (bet. Columbia & Kalorama Rds.) | 202-332-3077

The "faithful if somewhat quirky clients" of this "reliable" Adams Morgan fixture feel like they're "stepping into a bistro in Paris" –

"huge murals on the wall" add a Gallic "arty feel" and "most of the staff actually speaks French" and acts "a bit brusque"; the "old-style" ("heavy, buttery") classic fare, "decent wine" and "outdoor eating" complete the illusion, plus the popular brunch is a "good deal"; P.S. it's so "authentic", it closes for much of August.

NEW La Limeña *Cuban/Peruvian*

`- | - | - | I`

Rockville | Ritchie Ctr. | 765 Rockville Pike (1st St.), MD | 301-424-8066
Homestyle Cuban and Peruvian fare is served in this spare store-front on Rockville Pike, where sizzling meat on the rotisserie and grill pass for decor; earthy choices like tripe and beef hearts (or standards like pork and seafood) can be paired with sides or stuffed into hefty sandwiches; N.B. until it gets its liquor license, try one of the unusual maize- and fruit-based drinks.

La Madeleine Bakery Café & Bistro *French*

`17 | 16 | 11 | $17`

Georgetown | 3000 M St. NW (30th St.) | 202-337-6975
Bethesda | 7607 Old Georgetown Rd. (Commerce Ln.), MD | 301-215-9142
Rockville | Mid-Pike Plaza | 11858 Rockville Pike (Montrose Rd.), MD | 301-984-2270
Alexandria | 500 King St. (Pitt St.), VA | 703-739-2854
Falls Church | Bailey's Crossroads | 5861 Crossroads Center Way (bet. Columbia & Leesburg Pikes), VA | 703-379-5551
Reston | 1833 Fountain Dr. (bet. Baron Cameron Ave. & New Dominion Pkwy.), VA | 703-707-0704
McLean | 1915C Chain Bridge Rd. (Leesburg Pike), VA | 703-827-8833
www.lamadeleine.com
Queue up for "ooh-la-luscious" tomato soup, "fab breads", "butter-laden" "almond croissants, chocolate brioches" and "bottomless cups of coffee" at this "serve yourself, cafeteria-style French food chain" with "cheap and easy" fare that's "well worth carrying your own tray"; but purists "pass" on this "Americanized" "McFrance" with its "contrived" decor and "disorganized" service.

La Miche *French*

`22 | 20 | 21 | $49`

Bethesda | 7905 Norfolk Ave. (St. Elmo Ave.), MD | 301-986-0707 | www.lamiche.com
Bethesda diners feel "fortunate to have this delightful restaurant" nearby since they can easily drop in for the "whole French experience" in a "warm, quiet space" perfect "for an intimate dinner" or Sunday champagne brunch; the service "aims to please", and chef-owner Jason Tepper turns out "amazing crab cakes and fantastic chocolate soufflés" to the "baby boomer generation" that's been coming "for years for family celebrations", but a few critical cutting-edgers sigh "ho-hum" to this "staid" standard.

Landini Brothers *Italian*

`22 | 18 | 20 | $43`

Alexandria | 115 King St. (Union St.), VA | 703-836-8404 | www.landinibrothers.com
A "convivial hangout" for over three decades, this Tuscan is where Old Town Alexandria's "regular Virginians congregate at the bar"

"for all the gossip"; but they're also here for "excellent freshly made pasta", "wonderful veal chops" and some "cannoli for dessert" – as well as the "nice little piano bar upstairs"; opponents who find it "tired" tag it as "the place you'd bring a Midwest mom and dad."

NEW La Rue 123 ⑤ *French* — | — | — | M

Fairfax | Bailiwick Inn | 4023 Chain Bridge Rd. (Sager Ave.), VA | 703-691-2266 | www.larue123.com

One of the former owners of nearby Le Tire Bouchon has brought a similar menu of midpriced French fare to the Federal-period dining rooms in Fairfax's Bailiwick Inn; fresh yellow paint and colorful art now warm the space, while a soon-to-open outdoor patio is certain to exude a bit of Parisian charm.

NEW Las Canteras Ⓜ *Peruvian* — | — | — | I

Adams Morgan | 2307 18th St. NW (bet. Belmont & Columbia Rds.) | 202-265-1780

This bi-level Adams Morgan Peruvian serves not only well-priced authentic standards but updated quinoa dishes too; a red-walled, second-floor dining room accented with native crafts sets the stage for the cuisine, while a tile-fronted ground-floor bar dispenses pisco sours and a selection of wines.

La Sirenita *Mexican* — | — | — | I

Hyattsville | 4911 Edmonston Rd. (Decatur St.), MD | 301-864-0188

There's "real Mexican food" in Hyattsville's Little Mexico sigh Latin lovers of this "fabulous" cantina serving tacos seven meaty ways (including with chorizo, goat and oxtail) along with homestyle *platos* ranging from the usual (chiles rellenos) to the more adventurous (quail in salsa verde); "language may be a hurdle" when placing your order with the "friendly", mostly Spanish-speaking, staff, but the biggest problem may be that it "won't hear you" over the jukebox.

La Tasca *Spanish* 16 | 20 | 16 | $30

Chinatown | 722 Seventh St. NW (bet. G & H Sts.) | 202-347-9190
NEW **Rockville** | Row at Rockville Town Sq. | 141 Gibbs St. (Washington St.), MD | 301-279-7011
NEW **Alexandria** | 607 King St. (St. Asaph St.), VA | 703-299-9810
Arlington | 2900 Wilson Blvd. (Fillmore St.), VA | 703-812-9120 ◑
www.latascausa.com

These handsome hermanas (now including locations in Rockville, Alexandria and Baltimore's Inner Harbor) "transport you to a Spanish fiesta" with walls that are "decorated from floor to ceiling", flamenco dancers and a generally "lively atmosphere"; the "reasonably priced" "tasty tapas", "huge selection of sangrias" and a "happy hour with free paella", plus "friendly service", make it "great for big groups"; the less *enamorado,* however, dis the "noisy" "Disneyland" vibe.

ⓩ L'Auberge Chez François Ⓜ *French* 27 | 26 | 27 | $75

Great Falls | 332 Springvale Rd. (Beach Mill Rd.), VA | 703-759-3800 | www.laubergechezfrancois.com

"Special occasions" are made "memorable" at this "universally be-loved" "rustic" Alsatian in a "magical" country setting in Great Falls

	FOOD	DECOR	SERVICE	COST

that takes you to "pastoral" France; the "excellent" French fare is served by a staff that makes you "feel loved and taken care of" whether you're enjoying the "fireplace warmth" in winter or the garden "on a lovely summer night", so overall many find it a "top value."

☑ L'Auberge Provençale Ⓜ *French* | 25 | 26 | 26 | $86 |

Boyce | L'Auberge Provençale | 13630 Lord Fairfax Hwy. (Rte. 50), VA | 540-837-1375 | www.laubergeprovencale.com

"A fabulous setting" "for a romantic getaway", this "lovely" antiques-filled French inn brimming with "warm hospitality" in the Virginia countryside serves "memorable", "artfully arranged" multicourse dinners of "exceptional flavor", accompanied by impressive wines; sojourners suggest "spending the weekend, visiting local vineyards, snuggling in front of the fire and eating the sensational" breakfasts – it'll be "expensive", but what a "great escape."

☑ Lauriol Plaza *Mexican* | 19 | 19 | 16 | $28 |

Dupont Circle | 1835 18th St. NW (T St.) | 202-387-0035 | www.lauriolplaza.com

The "slightly more trendy" sister of Cactus Cantina, this multilevel Dupont East "fajita factory" is "somehow always packed" with the "young and young at heart" grazing on "amazing" homemade chips and salsa, "sneakily strong" margaritas and "satisfying" Mexican in "portions that could feed an army"; "loud", "lusty" and "festive", it's a summer "gold mine" with "sidewalk seating" and a "wonderful" rooftop deck; trend-avoiders label it "Lauriolpalooza."

Lavandou *French* | 21 | 19 | 19 | $41 |

Cleveland Park | 3321 Connecticut Ave. NW (bet. Macomb & Ordway Sts.) | 202-966-3002 | www.lavandourestaurant.net

A "*très charmant*" French "snuggled" into a "strip of chic" Cleveland Park restaurants, this "cozy" bistro serves "well-prepared" favorites to Francophilic fans willing to trade elbow room for "irresistable" mussels and frites; though fusspots find its "folksy ways outdated", others focus on "good deal" perks like corkage-fee-free Mondays.

Layalina Ⓜ *Mideastern* | ▽ 23 | 18 | 23 | $30 |

Arlington | 5216 Wilson Blvd. (bet. N. Emerson & N. Greenbrier Sts.), VA | 703-525-1170 | www.layalinarestaurant.com

"Prepare to be pampered" at this "veg-friendly" Middle Easterner in Arlington's Ballston area, where the "warm" chef makes patrons feel like "honored guests" when she "comes to every table to take your order"; the "lovingly prepared" menu features "delicious" lamb shanks, eggplant and "unique" Syrian dishes that reputedly draw the Saudi royal family, while the space – "cozy" to some, "claustrophobic" to others – has "enough cultural items to fill a Smithsonian exhibit."

Lebanese Butcher & Restaurant *Lebanese* | - | - | - | I |

Falls Church | 109 E. Annandale Rd. (bet. Hillwood & S. Maple Aves.), VA | 703-241-2012

"Superb" Lebanese can be found at this "hole-in-the-wall" eatery adjacent to a combination deli/grocer/halal butcher in Falls Church that's become something of a foodie destination; despite some-times "erratic service", customers return for well-priced "obviously fresh" dishes that include "great schwarmas, kebabs" and hummus.

☑ Lebanese Taverna *Lebanese*   22 | 17 | 18 | $26

Woodley Park | 2641 Connecticut Ave. NW (bet. Calvert St. & Woodley Rd.) | 202-265-8681

Rockville | Congressional Plaza | 1605 Rockville Pike (Congressional Ln.), MD | 301-468-9086

Silver Spring | 933 Ellsworth Dr. (Rte. 29), MD | 301-588-1192

Arlington | Pentagon Row | 1101 S. Joyce St. (Army Navy Dr.), VA | 703-415-8681

Arlington | 5900 Washington Blvd. (McKinley Rd.), VA | 703-241-8681

McLean | Tysons Galleria | 1840G International Dr. (Greensboro Dr.), VA | 703-847-5244

www.lebanesetaverna.com

It's an "adventure worth taking" when you "jump from dish to dish" of "mouthwatering" meze at this "family-owned" and "family-friendly" Lebanese chainlet that warrants "lengthy waits" for a spot in its "crowded", "noisy" dining rooms; many head straight for the "creamy hummus" and "awesome" chicken schwarma on the "extensive menu" of Middle Eastern "favorites", but more critical diners discern "no real Med flavor" and find the settings of mixed quality; N.B. a Baltimore branch opened post-Survey and a second Rockville location is planned for 2007.

Le Chat Noir *French*   18 | 15 | 18 | $35

Upper NW | 4907 Wisconsin Ave. NW (41st St.) | 202-244-2044 | www.lechatnoirrestaurant.com

This "pleasant" French bistro near American University in Upper NW fills up with locals (it's a "favorite of the French Embassy staff") who love the "homey, country" dishes like "hearty buckwheat crêpes" and moules frites; the "understated", "relaxed but refined" setting and "welcoming" vibe make up for the somewhat "uneven" service that prompts a few patrons to predict it may have become "too popular too soon."

Leftbank *American*   15 | 19 | 12 | $32

Adams Morgan | 2424 18th St. NW (bet. Belmont & Columbia Rds.) | 202-464-2100 | www.leftbankdc.com

"Dress fashionably" at this "hip" Adams Morgan New American bistro/lounge featuring "surprisingly good" sushi, a "tasty" brunch and "great cocktails" at happy hour; while some find the "futuristic" "Euro" vibe "refreshing", terrestrial types say they "try a little bit too hard" here and snipe that dishes "come with a side of snark" from "beautiful" servers who "could do a little less people-watching and a little more table-watching"; P.S. the "ultraminimalist decor" was freshened up in 2006.

☑ Legal Sea Foods *Seafood*   20 | 16 | 18 | $36

Penn Quarter | 704 Seventh St. NW (bet. G & H Sts.) | 202-347-0007

Golden Triangle | 2020 K St. NW (bet. 20th & 21st Sts.) | 202-496-1111 ⓢ

(continued)

(continued)

Legal Sea Foods

Bethesda | Montgomery Mall | 7101 Democracy Blvd., 3rd fl. (I-270), MD | 301-469-5900
Arlington | 2301 Jefferson Davis Hwy. (23rd St.), VA | 703-415-1200
McLean | Tysons Galleria | 2001 International Dr. (Chain Bridge Rd.), VA | 703-827-8900
www.legalseafoods.com

"When an oyster craving hits", sail into one of these "local outposts" of the Boston-based chain known for their "consistently good" catches that "taste like they just swam onto your plate"; it's all served in "clubby" digs dressed up with "crisp white linens" and staffed by folks who "get it"; but "disappointed" fin fans question the legality of this "cookie cutter" that's "too expensive for the quality"; N.B. the K Street location is expected to close in August 2007.

Le Gaulois *French*

| 19 | 18 | 18 | $42 |

Alexandria | 1106 King St. (bet. Fayette & Henry Sts.), VA | 703-739-9494 | www.legauloiscafe.com

A "lovely garden for summer dining" and two "fireplaces in winter" are highlights of this "reliable" Old Town Alexandria Gallic where patrons warm up with "honest" country French specialties in a bistro setting; it's "reasonably priced" and "very nice for an afternoon lunch", plus diners who've called the fare "dull" will be pleased to know that chef Tom Meyers (ex Pesce) took over the reins post-Survey.

Le Mistral *French*

| 24 | – | 23 | $48 |

McLean | 6641 Old Dominion Dr. (Chain Bridge Rd.), VA | 703-748-4888 | www.lepetitmistral.com

"Fabulous" Med-inflected cuisine makes McLean's gentry "want to come back for more" at this "first-rate" French that's kept its "old-world charm" after a move down the street to more spacious quarters; despite the "Downtown DC" tabs, locals can expect to have a "delightful evening" or lunch with friends, especially given "excellent" prix fixe menus and "service that's hard to find at any price."

NEW Lemon Tree *Turkish*

| – | – | – | I |

Rockville | 1701 Rockville Pike (Halpine Rd.), MD | 301-984-0880 | www.lemontreemarket.com

Bright and airy, this Turkish cafe/market in Rockville tempts with Middle Eastern specialties that include housemade meze and pastries plus its native coffee and yogurt-based drinks; free WiFi, a working fireplace and cozy overstuffed chairs invite lingering.

Leopold's Kafe & Konditorei *Austrian*

| 21 | 21 | 14 | $32 |

Georgetown | Cady's Alley | 3318 M St. NW (bet. 33rd & 34th Sts.) | 202-965-6005 | www.kafeleopolds.com

Find "a touch of Vienna" hidden in Georgetown's Cady's Alley at this "postmodern" *konditorei* – cafe, coffeehouse and bakery – that may just look "too cool to be Austrian-cozy"; there's "excellent Wiener schnitzel", "wonderful hot chocolate" and a variety of sandwiches, along with a pastry display case of "nice indulgences", and "if you can

	FOOD	DECOR	SERVICE	COST

snag a table by the fountain" in the "beautiful" courtyard, it's even better; too bad the "snooty" "inept" service takes it down a notch.

Le Palais ⑧ French   — | — | — | E

Gaithersburg | 304 Main St. (Midtown Rd.), MD | 301-947-4051

It's "a family affair with husband, wife and son" turning out "lovely" "delicately prepared" French favorites, many rooted in their native Brittany, in this storefront eatery in Gaithersburg's Kentlands community; though the price structure, the "beautiful" appointments (Laguiole knives and crystal) and the formality may seem at odds with the location, loyalists insist that "superb" service and "great attention to detail" mean "you won't be disappointed."

⦿ Le Paradou ⑧ French   27 | 25 | 24 | $89

Penn Quarter | 678 Indiana Ave. NW (bet. 6th & 7th Sts.) | 202-347-6780 | www.leparadou.net

"Brilliant" chef Yannick Cam "has done it again" at this "unique and exquisite" New French Penn Quarter eatery that's risen to DC's "top echelon"; the "out-of-this-world" tasting menu can be paired with bottles from an "amazing wine bible" in a "sublime setting", presided over by "professional" (if sometimes "haughty") help; devotees are surprised it's "easy to get into", but that's probably because a meal here could cost "more than your mortgage payment"; N.B. prix fixe lunch and dinner options make its luxury more affordable.

Le Refuge ⑧ French   22 | 18 | 21 | $46

Alexandria | 127 N. Washington St. (bet. Cameron & King Sts.), VA | 703-548-4661 | www.lerefugealexandria.com

"Familiarity breeds content"-ment at this "intimate" Old Town Alexandria French bistro, where "the mouthwatering aroma of garlic butter greets you at the door and the food that follows does not disappoint"; yes, the decor is "kitschy" since "little has changed" in some 25 years, but this "aging belle of the ball" offers "authentic" fare "without pretense" in a setting most find "endearing" – "if you don't mind sharing conversation with adjacent diners."

Les Halles ⦿ French   19 | 17 | 17 | $40

Downtown | 1201 Pennsylvania Ave. NW (12th St.) | 202-347-6848 | www.leshalles.net

For "a taste of France", "save the airfare" and fly instead to this "bustling" Downtown brasserie that "lands you in Paris" with its "classic" steak frites, "wonderful" moules and "escargot dripping with tasty olive oil and garlic"; though it's more about the "atmosphere" than the "rich fatty food", this "celebrated" brasserie proves "très bien" "before the theater", "late at night" or "outdoors on sunny days" – though "in classic French style, service can be a little stiff."

Le Tire Bouchon Ⓜ Mediterranean   ▽ — | 20 | 22 | $53

Fairfax | 4009 Chain Bridge Rd. (Main St.), VA | 703-691-4747 | www.letirebouchon.com

New chef Tony Spagnoli (ex Henley Park Hotel) has taken the menu in a modern Mediterranean direction at this "intimate" Fairfax spot where the classic "decor maximizes a narrow, awkward space" and the service is "welcoming"; fans can still find some of their favorites here, so "be sure to place your order for the divine soufflé" early.

Levante's *Mediterranean/Turkish*

17 | 16 | 16 | $29

Dupont Circle | 1320 19th St. NW (Dupont Circle) | 202-293-3244
Bethesda | 7262 Woodmont Ave. (Elm St.), MD | 301-657-2441
www.levantes.com

"You'll be tempted to fill up" on "fabulous", "freshly baked" flatbread, but don't miss out on "tasty meze appetizers", "excellent" Turkish pizzas and other Pan-Med "favorites" "with a slight American twist" at these modern Middle Easterners that draw "cute", "young" crowds; Dupont's "great sidewalk patio" offers "no better place to linger over a glass of wine", while the Bethesda location is "full of natural light" and is a "perfect" "date-and-a-movie" choice.

NEW LIA'S *American*

- | - | - | M

Chevy Chase | 4435 Willard Ave. (Wisconsin Ave.), MD | 240-223-5427 | www.liasrestaurant.com

Geoff Tracy (Chef Geoff's) has expanded his neighborhood-friendly restaurant operations to burgeoning Chevy Chase, where a convivial bar, a spacious patio and contemporary yet rustic dining areas (a working fireplace, walls of wine) are the backdrop for Italian-accented New American comfort fare; prices that are reasonable for this upscale locale make this spot suitable for anything from a shopping break to a celebration.

NEW Liberty Tavern *American*

- | - | - | M

Arlington | 3195 Wilson Blvd. (Irving St.), VA | 703-465-9360 | www.thelibertytavern.com

Clarendon's historic Masonic Lodge building is the rustic, wood-trimmed setting for this Arlington-area New American that serves the same seasonal menu in its street-level bar/lounge as it does in its fancier upstairs dining room; N.B. use the Liberty-To-Go entrance on Irving Street for takeout.

Z Lightfoot *American*

22 | 25 | 21 | $45

Leesburg | 11 N. King St. (Market St.), VA | 703-771-2233 | www.lightfootrestaurant.com

Set in a "lovingly restored" "old bank building", this "drop-dead gorgeous" New American with "blazing" fireplaces and hand-painted Venetian chandeliers serves as "an oasis of culinary class" "in the heart of Leesburg"; though some question whether the "expensive", seasonal menu "measures up" to the "impressive" decor, the "over-the-top" service helps make it "a must" for business affairs, "ladies who lunch", "romantic" dates and "pull-out-all-the-stops" occasions.

Light House Tofu *Korean*

- | - | - | I

Rockville | 12710 Twinbrook Pkwy. (Ardennes Ave.), MD | 301-881-1178

It's "a good sign" that "lots of Koreans eat" at this Rockville restaurant where the signature soybean curd creations "couldn't be more authentic" and the made-to-order soups and BBQ entrees offer "excellent value for the price"; the decor goes heavy on natural materials like wood and rice paper, creating a down-to-earth setting for the country-style cuisine.

Lima ⑤ *Pan-Latin*

| - | - | - | M |

Downtown | 1401 K St. NW (14th St.) | 202-789-2800 | www.limarestaurant.com

This kinetic, ultramodern tri-level bar, lounge and restaurant has landed in Downtown lawyer/lobbyist territory, where it's aiming to loosen ties after work at its ground-floor bar and snacking area; upstairs, there's eclectic Latin dining at tables overlooking the K Street action, while later in the evening, a DJ spins in the lower lounge, which doubles as a private event space.

Little Fountain Cafe *Eclectic*

| 23 | 21 | 23 | $40 |

Adams Morgan | 2339 18th St. NW (bet. Belmont & Kalorama Rds.) | 202-462-8100 | www.littlefountaincafe.com

An "adorable" "hidden" "oasis" in "bustling Adams Morgan", this "subterranean" Eclectic offers "good, reasonably priced" fare and "amazing desserts" (the "chocolate-chip bread pudding will blow your mind"), while wine buffs can explore a "small but intelligent wine list" that's half-price on Wednesdays; an "intimate setting" with "really personal service" is "perfect for trysts", though the heartless haven't any warmth for the "spotty" service and "predictable" menu.

Little Viet Garden *Vietnamese*

| 19 | 13 | 16 | $21 |

Arlington | 3012 Wilson Blvd. (N. Garfield St.), VA | 703-522-9686

"Skip the dark, cramped dining room and head straight" for the "private" garden at this "decent-for-the-price" Arlington-area Vietnamese "hidden" "in the heart of" Clarendon near the Metro; "there's never a crowd" in the "quiet, no-frills" space and admirers "wax poetic" about clay pot dishes and "fab pho", though doubters can't decipher "anything creative or authentic" on the menu.

Local 16 *American*

| 15 | 19 | 15 | $32 |

U Street Corridor | 1602 U St. NW (16th St.) | 202-265-2828 | www.localsixteen.com

"If you are going for dinner" at this U Street hot spot, "be sure to get there before it turns into a bar scene", even though tipplers tout that as the best time to go; although the eclectic New American fare has "gotten much better", it's "not a place to eat" as much as "to hang out at night on weekends" for "a drink and a burger" before heading to the "excellent rooftop deck" "to see and be seen."

Logan Tavern *American*

| 17 | 18 | 17 | $31 |

Logan Circle | 1423 P St. NW (bet. 14th & 15th Sts.) | 202-332-3710 | www.logantavern.com

The old joke, "nobody goes there anymore – it's too crowded" aptly applies to this "laid-back" P Street hangout known for its "bustling, lively" brunch and "humongous portions" of "basic" American "comfort cooking" like "meatloaf that warms the heart and is easy on the wallet", "great burgers", the "best French toast ever" and "to-die-for" Bloody Marys during weekend brunch; but naysayers knock this "diner with pretensions" as simply "not worth the long wait"; N.B. look for a new Columbia Heights sister restaurant called Logan @ The Heights.

Louisiana Express Co. *Cajun* | 22 | 10 | 17 | $19 |

Bethesda | 4921 Bethesda Ave. (Arlington Rd.), MD | 301-652-6945 | www.louisianaexpressco.com

French Quarter Café *Cajun*

Germantown | 19847 Century Blvd. (Pinnacle Dr.), MD | 301-515-7693 | www.thefrenchquartercafe.com

Face it, "this ain't Emeril's", but that's part of the charm of these "warm" "diamonds in the rough" that dish up "inexpensive", "honest to goodness" "really good Cajun grandma cookin'"; the same "inviting" family that opened the Bethesda original and "definitely knows how to make a roux" now provides a "real taste of New Orleans" in Germantown; both outlets will "bring the French Quarter to your nose and mouth" and a "smile to your face."

L'oustalet *French* | 22 | 17 | 19 | $42 |

Rockville | 302 King Farm Blvd. (Grand Champion Dr.), MD | 301-963-3400 | www.loustaletrest.com

Suburbanites "delight" in the "traditional French cooking" at this "petite and romantic" bistro in Rockville's King Farm village, where "upscale" if "pricey" foie gras, tournedos, frites and daily specials are "artistically presented" by chef-owner Marcel Bernard (ex Les Halles); but "beware" that the service can be more "well intentioned" than competent and the "cramped" space gets especially "overcrowded on Saturday nights."

Lucky Strike *American* | 16 | 22 | 15 | $24 |

Chinatown | Gallery Pl. | 701 Seventh St. NW (bet. F & H Sts.) | 202-347-1021 | www.bowlluckystrike.com

"More than a bowling alley", this "posh playground for adults" in Chinatown's Gallery Place scores points for "creative" American bar food (fried macaroni and cheese balls), "kinky drinks, sweet tunes and fun times" in a "hip atmosphere" with slick "images flashing above the lanes"; it may cause "sensory overload" for some pin-crashers who also claim they "waited forever for a waitress", but the cocktails and apps are "much better than expected" and you can "shoot some pool" or catch a game on the big TVs.

Luigino *Italian* | 18 | 16 | 17 | $38 |

Downtown | 1100 New York Ave. NW (bet. 11th & 12th Sts.) | 202-371-0595 | www.luigino.com

Downtown devotees of this "very reliable" Italian are drawn in by "*deliciozo* pastas" like the "fabulously addictive" house-smoked salmon in pink vodka sauce served in "bright", "business-lunch appropriate" surroundings; even if the location is a bit "out of the way" now that the Convention Center has moved to Mt. Vernon Square, it's still "convenient for theatergoers" who give it "a solid B"; dour diners are distracted by "slow service" and "tired" decor.

	FOOD	DECOR	SERVICE	COST

Luna Grill & Diner *Diner/Vegetarian*   19 | 15 | 17 | $20

Adams Morgan | 1301 Connecticut Ave. NW (N St.) |
202-835-2280
Arlington | 4024 28th St. S. (Quincy St.), VA | 703-379-7173
www.lunagrillanddiner.com

"Vegetarians, vegans and meat eaters" unite at this pair of "dependable" "bohemian alternatives" in Adams Morgan and Arlington that are "as comfortable as your favorite yoga pants", serving up "huge portions of cheap food": "classic blue-plate specials", "excellent" tomato soup, "'green-plate specials' for non-meat eaters", breakfast all day and "half-price pasta on Sunday and Monday nights"; still, some wonder why you'd deal with the sometimes "surly" service when "you can make any of their dishes at home."

☑ Maestro ⑤ Ⓜ *Italian*   28 | 27 | 28 | $114

McLean | Ritz-Carlton Tysons Corner | 1700 Tysons Blvd. (International Dr.), VA | 703-821-1515 | www.maestrorestaurant.com

A "fabulous experience" awaits at this luxurious Italian in the Ritz-Carlton Tysons Corner, where the "tasting menus" are "works of art", the "skilled" sommelier is worthy of "trust" and the rest of the "incredibly attentive and welcoming" staff will make "you feel like a celebrity"; "soft lighting and subtle music" melt away stress, and if you sit by the open kitchen and watch the "concentrated creativity" of "genius" chef Fabio Trabocchi and his crew "plate food using tweezers", you'll get "an immediate appreciation" of why this one ranks so high.

Maggiano's Little Italy *Italian*   18 | 17 | 18 | $32

Upper NW | 5333 Wisconsin Ave. NW (Western Ave.) |
202-966-5500
McLean | Tysons Galleria | 2001 International Dr. (Rte. 123), VA |
703-356-9000
www.maggianos.com

"Wear stretchy pants" to these Upper NW and Tysons Corner chain Italians because pasta "portions are huge and they just keep it coming" ("doggy bags are encouraged"); "fun" if "noisy" "1930s-style" digs, background music that's seemingly "all Sinatra, all the time" and "family-style dining" make them "great places for a large party", but non-admirers inquire "why go" to this "parody" of Italy with "oily" fare when there are wonderful alternatives nearby – unless it's just "all about quantity."

Magnolias at the Mill *American*   ▽ 19 | 23 | 19 | $39

Purcellville | 198 N. 21st St. (Main St.), VA | 540-338-9800 |
www.magnoliasmill.com

Set in a "lovely" Purcellville mill oozing "old Virginia style", this outpost of Leesburg's Tuscarora Mill boasts a similar "eclectic" wine and beer selection that "perfectly complements" its "modernized Americana" fare; while exurbanites welcome this "pleasant place for everything from burgers to grilled seafood" to stone-baked flatbread pizza, perfectionists insist that the food is "not exactly memorable" even if the "visually fantastic" environs – wood floors and beams, ceilings covered with old mill wheels – are.

Mai Thai *Thai*

| 22 | 21 | 19 | $26 |

Dupont Circle | 1200 19th St. NW (M St.) | 202-452-6870
Alexandria | 6 King St. (Union St.), VA | 703-548-0600
www.maithai.us

With a "sophisticated, modern" second-story setting on a "prime" corner in Old Town Alexandria overlooking the Harbour, this "reasonably priced" Thai is lauded for its "very attentive staff", "great drinks and good people-watching" along with "well-prepared" standards, i.e. the "best" pad Thai and green papaya salad; P.S. its glitzy sister, below Dupont Circle, opened post-Survey and features fancier decor, a lush lounge, a patio and a similar "good buy" menu.

NEW Majestic *American*

| – | – | – | M |

Alexandria | 911 King St. (Alfred St.), VA | 703-837-9117 |
www.majesticcafe.com

Cathal and Meshelle Armstrong (Eve, Eammon's) have taken over Old Town Alexandria's Majestic Café and given it a suave, uptown look courtesy of warm tones, flattering lighting and a bar that shakes up classic mixed drinks; its down-home American menu reflects a commitment to seasonality and locally sourced ingredients.

⁊ Makoto   *Japanese*

| 28 | 21 | 27 | $65 |

Palisades | 4822 MacArthur Blvd. NW (U St.) | 202-298-6866

"Take off your shoes" and time travel "back to the 19th century" when you enter this "shoebox"-size Palisades eatery, reminiscent of a Kyoto *ryokan* (rustic inn) that feels "more Japanese than today's Japan"; its highlights include "exquisite", "authentic" omakase meals that are "almost too pretty to eat" and "witty sushi chefs" who create "a wonderful meal at the bar"; it's just the "horrendously uncomfortable" box seats that annoy.

Malaysia Kopitiam *Malaysian*

| 22 | 9 | 17 | $22 |

Golden Triangle | 1827 M St. NW (bet. 18th & 19th Sts.) | 202-833-6232 |
www.malaysiakopitiam.com

If "you like Chinese and Indian (and Thai), then Malaysian will rock your world" and this "dark" "subterranean find" in the Golden Triangle provides a "shockingly affordable", "most authentic" opportunity to try the "fascinating" cuisine; chef-owner Penny Phoon and her "friendly" staff are happy to "suggest or explain" her native dishes, and the "full-color pictures" in her "phonebook"-size menu save the "uninitiated" from "ordering disaster"; just ignore the "dumpy basement" digs and focus on your plate.

Mamma Lucia *Italian*

| 19 | 12 | 17 | $22 |

Bethesda | 4916 Elm St. (bet. Arlington Rd. & Woodmont Ave.), MD | 301-907-3399
Olney | Olney Village Mart | 18224 Village Center Dr. (Olney Sandy Spring Rd.), MD | 301-570-9500
College Park | College Park Plaza | 4734 Cherry Hill Rd. (47th Ave.), MD | 301-513-0605
Rockville | Federal Plaza | 12274M Rockville Pike (Twinbrook Pkwy.), MD | 301-770-4894

(continued)

Mamma Lucia

Rockville | Fallsgrove Village Shopping Ctr. | 14921J Shady Grove Rd. (bet. Blackwell Rd. & Fallsgrove Blvd.), MD | 301-762-8805
Silver Spring | Blair Shops | 1302 East-West Hwy. (Colesville Rd.), MD | 301-562-0693
www.mammaluciarestaurants.com

Tots and teens alike "love" this mini-chain of "family-friendly" "down-home" Italians scattered across Montgomery County (plus a "classed-up" Frederick location); portions are "huge", and despite the "fast-food"-like feel, there's the "sense that somebody's mamma is cooking in the back"; but perturbed paesani point to "hit-or-miss" pastas that are "nothing to write Rome about", and solemnly "stick with" the New York–style pizza instead.

Mandalay *Burmese*
24 | 13 | 17 | $22

Silver Spring | 930 Bonifant St. (bet. Fenton St. & Georgia Ave.), MD | 301-585-0500 | www.mandalayrestaurantcafe.org

An "adventure in eating", this "amazingly affordable", "masterful Burmese" in Downtown Silver Spring continues to "impress" with a "huge vegetarian selection" and "solicitous", though sometimes "a little overwhelmed", servers who "ensure that your dishes are at the 'heat' level you can tolerate"; this storefront location is "far more charming" than the previous space (the Decor score may not reflect a recent move), but "don't expect quiet" since its local followers "tote their kids everywhere."

M & S Grill *Seafood/Steak*
18 | 18 | 17 | $34

Downtown | 600 13th St. NW (F St.) | 202-347-1500
Reston | Reston Town Ctr. | 11901 Democracy Dr. (Discovery St.), VA | 703-787-7766
www.mandsgrill.com

The "dress-down relatives" of parent McCormick & Schmick's, these "stuffy yet suave" surf 'n' turf Americans offer enough of the "basics" to "satisfy anyone", and host "unbeatable", "low-priced" happy hours that are "packed to the gills"; "the business set" keeps the Downtown DC and Reston locations "always" busy, while families and tourists "flock" to see the Baltimore branch's Inner Harbor views; still, surly sorts snipe at "inattentive", "sloppy" service.

NEW Mandu *Korean*
- | - | - | M

Dupont Circle | 1805 18th St. NW (bet. S & Swann Sts.) | 202-588-1540 | www.mandudc.com

This Dupont Circle Korean serves homespun dishes like bibimbop and its namesake dumplings in an Asian-themed setting featuring paintings that depict rural life; if you're looking to liven up the evening, try one of the specialty soju-based cocktails.

Mannequin Pis *Belgian*
23 | 14 | 16 | $43

Olney | Olney Ctr. | 18064 Georgia Ave. (Olney Laytonsville Rd.), MD | 301-570-4800 | www.mannequinpis.com

Go for the mussels and frites prepared "every way you can imagine" at this "tiny" "out-of-the-way" Olney Belgian offering more than a

FOOD | DECOR | SERVICE | COST

dozen bivalve specialties to choose from each night ("lavender-scented", anyone?) and "unusual meat dishes" too (bison tenderloin, kangeroo, ostrich); you may "feel like you're double dating the people at the next table", but the staff is "very smart about pairing" the "incredible beer selection" (served in the correct glassware) with the "novel" fare.

☑ Marcel's *Belgian/French*

28 | 24 | 27 | $73

West End | 2401 Pennsylvania Ave. NW (24th St.) | 202-296-1166 | www.marcelsdc.com

"A class act" from the "exquisitely prepared" Belgian-French fare to the "first-rate" staff to the "door-to-door" sedan service to the Kennedy Center, this West End fine-dining venue oozes ambiance; chef-owner Robert Wiedmaier's cooking, including a "wonderful" pre-theater prix fixe, "makes your heart sing" (and the cash register ring) with selections like the "best boudin blanc (sausage) in the city"; but lovers beware, when it gets "loud" it's "not the place for intimacy."

Mar de Plata *Spanish*

▽ 21 | 15 | 19 | $42

NEW Golden Triangle | 1827 Jefferson Pl. NW (Connecticut Ave.) | 202-293-2650

Logan Circle | 1410 14th St. NW (bet. P St. & Rhode Island Ave.) | 202-234-2679

In the "heart" of the newly gentrified 14th Street corridor, this well-established storefront "gem" offers "satisfying" Spanish fare and "unpretentious gracious service" to Studio Theater patrons; amigos enjoy the "well-prepared" local Latin-style seafood and "sneakingly expensive" tapas, "mitigated by the best mojitos", in a "spirited and friendly" atmosphere, but trendies who trek to the other eateries "trying to excel" here may "leave this one behind"; N.B. the Golden Triangle branch opened post-Survey.

Mark and Orlando's *American*

24 | 14 | 24 | $41

Dupont Circle | 2020 P St. NW (Hopkins St.) | 202-223-8463 | www.markandorlandos.com

The "attention is on the details" at this "bright" two-level spot on Dupont Circle where Mark Medley and Orlando Hitzig have turned a former Asian noodle shop into a "subdued" dining room and "cozy" upstairs bar/cafe; expect a daily changing menu that is filled with "tasty interpretations of New American" fare and served by an "attentive" staff.

Market Street Bar & Grill *American*

18 | 18 | 18 | $40

Reston | Hyatt Regency Reston | 1800 Presidents St. (Market St.), VA | 703-925-8250 | www.msbg.net

Even if "there are better restaurants", "you really can't go wrong" with the "reliable" New American fare (prime rib, crab cakes) at this Reston hotel dining room, where "wood floors and simple decor" complement "a lovely view of Town Center" or of pretty people at its "great happy hour"; business types who don't mind a meal that's "overpriced" claim they can "talk with clients without others overhearing", while leisure lovers head for the "live jazz" Thursday–Saturday nights.

	FOOD	DECOR	SERVICE	COST

Mark's Duck House *Chinese* | 23 | 8 | 15 | $24 |

Falls Church | Willston Ctr. I | 6184A Arlington Blvd. (Patrick Henry Dr.), VA | 703-532-2125 | www.marksduckhouse.com

"As the name suggests", this "crowded" Cantonese "must-visit" in Falls Church boasts "incredible Peking duck" (served with unexpected "pomp and circumstance") as well as "spectacular" dim sum; "come early for the freshest selection" – you can "be adventurous" by ordering from the "'village menu'" or be "tame" (there's "won ton soup unlike any other") – but don't expect much from the "depressing atmosphere" or "disinterested service."

Mark's Kitchen *American*   ▽ 19 | 8 | 16 | $15 |

Takoma Park | 7006 Carroll Ave. (Laurel St.), MD | 301-270-1884 | www.markskitchen.com

The "busiest joint in the heart of Old Town Takoma Park", this "homey" and "quirky" "nuclear free zone diner" is a "pleasant" spot to enjoy an "informal crowded meal, elbow-to-elbow with liberally minded folk"; the American dishes "with interesting Korean touches" include "lots of great vegetarian options" and other selections reflecting a "hippie/granola heritage" ("be sure to order the ginger milkshake"), but the decor and the "slacking service" "could use some help."

NEW Marrakesh Palace *Moroccan*   – | – | – | M |

Dupont Circle | 2147 P St. NW (Twining Ct.) | 202-775-1882 | www.marrakeshpalace.com

Open the massive copper door off Dupont Circle and enter this Moroccan escape where colorful wall tiles, cushion-strewn banquettes and flickering candles set the stage for classic tagines and meze; nightly belly dancing is an added fillip, and a prix fixe menu option for two makes it promising as a date-night destination.

Martin's Tavern *American* | 18 | 18 | 19 | $29 |

Georgetown | 1264 Wisconsin Ave. NW (N St.) | 202-333-7370 | www.martins-tavern.com

"Jack and Jackie ate here" – and other presidents from Truman to George W. also haven't been able to resist the "straightforward burgers" and the "best Kentucky 'hot brown' east of Louisville" served at this Traditional American "old-school" Georgetown "institution" that's "still a favorite local hangout"; sure, the "weathered" "haunt's" "historic" seats, like "JFK's 'rumbleseat' booth near the front", "are nearly too small for an adult", and regulars treat it solely as a bar, but it's one of the "last great taverns" around.

Matchbox ⊠ *American* | 23 | 19 | 17 | $26 |

Chinatown | 713 H St. NW (bet. 7th & 8th Sts.) | 202-289-4441 | www.matchboxdc.com

"How can such little hamburgers have such big taste?" ask admirers who frequent this "cool" row house "in the heart of Chinatown" that's shaped less "like a matchbox" after a massive post-Survey expansion; they not only "wax poetic" over its sliders, but also its "addictive (if greasy)" fried onion strings, "seriously good" wood-fired pizza and other New American entrees; the "excellent 'girlie' or 'manly' martinis" spark a "lively" happy hour that pulses with an "urban vibe"; N.B. they've added an outdoor deck.

Maté ◐ *Asian Fusion*
▽ 17 | 20 | 15 | $38

Georgetown | 3101 K St. NW (31st St.) | 202-333-2006 | www.matelounge.com

It's the "hip lounge setting" "with space-age decor" that draws denizens to this Georgetowner, though the place "gets points for creativity" with "amazing" Latin-influenced Asian fusion items like "corn masa sushi"; still, some say "just because they can" create wild food combinations "doesn't mean they should", and given the "nasty" service that "outdoes NYC attitude", it's "clearly geared to the club crowd", so just "come for the scene and the cocktails."

Matisse ⊠ *French/Mediterranean*
20 | 21 | 18 | $50

Upper NW | 4934 Wisconsin Ave. NW (Fessenden St.) | 202-244-5222 | www.matisserestaurantdc.com

In "a lovely townhouse" "off the beaten path" in Upper Northwest, this "delightful neighborhood" French-Med paints a "pretty" picture of "'downtown' food in an uptown setting", making the "sophisticated" "older crowd" "feel special and comfortable"; but a smattering of critics say its image is smudged by "crowded" seating and "stubbornly authentic French bistro service [that] can be grating."

Matsuri ⊠ *Japanese*
▽ 20 | 18 | 19 | $27

Herndon | 150 Elden St. (Fairfax County Pkwy.), VA | 703-707-0367

Discover some of the "best sushi in western Fairfax County" plus "a great lunchtime buffet" at this Herndon Japanese run by chef-owner Heeman Lee; sip sakes and munch on delectables like agedashi tofu, shumai, tempura and teriyaki, plus a nice selection of raw fish, amid contemporary decor.

Matuba *Japanese*
21 | 12 | 19 | $27

Bethesda | 4918 Cordell Ave. (bet. Norfolk Ave. & Old Georgetown Rd.), MD | 301-652-7449
Arlington | 2915 Columbia Pike (Walter Reed Dr.), VA | 703-521-2811 ⊠
www.matuba-sushi.com

"Sit at the sushi bar" and "watch the chef create his wonders while you munch" on "ultra"-"fantastic" fruits of the sea at these "straightforward" "bare-bones" eateries with "friendly servers"; the Bethesda branch boasts an "all-you-can-eat sushi menu at unbelievable prices", while the Arlington spot remains an "all-time favorite" despite its "drab" interior and location in a "downright awful strip of shops."

NEW M Cafe & Bar *Italian*
- | - | - | M

Chevy Chase | The Collection at Chevy Chase | 5471 Wisconsin Ave. (Wisconsin Circle), MD | 301-986-4818 | www.mcafeandbar.com

Fashionistas cruising the 'Rodeo Drive East' of Chevy Chase find light, sophisticated fare at this midpriced Italian cafe and wine bar adjacent to its parent, MaxMara boutique; a modern setting with fashion photos on the wall and a tucked-away sculpture courtyard attract shoppers and nearby denizens for everything from a quick lunch to a leisurely dinner.

Z McCormick & Schmick's *Seafood* | 21 | 20 | 20 | $41 |

Penn Quarter | 901 F St. NW (9th St.) | 202-639-9330
Golden Triangle | 1652 K St. NW (bet. 16th & 17th Sts.) | 202-861-2233
Bethesda | 7401 Woodmont Ave. (Montgomery Ln.), MD | 301-961-2626
Arlington | 2010 Crystal Dr. (20th St.), VA | 703-413-6400
Reston | Reston Town Ctr. | 11920 Democracy Dr. (bet. Discovery & Library Sts.), VA | 703-481-6600
McLean | Ernst & Young Bldg. | 8484 Westpark Dr. (Leesburg Pike), VA | 703-848-8000
www.mccormickandschmicks.com

The "daily fresh-catch offering can't be beat" say habitués hooked on this "clubby" chain "classic" where the "plethora of choices" "cooked as simply or as complicated as one would like" and "knowledgeable servers" make it "a safe bet for a biz lunch" or "excellent for a family celebration"; though the "disappointed" suggest that the "over-priced", "uninspired" "fish factory" fare is a "let-down", barflies insist that "great specials" during happy hour deliver "real value."

NEW M'Dawg Haute Dogs ● *Hot Dogs* | – | – | – | I |

Adams Morgan | 2418 18th St. NW (bet. Belmont & Columbia Rds.) | 202-328-8284 | www.m-dawg.com

For a late-night pick-me-up, Adams Morgan revelers head to this counter-service comfort station for a definitive selection of upscale hot dogs that can be accessorized at the toppings bar; naturally, its storefront digs are decorated with photos of customers' pet pooches; N.B. open until 4 AM on weekends.

NEW Mei's Asian | – | – | – | M |
Bistro *Chinese/Japanese*

Arlington | 3434 Washington Blvd. (N. Kirkwood Rd.), VA | 703-516-0123 | www.meisasianbistro.com

A sushi bar, patio and cocktail lounge ensures there's something for everyone at this midpriced Chinese-Japanese addition in Arlington's Virginia Square area; the menu even offers vegetarian dishes featuring imitation meats and seafood, and the lively, sophisticated decor is spruced up with colorful Asian murals.

Meiwah *Chinese* | 20 | 16 | 18 | $26 |

Golden Triangle | 1200 New Hampshire Ave. NW (M St.) | 202-833-2888
Chevy Chase | 4457 Willard Ave. (Wisconsin Ave.), MD | 301-652-9882
www.meiwahrestaurant.com

"Fresh tasting" and "surprisingly satisfying" rave regulars of these Golden Triangle and Chevy Chase sisters serving the "best 'Americanized' Chinese in town" with a "vegetarian's paradise" of tofu selections, "the best" crispy fried shredded beef and "reliably delicious" hunan chicken; on "weekends, the wait can be a bear" and spoilsports scoff at "unimaginative", "fast-food-esque" selections and "slow service", but everyday eaters counter even if they're "not highbrow . . . who cares?"

	FOOD	DECOR	SERVICE	COST

Mendocino Grille & Wine Bar *American/Californian*

23 | 20 | 21 | $48

Georgetown | 2917 M St. NW (bet. 29th & 30th Sts.) | 202-333-2912 | www.mendocinodc.com

"Delicious" New American and seasonal Californian cuisine and a "terrific assortment of fine cheeses" are paired with a "sensational wine list" that focuses on West Coast labels at Georgetown's version of a "civilized adult bar scene"–cum–"yuppie hangout"; the "knowledgeable staff" keeps the surroundings "elegant" in a "classy room" that's "cramped" enough to feel "more Manhattan than Mendocino", but the simple-minded say dishes are "too complicated with too many unrecognizable ingredients."

Merkado Kitchen *Nuevo Latino*

19 | 20 | 18 | $34

Logan Circle | 1443 P St. NW (bet. 14th & 15th Sts.) | 202-299-0018 | www.merkadodc.com

East meets South at this "stylish", "roomy" Asian-inflected Latin with "great cocktails" in the "now trendy neighborhood" of Logan Circle; after-theater diners and gentrifyers "bored of eating out" ignore the "slow" service and focus on "inventive" dishes that "make the odd enjoyable" yet are "friendly enough for Yankee stomachs"; N.B. a post-Survey chef change may outdate the above Food score.

Meskerem *Ethiopian*

21 | 17 | 18 | $24

Adams Morgan | 2434 18th St. NW (bet. Belmont & Columbia Rds.) | 202-462-4100

"There's nothing like eating with your hands" at this Adams Morgan "fine introduction to Ethiopian" where "combo meals allow you to sample" and they all pair well with a "honey wine that's total bliss"; even if purists proclaim it "under-seasoned" for the "suburban palate", it's still "worth a stop when you're not in a rush" since you can sit "upstairs on cushions" and enjoy the "gracious service."

Mezè ● *Mideastern*

19 | 17 | 16 | $27

Adams Morgan | 2437 18th St. NW (bet. Belmont & Columbia Rds.) | 202-797-0017 | www.mezedc.com

"Turkish tapas rule" at this "cute, homey" Adams Morgan spot serving an "eclectic" menu of Middle Eastern fare (including a "blissful brunch") that's "best when you can sit outside" on the "tranquil" patio "on a warm summer afternoon"; "the place buzzes with energy" on weekend nights, but the "service is hit-or-miss" and the "noise level" "makes it hard to hear the person next to you" (especially in the "refurbished" upstairs room).

NEW Mia's Pizzas Ⓜ *Pizza*

– | – | – | I

Bethesda | 4926 Cordell Ave. (Norfolk Ave.), MD | 301-718-6427 | www.miaspizzas.com

An eye-catching wood-fired oven turns out gourmet pizzas plus roasted chicken and fish at this inexpensive Bethesda pie parlor and wine bar; its off-street patio leads into a colorful skylit room decorated with photos of Italy; N.B. be sure to finish your meal with one of the signature dessert cupcakes.

	FOOD	DECOR	SERVICE	COST

Z Mie N Yu *American* 18 | 27 | 18 | $47

Georgetown | 3125 M St. NW (bet. 31st St. & Wisconsin Ave.) |
202-333-6122 | www.mienyu.com

The "outrageously fabulous" setting of this Georgetown New
American – "intricate lanterns and pillows", belly dancers, "couples
lounging in a Bedouins' tent" – brings to mind a "quirky Marco Polo-
inspired trip"; groups can "sit in the 'birdcage'" for a "bird's-eye view
of the dining room" and enjoy a personalized chef's tasting menu,
while others opt for selections from the "innovative" "Silk Road–
inspired menu"; imbibers get a "wallet hangover", however, from the
"offensively overpriced" drinks and are further vexed by servers
"more interested in looking good" than doing their jobs.

Mikaku Ⓜ *Japanese* ▽ 27 | 17 | 22 | $29

Herndon | 3065J Centreville Rd. (McLearen Rd.), VA | 703-467-0220
With a name meaning 'sense of taste', this "inviting" Herndon
"strip-mall" spot serves some of the "best sushi in the area" along
with interesting "Japanese tapas", homestyle soups and a full menu
of traditional dishes; there's "warm", welcoming, "kid-friendly" service and a back room that can be reserved for large groups.

Mimi's American Bistro *American* 18 | 19 | 21 | $32

Dupont Circle | 2120 P St. NW (bet. 21st & 22nd Sts.) | 202-464-6464 |
www.mimisdc.com

"Who needs *American Idol,* when we've got Mimi's?" rave fans of this
"unique" Dupont Circle musicale/restaurant with its "singing" servers
that's "always a hit with out-of-town guests" who get to hear their
waiter "croon a tune and then run to the kitchen" to fetch "reasonably
priced, reliable" Med-accented New American fare and "fancy" cocktails; though it's all mostly "fun", the "numerous 'Happy Birthday'" ser-
enades "can be wearing" and you have to "dig Broadway show tunes."

Minerva *Indian* 22 | 11 | 15 | $20

NEW Gaithersburg | 16240 Frederick Rd. (Shady Grove Rd.), MD |
301-948-9898
Fairfax | 10364 Lee Hwy. (University Dr.), VA | 703-383-9200
Herndon | Village Center at Dulles | 2443G1 Centreville Rd.
(Sunrise Valley Dr.), VA | 703-793-3223
Chantilly | 14513B Lee Jackson Memorial Hwy. (Airline Pkwy.), VA |
703-378-7778
www.minervacuisine.com

The "red-hot" dishes can "light a fire in your belly as well as your heart"
at these South Asians that are "popular with Indian families" but can
be "too spicy" for novices; the service is "weak" and "there's no atmosphere whatsoever", but you'll be able to try "stuff you won't see
anywhere else" during one of the "finest" lunch buffets around.

Minh's Restaurant *Vietnamese* 22 | 16 | 18 | $23

Arlington | 2500 Wilson Blvd. (Cleveland St.), VA | 703-525-2828 |
www.minhsrestaurant.com

In the "serene" Arlington Courthouse area, this Saigonese boasts
"affordable", "creative dishes" that are "much more unusual" than

average and a dining room that's "prettier than in most Vietnamese" eateries; servers are pleased to "bring you some of their favorites" (and "you won't be sorry" when they do), so it's hard to understand why "it's always half empty" – perhaps it's the "odd location."

NEW **Mio** 🖼 *American*   – | – | – | M

Downtown | 1110 Vermont Ave. NW (L St.) | 202-955-0075 | www.miorestaurant.com

Located in the redeveloped area above Downtown's McPherson Square, this midpriced New American exudes a cosmopolitan vibe via a modern, white-brick-wall setting accented with wood partitions, local artwork and the requisite open kitchen; the front area sports a long bar and lounge seating, and a piano player adds to the experience several nights a week.

Mi Rancho *Tex-Mex*   22 | 15 | 19 | $22

Germantown | 19725A Germantown Rd. (Middlebrook Rd.), MD | 301-515-7480
Silver Spring | 8701 Ramsey Ave. (Cameron St.), MD | 301-588-4872
These "lively", "crowded" "no-frills" Tex-Mex "stalwarts" in Germantown and Silver Spring may look "like someone's basement", but they always "feel like there's a party going on" with "*muy fantastico*" margaritas and "huge portions" of "hot and sizzling" fare; maybe they "aren't adventurous", but with such "fast service" and "decent prices", they're even "good for families" if you go early.

Mitsitam Café *American*   ▽ 22 | 16 | 13 | $16

SW | National Museum of the American Indian | 4th St. & Independence Ave. SW | 202-633-7041 | www.nmai.si.edu
You'd "never dream" you'd find such an "amazing selection" of Native American fare in a museum eatery, but here it is at this "surprisingly good", "reasonably priced" lunch-only cafeteria in the National Museum of the American Indian, where each of five stations features a different indigenous culinary tradition; "long lines of tourists" tote their trays in a "pretty" "glass-walled room" with a "courteous staff", but if you're a local "go early to beat" the crowds.

Moby Dick *Persian*   22 | 5 | 14 | $13

Georgetown | 1070 31st St. NW (bet. K & M Sts.) | 202-333-4400
Golden Triangle | 1300 Connecticut Ave. NW (N St.) | 202-833-9788 🖼
Bethesda | 7027 Wisconsin Ave. (Leland St.), MD | 301-654-1838
Gaithersburg | Market Sq. | 105 Market St. (Kentlands Blvd.), MD | 301-987-7770
Germantown | 12844 Pinnacle Dr. (Century Blvd.), MD | 301-916-1555
NEW **Rockville** | Fallsgrove Village Shopping Ctr. | 14929A Shady Grove Rd. (bet. Blackwell Rd. & Fallsgrove Blvd.), MD | 301-738-0005
NEW **Silver Spring** | 909 Ellsworth Dr. (Fenton St.), MD | 301-578-8777
Arlington | 3000 Washington Blvd. (N. Garfield St.), VA | 703-465-1600
Fairfax | 12154 Fairfax Towne Ctr. (W. Ox Rd.), VA | 703-352-6226

(continued)

Moby Dick

McLean | 6854 Old Dominion Dr. (Chain Bridge Rd.), VA | 703-448-8448
www.mobysonline.com
Additional locations throughout the DC area

For that "quick Persian fix" "who needs the fancy places?" when you've got these area "kebab masters" providing "fast food as it should be": "perfectly grilled meat", "addictive" rice, "amazing" hummus and "crisp and stunning" bread, all at "unbeatable prices"; even if it's "mobbed at lunchtime", it's "always worth the wait" – though if you "crave atmosphere" as well, "carry out" and "eat a sumptuous meal at home."

Mon Ami Gabi *French*

19 | 20 | 18 | $39

Bethesda | 7239 Woodmont Ave. (Bethesda Ave.), MD | 301-654-1234 | www.monamigabi.com

Although most agree you'll find an "authentic" Gallic bistro ambiance at this Bethesda link in a national chain, views are mixed on the rest of the proceedings: proponents proclaim it's "perfect before or after the [nearby] movies" because it "gets the formula right" with "buttery soft and delicious hanger steak" and "nice wines by the glass", but contrarians counter that you'll find "mediocre" "pretend French" fare and "snobby service."

Monocle ☒ *American*

17 | 18 | 21 | $42

Capitol Hill | 107 D St. NE (1st St.) | 202-546-4488 | www.themonocle.com

"See what your senator is eating for lunch" at this "power" spot on the "doorsteps of the Capitol" – indeed, "you might just be seated next to" him or her at this "venerable" American where the "stories are better than the food"; "if you're looking for anything extraordinary" to eat, "it's not the place", but you can "feel the history" and that's all that matters; N.B. closed Saturdays and Sundays.

Montmartre ☒ *French*

23 | 19 | 19 | $40

Capitol Hill | 327 Seventh St. SE (Pennsylvania Ave.) | 202-544-1244

An open kitchen and "quaint" dining room "draw on rustic inspiration" at this "sometimes excellent" bistro on the "Left Bank of Capitol Hill" that "delights" with "unpretentious", "quintessential" Gallic fare like "addictive" braised rabbit in truffle oil; but it's "oh-so-French, in good ways and bad" say those who suffer the "noisy", "cramped quarters" and service that only "halfway measures up" to the fare.

NEW Montsouris ☒ *French*

- | - | - | M

Dupont Circle | 2002 P St. NW (20th St.) | 202-833-4180

There's a genuine Parisian feel to this midpriced French bistro near Dupont Circle, thanks in part to the tiled floor, marble-topped bar and dark-wood-accented setting that it inherited from the relocated Johnny's Half Shell; these days, however, locals are greeted by the likes of charcuterie, steak frites and a chalkboard list of interesting wines by the glass.

	FOOD	DECOR	SERVICE	COST

Morrison-Clark Inn *American* — 23 | 23 | 23 | $57

Downtown | Morrison-Clark Inn | 1015 L St. NW (bet. 11th St. & Massachusetts Ave.) | 202-898-1200 | www.morrisonclark.com

"Step back to a gentler era" for some "old-fashioned comfort" at this "charming" Downtown mansion (circa 1864) with an "elegant, updated Victorian" dining room serving "artistically presented" New American fare with a "creative" Southern spin; a few realists find this "off-the-beaten-track" "escape" to be "sleepy", but it may just pop onto the foodie radar screen courtesy of new chef Janis McLean (ex redDog Cafe).

Ⓩ Morton's, The Steakhouse *Steak* — 25 | 20 | 23 | $63

Georgetown | 3251 Prospect St. NW (bet. Potomac St. & Wisconsin Ave.) | 202-342-6258

Golden Triangle | Washington Sq. | 1050 Connecticut Ave. NW (L St.) | 202-955-5997

Bethesda | Hyatt Hotel | 7400 Wisconsin Ave. (Old Georgetown Rd.), MD | 301-657-2650

Arlington | Crystal City Shops | 1750 Crystal Dr. (bet. 15th & 18th Sts.), VA | 703-418-1444

Reston | Reston Town Ctr. | 11956 Market St. (Reston Pkwy.), VA | 703-796-0128

Vienna | Fairfax Sq. | 8075 Leesburg Pike (Gallows Rd.), VA | 703-883-0800

www.mortons.com

Be prepared to "loosen your belt and open your wallet" at these "great classic American" steakhouses, where the "slabs of meat" the "size of Cleveland" are "perfectly tender, juicy and tasty", and are served by "experts at their craft"; the chain's "dark", "clubby" DC locations appeal to "Washington's most powerful", while "up-and-coming" politicos go "to make a deal or find a wife" at the "great happy hour"; but overly cranky carnivores cavil there's "too much foreplay to order" "bland" fare.

NEW Morty's Delicatessen *Deli* — - | - | - | I

Upper NW | 4620 Wisconsin Ave. NW (Brandywine St.) | 202-686-1989

Mel and Morty Krupin are back at the Upper NW deli they once ran, helping the current owners dish out pastrami, smoked fish, knishes and other NY-style provisions; longtime customers, many of whose family photos decorate the walls, can settle into homey booths and tables as they dig into homemade baked goods and more.

Mourayo *Greek* — ▽ 23 | 16 | 22 | $43

Dupont Circle | 1732 Connecticut Ave. NW (bet. R & S Sts.) | 202-667-2100 | www.mourayous.com

Savor "Greek like you've never had it before" at this "unique" Dupont Circle "gem" that looks and feels more "like a trip to the islands" than "your typical taverna"; "ever-present" owner Natalina Koropoulos "really seems to care about her guests", and the "rich, astonishing" fare includes "impeccably fresh" grilled whole fish "paraded through the venue to be filleted and served tableside" and complemented by "fun Greek wines."

	FOOD	DECOR	SERVICE	COST

Murasaki *Japanese* | 22 | 14 | 21 | $33 |

Upper NW | 4620 Wisconsin Ave. NW (Brandywine St.) | 202-966-0023 | www.thebestsushi.com

"Attention to detail" is the hallmark of this somewhat "undiscovered" Upper NW sushi spot with "creative" rolls that "make you think you've died and gone to Osaka" and "welcoming" staffers who "always treat you like a longtime friend"; while the "understated Japanese interior" strikes the Zen crowd as "calm and soothing", the easily bored believe it has "all the ambiance of a Roy Rogers."

Myanmar 🅼 *Burmese* | ▽ 21 | 9 | 15 | $22 |

Falls Church | Merrifalls Plaza | 7810C Lee Hwy. (Hyson Ln.), VA | 703-289-0013

"If you don't know Burmese food", this "simple tiny place" tucked away in a "dark Falls Church strip mall" offers "a wonderful introduction" to chicken in coconut cream, crispy bean sprout shrimp and other "zesty, flavorful" dishes, "each distinctively different than the one before"; although it "lacks any ambiance" and the "service is erratic", "foodies" "pack" in for taste "sensations of the highest order."

My Bakery & Café *Bakery/S American* | ▽ 18 | 11 | 17 | $18 |

Georgetown | 2233 Wisconsin Ave. NW (bet. Calvert & W Sts.) | 202-464-4670 ●

NEW **Alexandria** | 3839 Mt. Vernon Ave. (Russell Rd.), VA | 703-842-7554

Falls Church | 3508 Courtland Dr. (Columbia Pike), VA | 703-933-7332

Manassas | 9229 Sudley Rd. (Rte. 28), VA | 703-361-8220

www.mybakerycafe.com

This burgeoning Bolivian cafe/bakery mini-chain "has a lot going for it" – besides "pastries galore", there are "great *salteñas*" (meat-filled empanadas), "outstanding tres leches cake" and a full menu of sandwiches, tacos and dinner platters; the colorful quarters offer "free wireless" connections, and a "friendly" staff serves interesting Latin drinks; N.B. the Alexandria branch has live entertainment.

Mykonos Grill 🅼 *Greek* | 21 | 19 | 19 | $33 |

Rockville | 121 Congressional Ln. (Rockville Pike), MD | 301-770-5999 | www.mykonosgrill.com

Whether the "cobalt-and-white decor accented by grapevines" reminds you of "sunny, bright" Mykonos or a "borderline gaudy" "Epcot-meets-Greece", "you'll feel as though you're in the isles" as soon as you feast on the "hearty", "first-rate" leg of lamb and "fresh fish done very well" at this "solid" Rockville Pike "favorite"; the "slow", somewhat "indifferent" service and "relatively high prices" don't seem to deter the "throngs that flock" here.

Myung Dong 🆂 *Korean* (aka Oriental Noodle) | – | – | – | I |

Beltsville | 11114B Baltimore Ave. (Powder Mill Rd.), MD | 301-595-4173

Be on the lookout for the 'Oriental Noodle' sign or you'll drive right by this low-visibility Korean that recently reopened in a renovated Beltsville shopping plaza; while housemade noodles are its star attraction – try them chilled (in summer) or in its signature chicken soup – other dishes, including fried chicken, round out the menu.

Nage *American/Seafood*   – | – | – | M

Scott Circle | Scott Circle Marriott Hotel | 1600 Rhode Island Ave. NW (bet. 16th & 17th Sts.) | 202-448-8005 | www.nage.bz

Now that a citified outpost of Rehoboth Beach's popular New American has nestled into the Scott Circle Marriott Hotel, sampling its seafood-strong bistro fare doesn't require trips to the shore; regulars pay attention to the chalkboard listings that feature the daily catch as well as rich meat and fowl preparations.

Nam-Viet *Vietnamese*   21 | 9 | 18 | $21

Cleveland Park | 3419 Connecticut Ave. NW (bet. Macomb & Ordway Sts.) | 202-237-1015

Arlington | 1127 N. Hudson St. (Wilson Blvd.), VA | 703-522-7110

www.namviet1.com

Lemongrass chicken that "doesn't taste like it came from your front lawn, monster bowls of pho", "amazing spring rolls and crispy fish" head the list of "knockout chow" at this Vietnamese duo in Cleveland Park and Arlington that "outpaces many of its pricier counterparts"; expect the "really cheap", really "authentic" eats to be delivered in an "offhand manner" in "homey", "casual" surroundings.

NEW Napoleon *French*   – | – | – | M

Adams Morgan | 1847 Columbia Rd. NW (bet. Biltmore St. & Mintwood Pl.) | 202-299-9630 | www.napoleondc.com

The Adams Morgan space formerly occupied by Mantis has been transformed into this chic midpriced French bistro boasting black-, red- and gold-accented decor with ornate neo-classical touches; like its parent, Café Bonaparte, it serves crêpes in addition to salads, sandwiches and hearty classics; N.B. its basement lounge, Metropolitain, specializes in elegant small plates.

NEW Nark Kara Thai *Thai*   – | – | – | I

Bethesda | 4928 Cordell Ave. (Old Georgetown Rd.), MD | 301-652-2635 | www.narkkarathai.com

This Bethesda Thai creates an exotic atmosphere via videos of traditional dancing plus seating at low tables (made user-friendly with wells to accommodate feet); its inexpensive, multiregional menu covers the usual range of soups, curries and noodle dishes.

Nathans *American*   18 | 17 | 18 | $37

Georgetown | 3150 M St. NW (Wisconsin Ave.) | 202-338-2000 | www.nathansgeorgetown.com

On Georgetown's busiest corner, this "great local joint" with a "very Washington", "old-school club" look attracts loyal locals who "always feel comfortable" either at its "people-watching bar" or in its "cozy" back dining room; "reasonably priced" American fare and a "fabulous brunch" keep regulars returning, and even foodies who insist it's "not for serious diners" find it "fun"; N.B. owner Carol Joynt interviews a 'who's who' of news-making personalities at her popular 'Q&A Cafe' lunches.

Negril ⊠ *Jamaican* — 21 | 8 | 11 | $14

Upper NW | 2301G Georgia Ave. NW (Bryant St.) | 202-332-3737
Silver Spring | 965 Thayer Ave. (Georgia Ave.), MD | 301-585-3000
www.negrileats.com

Take "an affordable and delicious jaunt to Jamaica" at these "homey" eat-in/take-out spots in Upper NW and Silver Spring, where the "jerk chicken is jumping with spices" and the "coco bread is heaven sent"; though there's "surly" service and not much scenery, the "long lines" at lunch for its "fast and hot", 'grab-and-go' goodies attest to its popularity.

Neisha Thai *Thai* — 21 | 18 | 20 | $25

Upper NW | 4445 Wisconsin Ave. NW (Albemarle St.) | 202-966-7088
McLean | 7924LB Tysons Corner Ctr. (Chain Bridge Rd.), VA | 703-883-3588
www.neisha.net

"Only the bones remain" after satiated "scavengers" have devoured the "scrumptious" whole fish in chile sauce at this popular Thai duo in Upper NW and Tysons Corner, where "helpful servers" will "make sure your food is spicier" if you want; the "strange" "kitschy" decor strikes some as *The Flintstones* meet Thailand – think "babbling fountains" – but most find "noticeably better fare" here than at other like-minded spots.

Neramitra *Thai* — ▽ 17 | 17 | 18 | $24

Arlington | 2200 Crystal Dr. (bet. 20th & 23rd Sts.), VA | 703-413-8886 | www.neramitra.com

"Just the right balance of flavors" coupled with a "hip location" on Restaurant Row in Arlington's Crystal City turn this "bargain" Thai into a "great" place "for a first date or drinks with clients"; even if the "quality" menu is "typical", the "colorful decor", including purple walls and booths, takes it up a notch.

New Fortune ● *Chinese* — 21 | 10 | 15 | $20

Gaithersburg | 16515 S. Frederick Ave. (Westland Dr.), MD | 301-548-8886
Gaithersburg's "big barn" of a Chinese may be "too noisy" and "desperately in need of a face-lift", but groups who "pack in" for the "wonderful" lunchtime "dim sum heaven" swear that all "the chatter" and the sound of "loads of carts being wheeled around" just add to the "great fun"; you can "ask for help navigating the overly large" dinner menu, but just beware that servers are "not particularly friendly."

New Heights *American* — 22 | 19 | 20 | $53

Woodley Park | 2317 Calvert St. NW (Connecticut Ave.) | 202-234-4110 | www.newheightsrestaurant.com

This "lovable little second-story" "treat" in Woodley Park has an "interesting" New American menu that "appeals to a range of tastes", a "kitchen deeply sensitive to special dietary needs" and a "tasteful" "unpretentious" art-filled dining room that's comfortable for "intimate" "special occasions"; some blame the "inconsistent" fare on "chefs who come and go", but those critics may be appeased by the June 2007 return of former toque John Wabeck.

	FOOD	DECOR	SERVICE	COST

New Orleans Bistro Ⓜ Cajun/Creole   18 | 15 | 18 | $33

Bethesda | 4907 Cordell Ave. (bet. Norfolk Ave. & Old Georgetown Rd.), MD | 301-986-8833 | www.neworleansbistro.org

If you "know your N'Awlins", you'll appreciate this Bethesdan's "quite delicious" étouffée, "smooth" Abita beer and "beignets as good as the original at Café Du Monde in the Quarter" served in a plain room adorned with pictures of the Big Easy as it used to be; "the staff aims hard to please" and "they come close in some areas", but "the distance" between DC and New Orleans "is evident in others"; still, given the "relative scarcity" of this fare, purists forgive the "kinks."

Neyla Lebanese   22 | 23 | 18 | $40

Georgetown | 3206 N St. NW (Wisconsin Ave.) | 202-333-6353 | www.neyla.com

"Sexy", "stylish" digs and a "cool, laid-back" vibe appeal to the "hip crowd" that frequents this Georgetown Lebanese to sip "amazing cilantro martinis" amid the "blaring music" and "haphazard service"; meze mavens marvel at the "glorious marriage of Mediterranean and Middle Eastern" dishes, maintaining this is one of their "favorite places to take out-of-towners" or a "date", even if it's "impossible to have a table conversation."

Nick's Chophouse Steak   17 | 19 | 18 | $44

Rockville | 700 King Farm Blvd. (bet. Gaither & Shady Grove Rds.), MD | 301-926-8869 | www.nickschophouse.com

Sure, it's "high-priced for the suburbs", but Rockville's "upscale steakhouse" – with its "romantic" chandeliers and linen-topped tables – aims to deliver a "DC dining experience without the drive Downtown"; supporters find a "wonderful party venue" with a "friendly and attentive" staff, but down-to-earth carnivores say this "only game in town" is "a bit too pretentious", especially given the "underwhelming" cuts.

Nirvana Ⓢ Indian   20 | 13 | 18 | $20

Golden Triangle | 1810 K St. NW (bet. 18th & 19th Sts.) | 202-223-5043

Let "the aromas greet you as you walk" into this "casual" K Street Indian, a "vegetarian haven" where "you can't go wrong no matter what day you visit" since it "features the cuisine of a different region every weekday" at its "bargain" "all-you-can-eat buffet"; don't worry if some of the "exotic" "uncommon flavors" seem a little "mysterious" because the "warm and welcoming" owners "enjoy explaining dishes."

Niwanohana Japanese   23 | 16 | 21 | $29

Rockville | Wintergreen Plaza | 887 Rockville Pike (Edmonston Dr.), MD | 301-294-0553 | www.niwanohana.com

With standouts that include "heaven-on-a-plate" otoro and perhaps the "best dragon roll in the area", as well as "unique" "daily specials listed on the blackboard", this Rockville Japanese is "a reliable choice for sushi"; the "strip-mall location" and cramped space are offset by "gracious, efficient" servers and an "engaging owner" who "remembers regulars and makes them feel at home."

	FOOD	DECOR	SERVICE	COST

Nizam's ⊠ *Turkish*
| | 22 | 17 | 20 | $38 |

Vienna | Village Green Shopping Ctr. | 523 Maple Ave. W. (Nutley St.), VA | 703-938-8948

For 30 years this "old-world" "classic" in Vienna has "kept up high standards" for Turkish cuisine, including "delectable lamb preparations" such as a doner kebab "that never fails to delight"; "homey" digs and "comforting" visits from the namesake host make it "great for dates", but critics contend that the "traditional-to-the-point-of-unexciting" meals are "overpriced."

Nooshi *Pan-Asian*
| | 19 | 14 | 16 | $22 |

Golden Triangle | 1120 19th St. NW (bet. L & M Sts.) | 202-293-3138 | www.nooshidc.com

A "nice alternative to the million sandwich places" in Golden Triangle, this "big", "noisy" Pan-Asian gets "crowded to the max" with "downtown lawyers and bankers" slurping "oodles" of "Americanized" Japanese, Thai and Chinese noodles; the staff "keeps things under control", so it works for a "fun lunch, quick dinner" or takeout; P.S. don't overlook the "dependable" raw-fish offerings – "they've gotten sushi right."

☑ Nora ⊠ *American*
| | 25 | 23 | 24 | $60 |

Dupont Circle | 2132 Florida Ave. NW (R St.) | 202-462-5143 | www.noras.com

Patrons head here to "celebrate anniversaries and birthdays or just to enjoy wonderful" New American cuisine courtesy of chef/co-owner Nora Pouillon, who uses "fresh organic ingredients" in her "inspired" dishes; although the "outstanding" "spot-on" servers move smoothly around the "enchanting" space – an old carriage house located "near the Dupont Circle galleries" – that "attracts movers, shakers" and legions of loyalists, a few nitpickers point to a certain luster that's "faded."

Notti Bianche *Italian*
| | 24 | 17 | 22 | $47 |

Foggy Bottom | George Washington University Inn | 824 New Hampshire Ave. NW (bet. H & I Sts.) | 202-298-8085 | www.nottibianche.com

At this "creative" Italian eatery near the Kennedy Center in Foggy Bottom, new chef Brendan Cox (Circle Bistro) does double duty as he oversees a kitchen that continues to turn out "superbly presented" seasonal fare; meanwhile, the "enthusiastic" staff tries "very hard" to make the best of a somewhat "antiseptic" space.

NEW Not Your Average Joe's *American*
| | - | - | - | I |

Lansdowne | Lansdowne Town Ctr. | 19307 Promenade Dr. (Belmont Ridge Rd.), VA | 571-333-5637 | www.nyajoes.com

This Boston-based mini-chain makes its DC-area debut in Lansdowne Town Center's mock-village-style mall; its inexpensive, something-for-everyone American menu stars hearth-baked pizza and other homestyle creations, all served in a comfortable setting sporting an open kitchen; N.B. it offers takeout with service to your car, so you can pull up, load up and go.

Oakville Grille & Wine Bar *American*   18 | 15 | 17 | $41

Bethesda | Wildwood Shopping Ctr. | 10257 Old Georgetown Rd.
(Democracy Blvd.), MD | 301-897-9100

A "terrific asset in an area short on interesting" eats, this Bethesda
"bistro" "tucked away" in the Wildwood Shopping Center lends a
"relaxed" "California feel" to "upscale" "New American dishes"
paired with a "good selection" of "fairly priced" West Coast wines;
but a fussy few find the "decor could use some work", the fare's "just
average" and a "limited" menu of labels available by the glass makes
"calling this a wine bar a joke."

☑ Obelisk 🆂 🅼 *Italian*   27 | 20 | 25 | $73

Dupont Circle | 2029 P St. NW (bet. 20th & 21st Sts.) | 202-872-1180

"Fanatic" chef-owner Peter Pastan "keeps you focused on the finest
Italian in the city" at his "intimate" Dupont Circle space; connoisseurs
swear his daily changing prix fixe menu "could pass a blind taste
test" with Italy's "best", and the "unique" dishes are "prepared and
served by people who clearly respect food" and want to "take very
good care of you"; just remember to reserve "well in advance" if you
want to "spend an evening with your true love" in this 30-seat room.

Occidental *American*   21 | 23 | 22 | $54

Downtown | Willard Plaza | 1475 Pennsylvania Ave. NW (bet. 14th &
15th Sts.) | 202-783-1475 | www.occidentaldc.com

"Photos of dignitaries line the walls" while beneath them "power
players" make "deals happen" in "clubby" booths at this Downtown
New American "old-schooler" serving "delicious steaks", seafood
and "interesting wines" with a side of "people-watching" for the
"upscale tourist" clientele; still, "stuffy, brisk" service has critics insisting it "doesn't live up to the hype", although naysayers may be
won over by an updated menu that takes advantage of the restaurant's newly renovated, state-of-the-art kitchen.

☑ Oceanaire Seafood Room *Seafood*   24 | 22 | 23 | $54

Downtown | 1201 F St. NW (bet. 12th & 13th Sts.) | 202-347-2277 |
www.theoceanaire.com

The "ocean-liner atmosphere" gives this Downtown seafooder a
"retro", "hip" "Hollywood" touch that serves as a backdrop for "impeccable" fare done as "simply or as complex as you want" with "fun
fixin's" on the side; the sea of "Washington elite" and those who
"rub elbows with them" sail "first-class" all the way, so even if this
"cruise is costly, it's worth the ticket"; N.B. a branch in Baltimore's
Inner Harbor opened in 2005.

Olazzo *Italian*   22 | 15 | 19 | $26

Bethesda | 7921 Norfolk Ave. (Cordell Ave.), MD | 301-654-9496 |
www.olazzo.com

"Yuppies" on dates "love" the "trendy vibe" of this "homestyle"
Bethesda "trattoria" that's their "favorite place to grab a bowl of
pasta" and other "great-tasting, cheap Italian" dishes "just like
mama's"; a "fabulously long martini list" and "Monday's half-price
wine" special take the edge off "cheesy" decor that includes a "fake

"fireplace" and "small tables all scrunched together"; N.B. a Silver Spring offshoot is expected to debut in 2007.

Old Angler's Inn 🅜 *American*   21 | 23 | 20 | $56

Potomac | 10801 MacArthur Blvd. (Clara Barton Pkwy.), MD | 301-365-2425 | www.oldanglersinn.com

A "great romantic getaway just 20 minutes outside of the city" in Potomac, this "special-occasion" New American features a "wooded setting" "near the C&O Canal" that's a "lovely" backdrop for "delightful alfresco" dining; come winter, "have a drink in front of a fire" in the "rustic" yet "classy" "cottage", then head upstairs for fare that may no longer strike critics as "stodgy" now that popular former chef Jeffrey Tomchek is back in its kitchen.

NEW Old Dominion Brewhouse *Pub Food*   - | - | - | I

Mt. Vernon Square/New Convention Center | 1219 Ninth St. NW (bet. M & N Sts.) | 202-289-8158 | www.olddominionbrewhouse.com

Fifteen beers on tap and 20 flat-screen TVs define this watering hole located in a gleaming storefront next to the Convention Center in booming Mt. Vernon Square; accompanying the house brews (which are available as samplers) is an American burgers-and-bar-food menu offering twists like create-your-own pasta.

☒ Old Ebbitt Grill ◗ *American*   20 | 22 | 21 | $37

Downtown | 675 15th St. NW (bet. F & G Sts.) | 202-347-4801 | www.ebbitt.com

"The only thing better" than eating at this "pure DC experience" would be "eating in the White House", but "half the folks" at this "Downtown legend" located a "stone's throw" away "work there anyway"; it's "wall-to-wall people", from early until late, with four "great" happy-hour bars and an "excellent variety" of "solid" (if sometimes "mediocre") Traditional American dishes served in a "classy" "brass, glass" and "beautiful polished wood" setting; but it's really more about the "feeling of belonging" than it is about the cuisine.

Old Glory All-American BBQ *BBQ*   19 | 15 | 17 | $24

Georgetown | 3139 M St. NW (bet. 31st St. & Wisconsin Ave.) | 202-337-3406 | www.oldglorybbq.com

Follow the "mouthwatering scent" of "finger-lickin'" ribs and pulled pork to this "popular" BBQ "hangout" where "college kids" and tourists "chill out" and dig into a "veritable carnivorgy" of "dry rub" meats and Southern-accented sides, washed down with "tasty mason-jar drinks"; it's "kitschy" and "loud" – "the bar makes you feel like you should have brought your six-shooter" – but kids of all ages anxious to "get away from the snooty Georgetown crowd" find it pure "fun."

Olives 🅩 *Mediterranean*   22 | 21 | 20 | $47

Golden Triangle | World Center Bldg. | 1600 K St. NW (16th St.) | 202-452-1866 | www.toddenglish.com

Tantalizing "aromas [from] the open kitchen" draw you into this White House-area Med, chef Todd English's "cool" Golden Triangle venue for the "hip and hungry" who can dine at the bar and watch the cooking show or head with their dates to the calmer lower level to "avoid the clamor"; most find "hearty", "innovative", even "sexy", plates along with "helpful service" and a "high-energy" vibe, but watchful eyes wonder if it's "too popular to care" that the "food has lost its edge."

NEW 1Gen Thai Cuisine Thai

– | – | – | M

Arlington | 4300 Wilson Blvd. (enter on Glebe Rd.), VA | 703-243-9669 | www.1genthaicuisine.com

This Thai's artful, moderately priced cuisine is matched by modern digs in Arlington's Ballston area that feature a wraparound bar, high-backed black leather banquettes and orange wall sculptures; the traditional, nouveau and vegetarian menus are supplemented by creative monthly specials and frequent live cooking demonstrations that come complete with a three-course fixed-price meal.

100 King American

– | 22 | 19 | $39

Alexandria | 100 King St. (Union St.), VA | 703-299-0076 | www.100king.com

Adding a "modern edge" that's "much needed" in Old Town Alexandria's "tourist zone", this "cosmopolitan" spot is now under new management, which has introduced a menu of American brasserie fare (think pastas, salads, sandwiches and grilled fish) to go with some 20 by-the-glass wine choices; they've also redecorated the ground-floor dining room, but rest assured: the upstairs fine-dining area has retained its "incredible crystal chandeliers."

Oohhs and Aahhs ⊠Ⓜ Southern

– | – | – | I

U Street Corridor | 1005 U St. NW (Vermont Ave.) | 202-667-7142

Aaaahh . . . "with food like this, who needs decor?" fawn fans who've found this simple storefront on U Street, where the owners – "old Howard grads" – "talk it up" while serving Southern soul food that's easy to "love"; order at the counter, then "take out or eat in" – and be sure to try the homestyle mac 'n' cheese that beats any others in town.

Open City ❶ Diner

17 | 18 | 16 | $20

Woodley Park | 2331 Calvert St. NW (24th St.) | 202-332-2331 | www.opencitydc.com

"The best part" of this "upscale" American diner "might be the hours" (6 AM until at least 2 AM daily) say partyers who make it their "late-night pit stop"; but it's just as "loved" for its "happening brunch" scene – and "anything in between" – when "Woodley Park dilettantes" tired of "crossing the bridge" for its sister standbys, Tryst and The Diner, pack in for "comfort foods."

NEW Orchid Thai Thai

– | – | – | I

Ashburn | 43150 Broadlands Center Plaza (Broadlands Blvd.), VA | 703-724-9555

Colorful orchids are painted on the walls of this Ashburn addition where stylish lighting, floral arrangements and a small bar create an upscale backdrop for inexpensive Thai cuisine; its twists on familiar dishes are spiced for the less adventurous, so hotheads may want to ask for 'raging fire' seasoning.

	FOOD	DECOR	SERVICE	COST

Oriental East *Chinese* — 21 | 12 | 14 | $20

Silver Spring | 1312 East-West Hwy. (Colesville Rd.), MD | 301-608-0030 | www.orientaleast.com

"Round-the-block" lines form for "wildly popular" daily dim sum that keeps the "staff jumping" at this "cavernous" Silver Spring Chinese, so you'll want to "get there close to opening to avoid a long wait"; the rest of the time, unless you know "how to order the real" "authentically" prepared dishes served to its largely Asian clientele, you'll be stuck with a "mediocre" "Americanized" menu.

Oval Room ⌧ *American* — 21 | 21 | 23 | $57

Golden Triangle | 800 Connecticut Ave. NW (bet. H & I Sts.) | 202-463-8700 | www.ovalroom.com

Just steps from the White House, this Golden Triangle New American raises the question: "does a 'power location' necessarily translate into an excellent dining experience?" – "almost" respond partisans who are pleased with "inventive", "well-prepared" dishes "served with panache" in a "low-key" environment that includes a "pleasant" outdoor patio; some are less enamored by the "tourists at dinner", but it remains a surefire place to "be seen with, and by, the 'in' crowd" – especially now that new chef Tony Conte (ex NYC's Jean Georges) is putting his own sophisticated spin on the menu.

NEW Overwood *American* — - | - | - | M

Alexandria | 220 N. Lee St. (bet. Cameron & Queen Sts.), VA | 703-535-3340 | www.theoverwood.com

This rustic American near Old Town Alexandria's waterfront serves midpriced comfort classics – some from a log-burning oven – in an exposed-brick dining room; meanwhile, a sandstone-topped bar dispenses craft brews and some interesting international wines.

⬘ Oya *Asian Fusion* — 18 | 26 | 18 | $53

Penn Quarter | 777 Ninth St. NW (H St.) | 202-393-1400 | www.oyadc.com

The "drop-dead decor", with plush white banquettes, a red crocodile-leather bar, a 2.5-ton chain curtain and a "waterfall wall", renders this "stylish spot" in Penn Quarter "a glamorous and posh" "place to see and be seen"; the "interesting menu" includes "inventive" French-accented Eurasian fare (including sushi), but due to "service missteps", a couple of merely "tolerable" dishes and "oh no" prices, a few find the results are "all icing, no cake."

NEW Oyamel ◗ *Mexican* — - | - | - | M

Penn Quarter | 401 Seventh St. NW (D St.) | 202-628-1005 | www.oyamel.com

Chef José Andrés' ode to modern Mexico has reopened in dramatic Penn Quarter digs where clever design elements – including a wall-sized photomural and market-scene videos that play above a ceviche bar – let diners pretend they are at a cafe in Mexico City; before you fill up on the menu's midpriced *antojitos* (street food–inspired small plates), be sure to sample the guacamole made tableside and the margaritas topped with a salty foam.

☑ Palena ⧖ Ⓜ American
26 | 22 | 22 | $57

Cleveland Park | 3529 Connecticut Ave. NW (bet. Ordway & Porter Sts.) | 202-537-9250 | www.palenarestaurant.com

Have "a night to remember" with "all-around excellence in food, wine and service" at this "casual" Cleveland Park New American, "whether supping in the bar"/cafe or dining in the "quieter and more romantic" formal space in back; "if you can get reservations", you'll be amazed at chef-owner Frank Ruta's "superbly prepared" "twists on classics" and his "ambitious" "attention to detail" from the "house-cured" charcuterie to the "produce from his garden."

Palette American
22 | 23 | 20 | $50

Downtown | 1177 15th St. NW (M St.) | 202-587-2700 | www.palettedc.com

A "sleek" setting in which you "actually hear the conversation at your table and not at all the others" is the "arty" Downtown backdrop for this New American's "creative" food offerings and "great happy-hour drink" specials; however, the staff isn't "quite up" to the "sophisticated tone", and apart from a "few winning dishes", some eaters seem more impressed with the "freebie" "cotton candy at the end of the meal."

Palm Seafood/Steak
23 | 19 | 23 | $60

Golden Triangle | 1225 19th St. NW (bet. M & N Sts.) | 202-293-9091
McLean | 1750 Tysons Blvd. (Rte. 123), VA | 703-917-0200
www.thepalm.com

"Power brokers" "expense" their "power beef" and "over-the-top three-pound lobsters" at this steakhouse "institution" that pairs the "hustle and attitude" of its "New York original" with "solicitous service"; Golden Triangle is "the place to rub elbows with the Washington elite" (if you're prepared for the "deafening" "noise level" when they're "holding court"), but Tysons Corner has the "posh" decor; still, a money-strapped minority maintains "in a city full of" meat palaces, this one's "not worth the dough."

Panino ⧖ Italian
▽ 26 | 20 | 24 | $44

Manassas | Manassas Shopping Ctr. | 9116 Mathis Ave. (Sudley Rd.), VA | 703-335-2566

For a "warm and wonderful" time, head to this Manassas Italian that's a "fabulous" "surprise" given its "strip-shopping-center" location; inside, atop white linen tablecloths, the "sparkling" fare – "homemade pastas", "wonderful" specials like osso buco – shines, but given it's "a bit pricey for the 'burbs", regulars recommend it "for a special occasion."

Panjshir Afghan
23 | 15 | 21 | $26

Falls Church | 924 W. Broad St. (West St.), VA | 703-536-4566 ⧖
Vienna | 224 W. Maple Ave. (Lawyers Rd.), VA | 703-281-4183 Ⓜ
www.panjshirrestaurant.com

"Scrumptious" "sautéed pumpkin" is just one of many vegetarian dishes with "wonderful flavors" at these "authentic" Afghans in Falls Church and Vienna that also boast "extremely tasteful" kebabs and lamb chops; the "old-world service" is headed up by the "personable and attentive owner" who "likes to interact with patrons", so it's just the plain decor that gets no raves.

Paolo's *Californian/Italian* | 18 | 17 | 18 | $32

Georgetown | 1303 Wisconsin Ave. NW (N St.) | 202-333-7353 ◗
Reston | Reston Town Ctr. | 11898 Market St. (Reston Pkwy.), VA |
703-318-8920
www.paolosristorante.com

Even those who "just go for" the "addictive" tapenade and bread sticks find themselves saving room for "great wood-fired pizza", "fresh and tasty" salads or the "crispy eggplant" appetizer at this "trendy" Cal-Ital chain in Georgetown, Reston and Towson, MD; they're "great for your everyday night out", but they "fail to impress" sticklers who ignore the "half-hearted attempts at Italian" and head to the "chic" bar and "wonderful" "outdoor seating" instead.

Park Cafe *Continental* | 22 | 20 | 20 | $38

Capitol Hill | 106 13th St. SE (bet. Independence & Massachusetts Aves.) |
202-543-0184 | www.parkcafedc.com

A "little-known find overlooking" Lincoln Park (in a yet-to-be-fully-gentrified Capitol Hill neighborhood), this "sweet" "eclectic" Continental eatery is at its best in spring when you can sit at "the table in the front window" and enjoy the view "facing the park"; chef-owner Alcione Vinet "has fun with the menu" infusing "incredible flavors in every dish", but "disappointed taste buds" disagree, no longer wondering why it's "not hard to get a table" – it's "not thrilling."

Parkway Deli *Deli* | 20 | 9 | 18 | $17

Silver Spring | Rock Creek Shopping Ctr. | 8317 Grubb Rd.
(East-West Hwy.), MD | 301-587-1427 | www.parkwaydeli.com

"The closest thing to a New York deli in Washington", this Silver Spring "institution" merits a visit "if only for the matzo ball soup" and the complimentary "pickle-bar access"; "efficient", "if occasionally brusque", servers deliver "killer sandwiches" and egg creams to a room "crowded with families, aging regulars" and "displaced" Manhattanites, some of whom kvetch it's "more diner than deli" – "you go for a taste of NY, you get a taste of Montgomery County."

Pasha Cafe *Mediterranean* | ▽ 21 | 16 | 22 | $24

Arlington | 3911 N. Lee Hwy. (N. Pollard St.), VA | 703-528-1111 |
www.pashacafe.com

"Appetizers stand out" at this "cozy" Med in Arlington's Cherrydale area, but there's also a "pleasing variety of sandwiches, main courses and salads" with a Middle Eastern slant too; the "cozy" interior incorporates dark cherry woods, high-stool tables and booths, while the "neighborhood" feel attracts families along with a mix of ages who agree this is one of the "best values" in the area.

Passage to India *Indian* | 24 | 22 | 20 | $33

Bethesda | 4931 Cordell Ave. (bet. Norfolk Ave. & Old Georgetown Rd.),
MD | 301-656-3373 | www.passagetoindia.info

Patrons take a "sweeping tour" of India when they "eat their way through" a menu "organized by region" at this "classy" Bethesdan that boasts a "wider-than-usual range" of "perfectly seasoned" dishes ("special kudos" to the "big vegetarian sampler" and the "bargain lunches"); the service is "punctual", and the "lovely" room, with carved wooden screens and original artwork, is serene enough "for diners who prefer talking to shouting."

Pasta Mia ⊠Ⓜ⇱ *Italian*

| 24 | 11 | 13 | $21 |

Adams Morgan | 1790 Columbia Rd. NW (18th St.) | 202-328-9114

"Sometimes the best things in life are worth the wait" say pastafarians who "line up outside" this "hole-in-the-wall" trattoria ("part of what helps Adams Morgan retain its charm") for "mammoth portions" of "classic, rustic Italian fare"; "the "cheap eats" "attract a broad range" of "cult followers" despite "slow", "disorganized" service and a "soup Nazi" approach that warns "no substitutions!"

Pasta Plus Ⓜ *Italian*

| 24 | 14 | 21 | $28 |

Laurel | Center Plaza | 209 Gorman Ave. (bet. Rtes. 1 & 198), MD | 301-498-5100 | www.pastaplusrestaurant.com

"When an Italian priest says it's the best pasta this side of Rome", "carb lovers" know they can expect "fresh" "homemade" lasagna and "tasty" tortellini along with thin-crust pizza and "fabulous" seafood; the "nondescript strip-mall" setting in Laurel "has the curb appeal of a dentist's office", so "close your eyes to enjoy the value" of chef Sabatino Mazziotti's "top-notch" fare as well as the "great rapport" with "his brother, Max", a host "who remembers his regulars."

Peacock Cafe *American*

| 21 | 19 | 20 | $32 |

Georgetown | 3251 Prospect St. NW (bet. Potomac St. & Wisconsin Ave.) | 202-625-2740 | www.peacockcafe.com

A "cool" "Euro Georgetown crowd does lunch" at this "chic, casual" eatery with a "simple" New American menu "that doesn't try to go overboard", so you "won't pay a fortune" for "yummy smoothies", "upscale sandwiches" and "the best tomato bisque in all DC"; it "gets pretty loud" at the "fun weekend brunch", but it's "worth the wait" to join the "beautiful people" at "an outdoor table in the sun."

Pearl Seafood *Mediterranean/Pan-Latin*

| - | - | - | M |

Wheaton | 11230 Grandview Ave. (Reede Dr.), MD | 301-962-8888 | www.pearlseafood.com

Miami's South Beach comes to Wheaton via this luxe, lofty, high-glam restaurant and lounge offering Med and Pan-Latin tapas, dinner and tasting menus; given that it has a slick passageway to its sister nightspot, Ocean Drive, a drink and a bite in the minimalist, modern lounge could be a convenient prelude to clubbing.

Peking Cheers *Chinese*

| - | - | - | I |

Gaithersburg | 519 Quince Orchard Rd. (bet. Firstfield Rd. & W. Diamond Ave.), MD | 301-216-2090 | www.pekingcheers.com

The arrival of chef Tian Wen Pei from Joe's Noodle House has put this Gaithersburg shopping-center Chinese on the foodie roadmap; adventurous types are advised to ask the server about the selection of Szechuan specialties.

	FOOD	DECOR	SERVICE	COST

☑ Peking Gourmet Inn *Chinese* | 25 | 14 | 20 | $31 |

Falls Church | Culmore Shopping Ctr. | 6029 Leesburg Pike (Glen Carlyn Rd.), VA | 703-671-8088 | www.pekinggourmet.com

"Masterful tableside carving" "makes a show" of the "house specialty" at Falls Church's "old-school" Chinese, where "dependably good" "Americanized" dishes "can't rival" the "crisp, juicy" Peking duck that's "made every day, so you don't have to pre-order"; "picture-strewn walls of famous former patrons" ("all the Republican luminaries") "keep watch" over an "enormous" "factory" of a room accented by "cheesy", "stuck-in-the-'60s" "tired" decor.

Penang *Malaysian* | 19 | 19 | 16 | $28 |

Dupont Circle | 1837 M St. NW (19th St.) | 202-822-8773 | www.penangusa.com

"Mango chicken, snazzy drinks and a great-looking crowd" make this "fun" "south Dupont hot spot" – a cross "between a classy restaurant and a lounge" – "perfect for a Friday night", even if it may be "difficult to get the staff's attention"; add in "fabulous three-course lunch specials" and "$5 happy-hour martinis" and "what more could you want?"; but rivals retort it's only "trendy, fusion seekers" who fall for this "dumbed down" Malaysian.

Perrys *American* | 19 | 21 | 18 | $39 |

Adams Morgan | 1811 Columbia Rd. NW (Biltmore St.) | 202-234-6218 | www.perrysadamsmorgan.com

Known for "rooftop sushi" "under the stars", its "out-of-control" Drag Queen brunch that's "worth seeing once" and "the scene that comes along with dinner", this "edgy" Adams Morgan New American for "the young on the make" is "quite a unique experience"; though discerning diners dis an "assembly-line kitchen", it's really more about the crowd and the setting ("aim for a couch near the windows" or the "fantastic" outdoor terrace that "can't be beat on a nice night") than it is about the fare.

☑ Persimmon *American* | 26 | 18 | 22 | $52 |

Bethesda | 7003 Wisconsin Ave. (bet. Leland & Walsh Sts.), MD | 301-654-9860 | www.persimmonrestaurant.com

There's "no better restaurant in Bethesda" for celebrating "something special with someone special" than this "charming" New American with an "attentive staff" that creates "wonderful", "seasonal specialties in interesting and delicious ways" complemented by a "well-thought-out wine list", with "nice flights"; "improved" decor makes the most of its storefront space with "warm persimmon" tones and "inviting" yellows (more renovations are planned for 2007), and though it's "tightly packed", "sardines never ate so well."

Pesce *Seafood* | 25 | 15 | 20 | $43 |

Dupont Circle | 2016 P St. NW (bet. Hopkins & 20th Sts.) | 202-466-3474 | www.pescebistro.com

Finatics sigh "so many fish, so little time" when they visit this "cute" Dupont Circle seafood bistro where the chalkboard menu of "sparkling fresh" sea bounty "cooked just right" "changes daily"; new chef

	FOOD	DECOR	SERVICE	COST

Bernard Marchive (ex Le Paradou) continues to bring the ocean "flavors to life", but despite the "friendly welcome" from its "practiced" help, its "close-knit seating" ("typical" of storefront restaurants in the area) may not sit well with surveyors.

Pesto Ristorante ☒ *Italian*

▽ 17	16	17	$32

Woodley Park | 2915 Connecticut Ave. NW (Cathedral Ave.) | 202-332-8300 | www.pestodc.com

"Chatty" chef-owner Vincenzo Belvito "turns out terrific" favorites like homemade pasta, lamb osso buco and tiramisu in a "low-key" spot "hidden" in Woodley Park "just north of all the action on Connecticut Avenue"; for some picky diners, however, the "inconsistency from night to night" and "prices too expensive for the food you receive" mar what feels like the quintessential "little hole-in-the-wall Italian."

Petits Plats *French*

22	19	21	$38

Woodley Park | 2653 Connecticut Ave. NW (bet. Calvert St. & Woodley Rd.) | 202-518-0018 | www.petitsplats.com

"*Bon appetit*" salute fans of this "adorable little piece of Paris" "hidden" among the Woodley Park eateries that mostly cater to "convention crowds"; this one rises above the rest with "simple" French dishes – the "mussels with frites are worth many return trips" and the molten chocolate cake is "unforgettable" – served in a "cozy", "candlelit" environment where the "brother and sister owners make you feel like family"; however, if can be "noisy" when it's busy.

☑ P.F. Chang's China Bistro *Chinese*

19	19	18	$27

Rockville | White Flint Mall | 11301 Rockville Pike (Nicholson Ln.), MD | 301-230-6933

NEW **Arlington** | Arlington Gateway | 901 N. Glebe Rd. (Fairfax Dr.), VA | 703-527-0955

Fairfax | Fairfax Corner | 4250 Fairfax Corner Ave. (Monument Dr.), VA | 703-266-2414

McLean | Tysons Galleria | 1716M International Dr. (Chain Bridge Rd.), VA | 703-734-8996

www.pfchangs.com

Although some say "chain Asian dining" isn't needed in a big city, these "yuppified" bistros "pull it off" with "elegant, fun" interiors – "modern industrial meets shinto shrine" – and "solid, flavorful entrees" (their "amazing chicken lettuce wraps" aren't authentic, but "they're darn tasty"); while their mall locations are "reliable and convenient", impatient shoppers snap that "ridiculously long waits" and "slow service" "make it almost not worth going."

PGA Tour Restaurant ☒ *American*

-	-	-	M

Rockville | 1699 Rockville Pike (Research Blvd.), MD | 301-770-3312

A big stone fireplace, an inviting bar/lounge and a glass-walled conservatory-style dining room set the stage for wood-fired pizza, roasted chicken and other American fare at this Professional Golf Association–backed restaurant on Rockville Pike; although there are no grassy links in sight, golf-themed art and memorabilia encourage aficionados to tee off at this 19th hole.

	FOOD	DECOR	SERVICE	COST

Phillips *Seafood* — 15 | 15 | 16 | $33

SW | 900 Water St. SW (7th St.) | 202-488-8515 |
www.phillipsseafood.com
See review in the Baltimore Directory.

Pho 75 ⊅ *Vietnamese* — 23 | 5 | 14 | $11

Langley Park | 1510 University Blvd. E. (New Hampshire Ave.), MD |
301-434-7844
Rockville | 771 Hungerford Dr. (Mannakee St.), MD |
301-309-8873
Arlington | 1721 Wilson Blvd. (Quinn St.), VA | 703-525-7355
Falls Church | 3103 Graham Rd. (Arlington Blvd.), VA |
703-204-1490
Herndon | 382 Elden St. (Herndon Pkwy.), VA | 703-471-4145
Come to these Vietnamese soup kitchens for "cheap", "aromatic"
"comfort in a bowl"; while the "long communal tables" will either
"remind you of a mess hall", "your high-school cafeteria" or a "poor
community church basement" and the "brusque" service isn't much
better, the "always excellent" namesake dish (broth with basil, lime,
noodles and "your choice of meat and sauces") "can't be beat";
N.B. cash-only.

Pinzimini *Italian* — - | - | - | E

Arlington | Westin Arlington Gateway Hotel | 801 N. Glebe Rd.
(Wilson Blvd.), VA | 703-537-4200 | www.pinzimini.com
Named for the herb-infused olive oil (called *pinzimonio* in Italian)
that graces its handsome wooden tables, this Tuscan in the Westin
Arlington Gateway Hotel in Ballston specializes in similarly rustic
regional pastas and grilled meats; a bar with an extensive antipasto
display and a contemporary lounge offer upscale yet casual get-
together possibilities for members of the area's vibrant business
and social scenes.

NEW Piratz Tavern � *Eclectic* — - | - | - | M

Silver Spring | 8402 Georgia Ave. (Bonifant St.), MD | 301-588-9001 |
www.piratztavern.com
At this fanciful, glitter-filled pirates' lair in Silver Spring, the Eclectic
grub (e.g. piri piri chicken or cook-your-own steak on a stone) is
based on recipes pillaged from Iberia, Africa, the Caribbean and
other spots where the skull and crossbones once sailed; scurvy
dogs – aka customers – can swig rum at its convivial back bar, where
polished planks form a communal table and you may find a sword-
swallowing bartendress who takes it to the hilt.

NEW Pizza Zero *Pizza* — - | - | - | I

Bethesda | 4925 Bethesda Ave. (bet. Arlington & Clarendon Rds.), MD |
240-497-0751 | www.pizzazero.com
From the owners of Divino, this inexpensive Argentinean pie parlor
brings Buenos Aires to Bethesda in the form of wood-fired pizzas
topped with Spanish sausage and spicy chimichurri sauce; a striking
red-and-orange mosaic above the bar draws attention to the display
of reasonably priced vinos sourced from the motherland.

Ⓩ Pizzeria Paradiso *Pizza* | 24 | 15 | 18 | $23 |

Dupont Circle | 2029 P St. NW (bet. 20th & 21st Sts.) | 202-223-1245

Georgetown | 3282 M St. NW (bet. 32nd & 33rd Sts.) | 202-337-1245

www.eatyourpizza.com

It's "pizza nirvana" at these "dressed-down" Dupont Circle and Georgetown eateries where the "slightly chewy" yet "crisp" wood-oven-baked pies come topped with the "very freshest ingredients", accompanied by "wonderful salads" and "rustic wines by the tumbler"; since they're "always bustling" with a "lock on fun with style", you should "get there early and be prepared to wait"; N.B. the Georgetown branch's cozy basement is now a birreria boasting 90-plus brews from around the world.

Pollo Campero *Central American* | 17 | 7 | 11 | $10 |

NEW Columbia Heights | 3229 14th St. NW (Park Rd.) | 202-745-0078

NEW Gaithersburg | Lake Forest Mall | 703 Russell Ave. (Lakeforest Blvd.), MD | 240-403-0135

Hyattsville | 1355 E. University Blvd. (New Hampshire Ave.), MD | 301-408-0555

Wheaton | 11420 Georgia Ave. (Hickerson Dr.), MD | 301-942-6868

Falls Church | 5852 Columbia Pike (Moncure Ave.), VA | 703-820-8400

Herndon | 496 Elden St. (Grant St.), VA | 703-904-7500

www.campero.com

Before this Central American fried chicken chain opened outlets in the DC area, "flights into Dulles were filled with buckets" of the "spiced up", "tasty" birds that are "marinated and then battered and fried"; "Latins are still crazy" for "this step-up from KFC", and their "unique sides", though some skeptics suggest that the "greasy" "salted" fare "isn't as great as all the hype."

Portabellos *American* | 19 | 13 | 19 | $30 |

Arlington | Cherrydale Shopping Ctr. | 2109 N. Pollard St. (Lee Hwy.), VA | 703-528-1557 | www.portabellosrestaurant.com

True to its name, "fantastic panko-crusted" mushrooms headline the New American fare at this "cozy" "little" Arlington bistro tucked away in "a small strip mall off the main road"; "sincere service" and a "something-for-everyone" approach make this a "pleasant neighborhood" spot despite "disappointment" over fare that's "not as good as in the early days."

NEW Posh Ⓢ Ⓜ *American* | – | – | – | E |

Downtown | 730 11th St. NW (bet. G & H Sts.) | 202-393-0975 | www.poshdc.com

This Downtown New American evokes a '30s/'40s-era supper club with its elegant art deco design (curved, high-backed booths and golden draperies) and its updates of classic dishes like rock shrimp bisque and Kobe beef filet; a piano player and late-evening DJ set a lively retro mood that's enhanced with occasional classic movie clips shown above the bar.

Poste Moderne Brasserie *American* | 21 | 22 | 21 | $45 |

Penn Quarter | Hotel Monaco | 555 Eighth St. NW (bet. E & F Sts.) | 202-783-6060 | www.postebrasserie.com

"It's all about the truffle fries" and the "ever-changing martini menu" during happy hour note noshers at this "lovely bistro in a restored historic setting" (the Old Post Office) in Penn Quarter, although the "unique and delicious" New American entrees and the "airy" space also win praise; the "reasonably priced prix fixe" is "perfect for pre-theater" or pre-event meals before heading to the Verizon Center, but a few gripe over "uncoordinated" service.

Praline *American/Bakery* | - | - | - | M |

Bethesda | Sumner Pl. | 4611 Sangamore Rd. (Brookes Ln.), MD | 301-229-8180

This cheery New American bistro and bakery has transformed a two-story shopping-center space in a residential Bethesda enclave into a chic bar/lounge, an intimate hearth-centered dining room and a ground-floor market; sunlight bathes the tables in the upstairs atrium and outdoor patio, adding to the welcoming vibe.

⌷ Prime Rib ⌷ *Steak* | 27 | 24 | 26 | $62 |

Golden Triangle | 2020 K St. NW (bet. 20th & 21st Sts.) | 202-466-8811 | www.theprimerib.com

"Classy, swanky and all dressed up", these black-lacquered "old-fashioned supper clubs" in Golden Triangle and Baltimore's Downtown North are the quintessential spots to celebrate anniversaries or the "close of a big deal" over "massive cuts of buttery, beefy, masculine prime rib", the "most succulent" crab and "perfect" martinis brought to table by "impeccable" tuxedoed waiters; it's still a "powerhouse scene" in DC where "high-profile politicians" "wine and dine", but even sentimentalists think the leopard-print rug should "be retired to a '70s time capsule."

Primi Piatti ⌷ *Italian* | 21 | 18 | 20 | $45 |

Foggy Bottom | 2013 I St. NW (bet. 20th & 21st Sts.) | 202-223-3600 | www.primipiatti.com

Bordering Foggy Bottom and the West End, this "noisy" Italian appeals to "business power" types who enjoy an "authentic" variety of "delicious" pasta and Italian fare "on the company card"; even though a portion of picky patrons point to an "uppity staff" and decor that "needs a makeover", they find it "pleasant" dining on the outdoor patio.

NEW PS 7's ⌷ *American* | - | - | - | E |

Gallery Place | 777 I St. NW (bet. 7th & 8th Sts.) | 202-742-8550 | www.ps7restaurant.com

Chef-owner Peter Smith plays the numbers game at this upscale Gallery Place New American where a mix-and-match menu offers choices in seven price categories (and dessert in the form of seven deadly sins); it's all set in a big-windowed space done up in cocoa and cerulean blue, offset by an eye-catching yellow lava stone bar; N.B. you can also dine alfresco on the patio.

| | FOOD | DECOR | SERVICE | COST |

NEW Pyramids ⚑ Moroccan
| | - | - | - | I |

U Street Corridor | 600 Florida Ave. NW (T St.) | 202-232-6776
Embark on a wallet-friendly culinary adventure at this unprepossessing U Street Corridor Moroccan where a husband-and-wife team prepares tagines, b'steeyas (phyllo dough–covered savories) and harrira (a vegetable mélange) in the traditional manner; since this simply decorated, counter-service eatery has only a handful of tables, takeout is a popular option; N.B. cash-only.

Quarry House Tavern *American*
| ▽ 19 | 13 | 18 | $27 |

Silver Spring | 8401 Georgia Ave. (Bonifant St.), MD | 301-587-9406
A "favorite" "since Prohibition", this Silver Spring American neighborhood "dive" was resurrected in 2005 by the owner of nearby Jackie's, and she "aims to restore" its reputation for "the best burgers in town" (now made from farm-fresh organic beef); skeptics snarl that "higher prices" for food "served in plastic baskets" "doesn't feel like an improvement" so far, but others who "don't expect too much" too soon take a "wait-and-see" approach.

☑ Rabieng *Thai*
| 26 | 16 | 20 | $26 |

Falls Church | Glen Forest Shopping Ctr. | 5892 Leesburg Pike (Glen Forest Dr.), VA | 703-671-4222 | www.duangrats.com
This "unpretentious" Falls Church Thai "has been found" sigh those tight-lipped loyalists who had hoped the "zingy provincial dishes", including "exquisite" signature roast pork that "beats the socks" off the competition, would remain their little secret; instead, it now "overshadows its more celebrated sister, Duangrat's", around the corner, probably due to its much "more relaxed" setting and "unbeatable bargain" rates; P.S. be sure to "ask for the mango sticky rice for dessert."

Radius *Italian*
| ▽ 22 | 18 | 21 | $23 |

Mt. Pleasant | 3155 Mt. Pleasant St. NW (bet. Kenyon St. & Kilbourne Pl.) | 202-234-0808 | www.radiusdc.com
"Greasy is a good thing" at this Italian option that's part of "Mt. Pleasant's cool local grub scene"; the "gooiest New York–style pizza in town" created with "homemade ingredients" comes "named after Italian motorcycles" while "super healthy salads" take the edge off the fat; add in "reasonable prices", a "friendly staff" and a "relaxed" "hangout feel" and this is one "experience worth repeating."

Rail Stop Ⓜ *American*
| 20 | 16 | 19 | $40 |

The Plains | 6478 Main St. (Fauquier Ave.), VA | 540-253-5644 | www.railstoprestaurant.com
A "plain" "small-town" storefront in Virginia is the setting for this American "country place" in The Plains that's a perfect stop for the "horsey set" and folks galloping "out to their weekend place"; the "chef gets his strip steaks right" and the "kids' faces light up when the staff turns on the model train that runs around the dining room ceiling"; still, with prices a "bit too high" for ordinary folk, it's definitely not like the "old days."

	FOOD	DECOR	SERVICE	COST

NEW Rain ● _American_

| − | − | − | E |

Fairfax | 10418 Main St. (bet. Chain Bridge Rd. & University Dr.), VA | 703-865-6150 | www.fairfaxrain.com

Fairfax gets an injection of cool with this glitzy resto-lounge and dance club serving New American cuisine with Latin influences; an ultramodern setting – think cascading waterfalls and agua-inspired lighting – is also helping to lure NoVa's scenesters.

Raku _Pan-Asian_

| 21 | 17 | 16 | $29 |

Dupont Circle | 1900 Q St. NW (19th St.) | 202-265-7258
Bethesda | 7240 Woodmont Ave. (bet. Bethesda Ave. & Elm St.), MD | 301-718-8681

This "high-energy" pair of "funky" "Asian diners" with "consistently good" fare "draws a hip, young crowd" to Dupont and Bethesda for a "nice mix" of Eastern cuisines (including sushi), much of it served "tapas-style"; they're "frenetic on weekends" due to "totally reasonable" prices, but some say "waiting forever" to have "club music pounding" in their ears isn't their idea of fun; others opt to "sit outdoors on a sunny day and people-watch."

NEW Rangoli _Indian_

| − | − | − | M |

South Riding | Riding Plaza Mall | 24995 Riding Plaza (Riding Center Dr.), VA | 703-957-4900 | www.rangolirestaurant.us

A wide range of dishes is on offer at this South Riding Indian that makes its classic fare more accessible via contemporary updates (e.g. shredded tandoori chicken wrapped in a tortillalike roti); the moniker means 'mural', and the warm-toned space utilizes several of them to add to the festive atmosphere.

NEW Rarely Legal Grille 🅢 _Steak_

| − | − | − | M |

Bethesda | 7904 Woodmont Ave. (Fairmont Ave.), MD | 301-652-2229 | www.rarelylegalgrille.com

At this midpriced white-tablecloth steakhouse in Bethesda, meat eaters can choose their cut of beef, a sauce and two sides; diners people-watch through large front windows, while a video game-equipped upstairs bar exudes a youthful sociability.

Z Rasika 🅢 _Indian_

| 26 | 26 | 23 | $46 |

Penn Quarter | 633 D St. NW (bet. 6th & 7th Sts.) | 202-637-1222 | www.rasikarestaurant.com

Here's a "hip" Penn Quarter Indian that's in a "class by itself" say its sophisticated fans; expect a "sexy" setting, "exemplary service", "unique" tapas influenced by street cooking (you "must have" the "crispy" deep-fried spinach appetizer) and "innovative and thoughtful" wine pairings that work well with the "dynamic range" of "fabulous flavors"; indeed, from the "killer" cocktails to the "delectable dishes fit for the maharajah", they "seem to be doing everything right."

NEW Ray's The Classics 🅢 _American_

| ▽ 24 | 22 | 20 | $56 |

Silver Spring | 8606 Colesville Rd. (Georgia Ave.), MD | 301-588-7297

"Another home run for chef-owner Mike Landrum" (Ray's The Steaks), this Silver Spring eatery sports "classy", "streamlined decor" – white tablecloths, polished bar, dark-wood furnishings – to complement "tender, delicious steaks" and other "wonderful" American fare; some say "the establishment is a bit full of itself", but most "love it", citing generally "competent service" and an "affordable wine list"; N.B. the toque is currently doing double duty at both of his restaurants.

☑ Ray's The Steaks ⓜ Steak   27 | 10 | 22 | $43
Arlington | Colonial Village | 1725 Wilson Blvd. (bet. Quinn & Rhodes Sts.), VA | 703-841-7297

Chef-owner/butcher Mike 'Ray' Landrum is "a genius with a side of cow" – and the "no-frills ambiance" at his "bare-bones" meatery in an Arlington strip mall near the Courthouse metro "keeps the price down" for "some of the best red meat you'll eat anywhere", "cooked to perfection" and complemented by a "thoughtful, gently priced wine list"; still, "come early", as they don't take reservations; N.B. expect a move to more spacious quarters in Clarendon by the end of 2007.

redDog Cafe ⓜ American   19 | 18 | 17 | $25
Silver Spring | 8301A Grubb Rd. (East-West Hwy.), MD | 301-588-6300 | www.reddogcafe.com

You can "almost taste the passion" of the "great people" behind this "charming" Silver Spring cafe since their "simple but delicious" New American "home cooking" offers top-shelf "taste and quality for the $$$"; sure, it can get "noisy and crowded", but they've made the strip-mall space "as appealing as possible" using "warm" dark reds and offering "art for sale"; N.B. the outdoor patio is pooch-friendly.

Red Hot & Blue BBQ   19 | 14 | 17 | $20
Gaithersburg | Grove Shopping Ctr. | 16811 Crabbs Branch Way (Shady Grove Rd.), MD | 301-948-7333
Laurel | 677 Main St. (Rte. 216), MD | 301-953-1943
Alexandria | 6482 Landsdowne Ctr. (Beulah St.), VA | 703-550-6465
Rosslyn | 1600 Wilson Blvd. (Pierce St.), VA | 703-276-7427
Fairfax | 4150 Chain Bridge Rd. (Rte. 236), VA | 703-218-6989
Falls Church | Tower Sq. | 169 Hillwood Ave. (Douglass Ave.), VA | 703-538-6466
Manassas | 8366 Sudley Rd. (Irongate Way), VA | 703-367-7100
Leesburg | Bellwood Commons Shopping Ctr. | 541 E. Market St. (Plaza St.), VA | 703-669-4242
www.redhotandblue.com

"Pork rules" at this "family-friendly" chain of "Memphis barbecue joints" where folks "make hogs out of themselves" with "steaming hunks" of "pulled pig" and "dry-rub ribs that pack a punch" – plus "lip-smackin'" beans, "homemade" potato salad and "quart-sized cups of sweet tea"; connoisseurs, however, see red over "assembly-line" chow that's "nothing hot" and "leaves you blue."

Reef, The ● American   14 | 20 | 16 | $25
Adams Morgan | 2446 18th St. NW (Columbia Rd.) | 202-518-3800 | www.thereefdc.com

Staring at the "huge" fish tanks is "better than TV" at this aquarium-themed New American featuring "sustainable seafood and organic ingredients" on an "ever-changing menu"; but the "so-so" fare (perhaps "boiled in sea water"?) "is not the main attraction" here – it's the "rooftop bar that draws large crowds on summer evenings" with its "priceless" views of Adams Morgan and "eclectic beer list" served by an "attractive", though "uninspired", staff.

Regent, The   Thai   23 | 22 | 21 | $29

Dupont Circle | 1910 18th St. NW (bet. Florida Ave. & T St.) | 202-232-1781 | www.regentthai.com

Basic Thai "kicked up a notch" "never disappoints" Duponters who also enjoy the "visual delight" of this "staple's" "mood-setting" decor, including "dark-wood carvings" and teak seats; though the fare is "heavy on noodle dishes" and "not for the spice-phobic", it is a "fresh-feeling alternative in a sea" of Thai eateries, especially when "the line is too long at Lauriol Plaza."

Renato at River Falls   Italian   17 | 13 | 17 | $38

Potomac | 10120 River Rd. (Falls Rd.), MD | 301-365-1900

You're "bound to see someone you know" at this "informal" "neighborhood" Italian "gathering place" in Potomac that's "always busy" with "suburban ladies who lunch", local notables and families; in addition to "ample", "consistent" "home cooking" from the land of the red, white and green, there are now daily Med seafood specials courtesy of its new owners (the folks behind the next-door fish market), who have also given the interior a stylish update.

Rice   Thai   22 | 21 | 20 | $31

Logan Circle | 1608 14th St. NW (bet. Q & R Sts.) | 202-234-2400 | www.simplyhomedc.com

This "chic", "date"-friendly Logan Circle Asian exemplifies "the future of 14th Street" trill trendsters as they dig into "delicious" "imaginative" dishes featuring "interesting combinations of Thai and international ingredients" ("try anything with green tea") brought by a very "refreshing" staff; "wear black" to fit in with the "high-style" "Zen-like minimalism" ("exposed brick and dim lighting") that feels like it's "in NYC", but expect "long waits" for the "tiny", "loud" space.

Rí-Rá Irish Restaurant Pub   Pub Food   15 | 18 | 17 | $27

Bethesda | 4931 Elm St. (bet. Arlington Rd. & Woodmont Ave.), MD | 301-657-1122 ◗

Arlington | 2915 Wilson Blvd. (Fillmore St.), VA | 703-248-9888

www.rira.com

"Stop by for a pint" poured by bartenders "with brogues so thick you'll think you're in Dublin" instead of at one of these "cheery" Bethesda and Arlington hangouts that are outfitted with "authentic Irish pub" artifacts; "live music" and "fun" trivia nights "add to the atmosphere", so even if you "wish the mediocre pub food was better", "Guinness on draft washes away any bad taste."

Ristorante La Perla ◗   Italian   ▽ 19 | 19 | 20 | $52

Georgetown | 2600 Pennsylvania Ave. NW (26th St.) | 202-333-1767 | www.laperla.us

"Masterful" chef-owner Vittorio Testa "personally makes sure you're happy" at his bit of "old-world Italy" perched on the edge of

Georgetown, where cherubs and Murano chandeliers make you feel like you're "dining with Venus de Milo"; but some patrons who find the fare "out-of-date" proclaim "that's one pricey plate of penne" and others sigh over service that "can be spotty at times."

Ristorante Murali *Italian*

▽ 17 | 17 | 17 | $30

Arlington | Pentagon Row | 1201 S. Joyce St. (Army Navy Dr.), VA | 703-415-0411 | www.muraliva.com

Regulars run to this Pentagon Row trattoria for "decent" "basic Italian" paired with a good wine list at "reasonable prices", mentioning "simply perfect pumpkin ravioli" and helpful half-portions (though fussbudgets feel it "would be nice if they made friends with garlic and onion once in a while" to spice up the sometimes "bland" fare); the outdoor plaza cafe is particularly "nice for a shopping-mall" setting, but don't expect stellar service.

☑ Ritz-Carlton, The Grill (Pentagon City) *American*

25 | 25 | 26 | $62

Arlington | Ritz-Carlton Pentagon City | 1250 S. Hayes St. (bet. Army Navy Dr. & 15th St.), VA | 703-412-2760 | www.ritzcarlton.com

A "wonderful spot" to enjoy "tea for two", an "elegant luncheon" or an "extensive and superb brunch", this New American hotel dining room near the Pentagon offers "outstanding" fare all around; expect "top-notch" service in a "formalized, staid" environment.

Rock Creek *American*

23 | 21 | 21 | $43

Bethesda | 4917 Elm St. (bet. Arlington Rd. & Woodmont Ave.), MD | 301-907-7625 | www.rockcreekrestaurant.com

"Wanna eat healthy" and still "enjoy the food"? – head to this Bethesda New American with an "elegant" setting that includes a waterfall and a lovely wall mural of its namesake park; "the word is spreading" quickly on this "classy" "low-cal" gem with "sensible"-sized filet mignon, "to-die-for" molten chocolate cake and "considerate" servers who help you "feel virtuous"; still, some say this spot serves up "more than you want to know about carbs and cals"; N.B. a sibling (featuring maitre d' Ralph Fredericks) will debut in summer 2007 in Chevy Chase's Mazza Gallerie.

Rocklands *BBQ*

22 | 11 | 15 | $17

Glover Park | 2418 Wisconsin Ave. NW (Calvert St.) | 202-333-2558
Rockville | Wintergreen Plaza | 891A Rockville Pike (Wootton Pkwy.), MD | 240-268-1120
Alexandria | 25 S. Quaker Ln. (Duke St.), VA | 703-778-9663
www.rocklands.com

The "mouthwatering" "pulled pork sammies" and the "flawless", "fall-off-the-bone delicious" babyback ribs at these "no-frills" "joints" "will satisfy any craving", especially when you can "scoop a ladle" of "flat-out good" "tangy sauce" from the "help-yourself vat" ("you'll find yourself licking the plate" clean); "counter service" and "limited seating" make these "smoky" "holes-in-the-wall" "best for takeout", however; N.B. a fourth location is expected to open in Arlington in July 2007.

	FOOD	DECOR	SERVICE	COST

Roof Terrace at the Kennedy Center *American*

| 17 | 20 | 17 | $48 |

Foggy Bottom | Kennedy Ctr. | 2700 F St. NW (bet. New Hampshire & Virginia Aves.) | 202-416-8555 | www.kennedy-center.org

"Breathtaking" views of the DC skyline are the highlight of this New American "banquet hall" perched atop the Kennedy Center in Foggy Bottom, since some say "it's all about pre-show convenience" and not the "overpriced" fare that's "surprisingly bland given the grandeur" of the location; optimists, however, continue to find signs of "improvement" after post-Survey chef changes; N.B. it serves dinner only Monday–Sunday on performance nights, plus brunch starting at 11 AM on Sunday.

Rosa Mexicano *Mexican*

| 20 | 23 | 19 | $40 |

Penn Quarter | Terrel Pl. | 575 Seventh St. NW (F St.) | 202-783-5522 | www.rosamexicano.com

A "young crowd" packs this "high-energy" Penn Quarter Mexican, the DC link in a national chain known for "visually delicious decor" – in this case, a "back wall waterfall" – along with "high-end", "south-of-the-border" fare including "killer" guacamole made tableside and the "best margaritas in town" ("you gotta have the pomegranate" one); desperados "disappointed" with "over-accessorized, underwhelming entrees" at prices that must help these folks "pay their lease" for the prime location don't have as much "fun."

RT's *Cajun/Creole*

| 22 | 13 | 19 | $35 |

Alexandria | 3804 Mt. Vernon Ave. (Glebe Rd.), VA | 703-684-6010 | www.rtsrestaurant.net

"Addictive" crawfish étouffée, "the best she-crab soup in town", "flawless" pecan pie and other "Louisiana-style" "cooking that kicks it up a notch" have delivered "Cajun comfort" to Alexandria's "neighborhood hangout" "for the past 20-plus years"; just "don't be scared away" by the "strange location", "'50s exterior facade" and "fading" "decor that falsely screams 'mediocre.'"

Ruan Thai *Thai*

| – | – | – | I |

Wheaton | 11407 Amherst Ave. (University Blvd. W.), MD | 301-942-0075

This Wheaton Southeast Asian doesn't spare the spice when customers ask for their dishes 'Thai hot' – the duck with basil is a popular scorcher; besides complex curries and noodle dishes, it also offers traditional salads and appetizers not often found elsewhere, all served up in a simple storefront setting that may seem a startling contrast to the incendiary fare.

NEW Rugby Café *Eclectic*

| – | – | – | M |

Georgetown | 1065 Wisconsin Ave. NW (M St.) | 202-298-6894

It didn't take long for Georgetown denizens to discover this classy Eclectic cafe adjoining Ralph Lauren's rugby-themed clothing store, where salads, burgers and panini are served amid leather couches, sports memorabilia and other masculine trappings; its hearty breakfasts are a suitable warm-up for a match, while its full bar attracts more of a post-game party scene.

FOOD | DECOR | SERVICE | COST

Rustico *American*

| – | – | – | M |

Alexandria | 827 Slaters Ln. (Potomac Greens Dr.), VA | 703-224-5051 | www.rusticorestaurant.com

Despite a menu featuring boldly seasoned pizzas and grilled meats pulled from a wood-fired oven, the beer takes pride of place at this handsome, modern, brick-walled American near Potomac Yards in Alexandria; sure, there are wines and trendy cocktails, but the hearty fare from new chef Frank Morales (ex Zola) is meant to be matched with microbrews and cask ales, including 30 choices on tap and some 250 bottle selections.

🛂 Ruth's Chris Steak House *Steak*

| 24 | 21 | 23 | $57 |

Penn Quarter | 724 Ninth St. NW (H St.) | 202-393-4488
Dupont Circle | 1801 Connecticut Ave. NW (S St.) | 202-797-0033
Bethesda | 7315 Wisconsin Ave. (Elm St.), MD | 301-652-7877
Arlington | Crystal Park | 2231 Crystal Dr., 11th fl. (23rd St.), VA | 703-979-7275
NEW Fairfax | 4100 Monument Corner Dr. (Palace Way), VA | 703-226-1004
www.ruthschris.com

"Everything is big" at these "high-end" "budget-busting" houses of beef – the steaks "sizzling in butter, the sides, the drinks, the bill!" but "so what?" since you'll "check your diet at the door and rip into" a slab that "melts in your mouth", augmented by a "great bottle of wine"; the "well-timed" service further "pampers" and the dark-wood interiors are just right for business, but some insist these choices are "not as good" as the city's other chophouse options.

Saigon Saigon *Vietnamese*

| ▽ 18 | 16 | 18 | $23 |

Arlington | Pentagon Row | 1101 S. Joyce St. (Army Navy Dr.), VA | 703-412-0822

Shoppers taking a soul-warming break from Pentagon Row retail report "on a cold day, a big bowl of pho hits the spot" at this "consistently good" Vietnamese with "pleasant" service and "big portions"; purists wouldn't go out of their way for this one, though, finding "nothing special that would bring them back."

Sakana 🛂 *Japanese*

| 22 | 16 | 19 | $28 |

Dupont Circle | 2026 P St. NW (bet. 20th & 21st Sts.) | 202-887-0900

"Shhhh – don't let the word out on this Dupont jewel" plead patrons of this already "crowded basement eatery" where a "simple setting" doesn't distract from "wonderfully fresh" signature sushi, "truly delicious" shrimp tempura rolls and "surprisingly good Japanese classics (pork ramen, cold soba)"; the "small", "cramped location" may inspire "to-go" orders, but "friendly owners" and "reasonable prices" ensure "complete loyalty."

🛂 Sake Club 🛂 *Japanese*

| 23 | 25 | 19 | $38 |

Woodley Park | 2635 Connecticut Ave. NW (bet. Calvert St. & Woodley Rd.) | 202-332-2711 | www.sakeclub.net

"Hipper than a typical Japanese" eatery, this hideout in "Woodley Park's ethnic row" offers "sophisticated packaging" – dark "romantic" lighting, modern concrete tabletops and Asian antiques – and serves up a "dizzying array" of "innovative" if "pricey" small plates "ranging from sushi to beef BBQ" along with an equally "large collection" of the namesake rice wine (just "don't expect the servers to know more about the menu than you do"); P.S. the "half-price sake flights" from 5-7 PM are a steal.

Saki *Pan-Asian*

| 19 | 19 | 17 | $32 |

Adams Morgan | 2477 18th St. NW (bet. Belmont & Columbia Rds.) | 202-232-5005 | www.sakidc.com

The "super-chic" "mood-lit bar" attracts a "hip" crowd for "half-priced sushi" during happy hours at this Adams Morgan bi-level Pan-Asian with an "identity crisis": upstairs is "a cool place to go for dinner and drinks" before it "slowly transforms into a nightspot", while the "downstairs dance club" is a "weekend hot spot" with "dancing and good DJs"; aesthetes decry a "crowded bus-terminal" setting that's "fine for a late-night martini" and "amusing people-watching" but "not a meal."

Sakoontra *Thai*

| 22 | 20 | 19 | $21 |

Fairfax | Costco Plaza | 12300C Price Club Plaza (W. Ox Rd.), VA | 703-818-8886 | www.sakoontra.com

"Whoever goes to the Fairfax Costco or Home Depot and passes this by just doesn't know what they're missing" say shoppers smitten with the "wide variety" of "amazing", "affordable" Thai dishes in this "sleek" tiny space tucked into an area they call "the black hole of restaurants"; order the "ducky" signature duck, the "yummy" yum watercress or "any beef dish" from the "helpful" staff, and this spot may become one of your "favorites."

Sala Thai *Thai*

| 19 | 14 | 18 | $22 |

Dupont Circle | 2016 P St. NW (bet. 20th & 21st Sts.) | 202-872-1144
U Street Corridor | 1301 U St. NW (13th St.) | 202-462-1333
Cleveland Park | 3507 Connecticut Ave. NW (Ordway St.) | 202-237-2777
Bethesda | 4828 Cordell Ave. (Wisconsin Ave.), MD | 301-654-4676
Arlington | 2300 Wilson Blvd. (Veitch St.), VA | 703-807-5860
Arlington | 2900 N. 10th St. (Washington Blvd.), VA | 703-465-2900
www.salathaidc.com

"Chain Thai? - it works, and it works well" at these "safe bets" that "can't be beat for the price", especially the "huge bargains at lunch"; the staff "tries very hard" at the "workmanlike" empire that varies from the "bare-bones barracks" of Dupont's "basement" digs to the "stylish" ambiance of the "swanky" Bethesda outpost; still, picky patrons wish the menu's "marginal" standards "were more memorable."

Sam & Harry's 🅢 *Steak*

| 21 | 20 | 23 | $59 |

Golden Triangle | 1200 19th St. NW (M St.) | 202-296-4333 | www.samandharrys.com

An "inconspicuous joint" in the middle of Golden Triangle's steakhouse row "takes the prize" for "no gimmicks" meat - its "oxymoronic 'bone-in' filet" could be the "best" cut in town; add in a "world-class"

	FOOD	DECOR	SERVICE	COST

wine list, a "knowledgeable staff" and a "dark", clubby setting "populated with Washington power-lunchers" and most find it "lives up to the hype"; but bored beef eaters search vainly for "an injection of excitement" and find "uninspired" dishes instead.

Samantha's *Mexican/Salvadoran*   22 | 12 | 20 | $24

Silver Spring | 631 E. University Blvd. (Piney Branch Rd.), MD | 301-445-7300

Find "surprisingly good" seafood pupusas and other "exotic Salvadoran" dishes along with more "standard" Mexican fare at this "out-of-the-way" "jewel" in Silver Spring, where the iffy location and "hard-to-find" parking give way to a "quiet" "charming interior"; it's a good thing the staff "lets you linger" because "you won't want to move" when they start serving "some of the best" ceviche and most "perfect" *masitas de puerco* you've ever had.

San Vito *Italian*   20 | 16 | 17 | $24

Herndon | The Franklin Farm Shopping Ctr. | 13340 Franklin Farm Rd. (Fairfax County Pkwy.), VA | 703-707-6400

Springfield | King's Park Shopping Ctr. | 8944 Burke Lake Rd. (Braddock Rd.), VA | 703-250-0171

Ashburn | Broadlands Center Plaza | 43150 Broadlands Center Plaza (Broadlands Blvd.), VA | 571-223-2245

www.sanvitorestaurant.com

Loyalists of this suburban Virginia strip-mall pizza-pasta trio tout the "high-end", "wonderful" Italian dishes and "inventive" pies served in a "friendly, family atmosphere" for "surprisingly low prices"; the less-impressed, however, deem it merely "a cut above the chains" and warn that you should "be prepared for children running around your table."

NEW Saravana Palace *Indian/Vegetarian*   - | - | - | I

Fairfax | 11725 Lee Hwy. (McKenzie Ave.), VA | 703-218-4182 | www.saravanapalaceva.com

At this mod Fairfax Indian, the vegetarian fare is spiced for its countrymen, who fill its padded turquoise booths for affordable culinary adventures; in addition to an ever-changing lunchtime buffet ($7.95 on weekdays and $9.95 on weekends), there's also a wide-ranging menu that includes hard-to-find Indo-Chinese dishes, along with curries, dosas and even flavorful preparations made without onions or garlic, which some Hindus shun.

SBC Café ⬛ *American*   ▽ 24 | 13 | 18 | $23

Herndon | Herndon Clock Tower | 2501-08 McNair Farms Rd. (Centerville Rd.), VA | 703-793-7388

A "great find in an unlikely location" in Herndon, this "reasonably priced" New American "boutique" "serves up delicious" "gourmet" dishes with "character" (sensitive tongues should "ask them to lighten up on the spices"); the "decor and service need work" since the strip-mall "space gets full" and "disorganized" when busy, but adventurous types appreciate that half the menu consists of "specials listed on the blackboard."

	FOOD	DECOR	SERVICE	COST

Sea Catch 🛇 *Seafood*
21 | 20 | 20 | $48

Georgetown | Canal Sq. | 1054 31st St. NW (M St.) | 202-337-8855 |
www.seacatchrestaurant.com

You'll "feel more like you're in Amsterdam" than Georgetown when
you're "sitting outside overlooking the canal on a balmy summer night"
at this "classy" seafooder that's "great for an intimate evening or good
conversation" "when the old folks come to visit"; "super-friendly"
staffers help you choose between "delicious" crab cakes, "fresh
catches" and the "best oyster bar in town", but cynics suggest there's
something fishy about "average" fare for "above-average prices."

🛂 Seasons *American*
27 | 25 | 27 | $64

Georgetown | Four Seasons Hotel | 2800 Pennsylvania Ave. NW
(28th St.) | 202-944-2000 | www.fourseasons.com

The Georgetown Four Seasons' "elegant" "high standards pay off" at
its New American restaurant where the "out-of-this-world" fare,
"quiet ambiance, terrific service and tables spaced so that you're
not afraid to tell the person you're with what you're thinking about"
draw a "diplomatic and senior policy crowd"; it's *the* business hotel
in DC", so "having breakfast anywhere else before you've been
elected (or after you've been impeached) is just plain silly", plus
there's a "mind-boggling" weekend brunch.

Sequoia *American*
15 | 23 | 15 | $41

Georgetown | Washington Harbour | 3000 K St. NW (30th St.) |
202-944-4200 | www.arkrestaurants.com

"Fabulous waterfront" vistas and a "lively atmosphere" make this
Washington Harbour New American's "beautiful" tiered balcony and
its "posh" dining room a "mandatory stop for out-of-town guests"
(it's "an excellent choice for brunch" when "parents or in-laws" are
visiting); sure, the service is "disinterested" "at best" and the fare is
"mediocre", but "you pay for the views" (and perhaps the people-
watching at the "crazy bar scene"), which are "unbelievable."

Sesto Senso 🛇 *Italian*
20 | 16 | 19 | $41

Golden Triangle | 1214 18th St. NW (bet. Jefferson Pl. & M St.) |
202-785-9525 | www.sesto.com

"Huge bowls of olives on the bar begin the bacchanal" at this Golden
Triangle Italian where "ambassadors and other leading DC lights"
"treat themselves" to "traditionally prepared" pastas during "meet-
ings over lunch"; come nightfall, it's more of a "very loud" "singles bar
scene", "packed full" with "Euro clubbers" and partyers; any time you
go, however, expect "small plates" and service "with a little 'tude."

Sette Bello ➊ *Italian*
21 | 21 | 15 | $39

Arlington | 3101 Wilson Blvd. (N. Highland St.), VA | 703-351-1004 |
www.settebellorestaurant.com

Adding some "Euro class" to Arlington's burgeoning Clarendon corridor, this "haute and hip" "high-end Italian" boasts "cool" bar
perches for the "established crowd" and a similar "upscale" menu
(with "creative additions") as its older sibling, Cafe Milano; "sit outside on a nice day" to escape the "cavernous" space that's "too noisy

for conversation", and ignore its few "kinks", including a "chaotic" atmosphere and an "inattentive staff."

Sette Osteria ● *Italian* | 20 | 17 | 16 | $32 |

Dupont Circle | 1666 Connecticut Ave. NW (R St.) | 202-483-3070 | www.setteosteria.com

A Dupont Circle "magnet for energetic, attractive folks", this "noisy", "casual sibling of Georgetown's Cafe Milano" is "always packed" with an "international clientele" who come for "simple and solid" pasta, "thin-crust pizza with unusual toppings" and, of course, "great people-watching" whether perched on the "outdoor patio" or gazing through the "huge" open windows; but "what's with the attitude" of the "inexperienced" "lax" servers?

701 ● *American* | 23 | 22 | 23 | $49 |

Penn Quarter | 701 Pennsylvania Ave. NW (7th St.) | 202-393-0701 | www.701restaurant.com

Overlooking the Navy Memorial's cascading fountains, this "civilized, sophisticated" Penn Quarter New American "does power lunches and romantic dinners with equal ease" in "classy" modern surroundings; the pre-theater menu "steals the show", but regulars go for the martini bar, where they can "chat with 'Mo' (Taheri), the city's primo bartender", or linger over nightly "jazz and caviar"; N.B. expect new chef Alexander Powell (ex NYC's Jean Georges and JoJo) to put his own spin on the cuisine.

Seven Seas *Chinese/Japanese* | 18 | 13 | 16 | $23 |

College Park | 8503 Baltimore Ave. (Quebec St.), MD | 301-345-5807 | www.sevenseascp.com

Rockville | Federal Plaza | 1776 E. Jefferson St. (bet. Montrose Rd. & Rollins Ave.), MD | 301-770-5020 | www.sevenseasrestaurant.com

Ask for the "Chinese-only red menu" at these College Park and Rockville Asians known for "cheap" "authentically" prepared whole fish, plus "decent" Japanese sushi and tempura; the interiors are "dated" and the service can be "lacking", but the cuisine is "tasty"; P.S. "don't ask for extra spicy unless you want to blow your head off."

⊠ 1789 *American* | 26 | 25 | 25 | $61 |

Georgetown | 1226 36th St. NW (Prospect St.) | 202-965-1789 | www.1789restaurant.com

"Everything" about this "elegant" Georgetowner "screams quality and class": the "excellent" seasonal New American fare, the "impeccable" service and the "classic" Federal period dining rooms favored for "romance" "by the fireplace"; the 2006 departure of longtime chef Ris Lacoste concerned loyalists, but early reports say her replacement, Nathan Beauchamp (ex Eve), has been able to "liven up the menu while still keeping true to the standards."

Shamshiry *Persian*   ▽ | 23 | 12 | 17 | $21 |

Falls Church | 8607 Westwood Center Dr. (Leesburg Pike), VA | 703-448-8883 | www.shamshiry.com

Expat "extended families" feasting on "succulent" kebabs "grilled to perfection" and "aromatic rice dishes" "attest to the authenticity of the simple but excellent" fare at this Falls Church Persian "tucked behind car dealerships in a low-rise office building"; "even though they don't serve alcohol", they deliver "generous portions" "quickly", offering "true value for your money."

Shula's Steak House 🖪 *Steak* — 18 | 17 | 18 | $54

Vienna | Tysons Corner Marriott Hotel | 8028 Leesburg Pike (Towers Crescent Dr.), VA | 703-506-3256 | www.donshula.com

If you "order the 48-oz. porterhouse" they'll "put your name on a plaque" at Tysons Corner's gridiron-themed grill with "a wall of memorabilia" honoring the namesake owner's storied stint as coach of the NFL Colts and Dolphins; though it (and its Downtown Baltimore sibling) scores points with some fans for "decent" chops, others insist it "needs to draft some new service talent" and cry foul over the "absurdly priced" fare – as for the "novelty" "pigskin menu", "drop kick that football outta here."

Simply Fish *Seafood* — ▽ 19 | 17 | 15 | $32

Alexandria | Fairlington Ctr. | 1700 Fern St. (Kenwood St.), VA | 703-778-3474 | www.simplyfish.biz

"Have it your way" when you "pick your fish, pick your sauce and pick your sides" at this Alexandria seafooder that makes a "cool concept" out of "à la carte ordering" "without having to mortgage the farm"; it's too bad the "limited wine selection", "uneven execution" and "grumpy" service lead some to simply "skip this one."

Simply Home *Thai* — - | - | - | M

U Street Corridor | 1410 U St. NW (bet. 14th & 15th Sts.) | 202-232-8424 | www.simplyhomedc.com

A popular U Street carryout spot – noted for its serene minimalist setting and full-flavored Thai cuisine – is reborn in a nearby storefront as a sophisticated restaurant and lounge, where a marvelously twisted tree root and other natural materials create a soigné setting for both traditional dishes and Thai-accented takes on ceviche, sashimi, martinis and more; N.B. an adjacent market sells similarly chic gifts and home accessories.

Siné ● *Pub Food* — 15 | 16 | 16 | $22

Arlington | Pentagon Row | 1301 S. Joyce St. (Army Navy Dr.), VA | 703-415-4420 | www.sineirishpub.com

There's "no blarney here" chirp chums of this "fun" Pentagon Row pub with "kitschy decor", "service with a smile" and a menu "that lists a pint of Guinness as an appetizer", in addition to "typical Irish fare"; head here "after work" or to "watch a Notre Dame football game" and keep an eye out for those "Pentagon staffers and active-duty" officers who make this their "favorite watering hole" – who knows, "you just may be rubbing elbows with a special forces operative."

Skewers/Café Luna ● *Italian/Mideastern* — 18 | 15 | 18 | $22

Dupont Circle | 1633 P St. NW (bet. 16th & 17th Sts.) | 202-387-7400 | www.skewers-cafeluna.com

This "unpretentious" pair of "neighborhood favorites" share ownership and location in Dupont Circle but sport "very different" menus and decor: downstairs, Café Luna is a "lovable hole-in-the-wall" Italian with "solid pizza" and pasta, while upstairs at Skewers, "attentive servers" deliver "tasty" Middle Eastern meze at "comfy banquettes littered with pillows"; nitpickers note the latter is "more consistent", but with low prices and regular "half-price specials" at both, you'll "come away pleasantly satiated."

Smith & Wollensky ● *Steak* 21 | 19 | 21 | $57

Golden Triangle | 1112 19th St. NW (bet. L & M Sts.) | 202-466-1100 | www.smithandwollensky.com

The waiters "do a good job channeling the New York original" steakhouse at this Golden Triangle outpost filled with lawyers and lobbyists feasting on "big, juicy, bloody prime ribs", "beautifully prepared" chops and shellfish and "exceptional wines"; the "old-school" decor is "not as dark and gloomy" as some other branches, perhaps explaining the "surprisingly young crowd", but a minority reports "disappointment" in beef that's "not worth half of what they charge."

SoBe Seafood Co. Ⓜ *Seafood* ▽ 17 | 11 | 17 | $27

Arlington | 3100 Clarendon Blvd. (bet. Highland & Washington Sts.), VA | 703-528-0033

Though it's "still close to the Clarendon nightlife", the Arlington area's dinner-only Floribbean "favorite" is far enough away that it's "rarely full" despite the "reasonable prices" for "terrific" seafood and mango chutney dipping sauce; seasick sorts "feel like they're eating inside a fish tank" in the blue-walled dining room, but they can sit in the "beautiful courtyard" "when the weather permits."

Sol de España ● *Spanish* 23 | 18 | 24 | $37

Rockville | 838C Rockville Pike (Edmonston Dr.), MD | 240-234-1818

"Warm and welcoming" chef-owner Joaquin Serrano "cooks and hosts as though you were in his home" rather than "the morass of Rockville Pike" at this "amazing find" where you can enjoy Spanish fare including "expertly filleted" "fresh fish", paella and "sangria, sangria, sangria"; better yet, "they never pressure you to leave", so you can "linger", "close your eyes" and pretend you're "in Barcelona" as you listen to the flamenco guitar.

Sonoma Restaurant & Wine Bar *American* 21 | 21 | 19 | $39

Capitol Hill | 223 Pennsylvania Ave. SE (bet. 2nd & 3rd Sts.) | 202-544-8088 | www.sonomadc.com

"California comes to Capitol Hill" with this New American wine bar boasting an "artfully selected" list of 40-plus types by the glass and "fabulous charcuterie and cheese plates" that are "perfect for the grazer"; the "fashion-forward, minimalist" dining space, as well as "intimate" digs upstairs, are "always booked" with "see-and-be-seen" sorts enjoying "nontypical" plates with their vino, but a few gourmands gripe that the "overpriced" "portions are a tad too refined."

	FOOD	DECOR	SERVICE	COST

Sorak Garden *Korean* ▽ 22 | 16 | 16 | $30

Annandale | 4308 Backlick Rd. (Little River Tpke.), VA |
703-916-7600

It's a good sign when you see "lots of Koreans" in this Annandale
Asian featuring "interesting choices" including "fantastic side
dishes" and some of "the best" barbecue in Northern Virginia on its
"large" menu; the "friendly" attitude doesn't always make up for
"spotty service" however.

Sorriso *Italian* 20 | 18 | 19 | $31

Cleveland Park | 3518 Connecticut Ave. NW (Ordway St.) |
202-537-4800 | www.sorrisoristorante.net

Feel like you're "visiting a trattoria in Italy" as you step into this
"family-run" neighborhood spot just steps from the Cleveland Park
metro station, where the "owner greets everyone with a wide smile"
and sometimes pours a taste of the wines he sells "from his own
vineyards" in Friuli; *amici* appreciate the "smoky, crisp" wood-fired
pizzas as well as the other "hearty, flavorful" fare that's ferried by
staffers through the "funny little labyrinth of tables", but are less-
impressed with "painfully slow" service.

Spezie ⧄ *Italian* 19 | 18 | 20 | $41

Golden Triangle | 1736 L St. NW (bet. Connecticut Ave. & 18th St.) |
202-467-0777 | www.spezie.com

Chef-owner Enzo Livia dishes out "freshly made pasta" and "classic"
Italian entrees "with a slightly modern twist" at this Golden Triangle
trattoria that is "criminally underknown" according to fans; "moderate prices", "informal atmosphere" and a "friendly" staff are draws,
particularly to "suits" coming for business lunches, while others
"feel right at home just sitting at the bar" enjoying the appetizers;
P.S. "when the weather's good", the "windows open to the street."

Spices *Pan-Asian* 20 | 15 | 17 | $26

Cleveland Park | 3333A Connecticut Ave. NW (bet. Macomb &
Ordway Sts.) | 202-686-3833

"Top-notch" sushi plus "plenty of choices" for "anti-raw-fish" folks
make this "sleek", "funky" Cleveland Park Pan-Asian the "ultimate
yuppie first-date" destination as well as the spot to take "indecisive
people"; sure, it's "a little culturally confused" ("you get the feeling
they have Thais cooking Chinese and Vietnamese rolling sushi")
and it "tries way too hard to be trendy", but the "noisy" "twentysomethings" who "crowd" this "accommodating" "hot spot" don't
seem to mind.

Starfish Cafe *Seafood* 17 | 18 | 19 | $30

Capitol Hill | 539 Eighth St. SE (G St.) | 202-546-5006 |
www.starfishcafedc.com

You'll find a "pleasant surprise on Eighth Street" at this "simple", "vibrant" seafooder with "fun", "friendly" servers and a good-"value"
Sunday brunch; fin fans are mixed on the fare, however, enjoying
complimentary hushpuppies and "surf 'n' turf that's worth the cost",
but labeling some of the other fish as "mediocre"; nevertheless,

even if it's not exactly a star, it's "decent for something a little different on the Hill."

Sticky Fingers *Bakery/Vegan*

| - | - | - | I |

Columbia Heights | 1370 Park Rd. NW (bet. 13th & 14th Sts.) | 202-299-9700 | www.stickyfingersbakery.com

Overwhelming response to its stint on the Food Network's *Road Tasted* series has led this vegan bakery to relocate to burgeoning Columbia Heights; it's now ensconced in a modern cafe-style storefront where patrons can sample the likes of dairy-free soups and mac 'n' cheese as well as its popular sticky buns.

Stoney's Bar & Grill ◕ *Pub Food*

| - | - | - | I |

Logan Circle | 1433 P St. NW (bet. 14th & 15th Sts.) | 202-234-1818

After losing its divey digs to Downtown development, this beloved beer-and-burger joint has been reborn in happening Logan Circle; a polished wood bar with high tops greets patrons up front, while the familiar 'glory wall' of photos (and the signature grilled-cheese sandwiches) reminds them of where they are.

Straits of Malaya *Malaysian*

| 21 | 13 | 20 | $27 |

Dupont Circle | 1836 18th St. NW (T St.) | 202-483-1483 | www.straitsofmalaya.com

Serving "consistently tasty" Straits cuisine – an "interesting" mix of "classic Malay" with Chinese and Indian influences – has turned this Dupont East spot into a neighborhood "favorite"; locals just can't resist "filling up for pennies" on "homey fare, with homey service to match", and the "great" roof terrace means they can avoid the "nonexistent" interior decor and "dine in peace" while "laughing at all the people standing in line" below for a nearby eatery.

Sushi-Go-Round & Tapas *Asian Fusion*

| ▽ 21 | 14 | 18 | $24 |

Chinatown | Gallery Pl. | 705 Seventh St. NW (bet. F & H Sts.) | 202-393-2825 | www.sushigoroundatmci.com

"Chinatown sushi?" – yes, and some say "the joy of watching" the "variety of raw fish" "come at you on a conveyor belt" at this Asian fusion makes it "fun" as well; it's "perfect for pre-movie or bowling" if "you're in a rush" since "you can dip in and eat as soon as you sit down", though some say it "looks more exciting than it tastes"; P.S. "the outdoor patio is popular when the weather warms up."

Sushi-Ko *Japanese*

| 24 | 16 | 19 | $39 |

Glover Park | 2309 Wisconsin Ave. NW (south of Calvert St.) | 202-333-4187 | www.sushiko.us

"Burgundy and sushi – magic in your mouth" is the maxim at this Glover Park Japanese that brings "fine European wines" and raw-fish creations "together on the same page"; they "play with foods" here, so besides its "outstanding" "sushi with attitude", there are "creative" little fusion dishes that produce a "taste-bud orgy"; however, a few eaters are "not thrilled", and opinions vary about the decor ("minimalist" vs "airport cafeteria"); N.B. look for a more spacious Chevy Chase outpost in summer 2007.

	FOOD	DECOR	SERVICE	COST

Sushi Sushi *Japanese* | 19 | 12 | 18 | $24

Cleveland Park | 3714 Macomb St. NW (Wisconsin Ave.) | 202-686-2015
"Forget the few [entree] offerings from the kitchen and concentrate" instead on the "simple sushi at its best" from this "storefront shop" in Cleveland Park that's "not the most glamorous" spot, but is "reasonably priced" and "kid-friendly"; though service may be "slow, slow", there "are never any lines."

☑ Sushi Taro ☒ *Japanese* | 25 | 18 | 20 | $35

Dupont Circle | 1503 17th St. NW (P St.) | 202-462-8999 |
www.sushitaro.com
"Follow the Japanese diplomats" and "busloads of businessmen" to this "delightful" Duponter revered for an "extensive choice of non-Americanized" dishes, "assuredly fresh sushi", "superb" sashimi and "equally delicious" cooked items; there's a "very lively scene" at the bar, but you can opt for more peaceful "traditional" "floor seating on tatami mats" as well – "who knew a walk-up restaurant over a CVS could be so Zen-like?"; P.S "come early" to avoid "waiting outside for a while."

Sweet Basil *Thai* | 22 | 16 | 21 | $31

Bethesda | 4910 Fairmont Ave. (bet. Norfolk Ave. & Old Georgetown Rd.), MD | 301-657-7997 | www.sweetbasilland.com
You'll "love anything in the red or green curry" at this Bethesda "family favorite" where "arty" Asian fusion cuisine is a complement to "a tempting array of traditional Thai standards" that are "always good and sometimes sparkling"; even the "drab setting" (albeit one with outdoor seating) doesn't diminish from sweet "service that goes out of its way to please."

Sweet Ginger *Pan-Asian* | ▽ 24 | 19 | 22 | $29

Vienna | Danor Plaza | 120B Branch Rd. SE (Maple Ave.), VA | 703-319-3922
This "tiny jewel" glowing in a Vienna shopping strip offers "wonderful Asian fare and sushi" amid "sophisticated decor" that includes hand-painted lacquered tables, bamboo accents and a soothing water sculpture; there's an "excellent use of spices, flavorings and mixtures" in the "tasty Thai, Vietnamese and curries", and local loyalists who swear they serve the "best spicy tuna rolls in the area" proclaim "yes, Virginia, there *is* decent sushi in the suburbs!"

Sweetwater Tavern *Southwestern* | 22 | 19 | 21 | $28

Merrifield | 3066 Gatehouse Plaza (bet. Gallows Rd. & Rte. 50), VA | 703-645-8100
Centreville | 14250 Sweetwater Ln. (Multiplex Dr.), VA | 703-449-1100
Sterling | 45980 Waterview Plaza (bet. Loudon Tech Dr. & Rte. 7), VA | 571-434-6500
www.greatamericanrestaurants.com
"Great for after-work drinks as well as family dining", these "cavernous", "noisy" Northern Virginia brewpubs bring a Southwest slant to "amazing" pork chops, "yummy" lobster bisque and a "heavenly" "flourless chocolate waffle" – though it's the "little buns provided be-

fore dinner that may steal the show"; there are "no reservations" taken so avoid "unbearable waits" that can spoil the "overall experience" by "going at off-hours" or "learning to play the call-ahead game."

Tabaq Bistro *Mediterranean* | 19 | 24 | 16 | $35 |

U Street Corridor | 1336 U St. NW (bet. 13th & 14th Sts.) | 202-265-0965 | www.tabaqdc.com

Enjoy "incredible sunsets" and "breathtaking" "views of the city at night" atop this "trendy" "four-story townhouse" on U Street that sports an "amazing" retractable glass-enclosed roof deck and a recently redone basement lounge; the "tasty" contemporary Mediterranean tapas, brought to table by a "knowledgeable staff", may not quite live up to the atmosphere, but most focus on those unobstructed sights of the Monument that make up for any failings.

⊠ Tabard Inn *American* | 23 | 23 | 21 | $41 |

Dupont Circle | Hotel Tabard Inn | 1739 N St. NW (bet. 17th & 18th Sts.) | 202-331-8528 | www.tabardinn.com

Just off Dupont Circle is "one of the most adorable places for brunch" (don't miss the "homemade doughnuts") or for a "romantic" wintertime "fireside dinner" of "consistent yet adventurous" New American fare enhanced by some "unusual accessible wines"; indeed, any meal served by the "friendly staff" in the "lovely" courtyard of this "funky" hotel "hideaway" makes Washington and its "passionless policy wonks" "seem a continent away", so who cares if it's a bit "frayed on the edges"?

Taberna del Alabardero ⊠ *Spanish* | 24 | 24 | 23 | $59 |

World Bank | 1776 I St. NW (18th St.) | 202-429-2200 | www.alabardero.com

You'll "feel like you're blocks from the Puerta del Sol, rather than the White House" at this "sumptuously decorated" bastion of "old-world Madrid" near the World Bank, where the "excellent", "authentic" blend of "modern cuisine with Spanish tradition" means there are even some "Ferran Adrià–like" items (i.e. frozen olive oil) to try; "dress well" and experience "wonderfully civilized" cosseting that makes "special occasions" *"muy romantico"*, or for a "far less expensive evening out", try the bar's half-price happy-hour tapas.

Tachibana *Japanese* | 24 | 14 | 20 | $35 |

McLean | 6715 Lowell Ave. (Emerson Ave.), VA | 703-847-1771 | www.tachibana.us

"Sit at the bar for special treats" from the "super-friendly" chefs at this "cozy" McLean "favorite" "where lovers of traditional sushi have gathered" "for over a generation"; an "experienced staff turns out good – if unexciting – raw fish and cooked Japanese standards", but focus on the "huge portions" rather than the "frozen-in-the-'60s" decor.

Taipei Tokyo *Chinese/Japanese* | 18 | 9 | 13 | $16 |

Rockville | 11510 Rockville Pike (Nicholson Ln.), MD | 301-881-8388
Rockville | Fallsgrove Village Shopping Ctr. | 14921D Shady Grove Rd. (bet. Blackwell Rd. & Fallsgrove Blvd.), MD | 301-738-8813

(continued)

Taipei Tokyo

Rockville | 1596 Rockville Pike (Congressional Ln.), MD | 301-881-8533

"When you want a fast Asian meal and can't make up your mind", nothing beats this Maryland trio's "excellent quality for the price"; the "cafeteria-style" Chinese and Japanese fare is "cheap and tasty" (especially the "excellent noodle soups") and "fits the bill nicely when you need a simple wasabi wake-up", but with "minimal service" and "bad"-to-"modest" decor, "depending on location", you may want to consider carryout.

Tako Grill *Japanese*

24 | 16 | 20 | $32

Bethesda | 7756 Wisconsin Ave. (Cheltenham Dr.), MD | 301-652-7030 | www.takogrill.com

At this "friendly" Bethesda Japanese set in a "barn of a place on Wisconsin Avenue", you'll find "first-rate sushi", "terrific" "consistent" grilled items and a much "greater variety of dishes than you usually see"; a "sleek bar adds a hip" slant to a space otherwise "short on decor", and the "amazing choice of sakes" keeps it "loud."

Tallula *American*

22 | 23 | 22 | $38

Arlington | 2761 Washington Blvd. (Pershing Dr.), VA | 703-778-5051 | www.tallularestaurant.com

Find "delicious comfort food for the upwardly mobile" at this Clarendon New American that caters to Arlington's "younger crowd" with "inventive" casual fare in its gastropub, Eat Bar (serving nearly 60 wines by the glass), or in a "swanky" dining room; so many patrons like "tasting a bunch of things without breaking the bank or the diet" that it's often "jam-packed"; N.B. an in-house retail shop carries the hundreds of vinos available in the restaurant.

Tandoori Nights *Indian*

22 | 23 | 22 | $27

Gaithersburg | 106 Market St. (Kentlands Blvd.), MD | 301-947-4007
Arlington | 2800 Clarendon Blvd. (Fairfax Dr.), VA | 703-248-8333
www.tandoorinights.com

Known for its "beautiful" "polished decor" and "romantic" ambiance, this "standout" in the Kentlands complex in Gaithersburg serves "eclectic" modern Indian that's "easy on Americans", notably its vindaloo and namesake clay oven dishes; even if the food is "not 100 percent authentic", its setting and service are "always crowd-pleasing"; N.B. an equally decorative branch, with a buzzing lounge, opened post-Survey in Arlington's Clarendon corridor.

Tapatinis ●🗷Ⓜ *Mediterranean*

16 | 19 | 16 | $23

Capitol Hill | 711 Eighth St. SE (G St.) | 202-546-8272 | www.tapatinis.com

Attracting "hipsters new to the neighborhood" and "after-work" "Hill staffers" to a "really cute" Barracks Row location near the Capitol, this Mediterranean eatery features "simple", "tasty" tapas, a "huge menu of totally delish martinis" and "walls that pulsate with color by the minute"; there are "knock-your-socks-off drink specials" every night, leading to "noisy", "crowded" conditions, but the "very hospitable" staff and "fun" mood compensate.

Tapeo *Spanish*

- | - | - | M

Arlington | Pentagon Row | 1301 S. Joyce St. (Army Navy Dr.), VA | 703-416-6432 | www.tapeovirginia.com

A Latin sibling of the nearby Ristorante Murali, this Pentagon Row entry offers small-plates dining in chic surroundings; an extensive menu of Spanish tapas, along with hearty entrees, is served in a variety of settings: a tony bar, an outdoor patio and a trim tile-floored dining room accented by tomato-red seats.

Taqueria El Charrito Caminante ⊅ *Salvadoran*

▽ 22 | 4 | 16 | $9

Arlington | 2710A Washington Blvd. (N. Pershing Dr.), VA | 703-351-1177

"You'll wonder how they can produce something so fresh for so cheap" at this Salvadoran storefront "walk-up counter" in Arlington that gives locals a chance to sample "authentic" versions of "Central American and Mexican favorites" such as "goat meat (charrito) tacos, pupusas and burritos"; there's sometimes "a bit of a wait", but the "family that runs the business is extremely nice."

Taqueria el Poblano *Mexican*

20 | 15 | 19 | $20

Alexandria | 2400B Mt. Vernon Ave. (Oxford Ave.), VA | 703-548-8226

Arlington | 2503A N. Harrison St. (Lee Hwy.), VA | 703-237-8250 www.taqueriapoblano.com

Ask for the "homemade habanero sauce, it's a great addition" to the "California Baha-style" Mexican dishes served at this colorful pair in Alexandria and Arlington; "fabulous" tacos that come in fish, duck and veggie varieties "are a change" from the usual (both locations also feature a popular Sunday brunch), plus "some of the nicest people" offer "friendly" service in "noisy", "kid-friendly" quarters; N.B. the Alexandria branch is closed on Tuesdays.

Taqueria Tres Reyes *Mexican*

- | - | - | I

Riverdale | 5403 Kenilworth Ave. (Kennedy St.), MD | 301-779-6060

This pink-and-white counter-service taqueria is "part of Mexico" swear its admirers, leading them to assert it "just happens to be" located in Riverdale, MD; "English isn't spoken much", but the "real" south-of-the-border fare – tacos filled with goat, beef, pork or tongue and "great *menudo*" (tripe soup that supposedly cures hangovers) – speaks for itself.

Tara Thai *Thai*

20 | 19 | 18 | $25

Bethesda | 4828 Bethesda Ave. (bet. Arlington Rd. & Woodmont Ave.), MD | 301-657-0488

Gaithersburg | 9811 Washingtonian Blvd. (Sam Eig Hwy.), MD | 301-947-8330

Rockville | Montrose Crossing | 12071 Rockville Pike (Montrose Rd.), MD | 301-231-9899

Arlington | 4001 Fairfax Dr. (bet. Quincy & Randolph Sts.), VA | 703-908-4999

Falls Church | 7501E Leesburg Pike (Pimmit Dr.), VA | 703-506-9788

(continued)

Tara Thai

Vienna | 226 Maple Ave. W. (bet. Lawyers Rd. & Nutley St.), VA | 703-255-2467

Fans say "you can always count on" "reasonably priced", "tasty" Thai at this "mini-chain" where the emphasis on seafood carries through to "underwater"-themed decor that makes sitting at the "tight, close colorful tables" feel "a bit like dining in a fish tank"; though it tries "to please every taste", critics carp about "tara-ble" fare – "somewhat sanitized for American palates" – and "rushed" service.

NEW Taste of Burma *Burmese*

| – | – | – | I |

Sterling | Countryside Shopping Ctr. | 126 Edds Ln. (Cromwell Rd.), VA | 703-444-8510 | www.atasteofburma.com

Handmade tapestries adorn the walls of this shopping-center Burmese in Sterling that serves its rarely found cuisine – including classic rice-noodle dishes and distinctively flavored curries – in a simple, serene setting; the inexpensive menu features over 100 items (including dozens of vegetarian choices) that may just entice adventure-seekers to return again and again.

Taste of Jerusaleum *Mideastern*

| – | – | – | M |

Silver Spring | 8123 Georgia Ave. (Sligo Ave.), MD | 301-495-3067

The Hawa family channels its Palestinian heritage into this Silver Spring storefront via pretty, decorative stained glass and Middle Eastern menu classics; here, familiar fare is given distinctive touches in dishes such as the housemade dip made from za'atar (dried thyme), lemon, olive oil and sesame seed.

Taste of Morocco *Moroccan*

| 20 | 19 | 17 | $30 |

Silver Spring | City Place Mall | 8661 Colesville Rd. (Fenton St.), MD | 301-588-4003 | www.tasteofmorocco.net
Arlington | 3211 N. Washington Blvd. (Wilson Blvd.), VA | 703-527-7468

This "enormously popular" Silver Spring Moroccan (and its long-time Arlington sibling) "transports" guests "from an aging urban mall to a North African salon" with "amazing" tagines and "rich" chicken b'steeya served in an "elegant and exotic environment" – "all that and belly dancers too!"; the somewhat "tired" Arlington original offers a homier experience where a "small dining space belies big taste", but service at both can be "poor."

Taste of Saigon *Vietnamese*

| 22 | 16 | 20 | $27 |

Rockville | 410 Hungerford Dr. (Beall Ave.), MD | 301-424-7222
McLean | 8201 Greensboro Dr. (International Dr.), VA | 703-790-0700
www.tasteofsaigon.com

Try "anything with the black pepper sauce" at these family-owned "commendable Vietnamese" in Rockville and Tysons Corner, and "you'll lick the plate" clean, but "just about everything else" on this "enormous" menu is also "divine" and a "steal" to boot; "enthusiastic servers" and "wonderful" outdoor patios ("so well landscaped you might not notice the parking lot") help overcome their "bland suburban settings."

	FOOD	DECOR	SERVICE	COST

NEW Tavern on the Lake *American* | - | - | - | M |

Reston | Lake Anne Village Ctr. | 1617 Washington Plaza N.
(North Shore Dr.), VA | 703-471-0121 | www.tavernonthelake.com
At this casual American in Reston, trendy martinis and globally inspired small plates are offered waterside at awning-shaded tables,
in a contemporary lounge or at a rock-walled bar; more substantial
Eclectic fare (including a kids' menu) is served in the mural-walled
dining room, and there's live music Thursday–Saturday.

Tavira *Portuguese* | 21 | 18 | 23 | $46 |

Chevy Chase | Chevy Chase Bank Bldg. | 8401 Connecticut Ave.
(Chevy Chase Lake Dr.), MD | 301-652-8684 | www.tavirarestaurant.com
"Bad location, wonderful restaurant" say "older folks" who dote on
this "hard-to-find" "find" – a "gourmet" Portuguese in a Chevy
Chase office building basement with an unfortunate "Holiday Inn"–
like setting; "if it was located anywhere else it would be packed", but
instead there's "no problem parking or getting a table" at this "un-
derutilized" "classic" offering "quiet" "intimacy", "highly attentive
service" and "sumptuous" Mediterranean dishes.

Teaism *Tearoom* | 19 | 16 | 15 | $16 |

Penn Quarter | 400 Eighth St. NW (D St.) | 202-638-6010
Dupont Circle | 2009 R St. NW (Connecticut Ave.) |
202-667-3827
Golden Triangle | 800 Connecticut Ave. NW (H St.) |
202-835-2233 🛎
www.teaism.com
These very "un-DC" "serve-yourself" tearooms dotting Downtown
and Dupont offer a "quick and cheap bite without sacrificing taste
and health" in Asian-inspired surroundings that can be "serene" or
"bustling" depending on the time of day; "dishes as good as they are
simple" range from "guilt-inducing to Zen lightness", and the "variety of food" "makes up for the long line at the counter during rush
hours"; N.B. the Golden Triangle branch is open on weekdays only.

Teatro Goldoni 🛎 *Italian* | 23 | 22 | 22 | $56 |

Golden Triangle | 1909 K St. NW (bet. 19th & 20th Sts.) | 202-955-9494 |
www.teatrogoldoni.com
"Dramatic Fellini-esque decor" sets the stage for the "incredibly
rich" fare at this "elegantly decadant" Golden Triangle Italian where
the "chef's table tasting menu will blow you away" and you'll swear
by the "best lobster risotto in the city"; it's "worth the money if
you're entertaining" or celebrating a "special occasion", since you'll
"feel the trendiness when you walk in the door" and be doted on by
service that's a "tad overbearing"; P.S. "the $12.50 lunch at the bar
is an outstanding value."

Ted's Montana Grill *American* | 18 | 18 | 18 | $27 |

Alexandria | Alexandria-Hoffman | 2451 Eisenhower Ave. (Swamp Fox Rd.),
VA | 703-960-0500
Arlington | 2200 Crystal Dr. (bet. 20th & 23rd Sts.), VA | 703-416-8337
Arlington | Ballston Pt. | 4300 Wilson Blvd. (Rte. 120), VA | 703-741-0661

FOOD | DECOR | SERVICE | COST

(continued)

Ted's Montana Grill

NEW **Sterling** | Market Plaza | 46300 Cranston St. (Whitefield Pl.), VA | 703-444-8611

www.tedsmontanagrill.com

"Big sky meets big taste" at "Ted Turner's restaurants" where nearly "a whole page of burger options" "tops" a "broad" American menu including signature buffalo dishes that get mixed reviews (from "tough and tasteless" to "outstanding"); their "rustic" "Old West" settings are "great for groups" and have a "family-friendly" vibe, but cowboys cringe over decor that "screams chain" and a "bubbly twentysomething staff" that "tries too hard."

Temel *Mediterranean/Turkish*

▽ 21 | 19 | 19 | $30

Fairfax | 3232 Old Pickett Rd. (Old Lee Hwy.), VA | 703-352-5477 | www.temelrestaurant.com

It's "worth seeking out" this "unexpectedly good" Mediterranean-Turkish restaurant "hidden in a tiny" Fairfax strip mall for its "nice menu selections", including "yummy cigars" (phyllo-wrapped deep-fried pastries), "yogurt-based dishes" and "doner kebabs that rival the best"; "excellent value" and a relaxing atmosphere make it a "family favorite" as well.

Temperance Hall *American*

- | - | - | M

Petworth | 3634A Georgia Ave. NW (Princeton Pl.) | 202-722-7669 | www.temperancehalldc.com

This '20s speakeasy–themed American restaurant and bar in the rapidly gentrifying Petworth neighborhood has an eclectic, old-timey feel (antique chandeliers, worn wooden booths) well-calibrated to the hipsters and young professionals already knocking back its rye whiskey Manhattans and amusing riffs on bar fare (e.g. sloppy joe sliders); an expanded comfort-food menu, brunch service and outdoor patio add to its appeal.

Tempo *French/Italian*

22 | 16 | 20 | $34

Alexandria | 4231 Duke St. (Gordon St.), VA | 703-370-7900 | www.temporestaurant.com

The "eclectic menu" of French and Northern Italian dishes emphasizing "excellent fish" plays well with Alexandria's "over-65 crowd", a demographic that flocks to this "converted gas station" turned "New York supper club" run by a couple that "cares"; "if you can get past the lack of atmosphere" and take advantage of the weekly special (check their Web site), you'll find it "totally reliable."

☑ TenPenh ☒ *Pan-Asian*

24 | 24 | 23 | $48

Downtown | 1001 Pennsylvania Ave. NW (10th St.) | 202-393-4500 | www.tenpenh.com

"Everyone looks beautiful" at this Downtowner and "the food is just as pretty": a "killer menu of tongue-tingling favorites" from chef Jeff Tunks "pushes the Pan-Asian envelope without straying into truly rebellious territory", and the "dramatic, colorful atmosphere" is as "stylish" as its crowd; even though pensive types pout it "gets really loud" and the "tables are too close together", seasoned vets say the "biggest problem will be getting past the appetizers" – they're the "winners."

T.H.A.I. *Thai*   21 | 19 | 20 | $25

Arlington | Village at Shirlington | 4029 28th St. S. (Randolph St.), VA | 703-931-3203 | www.thaiinshirlington.com

Loyalists find that the initials of this Thai in the Village at Shirlington clearly stand for "this has all ingredients" – from "excellent" food to "super-fast preparation" to a "lovely staff" to decor that's "not your everyday cookie-cutter" variety (there's a "nice outdoor patio" too); even those who insist there's "better elsewhere" admit the 'big bowl' lunch specials are "one of the best deals" around.

Thai at Silver Spring *Thai*   ▽ 19 | 17 | 17 | $21

Silver Spring | 921E Ellsworth Dr. (Fenton St.), MD | 301-650-0666 | www.thaiatsilverspring.com

A "welcome" alternative in redeveloped Downtown Silver Spring, this "charming" Thai offers "something a little exotic" in its "tasty fare" "served with a smile"; it "manages an elegant ambiance" in what is "essentially an open-air mall", but critics contend it could use "more helping hands" during busy hours and admit "with the competition" in this cuisine category, it "doesn't stand out."

Thai Basil *Thai*   ▽ 22 | 12 | 20 | $21

Chantilly | 14511P Lee Jackson Memorial Hwy. (Airline Pkwy.), VA | 703-631-8277 | www.thaibasilchantilly.com

"Don't be put off" by the "no-frills" "industrial park location" of "one of the best Thais in Northern Virginia", since this Chantilly Asian, just south of Dulles Airport, is the "perfect spot for a before- or after-flight" meal; the majority finds the "most authentic" signature noodles and curries in a "soothing" atmosphere; N.B. chef-owner (and cookbook author) Nongkran Daks offers cooking and catering classes at the restaurant.

Thai Chili *Thai*   ▽ 20 | 16 | 18 | $24

Chinatown | Gallery Pl. | 701 Seventh St. NW (bet. F & H Sts.) | 202-393-2905

Conveniently located near the movie entrance in Chinatown's Gallery Place, this "really friendly" and "pretty" Thai "satisfies cravings" for traditional dishes and "creative" options as well as mai tais that are "especially delicious"; plus, nearby homebodies and office workers "love that they deliver"; P.S. you can get a "discount when you show your movie ticket."

Thai Farm *Thai*   ▽ 19 | 21 | 21 | $22

Rockville | 800 King Farm Blvd. (Redland Blvd.), MD | 301-258-8829 | www.thaifarmrestaurant.com

Crops no longer grow in Rockville's King Farm town center and housing complex, but this "solid" family Thai harvests local support with "beautiful murals" of its native farmland and "friendly" hospitality; its "menu allows for hundreds of combinations of meat, seafood and vegetarian dishes", making it just the place for "quiet get-togethers" with friends.

	FOOD	DECOR	SERVICE	COST

Thaiphoon *Thai* | 20 | 16 | 17 | $24 |

Dupont Circle | 2011 S St. NW (20th St.) | 202-667-3505
Arlington | Pentagon Row | 1301 S. Joyce St. (Army Navy Dr.), VA | 703-413-8200
www.thaiphoon.com

"Brushed steel, swank lighting" and huge "froufrou" "bargain" cocktails set the mood for the "lively young crowd" that "squeezes into the sardine can of a dining room" at this "trendy" Dupont Thai where the "waits on weekends can be a drag"; here, and at a "chic" Pentagon Row counterpart, the "consistently good" fare is "easy on the wallet", but a few who find it "so Americanized that it tastes like Chinese takeout" suggest "asking them to up the heat if you like spicy."

☑ Thai Square *Thai* | 26 | 10 | 18 | $22 |

Arlington | 3217 Columbia Pike (S. Highland St.), VA | 703-685-7040

"Hot means hot for a change" at this "authentic" Arlington "hole-in-the-wall" "where Thais go for Thai food"; it "doesn't put on airs, decorwise" – the "space is cramped" and service can be "surly" – but "in terms of pricing and quality" "no other place can match" the "exciting blend of texture and flavors" in the "simply wonderful" dishes.

Thai Tanic *Thai* | 19 | 13 | 18 | $22 |

Logan Circle | 1326A 14th St. NW (bet. N St. & Rhode Island Ave.) | 202-588-1795 | www.thaitanic.net

"No sinking feelings here, the food is as buoyant as ever" say locals of this "no-frills" place near Logan Circle with a "tragically unhip name" offering "consistently good" Thai "without a wait", along with a "menu of lush cocktails"; "unusual funky decor" that "appears to have been decorated by a glitter-happy teenybopper" garners groans, but there's no doubting this ship "soothes cravings without taking a large chunk from the wallet" (plus there's "fast" take-out delivery).

Thyme Square *American* | 16 | 15 | 15 | $32 |

Bethesda | 4735 Bethesda Ave. (Woodmont Ave.), MD | 301-657-9077 | www.thymesquarecafe.com

Vegetarians can be "happy" at this Bethesda staple with a "healthy flair" (nothing fried) to its hippie-fied, "sometimes weird" New American menu that also offers enough "fine choices" for meat and seafood eaters plus "favorite" pizzas from a wood-burning oven; the "execution varies widely" and the "very slow" service is "dismal", but it's still good for a bite "before or after taking in a nearby movie."

Tiffin *Indian* | ▽ 21 | 13 | 19 | $23 |

Takoma Park | 1341 University Blvd. (14th Ave.), MD | 301-434-9200 | www.tiffinrestaurant.com

Signature Kashmiri *rogan josh,* or lamb curry, headlines a "nice if narrow array" of "beautifully prepared" dishes served in Takoma Park's "best-kept secret", this modest North Indian that "proves you don't have to spend a lot of money for great food"; "bland" "Holiday Inn breakfast-room" decor won't impress, but that "delicious bread" and tandoori chicken brings 'em back "time and again."

Timpano Chophouse *Italian/Steak* | 18 | 19 | 18 | $36 |

Rockville | 12021 Rockville Pike (Montrose Rd.), MD | 301-881-6939 | www.timpanochophouse.net

"Young professionals (and some not so young) make the scene" at this "dimly lit", "blast-to-the-past" Rockville Italian that "defies its White Flint strip-mall" surrounds with a "barnlike", "loud" space, "breezy" vibe and "live jazz" most nights; they've got "some of the best veal you'll find anywhere", not to mention roasted mussels, but skeptics quip that the "overpriced" "à la carte menu" makes this "the most expensive pasta-from-a-box in town."

Tivoli Ⓢ *Italian* | 22 | 17 | 22 | $40 |

Rosslyn | 1700 N. Moore St. (Wilson Blvd.), VA | 703-524-8900 | www.tivolirestaurant.com

This "enclave of hospitality in the cold concrete canyons of Rosslyn" may be the "quintessential prom date" old-schooler ("you expect to see an orchestra start playing"), but it's also quite the "bargain for high-end" Northern Italian fare, with a three-course pre-theater menu for under 25 bucks; critics contend it "needs a makeover", but others agree it's "excellent for groups, special occasions" or a business lunch.

Tonic *American* | 18 | 18 | 17 | $24 |

Mt. Pleasant | 3155 Mt. Pleasant St. NW (bet. Kenyon St. & Kilbourne Pl.) | 202-296-0211

Tonic at Quigley's Pharmacy *American*

NEW Foggy Bottom | Quigley's Pharmacy | 2036 G St. NW (bet. 20th & 21st Sts.) | 202-296-0211
www.tonicrestaurant.com

With a "friendly staff" and "familiar faces" punctuating the "casual atmosphere", the downstairs bar of this American comfort-food haven is "the closest thing to *Cheers* in Mt. Pleasant"; head upstairs for a "bright" yellow dining space that's a "sunny refuge even on the grayest DC day", but since most say "flipping a mean hamburger and pouring a fresh cold beer is what it does best", you may want to "stick with the basics"; N.B. an ambitious sibling opened post-Survey in Foggy Bottom's former Quigley's Pharmacy space.

Tono Sushi *Japanese* | 21 | 14 | 19 | $26 |

Woodley Park | 2605 Connecticut Ave. NW (Calvert St.) | 202-332-7300 | www.tonosushi.com

"Get your sushi craving filled at a reasonable price" at this "unassuming" Woodley Park Japanese with a happy-hour $1-per-piece "bargain" that will "put a smile on your face"; it may be "unremarkable" overall, but "friendly" waiters take you through a "strong" menu that also includes Vietnamese, Thai and Chinese selections, and outdoor tables allow you to escape the "lack of atmosphere" inside.

Tony & Joe's Seafood Place *Seafood* | 14 | 16 | 15 | $37 |

Georgetown | Washington Harbour | 3000 K St. NW (30th St.) | 202-944-4545 | www.tonyandjoes.com

You "pay for the view" at this Washington Harbour "hangout" where the "after-work yuppie crowd lets loose" at a "fun", "crowded" "bar on the water"; indoors or out, Maryland-style crab cakes and "fresh" fish satisfy some, but the "unimpressed" imply "all it has going for it is the location" since the fare "makes Mrs. Paul's sound good."

Tony Cheng's *Chinese*
20	13	18	$26

Chinatown | 619 H St. NW (bet. 6th & 7th Sts.) | 202-371-8669
This "split-personality" "Chinatown fixture" serves "refined" seafood and "solid" dim sum ("little mouthfuls of joy") upstairs, while below, the "Mongolian wok" barbecue accompanied by the chef's "floor show" is "best enjoyed in a large" family group; on either level, "cheap eats" "get the job done", but you'll have to ignore the "massive" amounts of tourists, "perfunctory" service and "past-its-prime" decor.

Topaz Bar *Pan-Asian*
▽ 19	23	20	$28

Dupont Circle | Topaz Hotel | 1733 N St. NW (bet. 17th & 18th Sts.) | 202-393-3000 | www.topazhotel.com
"More of a hotel lounge than a restaurant", this "ultrahip, candlelit" Dupont Circle bar with "lounging couches and cozy corners" offers "inventive cocktails" and Asian-inspired small plates with "unusual touches" to a "lively after-work crowd"; it's "a great place to meet friends", but teetotalers warn "beware the drinks" for two reasons: "they don't skimp on liquor" and "New York–priced martinis" will "break your piggy bank."

☑ Tosca ☒ *Italian*
26	23	25	$59

Penn Quarter | 1112 F St. NW (bet. 11th & 12th Sts.) | 202-367-1990 | www.toscadc.com
Celebrated for "inventive modern interpretations of Northern Italian", this "understated and elegant" Penn Quarterite is set in a "serene, monochromatic" space that's usually "buzzing with 'heavy hitters'"; it "always lives up" to "expectations of the highest quality in food and service" with "amazing dishes and beautiful presentations", but it can be a "somewhat expensive date" unless you opt for the "absolute steal" $35 pre-theater three-course dinner.

Tragara *Italian*
22	19	20	$53

Bethesda | 4935 Cordell Ave. (bet. Norfolk Ave. & Old Georgetown Rd.), MD | 301-951-4935 | www.tragara.com
If you "order right, you'll be delighted" at this "old-world" Bethesda Northern Italian where some dishes – notably pasta with lobster and osso buco – are "truly delicious" and others strike some as "boring and old hat"; no matter what you order, it's "served with style" in a "sedate, quiet" atmosphere suited to "an intimate dinner or private discussion"; P.S. they can do "lovely" catered "parties upstairs."

Tryst ● *Coffeehouse*
18	21	16	$17

Adams Morgan | 2459 18th St. NW (bet. Belmont & Columbia Rds.) | 202-232-5500 | www.trystdc.com
Trysters trot to this "eclectic, chill" Adams Morgan cafe with free WiFi, "1950s couches" and a "hazy ambiance" that's a "slightly indie" "place to meet and greet" "without the pretension"; by day, it's a "good place to study" or work say "students, the self-employed

and the unemployed armed with laptops" who nosh on sandwiches and drink coffee from "cups that are more like bowls", but at night it turns into a "fun bar"; just don't expect stellar service from the "distracted" staff – and "good luck getting a seat."

Tuscarora Mill *American* | 23 | 21 | 22 | $43 |

Leesburg | Market Station | 203 Harrison St. SE (Loudoun St.), VA | 703-771-9300 | www.tuskies.com

You can "dress up for a special occasion" in a dining room with historic "character" or "wear jeans and enjoy a beer" and burger in the bar at this "Leesburg classic" that offers "first-rate American food and service" and an "excellent choice of beers and wines by the glass" "no matter where you sit"; but it's such a "popular" destination that some folks get tired of "waiting" and will "fight you over their place in line for the first-come, first-served areas."

Tutto Bene *Italian* | 18 | 13 | 17 | $27 |

Arlington | 501 N. Randolph St. (N. Glebe Rd.), VA | 703-522-1005 | www.tuttobeneitalian.com

"Marble busts and other dated flourishes adorn this frozen-in-time" (1970s) eatery in Arlington's Ballston area that serves "satisfying" "South American–style Italian" (the red-sauce kind) at "accommodating prices"; cognoscenti consider the weekend "Bolivian lunches with great *salteñas* [meat-filled pastry] and soups" a "treat" and recommend returning on "live opera" or tango dancing nights, but a few sour sorts find a "tired menu and staff to match."

☑ 2941 Restaurant *American* | 27 | 28 | 25 | $77 |

Falls Church | 2941 Fairview Park Dr. (Arlington Blvd.), VA | 703-270-1500 | www.2941.com

"Manhattan meets the Beltway in this surprisingly sophisticated suburban enclave" set in a Falls Church office park, where "wonderful" French-inflected New American is served in "gorgeous" tall-windowed dining rooms overlooking koi ponds and waterfalls; chef-owner Jonathan Krinn "architects flavors masterfully", pairs them "excellently" with wines and has them served by a "gracious, pampering" staff; but with all those "generous" end-of-meal goodies (chocolates, cotton candy), you'll wonder "does 2941 refer to the bill or the calories from the extra desserts?"

☑ 2 Amys *Pizza* | 25 | 15 | 18 | $23 |

Cleveland Park | 3715 Macomb St. NW (Wisconsin Ave.) | 202-885-5700 | www.2amyspizza.com

At this Cleveland Park "hot spot", "divine wood-fired pizza" ("the only ones in town that come close to the true Italian" variety), "inspired" antipasto, "wonderful modestly priced wine" and "perhaps a too child-friendly" vibe beget "long waits" and a "noisy" "stroller-set" atmosphere at prime time; its black-and-white-tile decor is "a little spartan, as befits a Neapolitan pizzeria" – but this one is certified by the Italian pie-makers association and the pedigree shows in the "amazing" output; N.B. an upstairs dining room (which is not stroller accessible) is slated to open in summer 2007.

	FOOD	DECOR	SERVICE	COST

Two Quail *American*

	17	21	19	$44

Capitol Hill | 320 Massachusetts Ave. NE (bet. 3rd & 4th Sts.) | 202-543-8030 | www.twoquail.com

For some of the "most romantic dining to be found in the city", sentimentalists "ask for the curtained-off" bay-window table of this "quirky" Capitol Hill Traditional American comprised of three townhouses "crowded" with as much "chintzy" "froufrou" as "your Aunt Mary's over-decorated English living room"; "good" if sometimes "tired" fare "tries hard to please and mostly succeeds", but modernists maintain "the days are long past when it was a charmer" and beg that the "all-Liza-all-the-time playing on the speakers" be turned down "two notches."

Udupi Palace *Indian/Vegetarian*

	23	10	17	$18

Takoma Park | 1329 University Blvd. E. (New Hampshire Ave.), MD | 301-434-1531 | www.udupipalace.com

"If you can get over the strip-mall ambiance", you'll find the menu at this "friendly" Takoma Park South Indian vegetarian is "a breath of fresh air" – from the "light" dosas (filled pancakes) "accompanied by creative condiments" to the "authentic", "unique" preparations in an "ever-changing buffet"; but brace yourself for "highly spiced", "butter-rich cooking" – "the ghee flows like the waters of the Potomac."

Ugly Mug *Pub Food*

	17	11	16	$20

Capitol Hill | 723 Eighth St. SE (bet. G & I Sts.) | 202-547-8459 | www.uglymugdc.com

"It ain't pretty, that's for sure", but this "dive bar–esque" "Capitol Hill hangout" from the minds behind Matchbox lures locals with its mini-burgers, pizzas and other American fare that's "too good to be just pub food", plus "friendly bartenders" pouring a "beer selection that's just right" (24 on tap); with "tons of plasma TVs", "they're guaranteed to have your game on", so make it "the place" "to grab a casual bite before the Nats play."

Uncle Julio's *Tex-Mex*
(fka Rio Grande Cafe)

	19	16	17	$25

Bethesda | 4870 Bethesda Ave. (Arlington Rd.), MD | 301-656-2981
Gaithersburg | 231 Rio Blvd. (Washingtonian Blvd.), MD | 240-632-2150
Arlington | 4301 N. Fairfax Dr. (Glebe Rd.), VA | 703-528-3131
Fairfax | Fairfax Corner | 4251 Fairfax Corner Ave. (Monument Dr.), VA | 703-266-7760
Reston | Reston Town Ctr. | 1827 Library St. (New Dominion Pkwy.), VA | 703-904-0703
www.unclejulios.com

The "young crowd" flocks to this "festive", "friendly" Tex-Mex chain that's "still the best place for happy-hour drinks" ("start off with" a "killer" swirl) and "fabulous" tortilla chips, while families say "sí" to "sizzling" fajitas and "homemade" tortillas served up "fast" in a "faux cantina" setting that's "so loud you can bring your screaming kids and no one will mind"; only a few find the wait "ridiculous" and "just don't get" the appeal of "industrial portions" of "run-of-the-mill" fare.

Uni *Japanese*

20 | 15 | 19 | $29

Dupont Circle | 2122 P St. NW (bet. 21st & 22nd Sts.) | 202-833-8038

"New-school" chef-owner James Tan creates "interesting" "experiments in taste" – think "spicy crunchy crawfish" and other "fun fusion rolls" – at this "unassuming" second-story Japanese near Dupont Circle; habitués find the "hit-or-miss" dishes "worth the gamble", especially during the "$1-a-piece happy hour", while sake-seekers discover "lots to sample" among its "exhaustive selection."

NEW Urbana *French/Italian*

- | - | - | M

Dupont Circle | Hotel Palomar | 2121 P St. NW (bet. 21st & 2nd Sts.) | 202-956-6650 | www.urbanadc.com

At this latest entry from the Kimpton Hotel group (Firefly, Poste), backlit wine bottles, ornate sepia-toned detailing and low ceilings help to transform an underground space near Dupont Circle into a stylish, contemporary French-Italian eatery; patrons can also dine at a marble bar in front of a wood-burning pizza oven or enjoy a drink in the romantic, cavelike lounge; N.B. a new chef could mean menu changes are on the horizon.

Urban Bar-B-Que Company *BBQ*

24 | 12 | 19 | $16

Rockville | 2007 Chapman Ave. (Twinbrook Pkwy.), MD | 240-290-4827 | www.eataturban.com

Regulars rush to this "no-frills" "barbecue gold mine" in Rockville for "finger-licking-good" pulled pork and ribs with the perfect "compromise between wet and dry rubs", paired with "unique sides" like 'soul rolls' (BBQ egg rolls) and 'redneck fondue' (a three-cheese dip blended with chili); a "friendly, sassy staff" mans the counter at this former carryout that's added "retro-fun" seating but remains "a bit too crowded for lingering."

NEW Urban Burger Company *Hamburgers*

- | - | - | I

Rockville | Rockcreek Village Ctr. | 5566 Norbeck Rd. (Bauer Dr.), MD | 301-460-0050 | www.eataturban.com

The humble hamburger gets respect at this Rockville grill, an offshoot of Urban Bar-B-Que, where cooked-to-order patties can be accessorized with crunchy, spicy and cheesy toppings, and paired with salads, sodas and sides; the family-friendly, counter-service operation features a playroom for the kids and flat-screen TVs that show cartoons as well as sports.

U-topia ❶ *Eclectic*

16 | 20 | 17 | $29

U Street Corridor | 1418 U St. NW (bet. 14th & 15th Sts.) | 202-483-7669

While "the jazz is hot, the food is not" at this "funky" "U Street hideaway" where you can "unwind" to free live music nightly while nibbling "fine" but "less-than-stellar" Eclectic eats and sipping coffee drinks or vino from a "well-priced wine list"; just overlook the "pedestrian service" in favor of the "well-meaning staff", "vibrant" ambiance and "visual stimulation" that includes exposed-brick walls with "fabulous art everywhere"; P.S. the "brunch is awesome."

	FOOD	DECOR	SERVICE	COST

NEW Vapiano ◑ *Italian* — | - | - | - | I

Golden Triangle | 1800 M St. NW (18th St.) | 202-640-1868
Arlington | 4401 Wilson Blvd. (N. Glebe Rd.), VA | 703-528-3113
www.vapiano.com

This German-based, upscale Italian chain is hoping to score with hungry hockey fans, opening its first U.S. location right across from the Washington Capitals' practice facility in Arlington's Ballston area; chic decor elements make for a stylish setting in which to enjoy made-to-order salads, pizzas and pastas, while a similarly sleek Golden Triangle branch courts desk jockeys and happy-hour types; N.B. look for offshoots in Chinatown and Reston.

NEW Vaso's Kitchen *Greek* — | - | - | - | M

Alexandria | 1225 Powhatan St. (Bashford Ln.), VA |
703-548-2747

Set in the former Dixie Pig space, this quaint Alexandria eatery offers affordable Greek food that can be paired with wines from Italy and the homeland; its ebullient chef/co-owner Vasiliki Volioti has prettied up the dining room with curtains and fresh paint, but the neon BBQ sign outside is a protected landmark, so expect a menu that offers ribs as well as moussaka.

Vegetable Garden *Chinese/Vegetarian* — 19 | 11 | 18 | $18

Rockville | 11618 Rockville Pike (bet. Nicholson Ln. & Old Georgetown Rd.), MD | 301-468-9301 | www.thevegetablegarden.com

It "should have a beacon of light emanating from it" aver grateful vegetarians who think this "rare treat" "hidden in an unassuming" Rockville Pike strip mall should be honored for its "creative fake-meat dishes" that convincingly "interpret mainstream Chinese"; carnivores who frown on "efforts to make" "sawdust" "taste like meat" can still "earn brownie points with vegan visitors" – "they'll love" the "extensive menu covering everything veg", including "organic and macrobiotic choices."

Vegetate Ⓜ *American/Vegetarian* — ▽ 21 | 20 | 21 | $27

Mt. Vernon Square/New Convention Center | 1414 Ninth St. NW (bet. O & T Sts.) | 202-232-4585 | www.vegetatedc.com

Finally, "vegans have a place to go on an anniversary" thanks to this "hip" Convention Center–area arrival serving "refined" New American veg meals "so unique you forget they don't have meat"; a "swank" setting with "vibrant artwork" and "soothing electronica courtesy of owner Dominic Redd" (aka DJ Dredd) plays foil to "refreshing" concoctions ("ginger ale with real ginger") that now include organic wines, beers and cocktails; N.B. closed Mondays and Tuesdays.

Vermilion *American* — 20 | 21 | 20 | $36

Alexandria | 1120 King St. (bet. Fayette & Henry Sts.), VA | 703-684-9669 | www.vermilionrestaurant.com

Paint Old Town Alexandria "red-hot" at this "trendy spot" where the namesake color splashes the walls in a "dressed-up" dining room serving updated New American with "downtown tastes and suburban prices"; some say the "chichi" "downstairs bar is the place to be", however, with "swanky" red-velvet "benches and pillows" a plush backdrop to "wonderfully sweet mojitos", "specialty martinis" and "tasty" appetizers; N.B. new chef Anthony Chittum (ex Notti Bianche) came on board post-Survey.

Z Vidalia *American* 26 | 22 | 24 | $58

Golden Triangle | 1990 M St. NW (bet. 19th & 20th Sts.) | 202-659-1990 | www.vidaliadc.com

"It has its off nights, but when it's 'on'", this Golden Triangle "destination" "really delivers" via a "delicious, innovative" New American menu with "an upscale Southern touch"; the "ambrosial fare" is served by a "gracious" staff that provides "VIP treatment" and "excellent wine matches" in a "lovely" underground setting "made brighter" by a "beautiful remodeling"; there's also a "stylish bar" suitable for sampling small plates or one of the 40 "well-researched" vinos by the glass.

Village Bistro *Continental* 21 | 13 | 19 | $33

Arlington | Colonial Village | 1723 Wilson Blvd. (bet. Quinn & Rhodes Sts.), VA | 703-522-0284 | www.villagebistro.com

Some say it's "quaint", others "shabby", but this "nooklike bistro" "hidden among Arlington's high-rises" (near the Courthouse metro) spins out French-infused Continental cuisine that's "better than you might expect", with "surprisingly good seafood" and "superbly prepared dinner specials"; though the "inviting" "date place" may feel "cramped and crowded at peak" times with "the occasional cranky waiter", it's "nice for a pleasant lunch", when "you can walk in."

NEW Vintage 50 *American* - | - | - | M

Leesburg | 50 Catoctin Circle NE (E. Market St.), VA | 703-777-2169 | www.vintage50.com

At this glossy Leesburg addition, hopsheads can pair house-brewed beers with classic dishes or with seasonal New American small and large plates in a mahogany clad dining room that has a bistro feel; a well-stocked wine bar suits oenophiles just fine, while a 30-ft.-long banquette and an upper deck give the lounge some Big City cred.

Viridian *American* 20 | 24 | 18 | $41

Logan Circle | 1515 14th St. NW (Church St.) | 202-234-1400 | www.viridianrestaurant.com

A meal "in an art gallery" with "wonderful vegetables" is the "chic" concept behind this "fab" New American that's part of the "blossoming 14th Street culinary scene"; new chef Michael Hartzer (Ray's The Classics) has added many contemporary fish and meat dishes to a "refreshingly simple yet innovative" veg-friendly menu, and the soaring space features "floor-to-ceiling windows" and "walls decorated" with "rotating artwork."

Warehouse Bar & Grill *Seafood/Steak* 19 | 17 | 18 | $38

Alexandria | 214 King St. (bet. Fairfax & Lee Sts.), VA | 703-683-6868 | www.warehousebarandgrill.com

It's old-time "Old Town personified" at Alexandria's "white-tablecloth" surf 'n' turf "standby" with "caricatures on the walls" and a "Southern touch" to its cuisine and service; regulars keep coming back for the "very good seafood at the bar" – including some of the "best she-crab soup in town" – plus crab cakes and steak, though a few doubters dub it a "dated" "tourist spot" that's "lost its charm and needs to reinvent itself."

NEW Wasabi ☒ *Japanese*

`-` `-` `-` `I`

Golden Triangle | 908 17th St. NW (I St.) | 202-822-0646 | www.wasabisushi.com

NEW WasabiSito *Japanese*

Arlington | Lyon Village | 3129 Lee Hwy. (Rte. 66), VA | 703-907-0060 | www.wasabisito.com

This Golden Triangle storefront serves its modern Japanese fare *kaiten*-style – diners pluck color-coded plates ($2-$5 each, depending on the hue) of salads, udon and Asian- and Latin-accented sushi from a conveyor belt; there are also sake tastings every Thursday from 6-9 PM and a refrigerated case up front holds the full menu for easy carry-out lunches; N.B. WasabiSito, a mostly take-out branch in Arlington, offers a unique kids' menu.

☒ Willard Room *American*

`23` `27` `25` `$68`

Downtown | Willard InterContinental Washington | 1401 Pennsylvania Ave. NW (bet. 14th & 15th Sts.) | 202-637-7440 | www.washington.intercontinental.com

"You might find yourself seated next to a former president in this posh" Downtown "bastion of elegance" where lobbying got its start; patrons propose this is "fine dining at its finest" – "outstanding" New American with modern French touches, a "gorgeous" revamped room that is infused with "history" and a staff that "makes you feel like a VIP", especially given tableside service options; while the whole experience is "over the top" ("especially the prices"), it's also "why you own a tux"; N.B. it has recently instituted a lavish Sunday buffet brunch.

Willow ☒ *American*

`24` `21` `22` `$47`

Arlington | 4301 N. Fairfax Dr. (N. Taylor St.), VA | 703-465-8800 | www.willowva.com

For "real dining sophistication" in Arlington's Ballston area, head to this New American that takes an "imaginative approach to classic dishes" while "letting the fine ingredients shine"; the "handsome", "art nouveau" decor is "a nice backdrop" for sipping "impressive" wines at the bar or indulging in a "special-occasion" meal, but brace yourself for "terrible acoustics."

Wok & Roll *Chinese/Japanese*

`15` `7` `12` `$16`

Chinatown | 604 H St. NW (bet. 6th & 7th Sts.) | 202-347-4656

"Dine in the last residence of" John Wilkes Booth and his co-conspirators at this "tiny" Chinatown "value" that's "great for a sit-down lunch" of "decent, honest Chinese fare", "fresh sashimi" and "stupendous bubble tea"; "it did not rock my wok" say some, especially given the "boring interior", but it remains a "reliable" option for $1-a-piece weekday sushi happy hours.

Woo Lae Oak *Korean*

22 | 18 | 18 | $33

Vienna | 8240 Leesburg Pike (Chain Bridge Rd.), VA | 703-827-7300 | www.woolaeoak.com

Serving "authentic Korean BBQ" aimed at "those who want the 'real thing'" ("cuts of meat that challenge" you), this Tysons Corner eatery is a "spacious, well-appointed" setup that combines traditional "tabletop cooking" with a bar/lounge offering "awesome sushi" and Asian fusion tapas; even better say some is the "attentive service."

Woo Mi Garden *Korean*

▽ 22 | 18 | 16 | $28

Wheaton | 2423 Hickerson Dr. (bet. Elkin St. & Rte. 97), MD | 301-933-0100

"If you love Korean barbecue, you should love" this Wheaton Seoul food specialist that's "the place to bring your family" or "a few friends" for "personal" tabletop grilling of "flavorful, tender meat", "plentiful", "authentic" sides, "excellent soups and stews", and even sushi; if you find that your "pleasant" server "speaks very little English", sneak a peek at the handy photos on the menu.

Yama *Japanese*

23 | 16 | 20 | $29

Vienna | Vienna Plaza | 328 Maple Ave. W. (Nutley St.), VA | 703-242-7703

"Great sushi is in our backyard" enthuse Vienna raw-fish fanciers who find a "hidden gem" at this "local favorite" "tucked away in a strip center" on the main drag, where they "always make you feel welcome"; its "reasonable prices" "keep customers coming back" for "elaborately constructed rolls" and "authentic Japanese dishes" that also let them save on gas by avoiding the "trek to DC"; consequently, the "small dining room" "can get crowded."

Yamazato *Japanese*

▽ 22 | 18 | 20 | $29

Alexandria | Beauregard Sq. | 6303 Little River Tpke. (Beauregard St.), VA | 703-914-8877 | www.yamazato.net

"Thick, succulent" cuts of sashimi and sushi, along with "lots of special tastings and treats" for those sitting at the long, blond-wood bar, "leave you craving more" from this "hard-to-find" Japanese in an Alexandria office complex that also offers Pan-Asian fusion dishes for those averse to raw fish; a few find "it's not a place you want to linger" but others say they have no choice due to "slow service."

NEW Yazuzu *Mideastern*

- | - | - | I

Adams Morgan | 2120 18th St. NW (bet. California St. & Wyoming Ave.) | 202-319-8989 | www.yazuzu.com

It didn't take long for expats to catch on to the homestyle Middle Eastern eats on offer at this counter-service basement cafe in Adams Morgan; patrons take their plates to gleaming white tables in a futuristic red room with a rounded ceiling; N.B. late-night revelers can take advantage of the 5 AM weekend closing time.

Yin Yankee *Asian Fusion*

24 | 18 | 21 | $33

NEW Bethesda | 4936 Fairmont Ave. (Old Georgetown Rd.), MD | 301-718-3400 | www.yinyankee.com

See review in the Baltimore Directory.

	FOOD	DECOR	SERVICE	COST

Yoko *Japanese* ▽ 20 | 18 | 19 | $30

Herndon | Herndon Center V | 332 Elden St. (Herndon Pkwy.), VA | 703-464-7000

Oakton | Hunter Mill Plaza | 2946J Chain Bridge Rd. (Hunter Mill Rd.), VA | 703-255-6644

"Although they're known for their sushi", these "small", "unpretentious neighborhood gems" "also prepare excellent cooked Japanese" fare, including a "banana tempura that's a unique finish"; now under separate ownership, the "simple but stylish" Herndon location makes "a nice place for a quiet adult dinner", while the "child-friendly" Oakton branch puts a "modern" spin on things; "they're not the best" shrug critics, "but for local eateries, they're fine."

Yosaku *Japanese* 21 | 11 | 20 | $32

Upper NW | 4712 Wisconsin Ave. NW (Chesapeake St.) | 202-363-4453 | www.yosakusushi.com

"Get a lot for less" at the "$1-a-piece happy hours" (Monday-Thursday) hosted by this "steady old" Upper Northwest "neighborhood standby" for "mouthwatering sushi" and "well-executed" "cooked dishes", including "interesting specials" "that can surprise"; the decor's "a bit lacking" (the "cool upstairs" is better), but you'll "always get a warm welcome" from the "courteous" staffers whose service only gets more "highly personalized once you're known."

Yuan Fu *Chinese/Vegetarian* ▽ 22 | 8 | 20 | $18

Rockville | 798 Rockville Pike (Wootton Pkwy.), MD | 301-762-5937

"Putting this much flavor into vegetables isn't easy" exclaim aficionados who think the "delectable" meatless dishes at this Rockville Chinese "may be better than the real thing"; the "extremely helpful owners" have created a "vegan heaven" where the "healthy choices" ("try the pumpkin duck") are "great for different diets", but given all the "wows" on the plate, it "should have a better location."

Z Zaytinya ● *Mediterranean/Mideastern* 25 | 25 | 20 | $39

Penn Quarter | Pepco Bldg. | 701 Ninth St. NW (G St.) | 202-638-0800 | www.zaytinya.com

"Stunning, sleek white walls provide a dramatic background for a buzzing crowd" at this "fabulous" "fast-paced" Penn Quarter "meze heaven" where an "epic menu" of Med–Middle Eastern (Turkish, Greek and Lebanese) "unique" small plates encourages "sharing", and a "knowledgeable staff keeps it from being overwhelming"; its "divine" "big-city atmosphere" (one of the "best-looking restaurants in town"), "excellent" prices and limited reservations can make "tables hard to come by."

Zed's *Ethiopian* 20 | 17 | 19 | $27

Georgetown | 1201 28th St. NW (M St.) | 202-333-4710 | www.zeds.net

Although this M Street row house on the major tourist route into Georgetown looks a "bit formal" and "Colonial", you can still follow Ethiopian tradition and "eat with your hands", wrapping "hearty" stews in its "excellent" spongy bread – an experience that's especially enjoyable "with a large group"; its "convenient" location attracts "celebrities" whose photos are displayed on the "glory-wall", and while purists hiss it's "Americanized Ethiopian", it offers "fun" outdoor people-watching.

Zengo *Asian Fusion*

21 | 24 | 17 | $45

Chinatown | Gallery Pl. | 781 Seventh St. NW (bet. F & H Sts.) | 202-393-2929 | www.modernmexican.com

The plethora of "beautiful people sipping" in "gorgeous" "trendy splendor" makes this Chinatown sizzler's street-level bar a "great scene", while upstairs, "wasabi meets Pancho Villa" in the "quieter drop-dead-cool dining area emphasizing small-plates sharing"; boosters believe the "Asian-Latin fusion actually works" and the "decor hits" the theme "surprisingly well", but contrarians counter "what's with the modern art raisinettes hanging from the ceiling?" and are further annoyed by dishes that "arrive in any order the kitchen feels like making them."

NEW Zodiac Grill *American/BBQ*

– | – | – | M

Gaithersburg | Kentlands | 654 Center Point Way (Market St.), MD | 301-977-2213 | www.zodiac-grill.com

This two-story venue in Gaithersburg has something for everyone: a family-friendly eatery serving midpriced American and BBQ fare, three bars and an upstairs nightclub hosting live entertainment; warm yellow walls, granite tables and colorful zodiac accents add a touch of sophistication to the sprawling space.

Z Zola *American*

22 | 25 | 20 | $50

Penn Quarter | International Spy Museum | 800 F St. NW (8th St.) | 202-654-0999 | www.zoladc.com

"Black napkins", "hidden" doors, booths with peepholes into the kitchen – you feel like you're entering a "mysterious" world of "espionage" at this "swank" New American attached to Penn Quarter's International Spy Museum, where "stylish" somebodies go for "creative cocktails" in the "stunning" bar or arrange a "perfect" "secret rendezvous"; with "less of a wait and more attention" by the staff during the day, it's become a lunchtime destination for the "up-and-coming power crowd" that digs into "fun twists on American cuisine."

WASHINGTON, DC
INDEXES

Cuisines

Includes restaurant names, neighborhoods and Food ratings. ☑ indicates places with the highest ratings, popularity and importance.

AFGHAN

Afghan | **Alexandria**	20
Bamian | **Falls Ch**	–
Faryab | **Bethesda**	22
Panjshir | **multi. loc.**	23

AMERICAN (NEW)

Addie's | **Rockville**	23
Agraria | **Georgetown**	–
Ardeo | **Cleve Pk**	21
Bardeo Wine | **Cleve Pk**	21
Bazin's/Church | **Vienna**	–
NEW Beacon B&G | **Scott Cir**	–
Black Market | **Garrett Pk**	24
☑ BlackSalt | **Palisades**	26
Black's Bar | **Bethesda**	23
NEW BLT Steak | **Gldn Triangle**	–
Blue Duck | **West End**	26
Buck's Fishing | **Upper NW**	20
Butterfield 9 | **D'town**	22
☑ Café MoZU | **SW**	22
NEW Café Panache | **Ashburn**	–
☑ Carlyle | **Arlington**	24
☑ Cashion's Eat | **Adams Mor**	25
Caucus Room | **Penn Qtr**	21
NEW Central M. Rich. | **Penn Qtr**	–
Charlie Palmer | **Cap Hill**	23
Chef Geoff's | **multi. loc.**	18
NEW Circa | **Dupont Cir**	–
Circle Bistro | **West End**	21
☑ CityZen | **SW**	26
Coeur de Lion | **Mt. Vernon Sq**	23
Colorado Kit. | **Upper NW**	24
☑ Colvin Run | **Vienna**	25
Comus Inn | **Dickerson**	20
☑ Corduroy | **D'town**	25
Crème | **U St**	23
Dahlia | **Upper NW**	21
David Craig | **Bethesda**	25
☑ DC Coast | **D'town**	24
Del Merei Grille | **Alexandria**	23
Dish + Drinks | **Foggy Bottom**	19
DuPont Grille | **Dupont Cir**	19
Eleventh St. | **Arlington**	–
Equinox | **Gldn Triangle**	25
☑ Eve | **Alexandria**	27
Evening Star | **Alexandria**	22
☑ Fahrenheit/Degrees | **Georgetown**	22
NEW Farrah Olivia | **Alexandria**	–
Felix | **Adams Mor**	18

15 ria | **Scott Cir**	19
Firefly | **Dupont Cir**	21
NEW Food Matters | **Alexandria**	–
Foti's | **Culpeper**	27
Grapeseed | **Bethesda**	24
Greystone Grill | **Rockville**	20
Grille, The | **Alexandria**	25
NEW Hook | **Georgetown**	–
Indigo Landing | **Alexandria**	–
☑ Inn/Little Washington | **Washington**	29
Jackie's | **Silver Spring**	20
NEW Jack's Rest. | **Dupont Cir**	–
Johnny's Half Shell | **Cap Hill**	23
Juniper | **West End**	19
Kolumbia | **Gldn Triangle**	18
☑ Komi | **Dupont Cir**	26
Lafayette Rm. | **Gldn Triangle**	24
Leftbank | **Adams Mor**	15
NEW LIA'S | **Chevy Chase**	–
NEW Liberty Tav. | **Arlington**	–
☑ Lightfoot | **Leesburg**	22
Local 16 | **U St**	15
Magnolias/Mill | **Purcellville**	19
Mark/Orlando's | **Dupont Cir**	24
Market St. B&G | **Reston**	18
Matchbox | **Chinatown**	23
Mendocino Grille | **Georgetown**	23
☑ Mie N Yu | **Georgetown**	18
Mimi's | **Dupont Cir**	18
NEW Mio | **D'town**	–
Morrison-Clark Inn | **D'town**	23
Nage | **Scott Cir**	–
New Heights | **Woodley Pk**	22
☑ Nora | **Dupont Cir**	25
Oakville Grille | **Bethesda**	18
Occidental | **D'town**	21
Old Angler's | **Potomac**	21
100 King | **Alexandria**	–
Oval Room | **Gldn Triangle**	21
☑ Palena | **Cleve Pk**	26
Palette | **D'town**	22
Peacock Cafe | **Georgetown**	21
Perrys | **Adams Mor**	19
☑ Persimmon | **Bethesda**	26
Portabellos | **Arlington**	19
NEW Posh | **D'town**	–
Poste Moderne | **Penn Qtr**	21
Praline | **Bethesda**	–
NEW PS 7's | **Gallery Pl**	–

NEW Rain	**Fairfax**	⌐
redDog Cafe	**Silver Spring**	19
Reef, The	**Adams Mor**	14
☑ Ritz, Grill (Pent. City)	**Arlington**	25
Rock Creek	**Bethesda**	23
Roof Terr./JFK Ctr.	**Foggy Bottom**	17
Rustico	**Alexandria**	⌐
SBC Café	**Herndon**	24
☑ Seasons	**Georgetown**	27
Sequoia	**Georgetown**	15
701	**Penn Qtr**	23
☑ 1789	**Georgetown**	26
Sonoma	**Cap Hill**	21
☑ Tabard Inn	**Dupont Cir**	23
Tallula	**Arlington**	22
Thyme Square	**Bethesda**	16
☑ 2941 Rest.	**Falls Ch**	27
Vegetate	**Mt. Vernon Sq**	21
Vermilion	**Alexandria**	20
☑ Vidalia	**Gldn Triangle**	26
NEW Vintage 50	**Leesburg**	⌐
Viridian	**Logan Cir**	20
☑ Willard Room	**D'town**	23
Willow	**Arlington**	24
☑ Zola	**Penn Qtr**	22

AMERICAN (TRADITIONAL)

Artie's	**Fairfax**	23
Ashby Inn	**Paris**	22
Bar Pilar	**Logan Cir**	16
Ben's Chili Bowl	**U St**	21
Blvd. Woodgrill	**Arlington**	19
Busboys & Poets	**U St**	18
Cafe Deluxe	**multi. loc.**	18
☑ Cheesecake Fact.	**multi. loc.**	18
☑ Clyde's	**multi. loc.**	18
Colorado Kit.	**Upper NW**	24
D.C. Boathse.	**Palisades**	14
NEW Dock/Lansdowne	**Lansdowne**	⌐
☑ Five Guys	**multi. loc.**	24
Franklin's	**Hyattsville**	17
Grillfish	**Gldn Triangle**	18
Hank's Oyster	**Dupont Cir**	23
Hard Times Cafe	**multi. loc.**	19
Harry's Tap Rm.	**Arlington**	21
Kramerbooks	**Dupont Cir**	17
Logan Tav.	**Logan Cir**	17
Lucky Strike	**Chinatown**	16
Luna Grill	**multi. loc.**	19
NEW Majestic	**Alexandria**	⌐
M & S Grill	**multi. loc.**	18
Mark's Kit.	**Takoma Pk**	19

Martin's Tav.	**Georgetown**	18
NEW M'Dawg	**Adams Mor**	⌐
Mitsitam	**SW**	22
Monocle	**Cap Hill**	17
Nathans	**Georgetown**	18
NEW Not Your Ave. Joe's	**Lansdowne**	⌐
NEW Old Dominion	**Mt. Vernon Sq**	⌐
☑ Old Ebbitt	**D'town**	20
Open City	**Woodley Pk**	17
NEW Overwood	**Alexandria**	⌐
PGA Tour	**Rockville**	⌐
Quarry House	**Silver Spring**	19
Rail Stop	**Plains**	20
NEW Ray's/Classics	**Silver Spring**	24
Stoney's B&G	**Logan Cir**	⌐
Sweetwater Tav.	**multi. loc.**	22
NEW Tavern/Lake	**Reston**	⌐
Ted's Montana	**multi. loc.**	18
Temperance Hall	**Petworth**	⌐
Tonic	**Foggy Bottom**	18
Tuscarora Mill	**Leesburg**	23
Two Quail	**Cap Hill**	17
Ugly Mug	**Cap Hill**	17
NEW Urban Burger	**Rockville**	⌐
NEW Vintage 50	**Leesburg**	⌐
NEW Zodiac Grill	**Gaith'burg**	⌐

ARGENTINEAN

Divino	**Bethesda**	20
NEW Pizza Zero	**Bethesda**	⌐

ASIAN FUSION

NEW Bezu	**Potomac**	⌐
Cafe Japoné	**Dupont Cir**	17
Maté	**Georgetown**	17
☑ Oya	**Penn Qtr**	18
Sushi-Go-Round	**Chinatown**	21
NEW Wasabi	**Arlington**	⌐
Yin Yankee	**Bethesda**	24
Zengo	**Chinatown**	21

AUSTRIAN

Café Monti	**Alexandria**	22
Leopold's Kafe	**Georgetown**	21

BAKERIES

Au Bon Pain	**multi. loc.**	16
Bread Line	**World Bank**	24
NEW Buzz	**Alexandria**	⌐
La Madeleine	**multi. loc.**	17
Leopold's Kafe	**Georgetown**	21
My Bakery & Café	**multi. loc.**	18
Praline	**Bethesda**	⌐
Sticky Fingers	**Columbia Hts**	⌐

BARBECUE

Ches. Chicken/Ribs | Bethesda	-
Old Glory BBQ | Georgetown	19
Red Hot & Blue | multi. loc.	19
Rocklands | multi. loc.	22
Urban BBQ | Rockville	24
NEW Zodiac Grill | Gaith'burg	-

BELGIAN

Belga Café | Cap Hill	21
NEW Brass. Beck | D'town	-
Mannequin Pis | Olney	23
☑ Marcel's | West End	28

BRAZILIAN

NEW Chima | Vienna	-
Fogo de Chão | D'town	23
Green Field | Rockville	19
Grill/Ipanema | Adams Mor	20

BRITISH

Elephant & Castle | D'town	13
Hunter's Head | Upperville	20

BURMESE

Burma | Chinatown	21
Mandalay | Silver Spring	24
Myanmar | Falls Ch	21
NEW Taste of Burma | Sterling	-

CAJUN

Acadiana | Mt. Vernon Sq	23
French Qtr./Louisiana | multi. loc.	22
New Orleans Bistro | Bethesda	18
RT's | Alexandria	22

CALIFORNIAN

Mendocino Grille | Georgetown	23
Paolo's | multi. loc.	18

CARIBBEAN

Islander Carib. | U St	20

CENTRAL AMERICAN

Pollo Campero | multi. loc.	17

CHINESE

(* dim sum specialist)

A&J* | multi. loc.	22
NEW Bob's 88 | Rockville	-
Bob's Noodle | Rockville	22
China Garden* | Rosslyn	19
China Star | Fairfax	20
Chinatown Express | Chinatown	22
City Lights | multi. loc.	18
Eat First | Chinatown	22
Fortune* | Falls Ch	19
Full Kee (VA) | Falls Ch	22
Full Kee (DC) | Chinatown	22

Full Key | Wheaton	20
Fu Shing | Gaith'burg	18
Good Fortune* | Wheaton	21
Hollywood East* | Wheaton	24
Hunan Dynasty | Cap Hill	-
Hunan Lion | Vienna	21
Joe's Noodle Hse. | Rockville	22
Kam Po | Falls Ch	-
Mark's Duck Hse.* | Falls Ch	23
NEW Mei's Asian | Arlington	-
Meiwah | multi. loc.	20
New Fortune* | Gaith'burg	21
Oriental East* | Silver Spring	21
Peking Cheers | Gaith'burg	-
☑ Peking Gourmet | Falls Ch	25
☑ P.F. Chang's | multi. loc.	19
Seven Seas | multi. loc.	18
Taipei Tokyo | Rockville	18
Tony Cheng's | Chinatown	20
Vegetable Gdn. | Rockville	19
Wok & Roll | Chinatown	15
Yuan Fu | Rockville	22

COFFEEHOUSES

NEW Buzz | Alexandria	-
Café Bonaparte | Georgetown	22
Leopold's Kafe | Georgetown	21
Tryst | Adams Mor	18

COFFEE SHOPS/DINERS

Ben's Chili Bowl | U St	21
Bob & Edith's | Arlington	16
Diner, The | Adams Mor	18
Florida Ave. Grill | U St	21
Luna Grill | multi. loc.	19
Open City | Woodley Pk	17

CONTINENTAL

NEW Jack's Rest. | Dupont Cir	-
Park Cafe | Cap Hill	22
Village Bistro | Arlington	21

CREOLE

Acadiana | Mt. Vernon Sq	23
French Qtr./Louisiana | multi. loc.	22
New Orleans Bistro | Bethesda	18
RT's | Alexandria	22

CUBAN

Banana Café | Cap Hill	18
Cuba de Ayer | Burtonsville	19
Cubano's | Silver Spring	21
NEW La Limeña | Rockville	-

DELIS

Chutzpah | multi. loc.	19
NEW Morty's Deli | Upper NW	-
Parkway Deli | Silver Spring	20

EASTERN EUROPEAN

Domku	**Petworth**	26

ECLECTIC

Busboys & Poets	**U St**	18
Café Saint-Ex	**Logan Cir**	19
C.F. Folks	**Gldn Triangle**	23
Dean & DeLuca	**Georgetown**	21
Kolumbia	**Gldn Triangle**	18
Little Fountain	**Adams Mor**	23
NEW Piratz Tav.	**Silver Spring**	‑
NEW Rugby Café	**Georgetown**	‑
NEW Tavern/Lake	**Reston**	‑
U-topia	**U St**	16

ETHIOPIAN

Dukem	**U St**	23
Etete	**U St**	21
Meskerem	**Adams Mor**	21
Zed's	**Georgetown**	20

FRENCH

NEW Bastille	**Alexandria**	‑
El Manantial	**Reston**	21
Jean-Michel	**Bethesda**	24
☑ La Bergerie	**Alexandria**	26
La Chaumiere	**Georgetown**	24
La Côte d'Or	**Arlington**	21
La Ferme	**Chevy Chase**	22
La Fourchette	**Adams Mor**	21
La Madeleine	**multi. loc.**	17
La Miche	**Bethesda**	22
NEW La Rue 123	**Fairfax**	‑
☑ L'Aub./François	**Grt Falls**	27
☑ L'Aub. Provençale	**Boyce**	25
Lavandou	**Cleve Pk**	21
Le Mistral	**McLean**	24
Le Palais	**Gaith'burg**	‑
L'oustalet	**Rockville**	22
☑ Marcel's	**West End**	28
Matisse	**Upper NW**	20
☑ Oya	**Penn Qtr**	18
Tempo	**Alexandria**	22
Tonic	**Mt. Pleasant**	18
NEW Urbana	**Dupont Cir**	‑

FRENCH (BISTRO)

Bis	**Cap Hill**	24
Bistro D'Oc	**D'town**	20
Bistro Français	**Georgetown**	19
Bistro 123	**McLean**	19
Bistrot du Coin	**Dupont Cir**	19
Bistrot Lafayette	**Alexandria**	21
Bistrot Lepic	**Georgetown**	24
NEW Brass. Beck	**D'town**	‑
Café Bonaparte	**Georgetown**	22

NEW Café du Parc	**D'town**	‑
NEW Central M. Rich.	**Penn Qtr**	‑
NEW French Hound	**Mid'burg**	‑
Le Chat Noir	**Upper NW**	18
Le Gaulois	**Alexandria**	19
Le Refuge	**Alexandria**	22
Mon Ami Gabi	**Bethesda**	19
Montmartre	**Cap Hill**	23
NEW Montsouris	**Dupont Cir**	‑
NEW Napoleon	**Adams Mor**	‑
Petits Plats	**Woodley Pk**	22
Praline	**Bethesda**	‑

FRENCH (BRASSERIE)

Brass. Monte Carlo	**Bethesda**	22
Les Halles	**D'town**	19

FRENCH (NEW)

Bis	**Cap Hill**	24
☑ Café 15	**D'town**	25
☑ Citronelle	**Georgetown**	28
☑ Gerard's Place	**D'town**	27
☑ Le Paradou	**Penn Qtr**	27

GREEK

NEW Cava	**Rockville**	‑
Mourayo	**Dupont Cir**	23
Mykonos Grill	**Rockville**	21
NEW Vaso's Kit.	**Alexandria**	‑

HAMBURGERS

☑ Clyde's	**multi. loc.**	18
Elevation Burger	**Falls Ch**	21
☑ Five Guys	**multi. loc.**	24
Matchbox	**Chinatown**	23
☑ Morton's	**multi. loc.**	25
☑ Old Ebbitt	**D'town**	20
Stoney's B&G	**Logan Cir**	‑
Ted's Montana	**multi. loc.**	18
NEW Urban Burger	**Rockville**	‑

HONDURAN

Irene's Pupusas	**multi. loc.**	‑

HOT DOGS

NEW M'Dawg	**Adams Mor**	‑

INDIAN

Amma Veg.	**multi. loc.**	22
Bombay	**Silver Spring**	24
Bombay Bistro	**multi. loc.**	23
Bombay Club	**Gldn Triangle**	25
Bombay Palace	**Gldn Triangle**	23
Bombay Tandoor	**Vienna**	20
Café Spice	**Gaith'burg**	18
Cafe Taj	**McLean**	19
Curry Club	**Glover Pk**	24
Delhi Club	**Arlington**	22

Delhi Dhaba	multi. loc.	17
Haandi	multi. loc.	23
Heritage India	multi. loc.	23
☑ IndeBleu	Penn Qtr	23
India Palace	Germantown	23
☑ Indique	multi. loc.	24
Jaipur	Fairfax	23
Minerva	multi. loc.	22
Nirvana	Gldn Triangle	20
Passage to India	Bethesda	24
NEW Rangoli	S Riding	-
☑ Rasika	Penn Qtr	26
NEW Saravana Palace	Fairfax	-
Tandoori Nights	multi. loc.	22
Tiffin	Takoma Pk	21
Udupi Palace	Takoma Pk	23

IRISH

NEW Eamonn's	Alexandria	-
Fadó Irish Pub	Chinatown	16
Irish Inn/Glen Echo	Glen Echo	17
Rí-Rá Irish Pub	multi. loc.	15
Siné	Arlington	15

ITALIAN

(N=Northern; S=Southern)

Agrodolce	Germantown	22
A La Lucia	Alexandria	22
Al Crostino	U St	22
Al Tiramisu	Dupont Cir	23
Amada Amante	Rockville	20
Amici Miei	Potomac	20
Argia's	Falls Ch	20
Arucola	Upper NW	18
NEW Bebo	Arlington	-
Buca di Beppo	multi. loc.	15
NEW Buona Sera	Bethesda	-
Cafe Milano	Georgetown	20
Café Mileto	Germantown	17
Café Monti	Alexandria	22
Capri	McLean	21
Centro Italian	Bethesda	21
Cesco	N	Bethesda	23
Coppi's Organic	N	U St	22
NEW D'Acqua	Penn Qtr	-
Da Domenico	McLean	21
Dino	N	Cleve Pk	19
Dolce Vita	Fairfax	22
El Manantial	Reston	21
NEW Emilio's	Lansdowne	-
Etrusco	N	Dupont Cir	20
Extra Virgin	Arlington	17
Faccia Luna	multi. loc.	21
NEW Famoso	N	Chevy Chase	-
Filomena	Georgetown	22
Finemondo	D'town	18

Fiore di Luna	N	Grt Falls	22
Fontina Grille	Rockville	17
Geranio	N	Alexandria	21
NEW Il Mulino	D'town	-
☑ Il Pizzico	Rockville	25
Il Radicchio	Arlington	18
i Ricchi	N	Dupont Cir	23
Landini Bros.	N	Alexandria	22
Luigino	D'town	18
☑ Maestro	McLean	28
Maggiano's	multi. loc.	18
Mamma Lucia	multi. loc.	19
NEW M Cafe	Chevy Chase	-
Notti Bianche	Foggy Bottom	24
☑ Obelisk	Dupont Cir	27
Olazzo	Bethesda	22
Panino	Manassas	26
Paolo's	multi. loc.	18
Pasta Mia	Adams Mor	24
Pasta Plus	Laurel	24
Pesto	Woodley Pk	17
Pinzimini	N	Arlington	-
Primi Piatti	Foggy Bottom	21
Radius	Mt. Pleasant	22
Renato at River Falls	Potomac	17
Rist. La Perla	Georgetown	19
Rist. Murali	Arlington	17
San Vito	multi. loc.	20
Sesto Senso	Gldn Triangle	20
Sette Bello	Arlington	21
Sette Osteria	Dupont Cir	20
Skewers/Luna	Dupont Cir	18
Sorriso	Cleve Pk	20
Spezie	Gldn Triangle	19
Teatro Goldoni	Gldn Triangle	23
Tempo	N	Alexandria	22
Timpano	N	Rockville	18
Tivoli	N	Rosslyn	22
Tonic	Mt. Pleasant	18
☑ Tosca	N	Penn Qtr	26
Tragara	N	Bethesda	22
Tutto Bene	N	Arlington	18
NEW Urbana	Dupont Cir	-
NEW Vapiano	multi. loc.	-

JAMAICAN

Caribbean Feast	Rockville	21
Negril	multi. loc.	21

JAPANESE

(* sushi specialist)

NEW Bob's 88*	Rockville	-
Cafe Japoné*	Dupont Cir	17
☑ Café MoZU*	SW	22
Chez Mama-San	Georgetown	21
Chopsticks*	Georgetown	19

Flying Fish* | **Alexandria**	19
Hakuba* | **Gaith'burg**	23
Hama Sushi/Obi* | **multi. loc.**	21
Hinode* | **multi. loc.**	20
Hunan Dynasty* | **Cap Hill**	–
NEW Kansai Sushi* | **Vienna**	–
Kaz Sushi* | **World Bank**	25
Konami* | **Vienna**	22
Kotobuki* | **Palisades**	24
Z Makoto | **Palisades**	28
Matsuri* | **Herndon**	20
Matuba* | **multi. loc.**	21
NEW Mei's Asian | **Arlington**	–
Mikaku* | **Herndon**	27
Murasaki* | **Upper NW**	22
Niwanohana* | **Rockville**	23
Z Oya* | **Penn Qtr**	18
Perrys* | **Adams Mor**	19
Sakana* | **Dupont Cir**	22
Z Sake Club | **Woodley Pk**	23
Saki* | **Adams Mor**	19
Seven Seas | **multi. loc.**	18
Spices* | **Cleve Pk**	20
Sushi-Go-Round* | **Chinatown**	21
Sushi-Ko* | **Glover Pk**	24
Sushi Sushi* | **Cleve Pk**	19
Z Sushi Taro* | **Dupont Cir**	25
Sweet Ginger* | **Vienna**	24
Tachibana* | **McLean**	24
Taipei Tokyo | **Rockville**	18
Tako Grill* | **Bethesda**	24
Tono Sushi* | **Woodley Pk**	21
Uni* | **Dupont Cir**	20
NEW Wasabi* | **multi. loc.**	–
Wok & Roll* | **Chinatown**	15
Woo Mi Gdn.* | **Wheaton**	22
Yama* | **Vienna**	23
Yamazato* | **Alexandria**	22
Yoko* | **multi. loc.**	20
Yosaku* | **Upper NW**	21

KOREAN

(* barbecue specialist)

Hee Been* | **Alexandria**	21
Light House Tofu | **Rockville**	–
NEW Mandu | **Dupont Cir**	–
Myung Dong | **Beltsville**	–
Sorak Garden* | **Annandale**	22
Woo Lae Oak* | **Vienna**	22
Woo Mi Gdn.* | **Wheaton**	22

LEBANESE

Lebanese Butcher | **Falls Ch**	–
Z Lebanese Tav. | **multi. loc.**	22
Neyla | **Georgetown**	22

MALAYSIAN

Malaysia Kopitiam | **Gldn Triangle**	22
Penang | **Dupont Cir**	19
Straits/Malaya | **Dupont Cir**	21

MEDITERRANEAN

NEW Bastille | **Alexandria**	–
Brass. Monte Carlo | **Bethesda**	22
Café Olé | **Upper NW**	21
Le Tire Bouchon | **Fairfax**	–
Levante's | **multi. loc.**	17
Matisse | **Upper NW**	20
Olives | **Gldn Triangle**	22
Pasha Cafe | **Arlington**	21
Pearl Seafood | **Wheaton**	–
Tabaq Bistro | **U St**	19
Tapatinis | **Cap Hill**	16
Taste/Jerusaleum | **Silver Spring**	–
Tavira | **Chevy Chase**	21
Temel | **Fairfax**	21
Z Zaytinya | **Penn Qtr**	25

MEXICAN

NEW Casa Oaxaca | **Adams Mor**	–
NEW El Limeño | **Petworth**	–
El Mariachi | **Rockville**	23
El Tapatio's | **Bladensburg**	–
Guajillo | **Arlington**	22
La Sirenita | **Hyattsville**	–
Z Lauriol Plaza | **Dupont Cir**	19
NEW Oyamel | **Penn Qtr**	–
Rosa Mexicano | **Penn Qtr**	20
Samantha's | **Silver Spring**	22
Taqueria/Charrito | **Arlington**	22
Taqueria/Poblano | **multi. loc.**	20
Taqueria/Reyes | **Riverdale**	–
Uncle Julio's | **Fairfax**	19

MIDDLE EASTERN

Amsterdam Falafel | **Adams Mor**	–
Kabob Palace | **Arlington**	25
Layalina | **Arlington**	23
Mezè | **Adams Mor**	19
Skewers/Luna | **Dupont Cir**	18
Taste/Jerusaleum | **Silver Spring**	–
NEW Yazuzu | **Adams Mor**	–
Z Zaytinya | **Penn Qtr**	25

MOROCCAN

NEW Marrakesh | **Dupont Cir**	–
NEW Pyramids | **U St**	–
Taste of Morocco | **multi. loc.**	20

NEW ZEALAND

Cassatt's | **Arlington**	20

NOODLE SHOPS

Bob's Noodle | **Rockville**	22
Chinatown Express | **Chinatown**	22
Full Key | **Wheaton**	20
Myung Dong | **Beltsville**	⎯
Nooshi | **Gldn Triangle**	19
Pho 75 | **multi. loc.**	23

NUEVO LATINO

Agua Ardiente | **West End**	17
☑ Café Atlántico | **Penn Qtr**	25
Café Salsa | **Alexandria**	20
☑ Ceiba | **D'town**	24
Ceviche | **Silver Spring**	23
Gua-Rapo | **Arlington**	17
Merkado Kit. | **Logan Cir**	19

PAKISTANI

Kabob Palace | **Arlington**	25

PAN-ASIAN

Asia Bistro/Zen | **Arlington**	19
☑ Asia Nora | **West End**	25
NEW Banana Leaves | **Dupont Cir**	⎯
Cafe Asia | **multi. loc.**	19
Ching Ching | **Georgetown**	19
Nooshi | **Gldn Triangle**	19
Raku | **multi. loc.**	21
Saki | **Adams Mor**	19
Spices | **Cleve Pk**	20
Sweet Ginger | **Vienna**	24
Teaism | **multi. loc.**	19
☑ TenPenh | **D'town**	24
Topaz Bar | **Dupont Cir**	19
Yamazato | **Alexandria**	22

PAN-LATIN

Azucar | **Silver Spring**	26
Café Citron | **Dupont Cir**	17
Caribbean Breeze | **Arlington**	17
Gallery | **Silver Spring**	⎯
NEW Guardado's | **Bethesda**	⎯
Lima | **D'town**	⎯
Pearl Seafood | **Wheaton**	⎯

PERSIAN

Moby Dick | **multi. loc.**	22
Shamshiry | **Falls Ch**	23

PERUVIAN

Crisp & Juicy | **multi. loc.**	24
El Chalan | **Foggy Bottom**	20
☑ El Pollo Rico | **multi. loc.**	25
Kam Po | **Falls Ch**	⎯
NEW La Limeña | **Rockville**	⎯
NEW Las Canteras | **Adams Mor**	⎯

PIZZA

Agrodolce | **Germantown**	22
Café Mileto | **Germantown**	17
NEW Comet Ping Pong | **Upper NW**	⎯
Coppi's Organic | **U St**	22
Dolce Vita | **Fairfax**	22
Ella's Pizza | **Penn Qtr**	19
NEW Emilio's | **Lansdowne**	⎯
Faccia Luna | **multi. loc.**	21
Fontina Grille | **Rockville**	17
Il Radicchio | **Arlington**	18
Levante's | **multi. loc.**	17
Mamma Lucia | **multi. loc.**	19
Matchbox | **Chinatown**	23
NEW Mia's Pizzas | **Bethesda**	⎯
Pasta Plus | **Laurel**	24
PGA Tour | **Rockville**	⎯
NEW Pizza Zero | **Bethesda**	⎯
☑ Pizzeria Paradiso | **multi. loc.**	24
Radius | **Mt. Pleasant**	22
Rustico | **Alexandria**	⎯
San Vito | **multi. loc.**	20
Sette Osteria | **Dupont Cir**	20
Sorriso | **Cleve Pk**	20
☑ 2 Amys | **Cleve Pk**	25
NEW Vapiano | **Arlington**	⎯

PORTUGUESE

Tavira | **Chevy Chase**	21

PUB FOOD

☑ Clyde's | **multi. loc.**	18
Dogfish Head | **Gaith'burg**	17
Elephant & Castle | **D'town**	13
Fadó Irish Pub | **Chinatown**	16
Franklin's | **Hyattsville**	17
Hunter's Head | **Upperville**	20
Irish Inn/Glen Echo | **Glen Echo**	17
NEW Old Dominion | **Mt. Vernon Sq**	⎯
Rí-Rá Irish Pub | **multi. loc.**	15
Siné | **Arlington**	15
Stoney's B&G | **Logan Cir**	⎯
Ugly Mug | **Cap Hill**	17

PUERTO RICAN

Banana Café | **Cap Hill**	18

SALVADORAN

El Gavilan | **Silver Spring**	23
NEW El Limeño | **Petworth**	⎯
Irene's Pupusas | **multi. loc.**	⎯
Samantha's | **Silver Spring**	22
Taqueria/Charrito | **Arlington**	22

SANDWICHES

Au Bon Pain	**multi. loc.**	16
Bread Line	**World Bank**	24

SCANDINAVIAN

Domku	**Petworth**	26

SEAFOOD

🆕 BlackSalt	**Palisades**	26
Black's Bar	**Bethesda**	23
Charlie Palmer	**Cap Hill**	23
Coastal Flats	**multi. loc.**	22
NEW D'Acqua	**Penn Qtr**	–
🆕 DC Coast	**D'town**	24
NEW Dock/Lansdowne	**Lansdowne**	–
Finn & Porter	**multi. loc.**	17
Flying Fish	**Alexandria**	19
Grillfish	**Gldn Triangle**	18
Hank's Oyster	**Dupont Cir**	23
Harry's Tap Rm.	**Arlington**	21
NEW Hook	**Georgetown**	–
Jerry's Seafood	**Seabrook**	24
Johnny's Half Shell	**Cap Hill**	23
Kam Po	**Falls Ch**	–
🆕 Kinkead's	**Foggy Bottom**	26
🆕 Legal Sea Foods	**multi. loc.**	20
M & S Grill	**multi. loc.**	18
Mar de Plata	**Logan Cir**	21
🆕 McCormick/Schmick	**multi. loc.**	21
Nage	**Scott Cir**	–
🆕 Oceanaire	**D'town**	24
Palm	**multi. loc.**	23
Pesce	**Dupont Cir**	25
Phillips	**SW**	15
NEW Ray's/Classics	**Silver Spring**	24
Sea Catch	**Georgetown**	21
Seven Seas	**multi. loc.**	18
Simply Fish	**Alexandria**	19
SoBe Seafood	**Arlington**	17
Starfish Cafe	**Cap Hill**	17
Tony & Joe	**Georgetown**	14
Warehouse B&G	**Alexandria**	19

SMALL PLATES

(See also Spanish tapas specialist)

Agua Ardiente	Nuevo Latino	**West End**	17
Asia Bistro/Zen	Asian	**Arlington**	19
Bardeo Wine	Amer.	**Cleve Pk**	21
NEW Café du Parc	French	**D'town**	–
Café Olé	Med.	**Upper NW**	21
NEW Cava	Greek	**Rockville**	–
Dino	Italian	**Cleve Pk**	19

Divino	Argent.	**Bethesda**	20
Gua-Rapo	Nuevo Latino	**Arlington**	17
Heritage India	Indian	**Dupont Cir**	23
🆕 Indique	Indian	**multi. loc.**	24
Mezè	Turkish	**Adams Mor**	19
Mikaku	Jap.	**Herndon**	27
100 King	Amer.	**Alexandria**	–
NEW Oyamel	Mex.	**Penn Qtr**	–
Pearl Seafood	Med.	**Wheaton**	–
🆕 Sake Club	Jap.	**Woodley Pk**	23
Sushi-Go-Round	Asian Fusion	**Chinatown**	21
Tallula	Amer.	**Arlington**	22
Tandoori Nights	Indian	**multi. loc.**	22
Tapatinis	Med.	**Cap Hill**	16
NEW Tavern/Lake	Eclectic	**Reston**	–
Topaz Bar	Asian	**Dupont Cir**	19
Yin Yankee	Asian Fusion	**Bethesda**	24
🆕 Zaytinya	Mideastern.	**Penn Qtr**	25

SOUL FOOD

Florida Ave. Grill	**U St**	21
Oohhs & Aahhs	**U St**	–

SOUTH AMERICAN

Chi-Cha Lounge	**U St**	16
El Golfo	**Silver Spring**	21
My Bakery & Café	**multi. loc.**	18
Tutto Bene	**Arlington**	18

SOUTHERN

Acadiana	**Mt. Vernon Sq**	23
B. Smith's	**Cap Hill**	19
Del Merei Grille	**Alexandria**	23
Florida Ave. Grill	**U St**	21
🆕 Georgia Brown's	**D'town**	23
Morrison-Clark Inn	**D'town**	23
Oohhs & Aahhs	**U St**	–
🆕 Vidalia	**Gldn Triangle**	26

SOUTHWESTERN

Sweetwater Tav.	**multi. loc.**	22

SPANISH

(* tapas specialist)

Andalucia	**Rockville**	18
NEW Guardado's*	**Bethesda**	–
🆕 Jaleo*	**multi. loc.**	23
La Tasca*	**multi. loc.**	16
Mar de Plata*	**multi. loc.**	21
Sol de España	**Rockville**	23
Taberna/Alabardero*	**World Bank**	24
Tapeo*	**Arlington**	–

STEAKHOUSES

NEW BLT Steak | **Gldn Triangle**	–
Bobby Van's Steak | **D'town**	20
Z Capital Grille | **multi. loc.**	25
Caucus Room | **Penn Qtr**	21
Charlie Palmer | **Cap Hill**	23
NEW Chima | **Vienna**	–
District ChopHse. | **Penn Qtr**	20
Finn & Porter | **multi. loc.**	17
Fleming's Steak | **McLean**	24
Fogo de Chão | **D'town**	23
Harry's Tap Rm. | **Arlington**	21
Les Halles | **D'town**	19
M & S Grill | **multi. loc.**	18
Z Morton's | **multi. loc.**	25
Nick's Chophse. | **Rockville**	17
Palm | **multi. loc.**	23
Z Prime Rib | **Gldn Triangle**	27
NEW Rarely Legal | **Bethesda**	–
NEW Ray's/Classics | **Silver Spring**	24
Z Ray's/Steaks | **Arlington**	27
Z Ruth's Chris | **multi. loc.**	24
Sam & Harry's | **Gldn Triangle**	21
Shula's | **Vienna**	18
Smith/Wollensky | **Gldn Triangle**	21
Timpano | **Rockville**	18
Warehouse B&G | **Alexandria**	19

TAIWANESE

Bob's Noodle | **Rockville**	22

TEAROOMS

Ching Ching | **Georgetown**	19
Teaism | **multi. loc.**	19

TEX-MEX

Austin Grill | **multi. loc.**	16
Cactus Cantina | **Cleve Pk**	18
Calif. Tortilla | **multi. loc.**	18
Guajillo | **Arlington**	22
Mi Rancho | **multi. loc.**	22
Uncle Julio's | **multi. loc.**	19

THAI

Z Bangkok54 | **Arlington**	25
Bangkok Joe's | **Georgetown**	20
Benjarong | **Rockville**	22
Busara | **multi. loc.**	20
NEW Cee Fine Thai | **Fairfax**	–
Crystal Thai | **Arlington**	23
Duangrat's | **Falls Ch**	23
Haad Thai | **D'town**	19
Mai Thai | **multi. loc.**	22
NEW Nark Kara Thai | **Bethesda**	–

Neisha Thai | **multi. loc.**	21
Neramitra | **Arlington**	17
NEW 1Gen Thai | **Arlington**	–
NEW Orchid Thai | **Ashburn**	–
Z Rabieng | **Falls Ch**	26
Regent, The | **Dupont Cir**	23
Rice | **Logan Cir**	22
Ruan Thai | **Wheaton**	–
Sakoontra | **Fairfax**	22
Sala Thai | **multi. loc.**	19
Simply Home | **U St**	–
Sweet Basil | **Bethesda**	22
Tara Thai | **multi. loc.**	20
T.H.A.I. | **Arlington**	21
Thai/Silver Spring | **Silver Spring**	19
Thai Basil | **Chantilly**	22
Thai Chili | **Chinatown**	20
Thai Farm | **Rockville**	19
Thaiphoon | **multi. loc.**	20
Z Thai Sq. | **Arlington**	26
Thai Tanic | **Logan Cir**	19

TURKISH

Cafe Divan | **Glover Pk**	20
Kazan | **McLean**	22
NEW Lemon Tree | **Rockville**	–
Levante's | **multi. loc.**	17
Nizam's | **Vienna**	22
Temel | **Fairfax**	21

VEGETARIAN

(* vegan)

Amma Veg. | **multi. loc.**	22
Amsterdam Falafel | **Adams Mor**	–
Luna Grill* | **multi. loc.**	19
Mandalay | **Silver Spring**	24
Mark's Kit. | **Takoma Pk**	19
Nirvana | **Gldn Triangle**	20
NEW Saravana Palace | **Fairfax**	–
Sticky Fingers* | **Columbia Hts**	–
Thyme Square | **Bethesda**	16
Udupi Palace | **Takoma Pk**	23
Vegetable Gdn.* | **Rockville**	19
Vegetate* | **Mt. Vernon Sq**	21
Yuan Fu* | **Rockville**	22

VIETNAMESE

Green Papaya | **Bethesda**	21
Huong Que | **Falls Ch**	23
Huong Viet | **Falls Ch**	23
Little Viet Garden | **Arlington**	19
Minh's | **Arlington**	22
Nam-Viet | **multi. loc.**	21
Pho 75 | **multi. loc.**	23
Saigon Saigon | **Arlington**	18
Taste of Saigon | **multi. loc.**	22

subscribe to zagat.com

Locations

Includes restaurant names, cuisines and Food ratings. 🄩 indicates places with the highest ratings, popularity and importance.

Washington, DC

ADAMS MORGAN/ MT. PLEASANT

Amsterdam Falafel	*Mideast.*	–
NEW Casa Oaxaca	*Mex.*	–
🄩 Cashion's Eat	*Amer.*	25
Diner, The	*Diner*	18
Felix	*Amer.*	18
Grill/Ipanema	*Brazilian*	20
La Fourchette	*French*	21
NEW Las Canteras	*Peruvian*	–
Leftbank	*Amer.*	15
Little Fountain	*Eclectic*	23
Luna Grill	*Diner/Veg.*	19
NEW M'Dawg	*Hot Dogs*	–
Meskerem	*Ethiopian*	21
Mezè	*Mideast.*	19
NEW Napoleon	*French*	–
Pasta Mia	*Italian*	24
Perrys	*Amer.*	19
Radius	*Italian*	22
Reef, The	*Amer.*	14
Saki	*Pan-Asian*	19
Tonic	*Amer.*	18
Tryst	*Coffee*	18
NEW Yazuzu	*Mideast.*	–

CAPITOL HILL

Au Bon Pain	*Bakery*	16
Banana Café	*Cuban/Puerto Rican*	18
Belga Café	*Belgian*	21
Bis	*French*	24
B. Smith's	*Southern*	19
Charlie Palmer	*Steak*	23
Hunan Dynasty	*Chinese*	–
Johnny's Half Shell	*Amer./Seafood*	23
Monocle	*Amer.*	17
Montmartre	*French*	23
Park Cafe	*Continental*	22
Sonoma	*Amer.*	21
Starfish Cafe	*Seafood*	17
Tapatinis	*Med.*	16
Two Quail	*Amer.*	17
Ugly Mug	*Pub*	17

CHINATOWN/ PENN QUARTER

(Including Gallery Place)

Au Bon Pain	*Bakery*	16
Austin Grill	*Tex-Mex*	16
Burma	*Burmese*	21
🄩 Café Atlántico	*Nuevo Latino*	25
Calif. Tortilla	*Tex-Mex*	18
🄩 Capital Grille	*Steak*	25
Caucus Room	*Amer.*	21
NEW Central M. Rich.	*Amer./French*	–
Chinatown Express	*Chinese*	22
🄩 Clyde's	*Amer.*	18
NEW D'Acqua	*Italian/Seafood*	–
District ChopHse.	*Steak*	20
Eat First	*Chinese*	22
Ella's Pizza	*Pizza*	19
Fadó Irish Pub	*Pub*	16
🄩 Five Guys	*Hamburgers*	24
Full Kee (DC)	*Chinese*	22
🄩 IndeBleu	*Indian*	23
🄩 Jaleo	*Spanish*	23
La Tasca	*Spanish*	16
🄩 Legal Sea Foods	*Seafood*	20
🄩 Le Paradou	*French*	27
Lucky Strike	*Amer.*	16
Matchbox	*Amer.*	23
🄩 McCormick/Schmick	*Seafood*	21
🄩 Oya	*Asian Fusion*	18
NEW Oyamel	*Mex.*	–
Poste Moderne	*Amer.*	21
NEW PS 7's	*Amer.*	–
🄩 Rasika	*Indian*	26
Rosa Mexicano	*Mex.*	20
🄩 Ruth's Chris	*Steak*	24
701	*Amer.*	23
Sushi-Go-Round	*Asian Fusion*	21
Teaism	*Tea*	19
Thai Chili	*Thai*	20
Tony Cheng's	*Chinese*	20
🄩 Tosca	*Italian*	26
Wok & Roll	*Chinese/Jap.*	15
🄩 Zaytinya	*Med./Mideast.*	25
Zengo	*Asian Fusion*	21
🄩 Zola	*Amer.*	22

DOWNTOWN

Au Bon Pain	*Bakery*	16
Bistro D'Oc	*French*	20
Bobby Van's Steak	*Steak*	20
NEW Brass. Beck	*Belgian/French*	–
Butterfield 9	*Amer.*	22
NEW Café du Parc	*French*	–
🄩 Café 15	*French*	25

☑ Ceiba	*Nuevo Latino*	24
Chef Geoff's	*Amer.*	18
☑ Corduroy	*Amer.*	25
☑ DC Coast	*Amer.*	24
Elephant & Castle	*Pub*	13
Finemondo	*Italian*	18
Finn & Porter	*Seafood/Steak*	17
Fogo de Chão	*Brazilian/Steak*	23
☑ Georgia Brown's	*Southern*	23
☑ Gerard's Place	*French*	27
Haad Thai	*Thai*	19
NEW Il Mulino	*Italian*	–
Les Halles	*French*	19
Lima	*Pan-Latin*	–
Luigino	*Italian*	18
M & S Grill	*Seafood/Steak*	18
NEW Mio	*Amer.*	–
Morrison-Clark Inn	*Amer.*	23
Occidental	*Amer.*	21
☑ Oceanaire	*Seafood*	24
☑ Old Ebbitt	*Amer.*	20
Palette	*Amer.*	22
NEW Posh	*Amer.*	–
☑ TenPenh	*Pan-Asian*	24
☑ Willard Room	*Amer.*	23

DUPONT CIRCLE

Al Tiramisu	*Italian*	23
NEW Banana Leaves	*Pan-Asian*	–
Bistrot du Coin	*French*	19
Buca di Beppo	*Italian*	15
Café Citron	*Pan-Latin*	17
Cafe Japoné	*Asian Fusion*	17
NEW Circa	*Amer.*	–
City Lights	*Chinese*	18
DuPont Grille	*Amer.*	19
Etrusco	*Italian*	20
Firefly	*Amer.*	21
Hank's Oyster	*Seafood*	23
Heritage India	*Indian*	23
i Ricchi	*Italian*	23
NEW Jack's Rest.	*Amer.*	–
☑ Komi	*Amer.*	26
Kramerbooks	*Amer.*	17
☑ Lauriol Plaza	*Mex.*	19
Levante's	*Med./Turkish*	17
Mai Thai	*Thai*	22
NEW Mandu	*Korean*	–
Mark/Orlando's	*Amer.*	24
NEW Marrakesh	*Moroccan*	–
Mimi's	*Amer.*	18
NEW Montsouris	*French*	–
Mourayo	*Greek*	23
☑ Nora	*Amer.*	25
☑ Obelisk	*Italian*	27
Penang	*Malaysian*	19

Pesce	*Seafood*	25
☑ Pizzeria Paradiso	*Pizza*	24
Raku	*Pan-Asian*	21
Regent, The	*Thai*	23
☑ Ruth's Chris	*Steak*	24
Sakana	*Jap.*	22
Sala Thai	*Thai*	19
Sette Osteria	*Italian*	20
Skewers/Luna	*Italian/Mideast.*	18
Straits/Malaya	*Malaysian*	21
☑ Sushi Taro	*Jap.*	25
☑ Tabard Inn	*Amer.*	23
Teaism	*Tea*	19
Thaiphoon	*Thai*	20
Topaz Bar	*Pan-Asian*	19
Uni	*Jap.*	20
NEW Urbana	*French/Italian*	–

FOGGY BOTTOM/
WORLD BANK

Au Bon Pain	*Bakery*	16
Bread Line	*Bakery*	24
Dish + Drinks	*Amer.*	19
El Chalan	*Peruvian*	20
Kaz Sushi	*Jap.*	25
☑ Kinkead's	*Seafood*	26
Notti Bianche	*Italian*	24
Primi Piatti	*Italian*	21
Roof Terr./JFK Ctr.	*Amer.*	17
Taberna/Alabardero	*Spanish*	24
Tonic	*Amer.*	18

GEORGETOWN/
GLOVER PARK

Agraria	*Amer.*	–
Amma Veg.	*Indian*	22
Bangkok Joe's	*Thai*	20
Bistro Français	*French*	19
Bistrot Lepic	*French*	24
Busara	*Thai*	20
Café Bonaparte	*French*	22
Cafe Divan	*Turkish*	20
Cafe Milano	*Italian*	20
Chez Mama-San	*Jap.*	21
Ching Ching	*Tea*	19
Chopsticks	*Jap.*	19
☑ Citronelle	*French*	28
☑ Clyde's	*Amer.*	18
Curry Club	*Indian*	24
Dean & DeLuca	*Eclectic*	21
☑ Fahrenheit/Degrees	*Amer.*	22
Filomena	*Italian*	22
☑ Five Guys	*Hamburgers*	24
Heritage India	*Indian*	23
NEW Hook	*Amer.*	–
La Chaumiere	*French*	24

La Madeleine | *French*	17
Leopold's Kafe | *Austrian*	21
Martin's Tav. | *Amer.*	18
Maté | *Asian Fusion*	17
Mendocino Grille | *Amer./Calif.*	23
☑ Mie N Yu | *Amer.*	18
Moby Dick | *Persian*	22
☑ Morton's | *Steak*	25
My Bakery & Café | *Bakery/S Amer.*	18
Nathans | *Amer.*	18
Neyla | *Lebanese*	22
Old Glory BBQ | *BBQ*	19
Paolo's | *Calif./Italian*	18
Peacock Cafe | *Amer.*	21
☑ Pizzeria Paradiso | *Pizza*	24
Rist. La Perla | *Italian*	19
Rocklands | *BBQ*	22
NEW Rugby Café | *Eclectic*	-
Sea Catch | *Seafood*	21
☑ Seasons | *Amer.*	27
Sequoia | *Amer.*	15
☑ 1789 | *Amer.*	26
Sushi-Ko | *Jap.*	24
Tony & Joe | *Seafood*	14
Zed's | *Ethiopian*	20

GOLDEN TRIANGLE

Au Bon Pain | *Bakery*	16
NEW BLT Steak | *Steak*	-
Bombay Club | *Indian*	25
Bombay Palace | *Indian*	23
Cafe Asia | *Pan-Asian*	19
C.F. Folks | *Eclectic*	23
Equinox | *Amer.*	25
Grillfish | *Seafood*	18
Kolumbia | *Amer.*	18
Lafayette Rm. | *Amer.*	24
☑ Legal Sea Foods | *Seafood*	20
Malaysia Kopitiam | *Malaysian*	22
Mar de Plata | *Spanish*	21
☑ McCormick/Schmick | *Seafood*	21
Meiwah | *Chinese*	20
Moby Dick | *Persian*	22
☑ Morton's | *Steak*	25
Nirvana | *Indian*	20
Nooshi | *Pan-Asian*	19
Olives | *Med.*	22
Oval Room | *Amer.*	21
Palm | *Seafood/Steak*	23
☑ Prime Rib | *Steak*	27
Sam & Harry's | *Steak*	21
Sesto Senso | *Italian*	20
Smith/Wollensky | *Steak*	21
Spezie | *Italian*	19

Teaism | *Tea*	19
Teatro Goldoni | *Italian*	23
NEW Vapiano | *Italian*	-
☑ Vidalia | *Amer.*	26
NEW Wasabi | *Jap.*	-

MT. VERNON SQUARE/ NEW CONVENTION CENTER

Acadiana | *Cajun/Creole*	23
Coeur de Lion | *Amer.*	23
☑ Five Guys | *Hamburgers*	24
NEW Old Dominion | *Pub*	-
Vegetate | *Amer./Veg.*	21

PALISADES

☑ BlackSalt | *Amer./Seafood*	26
D.C. Boathse. | *Amer.*	14
Kotobuki | *Jap.*	24
☑ Makoto | *Jap.*	28

PETWORTH/ BRIGHTWOOD/ COLUMBIA HEIGHTS

Domku | *E Euro./Scan.*	26
NEW El Limeño | *Mex./Salvadoran*	-
Pollo Campero | *Central Amer.*	17
Sticky Fingers | *Bakery/Vegan*	-
Temperance Hall | *Amer.*	-

SCOTT CIRCLE/ LOGAN CIRCLE

Bar Pilar | *Amer.*	16
NEW Beacon B&G | *Amer.*	-
Café Saint-Ex | *Eclectic*	19
15 ria | *Amer.*	19
Logan Tav. | *Amer.*	17
Mar de Plata | *Spanish*	21
Merkado Kit. | *Nuevo Latino*	19
Nage | *Amer./Seafood*	-
Rice | *Thai*	22
Stoney's B&G | *Pub*	-
Thai Tanic | *Thai*	19
Viridian | *Amer.*	20

SW

☑ Café MoZU | *Amer.*	22
☑ CityZen | *Amer.*	26
Mitsitam | *Amer.*	22
Phillips | *Seafood*	15

UPPER NW

Arucola | *Italian*	18
Buck's Fishing | *Amer.*	20
Cafe Deluxe | *Amer.*	18
Café Olé | *Med.*	21
☑ Cheesecake Fact. | *Amer.*	18

Chef Geoff's	*Amer.*	18
Colorado Kit.	*Amer.*	24
NEW Comet Ping Pong	*Pizza*	-
Dahlia	*Amer.*	21
Delhi Dhaba	*Indian*	17
Le Chat Noir	*French*	18
Maggiano's	*Italian*	18
Matisse	*French/Med.*	20
NEW Morty's Deli	*Deli*	-
Murasaki	*Jap.*	22
Negril	*Jamaican*	21
Neisha Thai	*Thai*	21
Yosaku	*Jap.*	21

U STREET CORRIDOR

Al Crostino	*Italian*	22
Ben's Chili Bowl	*Diner*	21
Busboys & Poets	*Amer./Eclectic*	18
Chi-Cha Lounge	*S Amer.*	16
Coppi's Organic	*Italian*	22
Crème	*Amer.*	23
Dukem	*Ethiopian*	23
Etete	*Ethiopian*	23
Florida Ave. Grill	*Diner*	21
Islander Carib.	*Carib.*	20
Local 16	*Amer.*	15
Oohhs & Aahhs	*Southern*	-
NEW Pyramids	*Moroccan*	-
Sala Thai	*Thai*	19
Simply Home	*Thai*	-
Tabaq Bistro	*Med.*	19
U-topia	*Eclectic*	16

WEST END

Agua Ardiente	*Nuevo Latino*	17
☑ Asia Nora	*Pan-Asian*	25
Blue Duck	*Amer.*	26
Circle Bistro	*Amer.*	21
Juniper	*Amer.*	19
☑ Marcel's	*Belgian/French*	28

WOODLEY PARK/
CLEVELAND PARK

Ardeo	*Amer.*	21
Bardeo Wine	*Amer.*	21
Cactus Cantina	*Tex-Mex*	18
Dino	*Italian*	19
☑ Indique	*Indian*	24
Lavandou	*French*	21
☑ Lebanese Tav.	*Lebanese*	22
Nam-Viet	*Viet.*	21
New Heights	*Amer.*	22
Open City	*Diner*	17
☑ Palena	*Amer.*	26
Pesto	*Italian*	17
Petits Plats	*French*	22
☑ Sake Club	*Jap.*	23

Sala Thai	*Thai*	19
Sorriso	*Italian*	20
Spices	*Pan-Asian*	20
Sushi Sushi	*Jap.*	19
Tono Sushi	*Jap.*	21
☑ 2 Amys	*Pizza*	25

Nearby Maryland

BETHESDA/
CHEVY CHASE

Austin Grill	*Tex-Mex*	16
Black's Bar	*Amer.*	23
Brass. Monte Carlo	*French/Med.*	22
NEW Buona Sera	*Italian*	-
Cafe Deluxe	*Amer.*	18
Calif. Tortilla	*Tex-Mex*	18
Centro Italian	*Italian*	21
Cesco	*Italian*	23
Ches. Chicken/Ribs	*BBQ*	-
City Lights	*Chinese*	18
☑ Clyde's	*Amer.*	18
David Craig	*Amer.*	25
Delhi Dhaba	*Indian*	17
Divino	*Argent.*	20
NEW Famoso	*Italian*	-
Faryab	*Afghan*	22
Grapeseed	*Amer.*	24
Green Papaya	*Viet.*	21
NEW Guardado's	*Pan-Latin/Spanish*	-
Haandi	*Indian*	23
Hard Times Cafe	*Amer.*	19
Hinode	*Jap.*	20
☑ Indique	*Indian*	24
☑ Jaleo	*Spanish*	23
Jean-Michel	*French*	24
La Ferme	*French*	22
La Madeleine	*French*	17
La Miche	*French*	22
☑ Legal Sea Foods	*Seafood*	20
Levante's	*Med./Turkish*	17
NEW LIA'S	*Amer.*	-
French Qtr./Louisiana	*Cajun*	22
Mamma Lucia	*Italian*	19
Matuba	*Jap.*	21
NEW M Cafe	*Italian*	-
☑ McCormick/Schmick	*Seafood*	21
Meiwah	*Chinese*	20
NEW Mia's Pizzas	*Pizza*	-
Moby Dick	*Persian*	22
Mon Ami Gabi	*French*	19
☑ Morton's	*Steak*	25
NEW Nark Kara Thai	*Thai*	-
New Orleans Bistro	*Cajun/Creole*	18

subscribe to zagat.com

Oakville Grille	*Amer.*	18
Olazzo	*Italian*	22
Passage to India	*Indian*	24
NEW Persimmon	*Amer.*	26
NEW Pizza Zero	*Pizza*	-
Praline	*Amer./Bakery*	-
Raku	*Pan-Asian*	21
NEW Rarely Legal	*Steak*	-
Rí-Rá Irish Pub	*Pub*	15
Rock Creek	*Amer.*	23
Z Ruth's Chris	*Steak*	24
Sala Thai	*Thai*	19
Sweet Basil	*Thai*	22
Tako Grill	*Jap.*	24
Tara Thai	*Thai*	20
Tavira	*Portug.*	21
Thyme Square	*Amer.*	16
Tragara	*Italian*	22
Uncle Julio's	*Tex-Mex*	19
Yin Yankee	*Asian Fusion*	24

GAITHERSBURG/ DICKERSON/ GERMANTOWN/OLNEY/ SHADY GROVE

Agrodolce	*Italian*	22
Buca di Beppo	*Italian*	15
Café Mileto	*Italian*	17
Café Spice	*Indian*	18
Calif. Tortilla	*Tex-Mex*	18
Comus Inn	*Amer.*	20
Dogfish Head	*Pub*	17
French Qtr./Louisiana	*Cajun*	22
Fu Shing	*Chinese*	18
Hakuba	*Jap.*	23
Hard Times Cafe	*Amer.*	19
India Palace	*Indian*	23
Le Palais	*French*	-
Mamma Lucia	*Italian*	19
Mannequin Pis	*Belgian*	23
Minerva	*Indian*	22
Mi Rancho	*Tex-Mex*	22
Moby Dick	*Persian*	22
New Fortune	*Chinese*	21
Peking Cheers	*Chinese*	-
Pollo Campero	*Central Amer.*	17
Red Hot & Blue	*BBQ*	19
Tandoori Nights	*Indian*	22
Tara Thai	*Thai*	20
Uncle Julio's	*Tex-Mex*	19
NEW Zodiac Grill	*Amer./BBQ*	-

POTOMAC/GLEN ECHO

Amici Miei	*Italian*	20
NEW Bezu	*Asian Fusion*	-
Calif. Tortilla	*Tex-Mex*	18

Irish Inn/Glen Echo	*Irish*	17
Old Angler's	*Amer.*	21
Renato at River Falls	*Italian*	17

PRINCE GEORGE'S COUNTY

Calif. Tortilla	*Tex-Mex*	18
Cuba de Ayer	*Cuban*	19
El Tapatio's	*Mex.*	-
Franklin's	*Pub*	17
Hard Times Cafe	*Amer.*	19
Irene's Pupusas	*Central Amer.*	-
Jerry's Seafood	*Seafood*	24
La Sirenita	*Mex.*	-
Mamma Lucia	*Italian*	19
Myung Dong	*Korean*	-
Pasta Plus	*Italian*	24
Pho 75	*Viet.*	23
Pollo Campero	*Central Amer.*	17
Red Hot & Blue	*BBQ*	19
Seven Seas	*Chinese/Jap.*	18
Taqueria/Reyes	*Mex.*	-

ROCKVILLE/GARRETT PARK/WHITE FLINT

A&J	*Chinese*	22
Addie's	*Amer.*	23
Amada Amante	*Italian*	20
Andalucia	*Spanish*	18
Benjarong	*Thai*	22
Black Market	*Amer.*	24
NEW Bob's 88	*Jap.*	-
Bob's Noodle	*Taiwanese*	22
Bombay Bistro	*Indian*	23
Calif. Tortilla	*Tex-Mex*	18
Caribbean Feast	*Jamaican*	21
NEW Cava	*Greek*	-
Z Cheesecake Fact.	*Amer.*	18
Z Clyde's	*Amer.*	18
Crisp & Juicy	*Peruvian*	24
El Mariachi	*Mex.*	23
Fontina Grille	*Italian*	17
Green Field	*Brazilian*	19
Greystone Grill	*Amer.*	20
Hard Times Cafe	*Amer.*	19
Hinode	*Jap.*	20
Z Il Pizzico	*Italian*	25
Joe's Noodle Hse.	*Chinese*	22
NEW La Limeña	*Cuban/Peruvian*	-
La Madeleine	*French*	17
La Tasca	*Spanish*	16
Z Lebanese Tav.	*Lebanese*	22
NEW Lemon Tree	*Turkish*	-
Light House Tofu	*Korean*	-
L'oustalet	*French*	22
Mamma Lucia	*Italian*	19

Moby Dick	*Persian*	22
Mykonos Grill	*Greek*	21
Nick's Chophse.	*Steak*	17
Niwanohana	*Jap.*	23
Z P.F. Chang's	*Chinese*	19
PGA Tour	*Amer.*	-
Pho 75	*Viet.*	23
Rocklands	*BBQ*	22
Seven Seas	*Chinese/Jap.*	18
Sol de España	*Spanish*	23
Taipei Tokyo	*Chinese/Jap.*	18
Tara Thai	*Thai*	20
Taste of Saigon	*Viet.*	22
Thai Farm	*Thai*	19
Timpano	*Italian/Steak*	18
Urban BBQ	*BBQ*	24
NEW Urban Burger	*Hamburgers*	-
Vegetable Gdn.	*Chinese/Veg.*	19
Yuan Fu	*Chinese/Veg.*	22

SILVER SPRING/ TAKOMA PARK/ WHEATON

Austin Grill	*Tex-Mex*	16
Azucar	*Pan-Latin*	26
Bombay	*Indian*	24
Calif. Tortilla	*Tex-Mex*	18
Ceviche	*Nuevo Latino*	23
Crisp & Juicy	*Peruvian*	24
Cubano's	*Cuban*	21
El Gavilan	*Salvadoran*	23
El Golfo	*S Amer.*	21
Z El Pollo Rico	*Peruvian*	25
Full Key	*Chinese*	20
Gallery	*Pan-Latin*	-
Good Fortune	*Chinese*	21
Hollywood East	*Chinese*	24
Irene's Pupusas	*Central Amer.*	-
Jackie's	*Amer.*	20
Z Lebanese Tav.	*Lebanese*	22
Mamma Lucia	*Italian*	19
Mandalay	*Burmese*	24
Mark's Kit.	*Amer.*	19
Mi Rancho	*Tex-Mex*	22
Moby Dick	*Persian*	22
Negril	*Jamaican*	21
Oriental East	*Chinese*	21
Parkway Deli	*Deli*	20
Pearl Seafood	*Med./Pan-Latin*	-
NEW Piratz Tav.	*Eclectic*	-
Pollo Campero	*Central Amer.*	17
Quarry House	*Amer.*	19
NEW Ray's/Classics	*Amer.*	24
redDog Cafe	*Amer.*	19
Ruan Thai	*Thai*	-

Samantha's	*Mex./Salvadoran*	22
Taste/Jerusaleum	*Mideast.*	-
Taste of Morocco	*Moroccan*	20
Thai/Silver Spring	*Thai*	19
Tiffin	*Indian*	21
Udupi Palace	*Indian/Veg.*	23
Woo Mi Gdn.	*Korean*	22

Nearby Virginia

ALEXANDRIA

Afghan	*Afghan*	20
A La Lucia	*Italian*	22
Austin Grill	*Tex-Mex*	16
NEW Bastille	*French*	-
Bistrot Lafayette	*French*	21
NEW Buzz	*Coffee*	-
Café Monti	*Austrian/Italian*	22
Café Salsa	*Nuevo Latino*	20
Z Clyde's	*Amer.*	18
Del Merei Grille	*Amer.*	23
NEW Eamonn's	*Irish*	-
Z Eve	*Amer.*	27
Evening Star	*Amer.*	22
Faccia Luna	*Pizza*	21
NEW Farrah Olivia	*Amer.*	-
Finn & Porter	*Seafood/Steak*	17
Z Five Guys	*Hamburgers*	24
Flying Fish	*Seafood*	19
NEW Food Matters	*Amer.*	-
Geranio	*Italian*	21
Grille, The	*Amer.*	25
Hard Times Cafe	*Amer.*	19
Hee Been	*Korean*	21
Indigo Landing	*Amer.*	-
Z La Bergerie	*French*	26
La Madeleine	*French*	17
Landini Bros.	*Italian*	22
La Tasca	*Spanish*	16
Le Gaulois	*French*	19
Le Refuge	*French*	22
Mai Thai	*Thai*	22
NEW Majestic	*Amer.*	-
My Bakery & Café	*Bakery/S Amer.*	18
100 King	*Amer.*	-
NEW Overwood	*Amer.*	-
Red Hot & Blue	*BBQ*	19
Rocklands	*BBQ*	22
RT's	*Cajun/Creole*	22
Rustico	*Amer.*	-
Simply Fish	*Seafood*	19
Taqueria/Poblano	*Mex.*	20
Ted's Montana	*Amer.*	18
Tempo	*French/Italian*	22

NEW Vaso's Kit. | *Greek* ⌐

Vermilion | *Amer.* 20

Warehouse B&G | *Seafood/Steak* 19

Yamazato | *Jap.* 22

ARLINGTON

Asia Bistro/Zen | *Pan-Asian* 19

Au Bon Pain | *Bakery* 16

☑ Bangkok54 | *Thai* 25

NEW Bebo | *Italian* ⌐

Bob & Edith's | *Diner* 16

Blvd. Woodgrill | *Amer.* 19

Cafe Asia | *Pan-Asian* 19

Calif. Tortilla | *Tex-Mex* 18

Caribbean Breeze | *Pan-Latin* 17

☑ Carlyle | *Amer.* 24

Cassatt's | *New Zealand* 20

☑ Cheesecake Fact. | *Amer.* 18

China Garden | *Chinese* 19

Crisp & Juicy | *Peruvian* 24

Crystal Thai | *Thai* 23

Delhi Club | *Indian* 22

Delhi Dhaba | *Indian* 17

Eleventh St. | *Amer.* ⌐

☑ El Pollo Rico | *Peruvian* 25

Extra Virgin | *Italian* 17

Faccia Luna | *Pizza* 21

Guajillo | *Mex.* 22

Gua-Rapo | *Nuevo Latino* 17

Hard Times Cafe | *Amer.* 19

Harry's Tap Rm. | *Seafood/Steak* 21

Il Radicchio | *Italian* 18

☑ Jaleo | *Spanish* 23

Kabob Palace | *Mideast.* 25

La Côte d'Or | *French* 21

La Tasca | *Spanish* 16

Layalina | *Mideast.* 23

☑ Lebanese Tav. | *Lebanese* 22

☑ Legal Sea Foods | *Seafood* 20

NEW Liberty Tav. | *Amer.* ⌐

Little Viet Garden | *Viet.* 19

Luna Grill | *Diner/Veg.* 19

Matuba | *Jap.* 21

☑ McCormick/Schmick | *Seafood* 21

NEW Mei's Asian | *Chinese/Jap.* ⌐

Minh's | *Viet.* 22

Moby Dick | *Persian* 22

☑ Morton's | *Steak* 25

Nam-Viet | *Viet.* 21

Neramitra | *Thai* 17

NEW 1Gen Thai | *Thai* ⌐

Pasha Cafe | *Med.* 21

☑ P.F. Chang's | *Chinese* 19

Pho 75 | *Viet.* 23

Pinzimini | *Italian* ⌐

Portabellos | *Amer.* 19

☑ Ray's/Steaks | *Steak* 27

Red Hot & Blue | *BBQ* 19

Rí-Rá Irish Pub | *Pub* 15

Rist. Murali | *Italian* 17

☑ Ritz, Grill (Pent. City) | *Amer.* 25

☑ Ruth's Chris | *Steak* 24

Saigon Saigon | *Viet.* 18

Sala Thai | *Thai* 19

Sette Bello | *Italian* 21

Siné | *Pub* 15

SoBe Seafood | *Seafood* 17

Tallula | *Amer.* 22

Tandoori Nights | *Indian* 22

Tapeo | *Spanish* ⌐

Taqueria/Charrito | *Salvadoran* 22

Taqueria/Poblano | *Mex.* 20

Tara Thai | *Thai* 20

Taste of Morocco | *Moroccan* 20

Ted's Montana | *Amer.* 18

T.H.A.I. | *Thai* 21

Thaiphoon | *Thai* 20

☑ Thai Sq. | *Thai* 26

Tivoli | *Italian* 22

Tutto Bene | *Italian* 18

Uncle Julio's | *Tex-Mex* 19

NEW Vapiano | *Italian* ⌐

Village Bistro | *Continental* 21

NEW Wasabi | *Jap.* ⌐

Willow | *Amer.* 24

FAIRFAX

Artie's | *Amer.* 23

Bombay Bistro | *Indian* 23

Calif. Tortilla | *Tex-Mex* 18

NEW Cee Fine Thai | *Thai* ⌐

China Star | *Chinese* 20

Chutzpah | *Deli* 19

Coastal Flats | *Seafood* 22

Dolce Vita | *Italian* 22

Jaipur | *Indian* 23

NEW La Rue 123 | *French* ⌐

Le Tire Bouchon | *Med.* ⌐

Minerva | *Indian* 22

Moby Dick | *Persian* 22

☑ P.F. Chang's | *Chinese* 19

NEW Rain | *Amer.* ⌐

Red Hot & Blue | *BBQ* 19

☑ Ruth's Chris | *Steak* 24

Sakoontra | *Thai* 22

NEW Saravana Palace | *Indian/Veg.* ⌐

Temel | *Med./Turkish* 21

Uncle Julio's | *Tex-Mex* 19

FALLS CHURCH

Argia's	*Italian*	20
Bamian	*Afghan*	-
Crisp & Juicy	*Peruvian*	24
Duangrat's	*Thai*	23
Elevation Burger	*Hamburgers*	21
Fortune	*Chinese*	19
Full Kee (VA)	*Chinese*	22
Haandi	*Indian*	23
Huong Que	*Viet.*	23
Huong Viet	*Viet.*	23
Kam Po	*Chinese/Peruvian*	-
La Madeleine	*French*	17
Lebanese Butcher	*Lebanese*	-
Mark's Duck Hse.	*Chinese*	23
Myanmar	*Burmese*	21
My Bakery & Café	*Bakery/S Amer.*	18
Panjshir	*Afghan*	23
☑ Peking Gourmet	*Chinese*	25
Pho 75	*Viet.*	23
Pollo Campero	*Central Amer.*	17
☑ Rabieng	*Thai*	26
Red Hot & Blue	*BBQ*	19
Shamshiry	*Persian*	23
Tara Thai	*Thai*	20
☑ 2941 Rest.	*Amer.*	27

GREAT FALLS

Fiore di Luna	*Italian*	22
☑ L'Aub./François	*French*	27

MCLEAN

Cafe Taj	*Indian*	19
Capri	*Italian*	21
Kazan	*Turkish*	22
Le Mistral	*French*	24
Moby Dick	*Persian*	22
Tachibana	*Jap.*	24

RESTON/HERNDON

Busara	*Thai*	20
☑ Clyde's	*Amer.*	18
El Manantial	*Italian/Spanish*	21
☑ Five Guys	*Hamburgers*	24
Hama Sushi/Obi	*Jap.*	21
Hard Times Cafe	*Amer.*	19
La Madeleine	*French*	17
M & S Grill	*Seafood/Steak*	18
Market St. B&G	*Amer.*	18
Matsuri	*Jap.*	20
☑ McCormick/Schmick	*Seafood*	21
Mikaku	*Jap.*	27
Minerva	*Indian*	22
☑ Morton's	*Steak*	25
Paolo's	*Calif./Italian*	18

Pho 75	*Viet.*	23
Pollo Campero	*Central Amer.*	17
San Vito	*Italian*	20
SBC Café	*Amer.*	24
🆕 Tavern/Lake	*Amer.*	-
Uncle Julio's	*Tex-Mex*	19
Yoko	*Jap.*	20

SPRINGFIELD/ ANNANDALE

A&J	*Chinese*	22
Austin Grill	*Tex-Mex*	16
☑ Five Guys	*Hamburgers*	24
Hard Times Cafe	*Amer.*	19
San Vito	*Italian*	20
Sorak Garden	*Korean*	22

TYSONS CORNER/ MERRIFIELD

Bistro 123	*French*	19
Bombay Tandoor	*Indian*	20
Busara	*Thai*	20
Cafe Deluxe	*Amer.*	18
☑ Capital Grille	*Steak*	25
☑ Cheesecake Fact.	*Amer.*	18
🆕 Chima	*Brazilian/Steak*	-
Chutzpah	*Deli*	19
☑ Clyde's	*Amer.*	18
Coastal Flats	*Seafood*	22
☑ Colvin Run	*Amer.*	25
Da Domenico	*Italian*	21
Fleming's Steak	*Steak*	24
Hunan Lion	*Chinese*	21
Konami	*Jap.*	22
La Madeleine	*French*	17
☑ Lebanese Tav.	*Lebanese*	22
☑ Legal Sea Foods	*Seafood*	20
☑ Maestro	*Italian*	28
Maggiano's	*Italian*	18
☑ McCormick/Schmick	*Seafood*	21
☑ Morton's	*Steak*	25
Neisha Thai	*Thai*	21
Palm	*Seafood/Steak*	23
☑ P.F. Chang's	*Chinese*	19
Shula's	*Steak*	18
Sweetwater Tav.	*SW*	22
Taste of Saigon	*Viet.*	22
Woo Lae Oak	*Korean*	22

VIENNA/OAKTON

Amma Veg.	*Indian*	22
Bazin's/Church	*Amer.*	-
🆕 Kansai Sushi	*Jap.*	-
Nizam's	*Turkish*	22
Panjshir	*Afghan*	23
Sweet Ginger	*Pan-Asian*	24

Tara Thai | *Thai* 20
Yama | *Jap.* 23
Yoko | *Jap.* 20

Exurban Virginia

BROADLANDS

🔲 Clyde's | *Amer.* 18

CENTREVILLE/
MANASSAS/PRINCE
WILLIAM COUNTY

🔲 Five Guys | *Hamburgers* 24
Hard Times Cafe | *Amer.* 19
My Bakery & Café | 18
  Bakery/S Amer.
Panino | *Italian* 26
Red Hot & Blue | *BBQ* 19
Sweetwater Tav. | *SW* 22

CHANTILLY

Minerva | *Indian* 22
Thai Basil | *Thai* 22

LEESBURG/LANSDOWNE

NEW Dock/Lansdowne | ⌐
  Amer./Seafood
NEW Emilio's | *Italian* ⌐
🔲 Lightfoot | *Amer.* 22

NEW Not Your Ave. Joe's | ⌐
  Amer.
Red Hot & Blue | *BBQ* 19
Tuscarora Mill | *Amer.* 23
NEW Vintage 50 | *Amer.* ⌐

PURCELLVILLE

Magnolias/Mill | *Amer.* 19

STERLING/ASHBURN/
SOUTH RIDING

NEW Café Panache | *Amer.* ⌐
NEW Orchid Thai | *Thai* ⌐
NEW Rangoli | *Indian* ⌐
San Vito | *Italian* 20
Sweetwater Tav. | *SW* 22
NEW Taste of Burma | *Burmese* ⌐
Ted's Montana | *Amer.* 18

Virginia Countryside

Ashby Inn | *Amer.* 22
Foti's | *Amer.* 27
NEW French Hound | *French* ⌐
Hunter's Head | *British* 20
🔲 Inn/Little Washington | 29
  Amer.
🔲 L'Aub. Provençale | *French* 25
Rail Stop | *Amer.* 20

Special Features

Listings cover the best in each category and include restaurant names, locations and Food ratings. Multi-location restaurants' features may vary by branch. ❷ indicates places with the highest ratings, popularity and importance.

ADDITIONS

(Properties added since the last edition of the book)

Amsterdam Falafel | **Adams Mor**	⌐
Banana Leaves | **Dupont Cir**	⌐
Bastille | **Alexandria**	⌐
Beacon B&G | **Scott Cir**	⌐
Bebo | **Arlington**	⌐
Bezu | **Potomac**	⌐
BLT Steak | **Gldn Triangle**	⌐
Bob's 88 | **Rockville**	⌐
Brass. Beck | **D'town**	⌐
Buona Sera | **Bethesda**	⌐
Buzz | **Alexandria**	⌐
Café du Parc | **D'town**	⌐
Café Panache | **Ashburn**	⌐
Casa Oaxaca | **Adams Mor**	⌐
Cava | **Rockville**	⌐
Cee Fine Thai | **Fairfax**	⌐
Central M. Rich. | **Penn Qtr**	⌐
Chima | **Vienna**	⌐
Circa | **Dupont Cir**	⌐
Comet Ping Pong | **Upper NW**	⌐
D'Acqua | **Penn Qtr**	⌐
Dock/Lansdowne | **Lansdowne**	⌐
Eamonn's | **Alexandria**	⌐
El Limeño | **Petworth**	⌐
Emilio's | **Lansdowne**	⌐
Famoso | **Chevy Chase**	⌐
Farrah Olivia | **Alexandria**	⌐
Food Matters | **Alexandria**	⌐
French Hound | **Mid'burg**	⌐
Guardado's | **Bethesda**	⌐
Hook | **Georgetown**	⌐
Hunan Dynasty | **Cap Hill**	⌐
Il Mulino | **D'town**	⌐
Irene's Pupusas | **multi. loc.**	⌐
Jack's Rest. | **Dupont Cir**	⌐
Kam Po | **Falls Ch**	⌐
Kansai Sushi | **Vienna**	⌐
La Limeña | **Rockville**	⌐
La Rue 123 | **Fairfax**	⌐
Las Canteras | **Adams Mor**	⌐
Lemon Tree | **Rockville**	⌐
LIA'S | **Chevy Chase**	⌐
Liberty Tav. | **Arlington**	⌐
Majestic | **Alexandria**	⌐
Mandu | **Dupont Cir**	⌐
Marrakesh | **Dupont Cir**	⌐
M Cafe | **Chevy Chase**	⌐
M'Dawg | **Adams Mor**	⌐
Mei's Asian | **Arlington**	⌐
Mia's Pizzas | **Bethesda**	⌐
Mio | **D'town**	⌐
Montsouris | **Dupont Cir**	⌐
Morty's Deli | **Upper NW**	⌐
Myung Dong | **Beltsville**	⌐
Napoleon | **Adams Mor**	⌐
Nark Kara Thai | **Bethesda**	⌐
Not Your Ave. Joe's | **Lansdowne**	⌐
Old Dominion | **Mt. Vernon Sq**	⌐
1Gen Thai | **Arlington**	⌐
Orchid Thai | **Ashburn**	⌐
Overwood | **Alexandria**	⌐
Oyamel | **Penn Qtr**	⌐
Peking Cheers | **Gaith'burg**	⌐
Piratz Tav. | **Silver Spring**	⌐
Pizza Zero | **Bethesda**	⌐
Posh | **D'town**	⌐
PS 7's | **Gallery Pl**	⌐
Pyramids | **U St**	⌐
Rain | **Fairfax**	⌐
Rangoli | **S Riding**	⌐
Rarely Legal | **Bethesda**	⌐
Ray's/Classics | **Silver Spring**	24
Ruan Thai | **Wheaton**	⌐
Rugby Café | **Georgetown**	⌐
Saravana Palace | **Fairfax**	⌐
Sticky Fingers | **Columbia Hts**	⌐
Stoney's B&G | **Logan Cir**	⌐
Taste of Burma | **Sterling**	⌐
Tavern/Lake | **Reston**	⌐
Urbana | **Dupont Cir**	⌐
Urban Burger | **Rockville**	⌐
Vapiano | **multi. loc.**	⌐
Vaso's Kit. | **Alexandria**	⌐
Vintage 50 | **Leesburg**	⌐
Wasabi | **multi. loc.**	⌐
Yazuzu | **Adams Mor**	⌐
Zodiac Grill | **Gaith'burg**	⌐

BREAKFAST

(See also Hotel Dining)

Ben's Chili Bowl | **U St**	21
Bob & Edith's | **Arlington**	16
Bread Line | **World Bank**	24
Dean & DeLuca | **Georgetown**	21
Diner, The | **Adams Mor**	18
Domku | **Petworth**	26

subscribe to zagat.com

Florida Ave. Grill | **U St**	21
Johnny's Half Shell | **Cap Hill**	23
La Madeleine | **multi. loc.**	17
Leopold's Kafe | **Georgetown**	21
French Qtr./Louisiana | **Bethesda**	22
Mark's Kit. | **Takoma Pk**	19
☑ Old Ebbitt | **D'town**	20
Parkway Deli | **Silver Spring**	20
Pho 75 | **multi. loc.**	23
Teaism | **multi. loc.**	19
Tryst | **Adams Mor**	18

BRUNCH

Ardeo | **Cleve Pk**	21
Artie's | **Fairfax**	23
Bangkok Joe's | **Georgetown**	20
Bis | **Cap Hill**	24
Black Market | **Garrett Pk**	24
Bombay Club | **Gldn Triangle**	25
B. Smith's | **Cap Hill**	19
Café Bonaparte | **Georgetown**	22
Cafe Deluxe | **multi. loc.**	18
Café Saint-Ex | **Logan Cir**	19
☑ Carlyle | **Arlington**	24
☑ Cashion's Eat | **Adams Mor**	25
Chef Geoff's | **multi. loc.**	18
☑ Clyde's | **multi. loc.**	18
Colorado Kit. | **Upper NW**	24
Duangrat's | **Falls Ch**	23
Evening Star | **Alexandria**	22
15 ria | **Scott Cir**	19
☑ Georgia Brown's | **D'town**	23
Hank's Oyster | **Dupont Cir**	23
Indigo Landing | **Alexandria**	–
☑ L'Aub. Provençale | **Boyce**	25
Morrison-Clark Inn | **D'town**	23
NEW Napoleon | **Adams Mor**	–
Nathans | **Georgetown**	18
Old Angler's | **Potomac**	21
☑ Old Ebbitt | **D'town**	20
Perrys | **Adams Mor**	19
☑ Rabieng | **Falls Ch**	26
Rail Stop | **Plains**	20
☑ Ritz, Grill (Pent. City) | **Arlington**	25
Roof Terr./JFK Ctr. | **Foggy Bottom**	17
☑ Seasons | **Georgetown**	27
Sequoia | **Georgetown**	15

BUSINESS DINING

Acadiana | **Mt. Vernon Sq**	23
Addie's | **Rockville**	23
Agraria | **Georgetown**	–
Artie's | **Fairfax**	23
Bamian | **Falls Ch**	–
Bazin's/Church | **Vienna**	–

NEW Beacon B&G | **Scott Cir**	–
Bis | **Cap Hill**	24
☑ BlackSalt | **Palisades**	26
NEW BLT Steak | **Gldn Triangle**	–
Blue Duck | **West End**	26
Bobby Van's Steak | **D'town**	20
Bombay Club | **Gldn Triangle**	25
Bombay Tandoor | **Vienna**	20
NEW Brass. Beck | **D'town**	–
Busara | **Reston**	20
Butterfield 9 | **D'town**	22
NEW Café du Parc | **D'town**	–
☑ Café 15 | **D'town**	25
☑ Capital Grille | **multi. loc.**	25
☑ Carlyle | **Arlington**	24
Caucus Room | **Penn Qtr**	21
NEW Cava | **Rockville**	–
NEW Cee Fine Thai | **Fairfax**	–
☑ Ceiba | **D'town**	24
NEW Central M. Rich. | **Penn Qtr**	–
Ceviche | **Silver Spring**	23
Charlie Palmer | **Cap Hill**	23
NEW Chima | **Vienna**	–
☑ Citronelle | **Georgetown**	28
☑ CityZen | **SW**	26
☑ Clyde's | **multi. loc.**	18
☑ Colvin Run | **Vienna**	25
Dahlia | **Upper NW**	21
☑ DC Coast | **D'town**	24
NEW Dock/Lansdowne | **Lansdowne**	–
Equinox | **Gldn Triangle**	25
☑ Eve | **Alexandria**	27
Extra Virgin | **Arlington**	17
NEW Farrah Olivia | **Alexandria**	–
Finn & Porter | **multi. loc.**	17
Fogo de Chão | **D'town**	23
☑ Georgia Brown's | **D'town**	23
☑ Gerard's Place | **D'town**	27
Grille, The | **Alexandria**	25
Harry's Tap Rm. | **Arlington**	21
NEW Hook | **Georgetown**	–
Hunan Dynasty | **Cap Hill**	–
NEW Il Mulino | **D'town**	–
Indigo Landing | **Alexandria**	–
☑ Indique | **Chevy Chase**	24
i Ricchi | **Dupont Cir**	23
Jackie's | **Silver Spring**	20
Johnny's Half Shell | **Cap Hill**	23
NEW Kansai Sushi | **Vienna**	–
Kaz Sushi | **World Bank**	25
☑ Kinkead's | **Foggy Bottom**	26
Konami | **Vienna**	22
Lafayette Rm. | **Gldn Triangle**	24
NEW La Rue 123 | **Fairfax**	–

Le Palais | Gaith'burg	–
NEW LIA'S | Chevy Chase	–
NEW Liberty Tav. | Arlington	–
Lima | D'town	–
Z Maestro | McLean	28
Magnolias/Mill | Purcellville	19
Mai Thai | Dupont Cir	22
M & S Grill | D'town	18
Z Marcel's | West End	28
Martin's Tav. | Georgetown	18
Matsuri | Herndon	20
Z McCormick/Schmick | multi. loc.	21
Monocle | Cap Hill	17
Z Morton's | multi. loc.	25
Nage | Scott Cir	–
Neramitra | Arlington	17
Notti Bianche | Foggy Bottom	24
NEW Not Your Ave. Joe's | Lansdowne	–
Occidental | D'town	21
Z Oceanaire | D'town	24
Z Old Ebbitt | D'town	20
Olives | Gldn Triangle	22
100 King | Alexandria	–
NEW Orchid Thai | Ashburn	–
Oval Room | Gldn Triangle	21
NEW Overwood | Alexandria	–
NEW Oyamel | Penn Qtr	–
Palm | multi. loc.	23
PGA Tour | Rockville	–
Pinzimini | Arlington	–
Poste Moderne | Penn Qtr	21
Z Prime Rib | Gldn Triangle	27
NEW PS 7's | Gallery Pl	–
NEW Rain | Fairfax	–
NEW Rangoli | S Riding	–
NEW Rarely Legal | Bethesda	–
Z Ritz, Grill (Pent. City) | Arlington	25
Rustico | Alexandria	–
Z Ruth's Chris | multi. loc.	24
Sam & Harry's | Gldn Triangle	21
Z Seasons | Georgetown	27
701 | Penn Qtr	23
Smith/Wollensky | Gldn Triangle	21
Taberna/Alabardero | World Bank	24
Taste of Morocco | Silver Spring	20
Teatro Goldoni | Gldn Triangle	23
Ted's Montana | Arlington	18
Thai/Silver Spring | Silver Spring	19
Z Tosca | Penn Qtr	26
Z 2941 Rest. | Falls Ch	27
NEW Urbana | Dupont Cir	–
Z Vidalia | Gldn Triangle	26

Z Willard Room | D'town	23
Willow | Arlington	24
Woo Lae Oak | Vienna	22
Zengo | Chinatown	21
Z Zola | Penn Qtr	22

CHEF'S TABLE

NEW Beacon B&G | Scott Cir	–
NEW Bezu | Potomac	–
Z BlackSalt | Palisades	26
Blue Duck | West End	26
NEW Brass. Beck | D'town	–
Z Citronelle | Georgetown	28
Z DC Coast | D'town	24
Z IndeBleu | Penn Qtr	23
NEW Jack's Rest. | Dupont Cir	–
Z Lightfoot | Leesburg	22
Matisse | Upper NW	20
Z Tosca | Penn Qtr	26
Z 2941 Rest. | Falls Ch	27

CHILD-FRIENDLY

(Alternatives to the usual fast-food places; * children's menu available)

Argia's | Falls Ch	20
Artie's* | Fairfax	23
Arucola | Upper NW	18
Austin Grill* | multi. loc.	16
Cactus Cantina* | Cleve Pk	18
Cafe Deluxe* | multi. loc.	18
Calif. Tortilla* | multi. loc.	18
Z Carlyle | Arlington	24
Chef Geoff's* | multi. loc.	18
Z Clyde's* | multi. loc.	18
Coastal Flats* | Fairfax	22
NEW Comet Ping Pong | Upper NW	–
Del Merei Grille* | Alexandria	23
Elevation Burger | Falls Ch	21
El Gavilan | Silver Spring	23
El Golfo* | Silver Spring	21
Ella's Pizza | Penn Qtr	19
15 ria* | Scott Cir	19
Z Five Guys | multi. loc.	24
NEW Food Matters | Alexandria	–
Hollywood East | Wheaton	24
Kabob Palace | Arlington	25
Z L'Aub./François* | Grt Falls	27
Z Lebanese Tav.* | multi. loc.	22
Z Legal Sea Foods* | multi. loc.	20
Maggiano's* | multi. loc.	18
Mark's Kit. | Takoma Pk	19
Minerva* | multi. loc.	22
Mi Rancho | multi. loc.	22
Old Glory BBQ* | Georgetown	19
Z P.F. Chang's | multi. loc.	19

Pizzeria Paradiso | **Dupont Cir** 24

Red Hot & Blue* | **multi. loc.** 19

Rí-Rá Irish Pub* | **Bethesda** 15

701 | **Penn Qtr** 23

Sweetwater Tav.* | **multi. loc.** 22

Taqueria/Poblano* | **multi. loc.** 20

Tara Thai* | **multi. loc.** 20

Ted's Montana* | **Alexandria** 18

🆉 2 Amys | **Cleve Pk** 25

Uncle Julio's* | **multi. loc.** 19

DESSERT

Black Market | **Garrett Pk** 24

🆉 BlackSalt | **Palisades** 26

Black's Bar | **Bethesda** 23

Blue Duck | **West End** 26

Bread Line | **World Bank** 24

Butterfield 9 | **D'town** 22

🆕 Buzz | **Alexandria** –

🆉 Café Atlántico | **Penn Qtr** 25

🆉 Café MoZU | **SW** 22

🆉 Carlyle | **Arlington** 24

🆉 Cashion's Eat | **Adams Mor** 25

🆉 Ceiba | **D'town** 24

🆉 Cheesecake Fact. | **multi. loc.** 18

🆉 Citronelle | **Georgetown** 28

🆉 CityZen | **SW** 26

🆉 Colvin Run | **Vienna** 25

🆉 DC Coast | **D'town** 24

Equinox | **Gldn Triangle** 25

🆉 Eve | **Alexandria** 27

🆕 Hook | **Georgetown** –

🆉 IndeBleu | **Penn Qtr** 23

Indigo Landing | **Alexandria** –

🆉 Inn/Little Washington | **Washington** 29

🆉 Jaleo | **multi. loc.** 23

Johnny's Half Shell | **Cap Hill** 23

🆉 Kinkead's | **Foggy Bottom** 26

🆕 Majestic | **Alexandria** –

🆉 Palena | **Cleve Pk** 26

Praline | **Bethesda** –

Roof Terr./JFK Ctr. | **Foggy Bottom** 17

🆉 1789 | **Georgetown** 26

🆉 TenPenh | **D'town** 24

🆉 2941 Rest. | **Falls Ch** 27

Willow | **Arlington** 24

🆉 Zaytinya | **Penn Qtr** 25

ENTERTAINMENT

(Call for days and times of performances)

Andalucia | flamenco/guitar | **Rockville** 18

Banana Café | piano | **Cap Hill** 18

Bombay Club | piano | **Gldn Triangle** 25

Cafe Asia | DJ | **Rosslyn** 19

Cafe Japoné | jazz/karaoke | **Dupont Cir** 17

Café Saint-Ex | DJ | **Logan Cir** 19

Café Salsa | salsa | **Alexandria** 20

Chi-Cha Lounge | DJ/Latin | **U St** 16

Coeur de Lion | piano | **Mt. Vernon Sq** 23

Duangrat's | Thai dancing | **Falls Ch** 23

Dukem | Ethiopian bands | **U St** 23

Evening Star | bands | **Alexandria** 22

🆉 Fahrenheit/Degrees | piano | **Georgetown** 22

Felix | varies | **Adams Mor** 18

🆉 Georgia Brown's | jazz | **D'town** 23

🆉 IndeBleu | DJ | **Penn Qtr** 23

Islander Carib. | varies | **U St** 20

🆉 Jaleo | flamenco dancing | **multi. loc.** 23

🆉 Kinkead's | jazz | **Foggy Bottom** 26

🆉 Marcel's | jazz/piano | **West End** 28

Mimi's | singing waiters | **Dupont Cir** 18

Neyla | DJ | **Georgetown** 22

Perrys | drag brunch | **Adams Mor** 19

Saki | DJ | **Adams Mor** 19

Sesto Senso | dancing/DJ | **Gldn Triangle** 20

701 | jazz/piano | **Penn Qtr** 23

Taste of Morocco | dancing | **Arlington** 20

Timpano | bands/jazz | **Rockville** 18

Tutto Bene | opera | **Arlington** 18

U-topia | blues/jazz | **U St** 16

FIREPLACES

Agraria | **Georgetown** –

Al Tiramisu | **Dupont Cir** 23

Ashby Inn | **Paris** 22

Bis | **Cap Hill** 24

Bistro D'Oc | **D'town** 20

🆕 Chima | **Vienna** –

Circle Bistro | **West End** 21

🆉 Clyde's | **multi. loc.** 18

Comus Inn | **Dickerson** 20

Dish + Drinks | **Foggy Bottom** 19

Dukem | **U St** 23

Fadó Irish Pub | **Chinatown** 16

15 ria | **Scott Cir** 19

Fogo de Chão | **D'town** 23

Foti's | **Culpeper** 27

Geranio | **Alexandria**	21
Harry's Tap Rm. | **Arlington**	21
⧉ IndeBleu | **Penn Qtr**	23
i Ricchi | **Dupont Cir**	23
Irish Inn/Glen Echo | **Glen Echo**	17
La Chaumiere | **Georgetown**	24
La Ferme | **Chevy Chase**	22
La Madeleine | **multi. loc.**	17
NEW La Rue 123 | **Fairfax**	-
⧉ L'Aub./François | **Grt Falls**	27
⧉ L'Aub. Provençale | **Boyce**	25
Le Gaulois | **Alexandria**	19
NEW Lemon Tree | **Rockville**	-
NEW LIA'S | **Chevy Chase**	-
Lightfoot | **Leesburg**	22
Matisse | **Upper NW**	20
Monocle | **Cap Hill**	17
Morrison-Clark Inn | **D'town**	23
Old Angler's | **Potomac**	21
⧉ Oya | **Penn Qtr**	18
Petits Plats | **Woodley Pk**	22
⧉ Ritz, Grill (Pent. City) | **Arlington**	25
Rustico | **Alexandria**	-
Sea Catch | **Georgetown**	21
Sette Bello | **Arlington**	21
⧉ 1789 | **Georgetown**	26
Siné | **Arlington**	15
Sonoma | **Cap Hill**	21
⧉ Tabard Inn | **Dupont Cir**	23
Tavira | **Chevy Chase**	21
Timpano | **Rockville**	18
NEW Vapiano | **Arlington**	-
⧉ Zaytinya | **Penn Qtr**	25

HISTORIC PLACES

(Year opened; * building)

1750 | Hunter's Head* | **Upperville**	20
1753 | L'Aub. Provençale* | **Boyce**	25
1800 | Overwood* | **Alexandria**	-
1829 | Ashby Inn* | **Paris**	22
1830 | La Rue 123* | **Fairfax**	-
1841 | Poste Moderne* | **Penn Qtr**	21
1851 | Willard Room* | **D'town**	23
1856 | Old Ebbitt | **D'town**	20
1860 | Old Angler's* | **Potomac**	21
1862 | Comus Inn* | **Dickerson**	20
1864 | Morrison-Clark Inn* | **D'town**	23
1876 | District ChopHse.* | **Penn Qtr**	20
1885 | Monocle* | **Cap Hill**	17
1887 | Tabard Inn* | **Dupont Cir**	23
1888 | Lightfoot* | **Leesburg**	22

1890 | Inn/Little Washington* | **Washington**	29
1890 | La Bergerie* | **Alexandria**	26
1890 | Nora* | **Dupont Cir**	25
1890 | Two Quail* | **Cap Hill**	17
1897 | Irish Inn/Glen Echo* | **Glen Echo**	17
1904 | Occidental* | **D'town**	21
1905 | Magnolias/Mill* | **Purcellville**	19
1907 | Liberty Tav.* | **Arlington**	-
1908 | B. Smith's* | **Cap Hill**	19
1909 | Ben's Chili Bowl* | **U St**	21
1932 | Fahrenheit/Degrees* | **Georgetown**	22
1932 | Majestic* | **Alexandria**	-
1933 | Martin's Tav. | **Georgetown**	18
1944 | Florida Ave. Grill | **U St**	21
1954 | L'Aub./François | **Grt Falls**	27

HOTEL DINING

Ashby Inn
Ashby Inn | **Paris**	22

Bailiwick Inn
NEW La Rue 123 | **Fairfax**	-

Beacon Hotel
NEW Beacon B&G | **Scott Cir**	-

Doubletree Hotel
15 ria | **Scott Cir**	19

Fairmont Hotel
Juniper | **West End**	19

Four Seasons Hotel
⧉ Seasons | **Georgetown**	27

George, Hotel
Bis | **Cap Hill**	24

George Washington Univ. Inn
Notti Bianche | **Foggy Bottom**	24

Hay-Adams
Lafayette Rm. | **Gldn Triangle**	24

Henley Park Hotel
Coeur de Lion | **Mt. Vernon Sq**	23

Hilton Alexandria
Finn & Porter | **Alexandria**	17

Hyatt Hotel
⧉ Morton's | **Bethesda**	25

Hyatt Regency Reston
Market St. B&G | **Reston**	18

Inn at Little Washington
⧉ Inn/Little Washington | **Washington**	29

Jurys Washington Hotel
DuPont Grille | **Dupont Cir**	19

Latham Hotel
⧉ Citronelle | **Georgetown**	28

L'Auberge Provençale
⧉ L'Aub. Provençale | **Boyce**	25

Mandarin Oriental
  Ⓩ Café MoZU | **SW** — 22
  Ⓩ CityZen | **SW** — 26
Monaco, Hotel
  Poste Moderne | **Penn Qtr** — 21
Morrison-Clark Inn
  Morrison-Clark Inn | **D'town** — 23
Morrison House
  Grille, The | **Alexandria** — 25
One Washington Circle Hotel
  Circle Bistro | **West End** — 21
Palomar, Hotel
  NEW Urbana | **Dupont Cir** — ⌐
Park Hyatt Hotel
  Blue Duck | **West End** — 26
Ritz-Carlton Georgetown
  Ⓩ Fahrenheit/Degrees | — 22
  Georgetown
Ritz-Carlton Pentagon City
  Ⓩ Ritz, Grill (Pent. City) | — 25
  Arlington
Ritz-Carlton Tysons Corner
  Ⓩ Maestro | **McLean** — 28
River Inn
  Dish + Drinks | **Foggy Bottom** 19
Scott Circle Marriott
  Nage | **Scott Cir** — ⌐
Sheraton Four Points
  Ⓩ Corduroy | **D'town** — 25
Sofitel Lafayette Sq.
  Ⓩ Café 15 | **D'town** — 25
Tabard Inn
  Ⓩ Tabard Inn | **Dupont Cir** 23
Topaz Hotel
  Topaz Bar | **Dupont Cir** — 19
Tysons Corner Marriott
  Shula's | **Vienna** — 18
Westin Arlington Gateway
  Pinzimini | **Arlington** — ⌐
Willard InterContinental
  NEW Café du Parc | **D'town** — ⌐
  Ⓩ Willard Room | **D'town** — 23

LATE DINING

(Weekday closing hour)

Amsterdam Falafel | varies | — ⌐
  Adams Mor
Austin Grill | 12 AM | **Silver Spring** 16
Bar Pilar | 12 AM | **Logan Cir** 16
Ben's Chili Bowl | 2 AM | **U St** 21
Bistro Français | 3 AM | — 19
  Georgetown
Bob & Edith's | 24 hrs. | **Arlington** 16
NEW Bob's 88 | 1 AM | **Rockville** — ⌐
Busboys & Poets | 12 AM | **U St** 18
NEW Buzz | 12 AM | **Alexandria** — ⌐
Cafe Japoné | 1 AM | **Dupont Cir** 17

NEW Circa | varies | **Dupont Cir** — ⌐
Ⓩ Clyde's | varies | **multi. loc.** 18
NEW D'Acqua | varies | **Penn Qtr** — ⌐
Diner, The | 24 hrs. | **Adams Mor** 18
Dukem | 1 AM | **U St** 23
Eat First | 2 AM | **Chinatown** 22
Eleventh St. | varies | **Arlington** — ⌐
Etete | 12 AM | **U St** 21
Full Kee (VA) | varies | **Falls Ch** 22
Full Kee (DC) | varies | **Chinatown** 22
Full Key | 12 AM | **Wheaton** 20
Good Fortune | 1 AM | **Wheaton** 21
Hard Times Cafe | varies | 19
  multi. loc.
Hollywood East | varies | **Wheaton** 24
Irene's Pupusas | 12 AM | — ⌐
  Wheaton
Kabob Palace | 12 AM | **Arlington** 25
Kramerbooks | 1:30 AM | 17
  Dupont Cir
La Tasca | 12 AM | **Arlington** 16
Les Halles | 12 AM | **D'town** 19
Maté | 12:30 AM | **Georgetown** 17
NEW M'Dawg | varies | — ⌐
  Adams Mor
Mezè | 1:30 AM | **Adams Mor** 19
My Bakery & Café | 12:30 AM | 18
  Georgetown
New Fortune | 1 AM | **Gaith'burg** 21
Ⓩ Old Ebbitt | 1 AM | **D'town** 20
Open City | 1:30 AM | **Woodley Pk** 17
NEW Rain | 2 AM | **Fairfax** — ⌐
Reef, The | 2 AM | **Adams Mor** 14
Rist. La Perla | 12 AM | 19
  Georgetown
Sette Osteria | 12 AM | **Dupont Cir** 20
701 | varies | **Penn Qtr** 23
Siné | varies | **Arlington** 15
Smith/Wollensky | 12 AM | 21
  Gldn Triangle
Sol de España | 2 AM | **Rockville** 23
Stoney's B&G | 12:45 AM | — ⌐
  Logan Cir
Tapatinis | varies | **Cap Hill** 16
Tryst | 1:30 AM | **Adams Mor** 18
NEW Vapiano | 12 AM | — ⌐
  Gldn Triangle
NEW Yazuzu | 12 AM | — ⌐
  Adams Mor

MEET FOR A DRINK

Acadiana | **Mt. Vernon Sq** 23
Banana Café | **Cap Hill** 18
Bardeo Wine | **Cleve Pk** 21
Bar Pilar | **Logan Cir** 16
NEW Bastille | **Alexandria** — ⌐
Bazin's/Church | **Vienna** — ⌐
NEW Beacon B&G | **Scott Cir** — ⌐

NEW Bebo | **Arlington**	‾
NEW Bezu | **Potomac**	‾
Bis | **Cap Hill**	24
Black's Bar | **Bethesda**	23
NEW BLT Steak | **Gldn Triangle**	‾
Blue Duck | **West End**	26
NEW Brass. Beck | **D'town**	‾
Buck's Fishing | **Upper NW**	20
Busboys & Poets | **U St**	18
Café Citron | **Dupont Cir**	17
NEW Café du Parc | **D'town**	‾
Cafe Milano | **Georgetown**	20
Café Saint-Ex | **Logan Cir**	19
Café Salsa | **Alexandria**	20
Caribbean Breeze | **Arlington**	17
NEW Casa Oaxaca | **Adams Mor**	‾
Caucus Room | **Penn Qtr**	21
Ⓩ Ceiba | **D'town**	24
NEW Central M. Rich. | **Penn Qtr**	‾
Ceviche | **Silver Spring**	23
Chef Geoff's | **D'town**	18
NEW Circa | **Dupont Cir**	‾
Ⓩ Citronelle | **Georgetown**	28
Ⓩ CityZen | **SW**	26
Ⓩ Clyde's | **multi. loc.**	18
NEW Comet Ping Pong | **Upper NW**	‾
Crème | **U St**	23
Dino | **Cleve Pk**	19
NEW Dock/Lansdowne | **Lansdowne**	‾
Domku | **Petworth**	26
Eleventh St. | **Arlington**	‾
Ⓩ Fahrenheit/Degrees | **Georgetown**	22
Finn & Porter | **D'town**	17
NEW Food Matters | **Alexandria**	‾
Gallery | **Silver Spring**	‾
NEW Guardado's | **Bethesda**	‾
Hank's Oyster | **Dupont Cir**	23
Harry's Tap Rm. | **Arlington**	21
NEW Hook | **Georgetown**	‾
Ⓩ IndeBleu | **Penn Qtr**	23
Indigo Landing | **Alexandria**	‾
Ⓩ Indique | **Chevy Chase**	24
Jackie's | **Silver Spring**	20
Ⓩ Jaleo | **multi. loc.**	23
Johnny's Half Shell | **Cap Hill**	23
Les Halles | **D'town**	19
NEW LIA'S | **Chevy Chase**	‾
NEW Liberty Tav. | **Arlington**	‾
Lima | **D'town**	‾
Local 16 | **U St**	15
Mai Thai | **Dupont Cir**	22
NEW Majestic | **Alexandria**	‾
Ⓩ Marcel's | **West End**	28
Mark/Orlando's | **Dupont Cir**	24
Maté | **Georgetown**	17
Merkado Kit. | **Logan Cir**	19
NEW Napoleon | **Adams Mor**	‾
Nathans | **Georgetown**	18
NEW Old Dominion | **Mt. Vernon Sq**	‾
Ⓩ Old Ebbitt | **D'town**	20
Olives | **Gldn Triangle**	22
100 King | **Alexandria**	‾
NEW Overwood | **Alexandria**	‾
Ⓩ Oya | **Penn Qtr**	18
NEW Oyamel | **Penn Qtr**	‾
Pearl Seafood | **Wheaton**	‾
Perrys | **Adams Mor**	19
Pinzimini | **Arlington**	‾
NEW Piratz Tav. | **Silver Spring**	‾
Poste Moderne | **Penn Qtr**	21
NEW PS 7's | **Gallery Pl**	‾
Ⓩ Rasika | **Penn Qtr**	26
NEW Rugby Café | **Georgetown**	‾
Rustico | **Alexandria**	‾
Sette Bello | **Arlington**	21
701 | **Penn Qtr**	23
Sonoma | **Cap Hill**	21
Stoney's B&G | **Logan Cir**	‾
Tabaq Bistro | **U St**	19
Tallula | **Arlington**	22
Tandoori Nights | **multi. loc.**	22
Tapatinis | **Cap Hill**	16
Temperance Hall | **Petworth**	‾
Ⓩ TenPenh | **D'town**	24
Tonic | **Foggy Bottom**	18
Topaz Bar | **Dupont Cir**	19
Tryst | **Adams Mor**	18
Ⓩ 2 Amys | **Cleve Pk**	25
Vegetate | **Mt. Vernon Sq**	21
Ⓩ Vidalia | **Gldn Triangle**	26
NEW Vintage 50 | **Leesburg**	‾
Viridian | **Logan Cir**	20
Willow | **Arlington**	24
Woo Lae Oak | **Vienna**	22
Ⓩ Zaytinya | **Penn Qtr**	25

OFFBEAT

Agua Ardiente | **West End**	17
Amsterdam Falafel | **Adams Mor**	‾
Ben's Chili Bowl | **U St**	21
Bob & Edith's | **Arlington**	16
Buca di Beppo | **multi. loc.**	15
Ⓩ Café Atlántico | **Penn Qtr**	25
Café Citron | **Dupont Cir**	17
Cassatt's | **Arlington**	20
Ching Ching | **Georgetown**	19
NEW Comet Ping Pong | **Upper NW**	‾

Dukem | **U St** _23_
Florida Ave. Grill | **U St** _21_
Franklin's | **Hyattsville** _17_
Gallery | **Silver Spring** _–_
Hunter's Head | **Upperville** _20_
Lima | **D'town** _–_
Malaysia Kopitiam | **Gldn Triangle** _22_
Mark's Kit. | **Takoma Pk** _19_
Matuba | **Bethesda** _21_
Meskerem | **Adams Mor** _21_
☑ Mie N Yu | **Georgetown** _18_
Mimi's | **Dupont Cir** _18_
Oohhs & Aahhs | **U St** _–_
Perrys | **Adams Mor** _19_
NEW Piratz Tav. | **Silver Spring** _–_
NEW Pyramids | **U St** _–_
☑ Tabard Inn | **Dupont Cir** _23_
NEW Taste of Burma | **Sterling** _–_
Vegetate | **Mt. Vernon Sq** _21_
☑ Zola | **Penn Qtr** _22_

OUTDOOR DINING

(G=garden; P=patio; S=sidewalk;
T=terrace)

Addie's | P | **Rockville** _23_
Arucola | S | **Upper NW** _18_
Ashby Inn | T | **Paris** _22_
Austin Grill | S | **multi. loc.** _16_
Bis | P | **Cap Hill** _24_
Blue Duck | P | **West End** _26_
Bombay Club | P | **Gldn Triangle** _25_
Bread Line | S | **World Bank** _24_
Busara | G | **Glover Pk** _20_
Cafe Deluxe | P, S | **multi. loc.** _18_
NEW Café du Parc | S | **D'town** _–_
☑ Café 15 | S | **D'town** _25_
Cafe Milano | P | **Georgetown** _20_
Café Mileto | P | **Germantown** _17_
Café Olé | P | **Upper NW** _21_
Café Saint-Ex | P | **Logan Cir** _19_
☑ Cashion's Eat | S | **Adams Mor** _25_
Circle Bistro | P | **West End** _21_
☑ Citronelle | S | **Georgetown** _28_
Comus Inn | T | **Dickerson** _20_
Dean & DeLuca | P | **Georgetown** _21_
DuPont Grille | P | **Dupont Cir** _19_
Equinox | S | **Gldn Triangle** _25_
Etrusco | S | **Dupont Cir** _20_
☑ Eve | P | **Alexandria** _27_
Evening Star | P | **Alexandria** _22_
15 ria | T | **Scott Cir** _19_
☑ Gerard's Place | S | **D'town** _27_
Hank's Oyster | S | **Dupont Cir** _23_
Indigo Landing | P | **Alexandria** _–_
Irish Inn/Glen Echo | P | **Glen Echo** _17_

☑ Jaleo | P | **Bethesda** _23_
Johnny's Half Shell | T | **Cap Hill** _23_
Juniper | G | **West End** _19_
Konami | P | **Vienna** _22_
La Fourchette | T | **Adams Mor** _21_
La Tasca | P | **Arlington** _16_
☑ L'Aub./François | G | **Grt Falls** _27_
☑ L'Aub. Provençale | T | **Boyce** _25_
☑ Lauriol Plaza | P, T | **Dupont Cir** _19_
Le Gaulois | G | **Alexandria** _19_
Leopold's Kafe | P | **Georgetown** _21_
Les Halles | P | **D'town** _19_
Levante's | S | **multi. loc.** _17_
Little Viet Garden | P | **Arlington** _19_
☑ Marcel's | S | **West End** _28_
Mezè | P | **Adams Mor** _19_
Mimi's | S | **Dupont Cir** _18_
Mon Ami Gabi | P | **Bethesda** _19_
Neyla | P | **Georgetown** _22_
Occidental | P | **D'town** _21_
Old Angler's | T | **Potomac** _21_
Open City | P | **Woodley Pk** _17_
Oval Room | S | **Gldn Triangle** _21_
☑ Palena | S | **Cleve Pk** _26_
Paolo's | P | **multi. loc.** _18_
Perrys | T | **Adams Mor** _19_
Pesto | T | **Woodley Pk** _17_
Poste Moderne | P | **Penn Qtr** _21_
Rail Stop | P, T | **Plains** _20_
Raku | P, S | **multi. loc.** _21_
Renato at River Falls | S | **Potomac** _17_
Rist. La Perla | T | **Georgetown** _19_
Rist. Murali | P | **Arlington** _17_
Sea Catch | P, T | **Georgetown** _21_
Sequoia | T | **Georgetown** _15_
Sette Bello | P | **Arlington** _21_
701 | P | **Penn Qtr** _23_
Straits/Malaya | P, T | **Dupont Cir** _21_
☑ Tabard Inn | G | **Dupont Cir** _23_
Taberna/Alabardero | S | **World Bank** _24_
☑ TenPenh | P | **D'town** _24_
Tony & Joe | P | **Georgetown** _14_
Tuscarora Mill | P | **Leesburg** _23_
☑ 2941 Rest. | G, P, T | **Falls Ch** _27_
☑ 2 Amys | P | **Cleve Pk** _25_
Uncle Julio's | P | **multi. loc.** _19_
☑ Zaytinya | P | **Penn Qtr** _25_

PEOPLE-WATCHING

Amsterdam Falafel | **Adams Mor** _–_
NEW Bebo | **Arlington** _–_
Bis | **Cap Hill** _24_
NEW Brass. Beck | **D'town** _–_
Bread Line | **World Bank** _24_
Busboys & Poets | **U St** _18_

Cafe Deluxe | **multi. loc.**	18
NEW Café du Parc | **D'town**	─
Cafe Milano | **Georgetown**	20
Café Saint-Ex | **Logan Cir**	19
NEW Casa Oaxaca | **Adams Mor**	─
Z Cashion's Eat | **Adams Mor**	25
Caucus Room | **Penn Qtr**	21
NEW Central M. Rich. | **Penn Qtr**	─
Charlie Palmer | **Cap Hill**	23
NEW Circa | **Dupont Cir**	─
Z Clyde's | **Broadlands**	18
NEW Comet Ping Pong | **Upper NW**	─
NEW D'Acqua | **Penn Qtr**	─
Z DC Coast | **D'town**	24
Dean & DeLuca | **Georgetown**	21
NEW Dock/Lansdowne | **Lansdowne**	─
Equinox | **Gldn Triangle**	25
Z Fahrenheit/Degrees | **Georgetown**	22
NEW Famoso | **Chevy Chase**	─
Firefly | **Dupont Cir**	21
Z Georgia Brown's | **D'town**	23
Hank's Oyster | **Dupont Cir**	23
NEW Hook | **Georgetown**	─
Z IndeBleu | **Penn Qtr**	23
Indigo Landing | **Alexandria**	─
Z Indique | **Chevy Chase**	24
Z Inn/Little Washington | **Washington**	29
Jackie's | **Silver Spring**	20
Z Jaleo | **multi. loc.**	23
Johnny's Half Shell | **Cap Hill**	23
Z Kinkead's | **Foggy Bottom**	26
Kramerbooks | **Dupont Cir**	17
Z Lauriol Plaza | **Dupont Cir**	19
NEW LIA'S | **Chevy Chase**	─
NEW Liberty Tav. | **Arlington**	─
Lima | **D'town**	─
Local 16 | **U St**	15
Lucky Strike | **Chinatown**	16
Mai Thai | **Dupont Cir**	22
Martin's Tav. | **Georgetown**	18
NEW M Cafe | **Chevy Chase**	─
Monocle | **Cap Hill**	17
NEW Napoleon | **Adams Mor**	─
Nathans | **Georgetown**	18
Z Nora | **Dupont Cir**	25
Z Old Ebbitt | **D'town**	20
Olives | **Gldn Triangle**	22
100 King | **Alexandria**	─
Oval Room | **Gldn Triangle**	21
Z Oya | **Penn Qtr**	18
NEW Oyamel | **Penn Qtr**	─
Palm | **Gldn Triangle**	23

NEW Piratz Tav. | **Silver Spring**	─
Poste Moderne | **Penn Qtr**	21
Rosa Mexicano | **Penn Qtr**	20
Sam & Harry's | **Gldn Triangle**	21
Z Seasons | **Georgetown**	27
Sequoia | **Georgetown**	15
Sette Bello | **Arlington**	21
701 | **Penn Qtr**	23
Simply Home | **U St**	─
Sonoma | **Cap Hill**	21
Tabaq Bistro | **U St**	19
Tallula | **Arlington**	22
Tandoori Nights | **Arlington**	22
Z TenPenh | **D'town**	24
Tryst | **Adams Mor**	18
Z 2941 Rest. | **Falls Ch**	27
Z Vidalia | **Gldn Triangle**	26
Viridian | **Logan Cir**	20
Z Zaytinya | **Penn Qtr**	25
Z Zola | **Penn Qtr**	22

POWER SCENES

Acadiana | **Mt. Vernon Sq**	23
Ardeo | **Cleve Pk**	21
Bamian | **Falls Ch**	─
Bis | **Cap Hill**	24
Bobby Van's Steak | **D'town**	20
Bombay Club | **Gldn Triangle**	25
NEW Brass. Beck | **D'town**	─
Z Capital Grille | **multi. loc.**	25
Caucus Room | **Penn Qtr**	21
NEW Central M. Rich. | **Penn Qtr**	─
Charlie Palmer | **Cap Hill**	23
Z Citronelle | **Georgetown**	28
Z CityZen | **SW**	26
Z Clyde's | **multi. loc.**	18
Z Colvin Run | **Vienna**	25
NEW D'Acqua | **Penn Qtr**	─
Z DC Coast | **D'town**	24
Equinox | **Gldn Triangle**	25
Etrusco | **Dupont Cir**	20
Z Eve | **Alexandria**	27
Hunan Dynasty | **Cap Hill**	─
Z IndeBleu | **Penn Qtr**	23
Z Inn/Little Washington | **Washington**	29
Johnny's Half Shell | **Cap Hill**	23
Z Kinkead's | **Foggy Bottom**	26
Z Komi | **Dupont Cir**	26
Z Maestro | **McLean**	28
Z Marcel's | **West End**	28
Monocle | **Cap Hill**	17
Z Morton's | **multi. loc.**	25
Nathans | **Georgetown**	18
Z Nora | **Dupont Cir**	25
Occidental | **D'town**	21

☑ Old Ebbitt | **D'town**	20
Olives | **Gldn Triangle**	22
Oval Room | **Gldn Triangle**	21
☑ Palena | **Cleve Pk**	26
Palm | **multi. loc.**	23
☑ Prime Rib | **Gldn Triangle**	27
Sam & Harry's | **Gldn Triangle**	21
☑ Seasons | **Georgetown**	27
701 | **Penn Qtr**	23
Sonoma | **Cap Hill**	21
Taberna/Alabardero | **World Bank**	24
Teatro Goldoni | **Gldn Triangle**	23
☑ Tosca | **Penn Qtr**	26
Tuscarora Mill | **Leesburg**	23
☑ 2941 Rest. | **Falls Ch**	27
☑ Vidalia | **Gldn Triangle**	26
☑ Willard Room | **D'town**	23
Willow | **Arlington**	24
Woo Lae Oak | **Vienna**	22
☑ Zaytinya | **Penn Qtr**	25
☑ Zola | **Penn Qtr**	22

PRE-THEATER DINING

(Call for prices and times)

Bistro D'Oc | **D'town**	20
Bistro Français | **Georgetown**	19
Butterfield 9 | **D'town**	22
☑ Café Atlántico | **Penn Qtr**	25
Chef Geoff's | **multi. loc.**	18
Circle Bistro | **West End**	21
Les Halles | **D'town**	19
☑ Marcel's | **West End**	28
Notti Bianche | **Foggy Bottom**	24
Occidental | **D'town**	21
701 | **Penn Qtr**	23
Tavira | **Chevy Chase**	21
☑ Tosca | **Penn Qtr**	26
☑ Willard Room | **D'town**	23

PRIVATE ROOMS

(Restaurants charge less at off
times; call for capacity)

Afghan | **Alexandria**	20
Ashby Inn | **Paris**	22
Bamian | **Falls Ch**	–
Bis | **Cap Hill**	24
Bistro D'Oc | **D'town**	20
Bistrot Lepic | **Georgetown**	24
NEW Brass. Beck | **D'town**	–
B. Smith's | **Cap Hill**	19
Cafe Milano | **Georgetown**	20
Caucus Room | **Penn Qtr**	21
☑ Ceiba | **D'town**	24
NEW Central M. Rich. | **Penn Qtr**	–
Charlie Palmer | **Cap Hill**	23
Chef Geoff's | **multi. loc.**	18

NEW Chima | **Vienna**	–
☑ Citronelle | **Georgetown**	28
☑ CityZen | **SW**	26
☑ Clyde's | **multi. loc.**	18
☑ DC Coast | **D'town**	24
Duangrat's | **Falls Ch**	23
Equinox | **Gldn Triangle**	25
Etrusco | **Dupont Cir**	20
Fiore di Luna | **Grt Falls**	22
Fleming's Steak | **McLean**	24
Fogo de Chão | **D'town**	23
Geranio | **Alexandria**	21
Heritage India | **Dupont Cir**	23
Irish Inn/Glen Echo | **Glen Echo**	17
Johnny's Half Shell | **Cap Hill**	23
☑ La Bergerie | **Alexandria**	26
La Chaumiere | **Georgetown**	24
La Ferme | **Chevy Chase**	22
☑ Lebanese Tav. | **Woodley Pk**	22
☑ Le Paradou | **Penn Qtr**	27
Les Halles | **D'town**	19
☑ Lightfoot | **Leesburg**	22
☑ Maestro | **McLean**	28
☑ Marcel's | **West End**	28
Matisse | **Upper NW**	20
Monocle | **Cap Hill**	17
☑ Morton's | **multi. loc.**	25
Nizam's | **Vienna**	22
☑ Nora | **Dupont Cir**	25
Occidental | **D'town**	21
Old Angler's | **Potomac**	21
Olives | **Gldn Triangle**	22
Oval Room | **Gldn Triangle**	21
☑ Oya | **Penn Qtr**	18
Palm | **multi. loc.**	23
Poste Moderne | **Penn Qtr**	21
☑ Rasika | **Penn Qtr**	26
Sam & Harry's | **Gldn Triangle**	21
Sequoia | **Georgetown**	15
701 | **Penn Qtr**	23
☑ 1789 | **Georgetown**	26
Smith/Wollensky | **Gldn Triangle**	21
Taberna/Alabardero | **World Bank**	24
Tavira | **Chevy Chase**	21
Teatro Goldoni | **Gldn Triangle**	23
☑ Tosca | **Penn Qtr**	26
Tragara | **Bethesda**	22
☑ 2941 Rest. | **Falls Ch**	27
☑ Vidalia | **Gldn Triangle**	26
Viridian | **Logan Cir**	20
☑ Willard Room | **D'town**	23
Woo Lae Oak | **Vienna**	22
☑ Zaytinya | **Penn Qtr**	25
Zengo | **Chinatown**	21
☑ Zola | **Penn Qtr**	22

PRIX FIXE MENUS

(Call for prices and times)

Bis | **Cap Hill**	24
Bistro Français | **Georgetown**	19
Bistrot Lafayette | **Alexandria**	21
Brass. Monte Carlo | **Bethesda**	22
☑ Café 15 | **D'town**	25
Charlie Palmer | **Cap Hill**	23
Ching Ching | **Georgetown**	19
☑ Citronelle | **Georgetown**	28
☑ Colvin Run | **Vienna**	25
Equinox | **Gldn Triangle**	25
☑ Eve | **Alexandria**	27
Fiore di Luna | **Grt Falls**	22
☑ Gerard's Place | **D'town**	27
Grapeseed | **Bethesda**	24
☑ Inn/Little Washington | **Washington**	29
☑ L'Aub./François | **Grt Falls**	27
☑ Maestro | **McLean**	28
☑ Makoto | **Palisades**	28
Matisse | **Upper NW**	20
☑ Nora | **Dupont Cir**	25
☑ Obelisk | **Dupont Cir**	27
Old Angler's | **Potomac**	21
☑ Palena | **Cleve Pk**	26
☑ Ritz, Grill (Pent. City) | **Arlington**	25
Taberna/Alabardero | **World Bank**	24
Teatro Goldoni | **Gldn Triangle**	23
☑ Tosca | **Penn Qtr**	26
☑ Willard Room | **D'town**	23

QUIET CONVERSATION

Ashby Inn | **Paris**	22
☑ Asia Nora | **West End**	25
NEW Bastille | **Alexandria**	–
Bombay Club | **Gldn Triangle**	25
NEW Brass. Beck | **D'town**	–
Butterfield 9 | **D'town**	22
Café Bonaparte | **Georgetown**	22
NEW Café du Parc | **D'town**	–
Caucus Room | **Penn Qtr**	21
Ching Ching | **Georgetown**	19
Circle Bistro | **West End**	21
☑ Citronelle | **Georgetown**	28
Coeur de Lion | **Mt. Vernon Sq**	23
☑ Eve | **Alexandria**	27
☑ Fahrenheit/Degrees | **Georgetown**	22
15 ria | **Scott Cir**	19
☑ Gerard's Place | **D'town**	27
Heritage India | **Glover Pk**	23
NEW Hook | **Georgetown**	–
☑ Indique | **multi. loc.**	24
☑ Inn/Little Washington | **Washington**	29

NEW La Rue 123 | **Fairfax**	–
NEW Las Canteras | **Adams Mor**	–
NEW Lemon Tree | **Rockville**	–
Leopold's Kafe | **Georgetown**	21
NEW Liberty Tav. | **Arlington**	–
Little Fountain | **Adams Mor**	23
☑ Maestro | **McLean**	28
☑ Makoto | **Palisades**	28
Morrison-Clark Inn | **D'town**	23
NEW Nark Kara Thai | **Bethesda**	–
New Heights | **Woodley Pk**	22
☑ Nora | **Dupont Cir**	25
☑ Obelisk | **Dupont Cir**	27
☑ Oceanaire | **D'town**	24
☑ Palena | **Cleve Pk**	26
Palette | **D'town**	22
☑ Rasika | **Penn Qtr**	26
☑ Ritz, Grill (Pent. City) | **Arlington**	25
Rock Creek | **Bethesda**	23
Sea Catch | **Georgetown**	21
☑ Seasons | **Georgetown**	27
☑ 1789 | **Georgetown**	26
Sonoma | **Cap Hill**	21
Taberna/Alabardero | **World Bank**	24
NEW Taste of Burma | **Sterling**	–
Temel | **Fairfax**	21
☑ Tosca | **Penn Qtr**	26
☑ Willard Room | **D'town**	23
Woo Lae Oak | **Vienna**	22

ROMANTIC PLACES

Al Tiramisu | **Dupont Cir**	23
Ashby Inn | **Paris**	22
☑ Asia Nora | **West End**	25
NEW Bezu | **Potomac**	–
NEW Bob's 88 | **Rockville**	–
Bombay Club | **Gldn Triangle**	25
NEW Casa Oaxaca | **Adams Mor**	–
NEW Cava | **Rockville**	–
Circle Bistro | **West End**	21
☑ Citronelle | **Georgetown**	28
Coeur de Lion | **Mt. Vernon Sq**	23
☑ Eve | **Alexandria**	27
Firefly | **Dupont Cir**	21
Green Papaya | **Bethesda**	21
NEW Hook | **Georgetown**	–
☑ IndeBleu | **Penn Qtr**	23
Indigo Landing | **Alexandria**	–
☑ Indique | **Chevy Chase**	24
☑ Inn/Little Washington | **Washington**	29
Kolumbia | **Gldn Triangle**	18
☑ La Bergerie | **Alexandria**	26
☑ L'Aub./François | **Grt Falls**	27

☒ L'Aub. Provençale | **Boyce**	25
☒ Le Paradou | **Penn Qtr**	27
Le Refuge | **Alexandria**	22
Little Fountain | **Adams Mor**	23
🆕 Majestic | **Alexandria**	–
🆕 Marrakesh | **Dupont Cir**	–
Montmartre | **Cap Hill**	23
New Heights | **Woodley Pk**	22
Neyla | **Georgetown**	22
☒ Nora | **Dupont Cir**	25
☒ Obelisk | **Dupont Cir**	27
Old Angler's | **Potomac**	21
☒ Oya | **Penn Qtr**	18
🆕 Oyamel | **Penn Qtr**	–
☒ Palena | **Cleve Pk**	26
Palette | **D'town**	22
Petits Plats | **Woodley Pk**	22
☒ Rasika | **Penn Qtr**	26
☒ Seasons | **Georgetown**	27
701 | **Penn Qtr**	23
☒ 1789 | **Georgetown**	26
☒ Tabard Inn | **Dupont Cir**	23
Taberna/Alabardero | **World Bank**	24
Two Quail | **Cap Hill**	17

SINGLES SCENES

Agua Ardiente | **West End**	17
Austin Grill | **multi. loc.**	16
Bardeo Wine | **Cleve Pk**	21
Bar Pilar | **Logan Cir**	16
🆕 Beacon B&G | **Scott Cir**	–
🆕 BLT Steak | **Gldn Triangle**	–
🆕 Brass. Beck | **D'town**	–
Café Citron | **Dupont Cir**	17
Cafe Deluxe | **multi. loc.**	18
Cafe Milano | **Georgetown**	20
Café Saint-Ex | **Logan Cir**	19
Café Salsa | **Alexandria**	20
🆕 Casa Oaxaca | **Adams Mor**	–
🆕 Central M. Rich. | **Penn Qtr**	–
Ceviche | **Silver Spring**	23
Chi-Cha Lounge | **U St**	16
🆕 Circa | **Dupont Cir**	–
☒ Clyde's | **multi. loc.**	18
Divino | **Bethesda**	20
🆕 Dock/Lansdowne | **Lansdowne**	–
Eleventh St. | **Arlington**	–
Felix | **Adams Mor**	18
Gua-Rapo | **Arlington**	17
🆕 Hook | **Georgetown**	–
☒ IndeBleu | **Penn Qtr**	23
☒ Indique | **Chevy Chase**	24
Kolumbia | **Gldn Triangle**	18
Kramerbooks | **Dupont Cir**	17
🆕 Liberty Tav. | **Arlington**	–

Lima | **D'town**	–
Local 16 | **U St**	15
Maté | **Georgetown**	17
Merkado Kit. | **Logan Cir**	19
☒ Mie N Yu | **Georgetown**	18
🆕 Mio | **D'town**	–
Nathans | **Georgetown**	18
Neyla | **Georgetown**	22
☒ Old Ebbitt | **D'town**	20
☒ Oya | **Penn Qtr**	18
🆕 Oyamel | **Penn Qtr**	–
Perrys | **Adams Mor**	19
🆕 PS 7's | **Gallery Pl**	–
Rustico | **Alexandria**	–
Saki | **Adams Mor**	19
Sequoia | **Georgetown**	15
Sesto Senso | **Gldn Triangle**	20
Straits/Malaya | **Dupont Cir**	21
Tabaq Bistro | **U St**	19
Tandoori Nights | **Arlington**	22
Tapatinis | **Cap Hill**	16
Temperance Hall | **Petworth**	–
Timpano | **Rockville**	18
Tony & Joe | **Georgetown**	14
Topaz Bar | **Dupont Cir**	19
Uni | **Dupont Cir**	20
U-topia | **U St**	16
☒ Zaytinya | **Penn Qtr**	25
Zengo | **Chinatown**	21
☒ Zola | **Penn Qtr**	22

SLEEPERS

(Good to excellent food, but little known)

Azucar | **Silver Spring**	26
Blue Duck | **West End**	26
Bombay | **Silver Spring**	24
Coeur de Lion | **Mt. Vernon Sq**	23
Curry Club | **Glover Pk**	24
David Craig | **Bethesda**	25
Domku | **Petworth**	26
El Gavilan | **Silver Spring**	23
Fiore di Luna | **Grt Falls**	22
Foti's | **Culpeper**	27
Grille, The | **Alexandria**	25
Hakuba | **Gaith'burg**	23
Huong Viet | **Falls Ch**	23
India Palace | **Germantown**	23
Jerry's Seafood | **Seabrook**	24
Kabob Palace | **Arlington**	25
Kotobuki | **Palisades**	24
Lafayette Rm. | **Gldn Triangle**	24
Layalina | **Arlington**	23
Mikaku | **Herndon**	27
Mitsitam | **SW**	22
Mourayo | **Dupont Cir**	23

Panino | **Manassas** — 26
Radius | **Mt. Pleasant** — 22
NEW Ray's/Classics | **Silver Spring** — 24
Regent, The | **Dupont Cir** — 23
SBC Café | **Herndon** — 24
Shamshiry | **Falls Ch** — 23
Sorak Garden | **Annandale** — 22
Sweet Ginger | **Vienna** — 24
Taqueria/Charrito | **Arlington** — 22
Thai Basil | **Chantilly** — 22
Woo Mi Gdn. | **Wheaton** — 22
Yamazato | **Alexandria** — 22
Yuan Fu | **Rockville** — 22

TEA SERVICE

Ching Ching | **Georgetown** — 19
Irish Inn/Glen Echo | **Glen Echo** — 17
Z Ritz, Grill (Pent. City) | **Arlington** — 25
Z Seasons | **Georgetown** — 27
Seven Seas | **Rockville** — 18
Teaism | **multi. loc.** — 19
Z Willard Room | **D'town** — 23

TRANSPORTING EXPERIENCES

Bombay Club | **Gldn Triangle** — 25
NEW Brass. Beck | **D'town** — –
Ching Ching | **Georgetown** — 19
Z Clyde's | **multi. loc.** — 18
Green Papaya | **Bethesda** — 21
Heritage India | **Glover Pk** — 23
Hunter's Head | **Upperville** — 20
Z IndeBleu | **Penn Qtr** — 23
Indigo Landing | **Alexandria** — –
Z Indique | **Chevy Chase** — 24
Z Inn/Little Washington | **Washington** — 29
Z L'Aub./François | **Grt Falls** — 27
Z Makoto | **Palisades** — 28
Z Mie N Yu | **Georgetown** — 18
Neyla | **Georgetown** — 22
Z Oya | **Penn Qtr** — 18
Pearl Seafood | **Wheaton** — –
Rock Creek | **Bethesda** — 23
Rosa Mexicano | **Penn Qtr** — 20
Tara Thai | **multi. loc.** — 20
Taste of Morocco | **Silver Spring** — 20
Topaz Bar | **Dupont Cir** — 19
Z Zaytinya | **Penn Qtr** — 25
Zengo | **Chinatown** — 21
Z Zola | **Penn Qtr** — 22

TRENDY

Acadiana | **Mt. Vernon Sq** — 23
Banana Café | **Cap Hill** — 18

Bangkok Joe's | **Georgetown** — 20
Bardeo Wine | **Cleve Pk** — 21
NEW Bastille | **Alexandria** — –
NEW Bebo | **Arlington** — –
Belga Café | **Cap Hill** — 21
Bis | **Cap Hill** — 24
NEW Brass. Beck | **D'town** — –
Buck's Fishing | **Upper NW** — 20
Busboys & Poets | **U St** — 18
Cafe Asia | **multi. loc.** — 19
Z Café Atlántico | **Penn Qtr** — 25
Café Citron | **Dupont Cir** — 17
NEW Café du Parc | **D'town** — –
Cafe Milano | **Georgetown** — 20
Café Saint-Ex | **Logan Cir** — 19
NEW Casa Oaxaca | **Adams Mor** — –
Z Ceiba | **D'town** — 24
NEW Central M. Rich. | **Penn Qtr** — –
Ceviche | **Silver Spring** — 23
NEW Circa | **Dupont Cir** — –
Z CityZen | **SW** — 26
Z Clyde's | **multi. loc.** — 18
NEW Comet Ping Pong | **Upper NW** — –
Z DC Coast | **D'town** — 24
Divino | **Bethesda** — 20
Domku | **Petworth** — 26
NEW Eamonn's | **Alexandria** — –
Eleventh St. | **Arlington** — –
Etete | **U St** — 21
Z Eve | **Alexandria** — 27
Z Fahrenheit/Degrees | **Georgetown** — 22
NEW Farrah Olivia | **Alexandria** — –
Felix | **Adams Mor** — 18
15 ria | **Scott Cir** — 19
Gua-Rapo | **Arlington** — 17
Hank's Oyster | **Dupont Cir** — 23
Heritage India | **multi. loc.** — 23
NEW Hook | **Georgetown** — –
Hunan Dynasty | **Cap Hill** — –
Z IndeBleu | **Penn Qtr** — 23
Z Indique | **Chevy Chase** — 24
Jackie's | **Silver Spring** — 20
Johnny's Half Shell | **Cap Hill** — 23
Z Komi | **Dupont Cir** — 26
Leopold's Kafe | **Georgetown** — 21
NEW Liberty Tav. | **Arlington** — –
Lima | **D'town** — –
Local 16 | **U St** — 15
NEW Mandu | **Dupont Cir** — –
Mark/Orlando's | **Dupont Cir** — 24
Merkado Kit. | **Logan Cir** — 19
Z Mie N Yu | **Georgetown** — 18
NEW Napoleon | **Adams Mor** — –

☑ Oya | **Penn Qtr**	18
NEW Oyamel | **Penn Qtr**	–
☑ Palena | **Cleve Pk**	26
Peacock Cafe | **Georgetown**	21
Pearl Seafood | **Wheaton**	–
Radius | **Mt. Pleasant**	22
NEW Rain | **Fairfax**	–
NEW Rarely Legal | **Bethesda**	–
☑ Rasika | **Penn Qtr**	26
NEW Ray's/Classics | **Silver Spring**	24
Reef, The | **Adams Mor**	14
Rice | **Logan Cir**	22
NEW Rugby Café | **Georgetown**	–
Rustico | **Alexandria**	–
Saki | **Adams Mor**	19
Sette Bello | **Arlington**	21
Stoney's B&G | **Logan Cir**	–
Tabaq Bistro | **U St**	19
Tallula | **Arlington**	22
Tandoori Nights | **Arlington**	22
Tapatinis | **Cap Hill**	16
Temperance Hall | **Petworth**	–
☑ TenPenh | **D'town**	24
Vermilion | **Alexandria**	20
Woo Lae Oak | **Vienna**	22
☑ Zaytinya | **Penn Qtr**	25
Zengo | **Chinatown**	21

VALET PARKING

Acadiana | **Mt. Vernon Sq**	23
Agua Ardiente | **West End**	17
Al Tiramisu | **Dupont Cir**	23
Ardeo | **Cleve Pk**	21
☑ Asia Nora | **West End**	25
Bardeo Wine | **Cleve Pk**	21
NEW Bebo | **Arlington**	–
Bis | **Cap Hill**	24
NEW BLT Steak | **Gldn Triangle**	–
Blue Duck | **West End**	26
Bobby Van's Steak | **D'town**	20
Bombay Club | **Gldn Triangle**	25
Bombay Palace | **Gldn Triangle**	23
Brass. Monte Carlo | **Bethesda**	22
NEW Buona Sera | **Bethesda**	–
Butterfield 9 | **D'town**	22
☑ Café Atlántico | **Penn Qtr**	25
Café Citron | **Dupont Cir**	17
NEW Café du Parc | **D'town**	–
☑ Café 15 | **D'town**	25
Cafe Milano | **Georgetown**	20
☑ Café MoZU | **SW**	22
☑ Capital Grille | **multi. loc.**	25
Caribbean Breeze | **Arlington**	17
☑ Cashion's Eat | **Adams Mor**	25
Caucus Room | **Penn Qtr**	21

☑ Ceiba | **D'town**	24
NEW Central M. Rich. | **Penn Qtr**	–
Centro Italian | **Bethesda**	21
Cesco | **Bethesda**	23
Charlie Palmer | **Cap Hill**	23
☑ Cheesecake Fact. | **Rockville**	18
Chef Geoff's | **D'town**	18
NEW Chima | **Vienna**	–
Circle Bistro | **West End**	21
☑ Citronelle | **Georgetown**	28
☑ CityZen | **SW**	26
Clyde's | **Vienna**	18
Coeur de Lion | **Mt. Vernon Sq**	23
☑ Colvin Run | **Vienna**	25
NEW D'Acqua | **Penn Qtr**	–
☑ DC Coast | **D'town**	24
Dish + Drinks | **Foggy Bottom**	19
District ChopHse. | **Penn Qtr**	20
DuPont Grille | **Dupont Cir**	19
Faccia Luna | **Alexandria**	21
☑ Fahrenheit/Degrees | **Georgetown**	22
15 ria | **Scott Cir**	19
Finemondo | **D'town**	18
Finn & Porter | **multi. loc.**	17
Firefly | **Dupont Cir**	21
Fleming's Steak | **McLean**	24
Fogo de Chão | **D'town**	23
Gallery | **Silver Spring**	–
☑ Georgia Brown's | **D'town**	23
Grapeseed | **Bethesda**	24
Green Field | **Rockville**	19
Grille, The | **Alexandria**	25
Hee Been | **Alexandria**	21
Heritage India | **multi. loc.**	23
NEW Il Mulino | **D'town**	–
☑ IndeBleu | **Penn Qtr**	23
Indigo Landing | **Alexandria**	–
☑ Indique | **Cleve Pk**	24
☑ Inn/Little Washington | **Washington**	29
i Ricchi | **Dupont Cir**	23
Irish Inn/Glen Echo | **Glen Echo**	17
☑ Jaleo | **multi. loc.**	23
☑ Kinkead's | **Foggy Bottom**	26
Lafayette Rm. | **Gldn Triangle**	24
La Miche | **Bethesda**	22
Leftbank | **Adams Mor**	15
☑ Legal Sea Foods | **Gldn Triangle**	20
Le Mistral | **McLean**	24
Les Halles | **D'town**	19
NEW LIA'S | **Chevy Chase**	–
Luigino | **D'town**	18
☑ Maestro | **McLean**	28
Maggiano's | **McLean**	18

Mai Thai | **Dupont Cir**	22
M & S Grill | **D'town**	18
🖪 Marcel's | **West End**	28
Market St. B&G | **Reston**	18
NEW Marrakesh | **Dupont Cir**	-
🖪 McCormick/Schmick | multi. loc.	21
Mimi's | **Dupont Cir**	18
NEW Mio | **D'town**	-
Mon Ami Gabi | **Bethesda**	19
Monocle | **Cap Hill**	17
Morrison-Clark Inn | **D'town**	23
🖪 Morton's | **multi. loc.**	25
Nage | **Scott Cir**	-
Neisha Thai | **McLean**	21
New Heights | **Woodley Pk**	22
New Orleans Bistro | **Bethesda**	18
Neyla | **Georgetown**	22
🖪 Nora | **Dupont Cir**	25
Notti Bianche | **Foggy Bottom**	24
Occidental | **D'town**	21
🖪 Oceanaire | **D'town**	24
🖪 Old Ebbitt | **D'town**	20
Olives | **Gldn Triangle**	22
100 King | **Alexandria**	-
Oval Room | **Gldn Triangle**	21
🖪 Oya | **Penn Qtr**	18
NEW Oyamel | **Penn Qtr**	-
Palette | **D'town**	22
Palm | **multi. loc.**	23
Passage to India | **Bethesda**	24
Perrys | **Adams Mor**	19
Pesce | **Dupont Cir**	25
Petits Plats | **Woodley Pk**	22
Pinzimini | **Arlington**	-
NEW Posh | **D'town**	-
Poste Moderne | **Penn Qtr**	21
🖪 Prime Rib | **Gldn Triangle**	27
Primi Piatti | **Foggy Bottom**	21
NEW PS 7's | **Gallery Pl**	-
NEW Rarely Legal | **Bethesda**	-
🖪 Rasika | **Penn Qtr**	26
Rist. La Perla | **Georgetown**	19
🖪 Ritz, Grill (Pent. City) | **Arlington**	25
Rosa Mexicano | **Penn Qtr**	20
🖪 Ruth's Chris | **multi. loc.**	24
Saki | **Adams Mor**	19
Sam & Harry's | **Gldn Triangle**	21
🖪 Seasons | **Georgetown**	27
Sesto Senso | **Gldn Triangle**	20
Sette Osteria | **Dupont Cir**	20
701 | **Penn Qtr**	23
🖪 1789 | **Georgetown**	26
Shula's | **Vienna**	18

Smith/Wollensky | **Gldn Triangle**	21
Sushi-Ko | **Glover Pk**	24
Tabaq Bistro | **U St**	19
🖪 Tabard Inn | **Dupont Cir**	23
Tara Thai | **Arlington**	20
Teatro Goldoni | **Gldn Triangle**	23
🖪 TenPenh | **D'town**	24
Topaz Bar | **Dupont Cir**	19
🖪 Tosca | **Penn Qtr**	26
Tragara | **Bethesda**	22
🖪 2941 Rest. | **Falls Ch**	27
NEW Urbana | **Dupont Cir**	-
🖪 Vidalia | **Gldn Triangle**	26
Viridian | **Logan Cir**	20
🖪 Willard Room | **D'town**	23
Woo Lae Oak | **Vienna**	22
Yin Yankee | **Bethesda**	24
🖪 Zaytinya | **Penn Qtr**	25
Zengo | **Chinatown**	21
🖪 Zola | **Penn Qtr**	22

VIEWS

(See also Waterside)

Ashby Inn | **Paris**	22
NEW Café du Parc | **D'town**	-
🖪 Café MoZU | **SW**	22
Café Spice | **Gaith'burg**	18
Charlie Palmer | **Cap Hill**	23
🖪 Clyde's | **Rockville**	18
Finn & Porter | **Alexandria**	17
Fontina Grille | **Rockville**	17
🖪 Inn/Little Washington | **Washington**	29
Irish Inn/Glen Echo | **Glen Echo**	17
Lafayette Rm. | **Gldn Triangle**	24
🖪 L'Aub./François | **Grt Falls**	27
Mai Thai | **Alexandria**	22
New Heights | **Woodley Pk**	22
Old Angler's | **Potomac**	21
Perrys | **Adams Mor**	19
🖪 Ruth's Chris | **Arlington**	24
🖪 Seasons | **Georgetown**	27
701 | **Penn Qtr**	23
Tabaq Bistro | **U St**	19

VISITORS ON EXPENSE ACCOUNT

Acadiana | **Mt. Vernon Sq**	23
Amada Amante | **Rockville**	20
Bazin's/Church | **Vienna**	-
NEW BLT Steak | **Gldn Triangle**	-
Blue Duck | **West End**	26
NEW Brass. Beck | **D'town**	-
Butterfield 9 | **D'town**	22
🖪 Café 15 | **D'town**	25
🖪 Capital Grille | **multi. loc.**	25

Capri | **McLean**	21
Caucus Room | **Penn Qtr**	21
NEW Central M. Rich. | **Penn Qtr**	–
Charlie Palmer | **Cap Hill**	23
Ⓩ Citronelle | **Georgetown**	28
Ⓩ CityZen | **SW**	26
Ⓩ Colvin Run | **Vienna**	25
NEW D'Acqua | **Penn Qtr**	–
Etrusco | **Dupont Cir**	20
Ⓩ Eve | **Alexandria**	27
Ⓩ Fahrenheit/Degrees | **Georgetown**	22
NEW Famoso | **Chevy Chase**	–
NEW Farrah Olivia | **Alexandria**	–
Ⓩ Gerard's Place | **D'town**	27
Grille, The | **Alexandria**	25
NEW Il Mulino | **D'town**	–
Ⓩ IndeBleu | **Penn Qtr**	23
Ⓩ Inn/Little Washington | **Washington**	29
i Ricchi | **Dupont Cir**	23
Ⓩ Kinkead's | **Foggy Bottom**	26
Lafayette Rm. | **Gldn Triangle**	24
Le Palais | **Gaith'burg**	–
Ⓩ Le Paradou | **Penn Qtr**	27
Ⓩ Maestro | **McLean**	28
Ⓩ Marcel's | **West End**	28
Ⓩ Morton's | **multi. loc.**	25
Ⓩ Oceanaire | **D'town**	24
Olives | **Gldn Triangle**	22
Ⓩ Palena | **Cleve Pk**	26
Palm | **multi. loc.**	23
Pinzimini | **Arlington**	–
Ⓩ Prime Rib | **Gldn Triangle**	27
NEW PS 7's | **Gallery Pl**	–
Ⓩ Ritz, Grill (Pent. City) | **Arlington**	25
Ⓩ Ruth's Chris | **multi. loc.**	24
Ⓩ 1789 | **Georgetown**	26
Shula's | **Vienna**	18
Ⓩ Tosca | **Penn Qtr**	26
Ⓩ 2941 Rest. | **Falls Ch**	27
Ⓩ Vidalia | **Gldn Triangle**	26
Ⓩ Willard Room | **D'town**	23
Willow | **Arlington**	24
Woo Lae Oak | **Vienna**	22

WATERSIDE

Indigo Landing | **Alexandria**	–
Phillips | **SW**	15
Roof Terr./JFK Ctr. | **Foggy Bottom**	17
Sea Catch | **Georgetown**	21
Sequoia | **Georgetown**	15
NEW Tavern/Lake | **Reston**	–
Tony & Joe | **Georgetown**	14
Ⓩ 2941 Rest. | **Falls Ch**	27

WINNING WINE LISTS

Amada Amante | **Rockville**	20
Ashby Inn | **Paris**	22
NEW Bastille | **Alexandria**	–
NEW Bebo | **Arlington**	–
Bis | **Cap Hill**	24
NEW BLT Steak | **Gldn Triangle**	–
Blue Duck | **West End**	26
Blvd. Woodgrill | **Arlington**	19
NEW Brass. Beck | **D'town**	–
Buck's Fishing | **Upper NW**	20
Ⓩ Café Atlántico | **Penn Qtr**	25
NEW Café du Parc | **D'town**	–
Ⓩ Café 15 | **D'town**	25
Ⓩ Capital Grille | **multi. loc.**	25
Ⓩ Carlyle | **Arlington**	24
Ⓩ Cashion's Eat | **Adams Mor**	25
Caucus Room | **Penn Qtr**	21
NEW Central M. Rich. | **Penn Qtr**	–
Charlie Palmer | **Cap Hill**	23
NEW Circa | **Dupont Cir**	–
Ⓩ Citronelle | **Georgetown**	28
Ⓩ CityZen | **SW**	26
Ⓩ Colvin Run | **Vienna**	25
NEW D'Acqua | **Penn Qtr**	–
Dino | **Cleve Pk**	19
Equinox | **Gldn Triangle**	25
Etrusco | **Dupont Cir**	20
Ⓩ Eve | **Alexandria**	27
Evening Star | **Alexandria**	22
Ⓩ Fahrenheit/Degrees | **Georgetown**	22
Fiore di Luna | **Grt Falls**	22
Fleming's Steak | **McLean**	24
Ⓩ Gerard's Place | **D'town**	27
Grapeseed | **Bethesda**	24
NEW Hook | **Georgetown**	–
Ⓩ Inn/Little Washington | **Washington**	29
Ⓩ Jaleo | **multi. loc.**	23
Johnny's Half Shell | **Cap Hill**	23
Ⓩ Kinkead's | **Foggy Bottom**	26
Ⓩ Maestro | **McLean**	28
Ⓩ Marcel's | **West End**	28
Mendocino Grille | **Georgetown**	23
Mon Ami Gabi | **Bethesda**	19
Nathans | **Georgetown**	18
New Heights | **Woodley Pk**	22
Ⓩ Nora | **Dupont Cir**	25
Oakville Grille | **Bethesda**	18
Ⓩ Obelisk | **Dupont Cir**	27
Occidental | **D'town**	21
Ⓩ Old Ebbitt | **D'town**	20
Oval Room | **Gldn Triangle**	21
NEW Overwood | **Alexandria**	–

☑ Palena | **Cleve Pk** — 26

Palm | **multi. loc.** — 23

☑ Prime Rib | **Gldn Triangle** — 27

☑ Rasika | **Penn Qtr** — 26

NEW Ray's/Classics | **Silver Spring** — 24

Sam & Harry's | **Gldn Triangle** — 21

☑ Seasons | **Georgetown** — 27

Smith/Wollensky | **Gldn Triangle** — 21

Sonoma | **Cap Hill** — 21

Sushi-Ko | **Glover Pk** — 24

Taberna/Alabardero | **World Bank** — 24

Tallula | **Arlington** — 22

Tivoli | **Rosslyn** — 22

☑ Tosca | **Penn Qtr** — 26

☑ 2941 Rest. | **Falls Ch** — 27

☑ 2 Amys | **Cleve Pk** — 25

☑ Vidalia | **Gldn Triangle** — 26

☑ Willard Room | **D'town** — 23

Willow | **Arlington** — 24

☑ Zaytinya | **Penn Qtr** — 25

☑ Zola | **Penn Qtr** — 22

WORTH A TRIP

Boyce, VA
  ☑ L'Aub. Provençale — 25

Culpeper, VA
  Foti's — 27

Paris, VA
  Ashby Inn — 22

The Plains, VA
  Rail Stop — 20

Washington, VA
  ☑ Inn/Little Washington — 29

BALTIMORE, ANNAPOLIS AND THE EASTERN SHORE

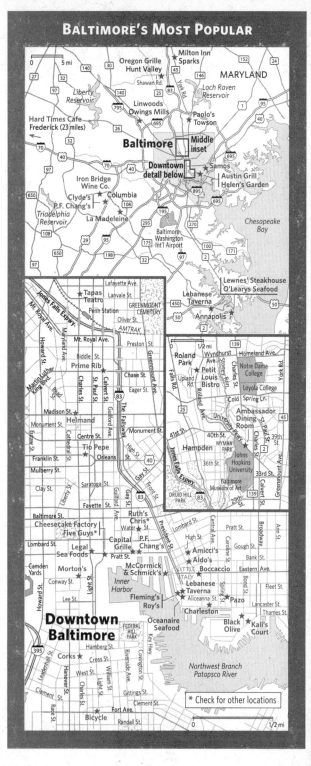

BALTIMORE'S MOST POPULAR

0   5 mi

Liberty Reservoir

Oregon Grille
Hunt Valley

Milton Inn
Sparks

Loch Raven
Reservoir

MARYLAND

Linwoods
Owings Mills

Shawan Rd.

Paolo's
Towson

Hard Times Cafe
Frederick (23 miles)

Baltimore

Middle
inset

Downtown
detail below

Samos

Austin Grill
Helen's Garden

Iron Bridge
Wine Co.

Clyde's
P.F. Chang's
Triadelphia
Reservoir

Columbia

La Madeleine

Chesapeake
Bay

Baltimore-
Washington
Int'l Airport

Lewnes' Steakhouse
O'Learys Seafood

Lebanese
Taverna

Annapolis

Lafayette Ave.

Tapas
Teatro

Lanvale St.

Jones Falls Espwy.

Penn Station

GREENMOUNT
CEMETERY

Mt. Royal Ave.

Oliver St.

AMTRAK

Preston St.

Roland
Park

1/2 mi

Wyndhurst
Ave.   Stoney Run

Homeland Ave.

Notre Dame
College

Mt. Royal Ave.

Prime Rib

Biddle St.

Upland
Rd.

Petit
Louis
Bistro

Loyola College

Chase St.

Cold Spring Ln.

Eager St.

Ambassador
Dining
Room

Madison St.

Helmand

Monument St.

University Pkwy.

41st St.

40th St.

Centre St.

Tio Pepe

Franklin St.

Orleans

Hampden

36th St.

WYMAN
PARK

39th
St.

Johns
Hopkins
University

33rd St.

Mulberry St.

Clay St.

Saratoga St.

Baltimore
Museum
of Art

29th
St.

Fayette St.

DRUID
HILL
PARK

Baltimore St.

Cheesecake Factory
Five Guys*

Ruth's
Chris*

Water St.

Lombard St.

Pratt St.

Capital
Grille

P.F.
Chang's

High St.

Amicci's

Aldo's

Lombard St.

Legal
Sea Foods

Boccaccio
LITTLE
ITALY

Camden
Yards

Morton's

McCormick
& Schmick's

Lebanese
Taverna

Conway St.

Inner
Harbor

Fleming's

Aliceanna St.

Pazo

Lee St.

Roy's

Charleston

**Downtown
Baltimore**

FEDERAL
HILL
PARK

Oceanaire
Seafood

Black
Olive

Kali's
Court

Corks

Hamberg St.

Northwest Branch
Patapsco River

Cross St.

West St.

Clement St.

* Check for other locations

Bicycle

0   1/2 mi

Baltimore's Most Popular

Each surveyor has been asked to name his or her five favorite places. This list reflects their choices. All restaurants are in the Baltimore area unless otherwise noted (A=Annapolis and E=Eastern Shore).

1. Clyde's
2. Ruth's Chris/A/BA
3. Prime Rib
4. Charleston
5. McCormick & Schmick's
6. Lebanese Taverna/A/BA
7. Capital Grille
8. Morton's Steak*
9. Legal Sea Foods
10. Oceanaire Seafood
11. Cheesecake Factory
12. Helmand
13. Pazo
14. Petit Louis Bistro
15. Five Guys/A/BA
16. P.F. Chang's
17. Ambassador Dining Rm.
18. Bicycle, The
19. Linwoods
20. Roy's

21. Fleming's Steak
22. Tio Pepe
23. Austin Grill
24. Oregon Grille
25. Black Olive
26. Iron Bridge Wine Co.*
27. Samos
28. Hard Times Cafe
29. Boccaccio
30. Helen's Garden
31. Kali's Court
32. Tapas Teatro*
33. Lewnes' Steak/A
34. Corks
35. Aldo's
36. O'Learys Seafood/A
37. La Madeleine
38. Milton Inn*
39. Paolo's*
40. Amicci's

Given the fact that both our surveyors and readers love to discover dining bargains, we have added a list of 40 Best Buys on page 194. These are restaurants that give real quality at extremely reasonable prices.

KEY NEWCOMERS

Our take on the most notable new arrivals of the past year. For a full list, see the Additions index on page 261.

Alabama BBQ
Cynthia's
Dogwood
Jack's Bistro
Kyma/A
Local/E

Nasu Blanca
Open Door Café
Osteria 177/A
Rocket to Venus
Rumor Mill
Three . . .

* Indicates a tie with restaurant above

Top Food Ratings

Ratings are to the left of names. Lists exclude places with low votes, unless indicated by a ▽.

<u>28</u> Sushi Sono
Joss Cafe/Sushi/A

<u>27</u> Charleston
Samos
Antrim 1844
Peter's Inn
Prime Rib
Lemongrass/A
Tersiguel's
Mari Luna

<u>26</u> Chameleon Cafe
O'Learys Seafood/A*
Trattoria Alberto
Aldo's
Helmand
Inn at Easton/E
Jalapeños/A
Abacrombie
Les Folies Brasserie/A
Linwoods

BY CUISINE

AMERICAN (NEW)
<u>27</u> Charleston
Antrim 1844
Peter's Inn
<u>26</u> Chameleon Cafe
Inn at Easton/E

AMERICAN (TRAD.)
<u>23</u> Brass Elephant
<u>21</u> Mealey's
Friendly Farm
<u>20</u> Dutch's Daughter
Hull St. Blues

CHINESE
<u>24</u> Szechuan House
Sonny Lee's Hunan
<u>22</u> Hunan Manor
Cafe Zen
Chinatown Café

CONTINENTAL
<u>25</u> Milton Inn
Josef's Country Inn▽
<u>24</u> Tio Pepe
<u>23</u> Northwoods/A
Kings Contrivance

CRAB HOUSE
<u>22</u> Cantler's Riverside Inn/A
Obrycki's Crab House
Costas Inn
<u>20</u> Crab Claw/E
<u>19</u> Harris Crab House/E

FRENCH
<u>27</u> Tersiguel's
<u>26</u> Les Folies Brasserie/A

<u>24</u> Petit Louis Bistro
Martick's
<u>23</u> Café de Paris

GREEK
<u>27</u> Samos
<u>26</u> Black Olive
<u>22</u> Paul's Homewood/A
Zorba's B&G
Ikaros

INDIAN
<u>25</u> Ambassador Dining Rm.
<u>22</u> Akbar
Mughal Garden
<u>21</u> Banjara

ITALIAN
<u>26</u> Trattoria Alberto
Aldo's
<u>25</u> Boccaccio
La Tavola
<u>24</u> La Scala

MEXICAN
<u>27</u> Mari Luna
<u>26</u> Jalapeños/A
<u>23</u> El Trovador
<u>22</u> Blue Agave
Cacique

SEAFOOD
<u>26</u> O'Learys Seafood/A
Black Olive
<u>25</u> Faidley's Seafood
<u>24</u> Oceanaire Seafood
Kali's Court

STEAKHOUSE

27 Prime Rib
26 Lewnes' Steak/A
25 Oregon Grille
   Capital Grille
   Morton's Steak

SUSHI

28 Sushi Sono
   Joss Cafe/Sushi/A

25 Edo Sushi
   Tsunami/A
24 Sushi King

THAI

27 Lemongrass/A
24 Thai Landing
23 Thai Arroy
   Thai
21 San Sushi/Thai

BY SPECIAL FEATURE

BOAT-ACCESSIBLE

23 Narrows, The/E
22 Cantler's Riverside Inn/A
21 Yellowfin/A
   Town Dock/E
20 Crab Claw/E

BREAKFAST

25 Blue Moon Cafe
23 Miss Shirley's
22 Stone Mill Bakery
19 Windows
18 City Cafe

BRUNCH

26 Abacrombie
25 Ambassador Dining Rm.
23 Helen's Garden
22 Gertrude's
20 Hull St. Blues

BUSINESS DINING

26 Roy's
25 Capital Grille
   Morton's Steak
24 Oceanaire Seafood
   Fleming's Steak

HISTORIC PLACES

26 Inn at Easton/E
24 Petit Louis Bistro
23 Kings Contrivance
21 Robert Morris Inn/E
   Reynolds Tavern/A

HOTEL DINING

25 Morton's Steak
   (Sheraton Inner Harbor)
24 Carlyle Club
   (Carlyle Inn & Suites)

23 Brightons Orangerie
   (InterContinental Harbor)
22 Pisces
   (Hyatt Regency)
19 Windows
   (Renaissance Harborplace)

MEET FOR A DRINK

25 Tasting Room
   Iron Bridge Wine Co.
23 Out of the Fire/E
   Wine Market
   Pazo

POWER SCENES

27 Charleston
26 Linwoods
25 Boccaccio
   Capital Grille
22 Harry Browne's/A

TRENDY

25 Tsunami/A
24 Mezze
23 Pazo
21 Brewer's Art
19 Red Maple

WORTH A TRIP

27 Antrim 1844
   Taneytown
23 Narrows, The/E
   Grasonville
22 Cantler's Riverside Inn/A
   Annapolis
19 Harris Crab House/E
   Grasonville
18 Baugher's
   Westminster

ANNAPOLIS

28 Joss Cafe/Sushi
27 Lemongrass
26 Jalapeños
   Les Folies Brasserie
25 Tsunami

COLUMBIA

28 Sushi Sono
25 Iron Bridge Wine Co.
   An Loi
24 Jesse Wong's Asean Bistro
   Sushi King

DOWNTOWN NORTH/ MT. VERNON

27 Prime Rib
26 Helmand
   Abacrombie
24 b
   Sotto Sopra

EASTERN SHORE

26 Inn at Easton
25 Bistro St. Michaels
23 Narrows, The
   Out of the Fire
   Mason's

EASTPORT

26 O'Learys Seafood
   Lewnes' Steak
24 Wild Orchid Café
   Ruth's Chris
22 Carrol's Creek Cafe

FELLS POINT

27 Peter's Inn
26 Black Olive
25 Pierpoint
   Henninger's Tavern
   Blue Moon Cafe

FREDERICK

25 Tasting Room
24 Isabella's
22 Cacique
20 Dutch's Daughter
19 Mamma Lucia

INNER HARBOR

25 Edo Sushi
   Capital Grille
   Morton's Steak
24 Ruth's Chris
23 Brightons Orangerie

INNER HARBOR EAST/ LITTLE ITALY

27 Charleston
26 Aldo's
   Roy's
25 Boccaccio
   La Tavola

LUTHERVILLE/TIMONIUM

25 Edo Sushi
24 Szechuan House
22 Christopher Daniel
21 San Sushi/Thai
   BlueStone

SOUTH BALTIMORE

25 Corks
24 SoBo Cafe
   Matsuri
23 Thai Arroy
21 Banjara

TOWSON

25 Atwater's
   Orchard Market
23 Sushi Hana
22 Café Troia
   Olive & Sesame

Top Decor Ratings

Ratings are to the left of names.

28 Pazo
Antrim 1844

26 Charleston
Ambassador Dining Rm.
Elkridge Furnace Inn
Ixia
Milton Inn

25 Brightons Orangerie
Red Maple
Oregon Grille

Louisiana
Saffron
Aldo's
Linwoods

24 Prime Rib
Blue Sea Grill
Sherwood's Landing/E
Brass Elephant
Metropolitan/A
Inn at Easton/E

OUTDOORS

Ambassador Dining Rm.
Arcos
Carrol's Creek Cafe/A
City Cafe
Gertrude's

Mason's/E
Reynolds Tavern/A
Stone Mill Bakery
Wine Market
Yin Yankee/A

ROMANCE

Ambassador Dining Rm.
Amicci's
Antrim 1844
Da Mimmo
Helen's Garden
Linwoods

Milton Inn
Paul's Homewood/A
Pazo
Petit Louis Bistro
Samos
Tersiguel's

ROOMS

Black Olive
Charleston
Inn at Easton/E
Ixia
Jesse Wong's Asean Bistro
Milton Inn

Pazo
Red Maple
Saffron
Sascha's 527
Taste
Vin

VIEWS

Brightons Orangerie
Carrol's Creek Cafe/A
Crab Claw/E
Fisherman's Inn/E
Gertrude's
Harris Crab House/E

Narrows, The/E
Pisces
Sherwood's Landing/E
Sushi Sono
Town Dock/E
Windows

Top Service Ratings

Ratings are to the left of names.

27 Antrim 1844
Charleston

26 Prime Rib
Tersiguel's

25 Aldo's
Linwoods

24 Jalapeños/A
Sushi Sono
Milton Inn
Lewnes' Steak/A

Brightons Orangerie
Capital Grille
Chameleon Cafe
Elkridge Furnace Inn
Orchard Market
Piccola Roma/A
Trattoria Alberto
Oregon Grille
Les Folies Brasserie/A
La Scala

Best Buys

In order of Bang for the Buck rating.

1. Five Guys/A/BA
2. Atwater's
3. Big Bad Wolf BBQ
4. An Loi
5. Baugher's
6. Chicken Rico
7. Attman's Deli
8. Jimmy's
9. Matthew's Pizzeria
10. Au Bon Pain
11. Blue Moon Cafe
12. Mari Luna
13. Szechuan House
14. Pho Dat Thanh
15. Samos
16. Finnerteas
17. Papermoon Diner
18. Chick & Ruth's/A
19. Hard Times Cafe
20. Holy Frijoles

OTHER GOOD VALUES

Amicci's
Arcos
Cafe Hon
City Cafe
El Trovador
Faidley's Seafood
Helmand
Ikaros
Jennings
Jesse Wong's Hong Kong

JJ's Everyday Café
Joss Cafe/Sushi/A
Mr. Bill's Terr. Inn
Orchard Market
Oriental Manor
Paul's Homewood/A
Peppermill
Pete's Grille
Sushi King
Zorba's B&G

BALTIMORE, ANNAPOLIS AND THE EASTERN SHORE RESTAURANT DIRECTORY

Baltimore

Abacrombie ☑ *American*   26 | 22 | 24 | $51

Mt. Vernon | Abacrombie Fine Food & Accommodations | 58 W. Biddle St.
(Cathedral St.) | 410-837-3630 | www.abacrombie.net

Although this Mt. Vernon B&B eatery continues to offer a menu of
New American dinner fare (plus a Sunday brunch), regulars should
expect big changes following the recent departure of inn and restaurant owner Sonny Sweetman – a move that may affect the above
scores; since pre-symphony diners are known to "overrun" the
"tiny", "subterranean" space, it's best to "reserve for 8 PM after the
crowds subside"; N.B. closed Mondays and Tuesdays.

Acacia Fusion Bistro *Asian Fusion*   - | - | - | E

Frederick | 129 N. Market St. (bet. Church & 2nd Sts.) | 301-694-3015 |
www.acacia129.com

Reopened in 2006 after a brief shuttering, this veteran venue is adding to Frederick's culinary diversity with Asian fusion dishes like sesame shrimp tempura as well as a few New American entrees; the
exotic fare is served in an elongated, multiroom space that's as casual as the chatty front bar; N.B. a Sunday brunch and garden views
are both pluses.

AIDA Bistro ☒ *Italian*   23 | 17 | 21 | $38

Columbia | Gateway Plaza | 7185A Gateway Dr. (Rte. 175) |
410-953-0500 | www.aidabistro.com

At this "drop of warmth" in "Columbia's suburban wasteland" – a
"nouveau Italiano" "hidden in a business park" – "fresh-made pastas"
and an "excellent" small-plates menu make up for what some call
"shopping-center decor"; it can get a bit "noisy" (especially on biweekly Wednesday jazz nights), so try one of the "informative" and
more subdued wine tasting dinners; N.B. lunch-only on Mondays.

Akbar *Indian*   22 | 15 | 20 | $23

Mt. Vernon | 823 N. Charles St. (bet. Madison & Read Sts.) | 410-539-0944
Columbia | 9400 Snowden River Pkwy. (Oakland Mills Rd.) | 410-381-3600
www.akbar-restaurant.com

Given "student discounts" and a "helpful" staff, admirers wonder
"who could blame the throngs for coming" to this duo serving "assertively spiced" North Indian fare in "minimalist" Mt. Vernon digs
and in an even more "stripped-down" space in Columbia; both feature
an "awesome" lunch buffet that's a "fantastic deal" ("as long as you
don't mind smelling like curry all day"), so "arrive when the doors
open", because they "fill up quickly."

NEW Alabama BBQ Company ☒ ☑ *BBQ*   - | - | - | I

Northeast Baltimore | 4311 Harford Rd. (Argonne Dr.) | 410-254-1440 |
www.alabamabbqcompany.com

Pit master Jay Belle has brought his love of BBQ from the contest circuit to this small row house in a burgeoning section of Northeast
Baltimore; though some of the cooking takes place off-premises,

'cue connoiseurs can expect a full menu of wood-smoked meats, hearty ribs and pulled pork sandwiches, plus down-home sides and a different whole smoked fish each Friday; N.B. there's only a few seats, so consider carryout at peak times.

Aldo's *Italian*

26 | 25 | 25 | $55

Little Italy | 306 S. High St. (Fawn St.) | 410-727-0700 | www.aldositaly.com
"Decadent" Southern Italian "indulgences" from woodworker-"turned-chef" and owner Aldo Vitale are "just part of the experience" at this Little Italy "special-occasion" destination that will make you "feel like a king" with "attentive" service and an "elegant" setting that's "like being in someone's exquisitely decorated home" with "lots of little rooms" and a colonnaded atrium; still, some nit-pickers note "you pay for the tux-and-luxe formula."

☑ Ambassador Dining Room *Indian*

25 | 26 | 24 | $33

Homewood | Ambassador Apts. | 3811 Canterbury Rd. (bet. 39th St. & University Pkwy.) | 410-366-1484 | www.ambassadordiningroom.com
In a "dark", "hushed" apartment house dining room that will "transport you to colonial India", patrons savor the "gourmet twists on traditional" dishes that make this the "best Indian in Baltimore"; its Homewood location is "hard to find", but once you do, "sit on the [enclosed] patio" – it's especially "romantic" "in winter with the fireplace roaring" – or in the "lush" garden "overlooking the fountain."

Amicci's ● *Italian*

22 | 15 | 20 | $23

Little Italy | 231 S. High St. (bet. Fawn & Stiles Sts.) | 410-528-1096 | www.amiccis.com
This "Little Italy bargain outpost" is a "family-friendly place" with a "lighthearted spirit" and "unpretentious Italian" fare that will "send you to garlic heaven" – as long as you "make sure your date has a bite as well"; "terrific lunch specials" attract swarms of "Downtown's worker bees", and those who note it's "not much to look at" should appreciate a recent expansion that's added a copper-topped bar serving a full menu until midnight.

Andy Nelson's BBQ ☒ *BBQ*

 - | - | - | I

Cockeysville | 11007 York Rd. (Wight Ave.) | 410-527-1226 | www.andynelsonsbbq.com
Cockeysville barbecue fans load up on porcine platters at this hickory smoke-filled shack that's fully stocked with Elvis tunes; the take-your-tie-off atmosphere isn't fancy, but if you crave "exceptional" "slow-cooked pulled pork", Memphis-style ribs with "meat falling off the bone" and "yummy sides", then this joint has your name all over it – right alongside that of the eponymous chef-owner and former Baltimore Colt; N.B. it also does catering.

An Loi *Vietnamese*

25 | 10 | 19 | $14

Columbia | 7104 Minstrel Way (Snowden River Pkwy.) | 410-381-3188
"If you've never had pho, get your feet wet" and order a "huge bowl of noodle soup" at this "excellent hole-in-the-wall" in Columbia, where new owners have added some Korean dishes to the mostly

Vietnamese menu; still, given "'80s Soviet bloc" decor and "fluorescent lighting", it's clear why most keep their focus on the "intoxicating broth" at "ridiculously low prices."

An Poitín Stil Irish Pub & Restaurant ● *Pub Food*

17 | 22 | 18 | $26

Timonium | 2323 York Rd. (Timonium Rd.) | 410-560-7900 | www.thestill.net

"Heavy" pub grub plays second fiddle to ambiance at this "little slice of Ireland" in Timonium that's "an escape from suburbia" with its "fun" "authentic decor"; "the blarney from the happy-hour crowd" and "good local music" nightly tempt tipplers to "grab a pint and be merry", and though it can be "loud and smoky", that's fine with those who say "this is where you drink your dinner."

⊠ Antrim 1844 *American/French*

27 | 28 | 27 | $70

Taneytown | 30 Trevanion Rd. (Rte. 140) | 410-756-6812 | www.antrim1844.com

"Even without an overnight stay" at this "beautiful" Taneytown country inn, you'll "fall in love" with its "romantic" New American-French "destination" restaurant, where walking the "lovely grounds" or "watching a wedding from the patio" is but a prelude to "being pampered" by a "gracious staff" serving chef Michael Gettier's "sublime" six-course prix fixe dinners; you'll "shell out big bucks" for the "experience", but it's "worth every penny."

Aquatica Ⓜ *Seafood*

▽ 24 | 19 | 20 | $38

Havre de Grace | 931 Pulaski Hwy./Rte. 40 (bet. Lewis Ln. & Otsego St.) | 410-939-7686 | www.aquaticarestaurant.com

In an "unlikely setting" along Route 40 in Havre de Grace, TV chef/co-owner Mark Laubner "explores" via seafood dishes that "titillate the taste buds"; a few deem it too "upscale for Harford County", but most have warmed to the "friendly staff" and the diners' choice entrees (select your fish, cooking method and sauce); N.B. dinner-only.

Arcos *Mexican*

19 | 24 | 17 | $22

East Baltimore | 129 S. Broadway (bet. Lombard & Pratt Sts.) | 410-522-4777

Set in an East Baltimore row house renovated by artisan-owner Nicolas Ramos, this "romantic" "warren of dark rooms" lures locals with "authentic Mexican" specialties plus a "gorgeous" patio reminiscent of an "Oaxacan courtyard"; "finding its legs" with an expanded menu, it may yet win over those who cite "inconsistent" service ("you'd have an easier time finding Godot than a server here").

Attman's Delicatessen *Deli*

24 | 8 | 14 | $13

East Baltimore | 1019 E. Lombard St. (bet. Central Ave. & S. President St.) | 410-563-2666 | www.attmansdeli.com

"No time to go to NYC?" – when the deli "craving hits", hit the "ridiculously long line" at this East Baltimore octogenarian, then "order quickly and know what you're doing", because the "Meg Ryan orgasm-inducing corned beef" and other sandwiches "come with a side of surliness" from the tongue-in-cheek staff; it's "nothing

	FOOD	DECOR	SERVICE	COST

fancy", but "great photos from the glory days" are a nice touch; P.S. "it's advisable to call ahead to place your order."

Atwater's *Bakery/Soup* — 25 | 12 | 20 | $12

York Road Corridor | Belvedere Square Mkt. | 529 E. Belvedere Ave. (York Rd.) | 410-323-2396
NEW Towson | 798 Kenilworth Dr. (Witherwood Ct.) | 410-938-8775
www.atwaters.biz

"Fortify yourself for shopping" in "trendy Belvedere Square" at proprietor Ned Atwater's soup bar and bakery where an "ever-changing menu" of "rib-stickin'" slurps ("extra points for vegan options") are paired with "huge hunks" of "chewy" bread and "interesting sandwiches"; a recent expansion of the original added "more tables" as well as cheese and coffee counters; N.B. a second location in Towson, with a drive-thru window, opened post-Survey.

Au Bon Pain Ⓢ *Bakery* — 16 | 10 | 12 | $11

Downtown | Commerce Pl. | 1 South St. (bet. Baltimore & Redwood Sts.) | 410-837-9814
Inner Harbor | 10 N. Calvert St. (Baltimore St.) | 410-727-9827
www.aubonpain.com
See review in the Washington, DC, Directory.

Austin Grill *Tex-Mex* — 16 | 15 | 16 | $22

Canton | American Can Company Bldg. | 2400 Boston St. (Hudson St.) | 410-534-0606 | www.austingrill.com
See review in the Washington, DC, Directory.

b Ⓜ *Eclectic* — 24 | 19 | 21 | $31

Downtown North | 1501 Bolton St. (Mosher St.) | 410-383-8600 | www.b-bistro.com

Bolton Hill's "local b-istro" feels like a "neighborhood restaurant, no matter where you're from", with a "hip but not pretentious" staff serving an "adventurous" and "varied" Eclectic menu complemented by a "reasonably priced wine list"; given "cozy" confines that can get "noisy", realists recommend you "don't go for intimate conversation", although "sitting outside in the summertime" makes for a "laid-back" alternative; N.B. dinner-only with a Sunday brunch.

Babalu Grill Ⓢ Ⓜ *Cuban* — 20 | 20 | 19 | $34

Inner Harbor | 32 Market Pl. (Water St.) | 410-234-9898 | www.babalugrill.com

"Lucy, I'm home!" crow "tourists and local young" things headed to émigré Steve de Castro's "fun" Market Place "hang" for "Cuban comfort food" in the evenings and dancing on weekends when it "turns into a nightclub"; while some say the eats could use "more commitment", other patrons find that the "festive" atmosphere may need less – the "congas-as-barstools" setting can get "noisy."

Baldwin's Station Ⓜ *American* — 20 | 21 | 18 | $40

Sykesville | 7618 Main St. (Rte. 32) | 410-795-1041 | www.baldwinsstation.com

"Take a ride in the country" to Sykesville to visit this "quaint" New American set in an 1883 "restored railroad station" overlooking the

Patapsco River; it's "fun to sit outside" on the deck "next to the tracks" and "watch the trains go by", and if spoilsports steam that the food and "spotty service" "aren't quite up to the prices", live music every other Thursday may help to "make it worth the trip."

Bamboo House ● *Chinese* | 19 | 13 | 20 | $27 |

Cockeysville | 26 Cranbrook Rd. (York Rd.) | 410-666-9550
Tucked into a Cockeysville strip mall, "this old standby gets overlooked" but is still "dependable after all these years" for "consistently good", "traditional Chinese"; maybe the decor could use "an update", but for most it remains a "great hole-in-the-wall" complete with live music and dancing Thursday–Saturday.

Banjara *Indian* | 21 | 12 | 19 | $23 |

South Baltimore | 1017 S. Charles St. (Hamburg St.) | 410-962-1554
This "reliable" Indian hidden in a South Baltimore row house provides "authentic" if "standard" Indian fare that utilizes a "flavorful", "right-on-the-money" "mix of spices" that "aren't overpowering"; some say the interior may "need a face-lift", but "attentive service" and "value prices" help to compensate.

Bân Thai ⊠ *Thai* | 21 | 12 | 19 | $19 |

Downtown North | 340 N. Charles St. (Mulberry St.) | 410-727-7971 | www.banthai.us
Boasting "decent prices" and "a great location" on Charles Street in the business district, this family-owned purveyor of "traditional Thai" easily makes up for what some dub "blah decor"; it's a "terrific lunch option" and "convenient pre-symphony", but the "mmm-good" fare can arrive "spiced for the timid", so don't hesitate to ask the "super-friendly" staff to "bring the condiment tray."

Baugher's *American* | 18 | 10 | 20 | $13 |

Westminster | 289 W. Main St. (Rte. 31) | 410-848-7413 | www.baughers.com
"Don't expect gourmet" – this "Westminster classic" serves up a side of "real Americana" with its "solid" "farmers' fare" like "fried chicken that's made to order"; whatever "great value" meal you choose, be sure to "save room" for their "calorie-worthy" "homemade pies and ice cream"; P.S. the eponymous Baugher family owns a nearby orchard, so "if it has apples in it, order it."

Bertha's *Seafood* | 19 | 15 | 17 | $26 |

Fells Point | 734 S. Broadway (Lancaster St.) | 410-327-5795 | www.berthas.com
"Real characters hang out" at this "maritime-themed", "old Fells Point" "institution" where – "surprise! – behind the bar is a cozy dining room" for downing seafood that includes the signature "mussels heard 'round the world" paired with "imaginative sauces"; "it's a little tired, but still popular", especially for its live music, Sunday brunch and reservations-only "afternoon high tea" (served Tuesdays, Fridays and Saturdays).

	FOOD	DECOR	SERVICE	COST

☑ Bicycle, The *Eclectic*
| - | 21 | 23 | $45 |

South Baltimore | 1444 Light St. (bet. Birckhead St. & Fort Ave.) | 410-234-1900 | www.bicyclebistro.com

Admirers who hoped that a recent ownership change would "not diminish the quality" of this "special place" in South Baltimore will be relieved to know that the current chef-owner has made only subtle alterations to the "inventive" Eclectic menu; it remains the type of "lighthearted" place that "buzzes" – due to its "small" setting *and* its "don't-miss 18 bottles for $18 wine list"; N.B. dinner-only.

Big Bad Wolf's House of Barbeque ☒ *BBQ*
| 25 | 7 | 20 | $12 |

Northeast Baltimore | 5713 Harford Rd. (White Ave.) | 410-444-6422 | www.bigbadwolfbarbeque.com

"Drawing people from all around", this "no-frills" "BBQ shack" in Northeast Baltimore serves up "real pit-smoked 'cue" from "the Q-men", chefs/co-owners Rick and Scott Smith (ex Charleston), whose culinary chops yield their "own version of authentic" regional grilled meats, "finger-lickin' sauces" and "don't-skip" sides; with only six stools, it's "strictly carryout" for some, although "a few outdoor tables" help to compensate.

Birches Restaurant ☒ *American*
| 24 | 18 | 16 | $29 |

Canton | 641 S. Montford Ave. (Foster Ave.) | 410-732-3000 | www.birchesrestaurant.com

Set in a "nondescript" Canton row house, this "cozy", dinner-only "corner hideaway" offers a "multi-tiered" New American menu with "choices for all budgets"; some surmise the "slow kitchen needs help" – "set aside two hours" – but "patience is rewarded with savory", wood-fire-grilled entrees that have "enough pizzazz to impress the adventurous"; P.S. "shady sidewalk" seating is a plus.

Black Olive, The *Greek/Seafood*
| 26 | 20 | 22 | $50 |

Fells Point | 814 S. Bond St. (Shakespeare St.) | 410-276-7141 | www.theblackolive.com

"Nicely renovated" twin Fells Point townhouses form the setting for this "cozy" Greek seafooder that has "a winning formula": a "market-style" icebox allows diners to "select their own fish", which is "filleted tableside", then "grilled to perfection" using "simple preparations" and mostly organic ingredients; of course, this "platonic ideal of a taverna" totals up to a "tsunami of a bill", although most conclude it's "worth the splurge."

Blue Agave Restaurante y Tequileria Ⓜ *Mexican*
| 22 | 20 | 18 | $31 |

Federal Hill | 1032 Light St. (Cross St.) | 410-576-3938 | www.blueagaverestaurant.com

An "authentic Mexican" menu "will make your tongue sizzle" at this "lively Federal Hill hot spot" specializing in "a mind-boggling variety of tequilas" – and "margaritas like you've never had"; although the setting is "festive" (read: "noisy") and the service "could be better", most say it's "worth the trek" to South Baltimore; N.B. dinner-only.

Blue Moon Cafe *American*

25 | 15 | 16 | $16

Fells Point | 1621 Aliceanna St. (bet. Bethel St. & B'way) | 410-522-3940

"Come two hours before you're hungry" because "tight" quarters mean "long lines" at this "funky" Fells Point breakfast spot, where "a colorful crowd" downs "homey" fare like "diet-crushing cinnamon rolls" and "big-as-your-head biscuits"; even those who say the kitchen is as "slow as molasses" and the setting a "throwback to the '60s" agree it's "a must", especially during their "late-night heaven" hours (Fridays and Saturdays, from 11 PM until 3 PM the next day).

Blue Sea Grill ☒ *Seafood*

24 | 24 | 22 | $46

Downtown | 614 Water St. (bet. Gay St. & Market Pl.) | 410-837-7300 | www.blueseagrill.com

This "chichi" Downtown seafooder from Ruth's Chris' Steve de Castro is done up in so many "shades of blue" that you may "think you're under the ocean as you dine" on "exceptionally fresh" fin fare amid schools of "see-and-be-seen" sorts; a few doubters deem the "reeeaally cool" environs "a little cold", although they admit "efficient service" and "mouthwatering lobster mac 'n' cheese" "make up for it"; P.S. "love the complimentary valet parking."

BlueStone *Seafood*

21 | 20 | 19 | $35

Timonium | 11 W. Aylesbury Rd. (Greenspring Dr.) | 410-561-1100 | www.bluestoneonline.net

"Off the beaten path" in Timonium near the Light Rail, this "nice catch for the suburbs" serves up "fresh seafood" "any style" – the fried green tomatoes with crab "requires a stop" – plus other New American dishes; it's a "casual" "date night" type of place, but the central bar can make it "noisy", and a few find that the "inconsistent service" "could use some finishing."

Bo Brooks *Crab House*

17 | 15 | 17 | $34

Canton | 2701 Boston St. (Lakewood Ave.) | 410-558-0202 | www.bobrooks.com

"Roll up your sleeves", then "get down and dirty" with "a yummy mess" of "large, plump, juicy" crustaceans and "cold beer" at this "crab house classic" located "right on the water" in Canton; some jaded locals, however, find it "noisy, crowded" and "overpriced", with "slow service" to boot – a "place to take tourists who can't tell this isn't the best in town."

Boccaccio *Italian*

25 | 21 | 23 | $53

Little Italy | 925 Eastern Ave. (bet. Exeter & High Sts.) | 410-234-1322 | www.boccaccio-restaurant.com

Catch this "solid performer" on "a good night" and the "flavorful" Northern Italian cuisine "will be the best you ever had", as will the "professional" service; with "tables far apart", it lends itself to "romance or closing the big deal", so while the unimpressed gripe about "mega bills", the majority agrees it's "a cut above the other Little Italy restaurants" and "worth it."

	FOOD	DECOR	SERVICE	COST

Brass Elephant *American*

| | 23 | 24 | 23 | $45 |

Mt. Vernon | 924 N. Charles St. (bet. Eager & Read Sts.) | 410-547-8480 | www.brasselephant.com

"A more refined era" lives on at this "Mt. Vernon mainstay" whose "brass and burnished wood" setting draws "an older crowd" – "take your parents" pre-symphony – for "wonderful" Traditional American plates in the dining room and "lighter-on-the-wallet" "mini-portions" upstairs in the "casual" Tusk Lounge; even those who say this "standby" is "past its prime" can't help but admit it's "still awfully good."

Brasserie Tatin *French*

| | 23 | 23 | 20 | $46 |

Homewood | Broadview Apts. | 105 W. 39th St. (Canterbury Rd.) | 443-278-9110 | www.brasserietatin.com

Sending you "back to Paris" with its "jazzy", "brash" "big-city decor" and "imaginative" brasserie fare, this "fabulous" Homewood French is "a great deal for lunch" but "tonier for dinner" – so "hold on to your wallet"; plus, it has a European-style Sunday brunch and also offers complimentary parking across the street; N.B. a post-Survey chef change may outdate the Food score.

Brewer's Alley *Pub Food*

| | 17 | 14 | 17 | $23 |

Frederick | 124 N. Market St. (bet. Church & 2nd Sts.) | 301-631-0089 | www.brewers-alley.com

All of Frederick "flocks" to this "casual", "dress-down" brewery, where the "decent yet typical" American pub grub "goes down nicely", "but the microbrews are what you go for": five year-round options plus seasonal varieties; the "tall-ceilinged" former town hall can turn into a "roaring" scene with "borderline service", however, so some warn "this is not the place for an intimate meal."

Brewer's Art ◗ *American*

| | 21 | 22 | 19 | $32 |

Mt. Vernon | 1106 N. Charles St. (bet. Biddle & Chase Sts.) | 410-547-6925 | www.belgianbeer.com

With a "wood-paneled dining room" and pub on the main floor and a "sultry" "dungeon" of a basement bar, "the environment is just as delicious" as the "handcrafted" brews at this "hipster" haven set in an "elegant" Mt. Vernon townhouse; there's "fancy" European-accented New American food, but "beer snobs unite" in believing that "the real reasons for coming here" are the "famous" "Resurrection Ale and garlic-rosemary fries"; P.S. the place can get "smoky", so "bring a gas mask."

Brightons Orangerie *American*

| | 23 | 25 | 24 | $44 |

Inner Harbor | InterContinental Harbor Court Hotel | 550 Light St. (bet. Conway & Lee Sts.) | 410-347-9750 | www.harborcourt.com

Now that its vaunted sister restaurant, Hampton's, has been transformed into a private events space, this "elegant" New American is the primary dining room at the InterContinental Harbor Court Hotel; it retains the same "fine views of the Baltimore Inner Harbor", but surveyors can expect dramatic changes in the kitchen (which may outdate the above Food score).

	FOOD	DECOR	SERVICE	COST

Broom's Bloom Dairy Ⓜ *Ice Cream*   ▽ 23 | 19 | 23 | $8

Bel Air | 1700 S. Fountain Green Rd./Rte. 543 (Rte. 136) | 410-399-2697 | www.bbdairy.com

Located "in the middle of a pasture" "in a pleasant country setting" four miles off I-95, this Bel Air dairy farm serves up "awesome", "made-on-site" ice cream that "can't be fresher" – particularly given the "short cow-to-customer distance"; there's also a small, home-spun cafe and an outdoor area for dining on a selection of "other food" (soups, cheeses, breads), but the "rich, amazing" scoops are the real draw.

Cacique *Mexican/Spanish*   22 | 20 | 19 | $22

Frederick | 26 N. Market St. (Patrick St.) | 301-695-2756 | www.caciquefrederick.com

This "valid date-night option" "on the main drag" in Downtown Frederick offers a "wonderful mix of Spanish" and "authentic Mexican food" plus "don't-miss sangria" to "sate your hunger and thirst"; it can "get busy early on the weekends", but it's "large" enough that "you can usually squeeze in" – literally, as the "tables are close together."

Caesar's Den *Italian*   22 | 16 | 23 | $38

Little Italy | 223 S. High St. (Stiles St.) | 410-547-0820 | www.caesarsden.com

As an "unassuming" "neighborhood standby", this "Little Italy survivor" is "not the fanciest", but like a "reliable old friend", it "never disappoints" locals with its "consistently terrific" Southern Italian savories; an "attentive staff" "appears and disappears at the perfect moment", punctuating a "special meal" that "makes you feel good."

Café de Paris *French*   23 | 19 | 21 | $43

Columbia | 8808 Centre Park Dr. (Rte. 108) | 410-997-3560 | www.cafedepariscolumbia.com

"*Parlez-vous* escargots?" – then be "wowed" by this "French bistro experience" set in an "unassuming" Columbia office park building, where "affable owner" "Erik Rochard is an absolute treasure": he "personally greets", "knows how to accommodate" and even plays jazz flute on Tuesdays, which adds up to "a memorable visit"; a "bargain" dinner prix fixe menu and an on-site crêperie/cafe are pluses; N.B. lunch-only on Mondays.

Cafe Hon *Diner*   15 | 18 | 17 | $19

Hampden | 1002 W. 36th St. (bet. Falls Rd. & Roland Ave.) | 410-243-1230 | www.cafehon.com

"Turn back the clock", "don your pink boa" and "learn Bawlmerese" at this "classic", "kitschy" "landmark Hampden eatery" that's "always a hoot" for "homestyle, campy comfort food" that's "bad for your thighs, good for your soul" and "the same as it ever was"; according to critics, that means it's "ok", "overpriced" American diner fare served up by "colorful", "endearingly ditzy" servers – just "avoid weekends if you want their full attention."

	FOOD	DECOR	SERVICE	COST

Café Troia ⑤ Italian
22 | 19 | 22 | $42

Towson | 28 W. Allegheny Ave. (Washington Ave.) | 410-337-0133 | www.cafetroia.com

"Save the drive Downtown" and follow the "local business and political" set to Towson, where this family-owned Italian spins out "competent" fare "cooked with quality ingredients" and served by an "experienced" staff; the "somewhat bland" setting has a "European ambiance", and while some find tabs "a bit on the pricey side", the $12.50 three-course lunch prix fixe is a "bargain."

Cafe Zen Ⓜ Chinese
22 | 12 | 18 | $19

North Baltimore | 438 E. Belvedere Ave. (York Rd.) | 410-532-0022 | www.cafezen.com

This "updated Chinese" in North Baltimore isn't "a looker" – more "a VFW hall" – but "who cares about decor" given dishes like the "not-to-be-missed" chicken Zen curry; it's "overwhelmed" by suburbanites headed to "a movie at the Senator", but at "prices that won't blow a hole in your pocket", it's "the place to go"; N.B. the owners recently opened Zen West, a Tex-Mex joint, in the space next door.

ⓩ Capital Grille, The Steak
25 | 24 | 24 | $58

Inner Harbor | 500 E. Pratt St. (Gay St.) | 443-703-4064 | www.thecapitalgrille.com

See review in the Washington, DC, Directory.

Carlyle Club, The Ⓜ Lebanese
24 | 24 | 22 | $33

Homewood | Carlyle Inn & Suites | 500 W. University Pkwy. (bet. 39th & 40th Sts.) | 410-243-5454

"You wouldn't know it from the name", but this "unexpected gem in an unlikely" Homewood apartment house plates up "complex", "satisfying" Lebanese cuisine befitting the "younger sister of the Ambassador" Dining Room; let an "attentive staff" serve you "alfresco on the patio" or in the "beautiful", "softly lit" interior that at times can feel "like a private dining room" – and a "decent value"; N.B. "parking's limited", making valet a "must."

NEW Cazbar ❶ Turkish
– | – | – | M

Downtown North | 316 N. Charles St. (Saratoga St.) | 410-528-1222 | www.cazbarbaltimore.com

A diverse crowd heads to this cozy, exotic Downtown North destination for quiet business lunches and late-night dates over hummus, kebabs and other Turkish fare, plus sandwiches, salads and panini; hookah smoking in the lounge and Saturday night belly dancing help to invigorate an otherwise languid atmosphere.

Chameleon Cafe ⑤Ⓜ American
26 | 18 | 24 | $37

Northeast Baltimore | 4341 Harford Rd. (3 blocks south of Cold Spring Ln.) | 410-254-2376 | www.thechameleoncafe.com

Husband-and-wife-team Jeffrey Smith and Brenda Wolf Smith's "dedication shines through" at this dinner-only Northeast Baltimore "foodie's find" featuring "innovative, artistic, delicious" French-inflected New American entrees; while the "small" setting strikes some as "too casual for the menu", an open kitchen and "adept" servers "with a lot of heart" make you feel like you're "eating in the owners' home"; N.B. sidewalk seating adds appeal.

☑ Charleston ☒ *American* · · · · · 27 | 26 | 27 | $74

Inner Harbor East | 1000 Lancaster St. (S. Exeter St.) | 410-332-7373 | www.charlestonrestaurant.com

"One of Baltimore's best" is "even better" thanks to a "strikingly elegant" makeover and a relatively new set-price format that lets diners "try more" of chef/co-owner Cindy Wolf's "cutting-edge", "Southern-style" New American small plates offered in three-, five- and six-course "create-your-own tasting menus"; though a few are perturbed about the now-"tiny portions", the "celestial" tabs at this Harbor East experience are justified by the "exceptional service" and an "exquisite wine list" from co-owner Tony Foreman.

☑ Cheesecake Factory *American* · · · 18 | 17 | 17 | $27

Inner Harbor | Harborplace Pratt Street Pavilion | 201 E. Pratt St. (South St.) | 410-234-3990 | www.thecheesecakefactory.com
See review in the Washington, DC, Directory.

Chiapparelli's *Italian* · · · · · · · 19 | 15 | 19 | $30

Little Italy | 237 S. High St. (Fawn St.) | 410-837-0309 | www.chiapparellis.com

The "eternally good" house salad may be the real "reason to go" to this "Little Italy mainstay", but diners can follow it up with "classic Italian favorites" "served up hot and heavy" by a "friendly" staff; it's "your parents' parents' restaurant" – "old-fashioned" with dishes that "haven't changed since the Carter administration" – but "affordable" tabs and "legendary portions" mean you can "bring the whole family."

Chicken Rico *Peruvian* · · · · · · · 20 | 5 | 14 | $11

Highlandtown | 3728 Eastern Ave. (bet. Dean & Eaton Sts.) | 410-522-2950
"It's a dive, but it's also the best rotisserie chicken in Baltimore" rave reviewers of this "minimalist" Highlandtown Peruvian whose dozen or so tables and "fluorescent lighting" give it that "cafeteria feel"; but "who cares" when "everyone's happy" with their "cheap", "South American–style" eats – "for $10, how can one complain?"; P.S. if you carry out, "don't forget the spicy green sauce."

Chinatown Café ◑ *Chinese* · · · · · 22 | 7 | 18 | $17

Downtown | 323 Park Ave. (W. Pleasant St.) | 410-727-5599
This "authentic" Chinese serves "tasty", "better-than-standard-issue" food including "amazing" weekend dim sum in, alas, a "bland" setting on the "sketchy" side of the Downtown business district; "inexpensive" prices work in its favor, and it's also "great for takeout"; N.B. it's closed on Wednesdays.

Chiu's Sushi *Japanese* · · · · · · · 21 | 16 | 22 | $30

Inner Harbor East | 608 S. Exeter St. (bet. Eastern Ave. & Fleet St.) | 410-752-9666
Raw-fish fanatics "choose Chiu's" for "top-notch sushi" and a "rich selection" of "interesting, unique rolls"; it makes up for what some

	FOOD	DECOR	SERVICE	COST

call a "nondescript" Harbor East location (next to Whole Foods) with "generous pieces", an "almost kitschy ambiance" and the "friendliest staff" – even "the owner greets you with a smile."

Christopher Daniel *American*
22 | 16 | 20 | $39

Timonium | Padonia Park Shopping Ctr. | 106 W. Padonia Rd. (Broad Ave.) | 410-308-1800 | www.christopher-daniel.com

At this Timonium "strip-mall surprise", suburbanites are split: fans say the chef-owners "know how to wow" with "delicious" New American food and "friendly service", while others opine its "mediocre" setting "could use warming up" and its staff a trip back from "la-la land", with a few foes finding it "not worth the cost"; P.S. the adjoining bar is "loud and crowded", so some advise "keep to the restaurant side."

Ciao Bella *Italian*
23 | 17 | 23 | $32

Little Italy | 236 S. High St. (bet. Fawn & Stiles Sts.) | 410-685-7733 | www.cbella.com

"Trying hard to be a cut above", this recently renovated "Little Italy favorite" serves up "solid", "earthy Italian" just "like from your mama's kitchen"; if some find "nothing to write home about", others point to "service that's just right, from pouring wine to ordering the next course", and ask "what's there not to like?"

City Cafe *American*
18 | 17 | 17 | $23

Mt. Vernon | 1001 Cathedral St. (Eager St.) | 410-539-4252 | www.citycafebaltimore.com

"Baltimore's most versatile restaurant" is this "bustling", "cool" Mt. Vernonite, where one side is an "airy" "urban coffeehouse" for "artists and grad students" to "hang out" and enjoy "bottomless cups of fla-vored" brews and "free WiFi", and the other half is a "funky, sleek" New American cafe; both are "loud", but fans say the service and food "ain't half bad", so "it's a safe bet" pre-theater or for a "lazy brunch."

☑ Clyde's ◑ *American*
18 | 21 | 19 | $30

Columbia | 10221 Wincopin Circle (Little Patuxent Pkwy.) | 410-730-2829 | www.clydes.com

See review in the Washington, DC, Directory.

Coburn's Tavern *American*
20 | 15 | 18 | $26

Canton | 2921 O'Donnell St. (Curley St.) | 410-342-0999 | www.coburnstavern.com

Offering "decent" American eats that are "a step above standard bar fare", this tavern is a "solid performer" in the midst of the Canton Square "scene"; locals stop by for "bargain" "specials throughout the week", but think twice Thursday–Saturday after 10 PM, when the upstairs morphs into a "loud" dance club and the "atmosphere takes a nose dive"; N.B. it serves breakfast on weekends.

Copra ☒ *American*
22 | 23 | 19 | $29

Downtown North | 313 N. Charles St. (bet. Mulberry & Saratoga Sts.) | 410-727-6080 | www.coprabaltimore.com

At this "hip spot" on Charles Street, the New American nibbles (in-cluding "fantastic wood-fired pizzas") are nearly as "tasty" as the ambiance, which features a "downstairs grotto with its own bar" and "lots of couches" – it "feels like hanging out at a friend's posh ski lodge"; it's "fun for groups" and "great after work", but it garners a few complaints for "snail-like service."

Corks ☑ American   25 | 19 | 23 | $51

South Baltimore | 1026 S. Charles St. (bet. Cross & Hamburg Sts.) | 410-752-3810 | www.corksrestaurant.com

This "hidden gem" in a South Baltimore row house keeps the "passionate" oenophile "in mind", pairing its "sublime", seasonally changing New American menu with an "outstanding" "all-American wine list" featuring "little-known vineyards"; "attentive, knowledgeable servers" help compensate for the "intimate (read: small, but nice)" space and "costly" tabs; N.B. dinner-only.

Cosmopolitan Bar & Grill American   18 | 16 | 17 | $30

Canton | 2933 O'Donnell St. (bet. Curley & Potomac Sts.) | 410-563-5000

"Generous portions" of New American fare are overshadowed by "over 50" "outstanding martinis" at this recently renovated, "upscale pub/restaurant" in Canton, where "the drink menu is more extensive than the food menu" – so some quip "eat elsewhere, but come back for after-dinner" sips; the "quaint but small" "converted row house" is also "popular", so "make sure to eat upstairs" away from the "hovering" barflies.

Costas Inn Crab House ◐ Crab House   22 | 9 | 19 | $35

Dundalk | 4100 N. Point Blvd. (New Battle Grove Rd.) | 410-477-1975 | www.costasinn.com

You may "run into high school friends" at this "real-deal" Dundalk "tradition", because "the only out-of-towners here are the crustaceans" – "heavy", "hot, spicy" blue crabs that are flown in from Texas and Louisiana; "always big and full of meat", the specialty's "served family-style" on paper-covered tables in a "utilitarian building" located near the Sparrows Point steel mill, making this "an all-around Baltimore experience"; P.S. "call ahead to reserve" your hardshells.

Crêpe du Jour ☑ French   21 | 16 | 17 | $22

Mt. Washington | 1609 Sulgrave Ave. (Kelly Ave.) | 410-542-9000 | www.crepedujour.com

If you're craving a "scrumptious", "gooey cheese-and-mushroom crêpe" served "Parisian-style", make a "roundtrip to France for about $20" at this "charming" "little bistro" in Mt. Washington that offers "lots of options" beside the namesake item; plus, there's a newly redone dining room to go with the already "pleasant", "civilized [back] patio."

NEW Cynthia's ☑ American   - | - | - | E

Severna Park | Park Plaza | 552 Ritchie Hwy. (bet. E. McKinsey & Robinson Rds.) | 410-315-8088 | www.cynthiassevernapark.com

At this quiet New American in Severna Park, husband-and-wife chef-owners Brian and Cindy Bennington (both have worked in top

U.S. kitchens) serve up a seasonal menu complete with house-baked breads; don't be deterred by its strip-mall locale, as it has a sophisticated, earth-toned setting, and there's also an intriguing wine list and a Sunday brunch.

Da Mimmo ● *Italian* | 22 | 18 | 22 | $54 |

Little Italy | 217 S. High St. (Stiles St.) | 410-727-6876 | www.damimmo.com

"See who's who in Baltimore" at this Little Italy "pearl" that's "romance personified", a "special-occasion" destination serving "delicious" Italian dishes that include what some consider the "best veal chop in town" "with service to match"; nonetheless, critics claim they're "resting on their laurels", with "overpriced" food and "decor that needs updating."

David Chu's China Bistro *Chinese* | 21 | 13 | 19 | $22 |

Pikesville | 7105 Reisterstown Rd. (bet. Glengyle Ave. & Seven Mile Ln.) | 410-602-5008

For "family-oriented" fressing, try this "kosher-but-great" Pikesville Chinese where "ample portions of tasty" tidbits come with "more beef and more quality control" but less heat according to those who say "they spice for the rest-home crowd"; "they're extremely strict" ("don't even bring baby milk"), so it may be "nicer to carry out", especially at peak hours, when it can get "noisy and crowded"; P.S. "not open Friday night or Saturday."

Della Notte *Italian* | 21 | 21 | 20 | $39 |

Little Italy | 801 Eastern Ave. (President St.) | 410-837-5500 | www.dellanotte.com

Some say the "ambiance is spellbinding", others "tacky", but "if you can get beyond" the "Roman pillars, marble busts and the tree in the middle of the dining room", this "special-occasion" spot "at the entrance to Little Italy" boasts a "diverse menu" of "solid" "upscale" (read: "pricey") Italian fare, plus "attentive service", an "extensive wine list" and a "lovely view" of the skyline at sunset; P.S. "free on-site parking is an added plus."

⬛NEW Dogwood *American* | - | - | - | M |

Hampden | 911 W. 36th St. (Roland Ave.) | 410-889-0952 | www.dogwooddeli.com

Although it began as a carry-out deli on Hampden's main drag, this subterranean seedling from chef-owner Galen Sampson (former executive toque at the late Hampton's) and his wife, Bridget, has grown into a nicely appointed New American restaurant; it offers a menu focused on natural foods and fresh ingredients that are sourced from local farms, and though it is currently BYO only, it plans to add a wine bar in fall 2007; N.B. a parking lot in back is an added bonus.

Dukem *Ethiopian* | 23 | 12 | 16 | $19 |

Mt. Vernon | 1100 Maryland Ave. (W. Chase St.) | 410-385-0318 | www.dukemrestaurant.com

See review in the Washington, DC, Directory.

Dutch's Daughter *American*

`20` `20` `20` `$35`

Frederick | 581 Himes Ave. (Rte. 40) | 301-668-9500 | www.dutchs.info

"Score some 'kid points'" and "take your mom" to this "oversized" "modern château" west of Frederick that "feels like a banquet facility" because it *is* one – its five dining areas "can support multiple rehearsal dinners" at once; while many find the "mainly seafood" American menu is "reliable", some say it "needs to be spiced up."

Edo Sushi *Japanese*

`25` `17` `23` `$26`

Inner Harbor | Harborplace Pratt Street Pavilion | 201 E. Pratt St. (South St.) | 410-843-9804

Timonium | Padonia Village Shopping Ctr. | 53 E. Padonia Rd. (York Rd.) | 410-667-9200

Owings Mills | Garrison Forest Plaza | 10347 Reisterstown Rd. (Rosewood Ln.) | 410-363-7720

Edo Mae Sushi *Japanese*

Owings Mills | Boulevard Corporate Ctr. | 10995 Owings Mills Blvd. (bet. I-795 & Reisterstown Rd.) | 410-356-6818
www.edosushimd.com

"Watch the chefs" as they create "beautifully prepared sushi" and sashimi at this Japanese quartet where the "innovative" specials are made from "fish that tastes like it just jumped out of the sea"; "attentive servers", a no-corkage-fee BYO policy at most locations and a drum you "bang for good luck" help diners ignore the "strip-mall atmosphere"; N.B. the Harborplace branch opened post-Survey.

Elkridge Furnace Inn Ⓜ *American/French*

`24` `26` `24` `$47`

Elkridge | 5745 Furnace Ave. (bet. Main St. & Race Rd.) | 410-379-9336 | www.elkridgefurnaceinn.com

"To close the big deal or tell your sweetie you love her", head to this "upscale" Elkridge New American–French set in a "charming" 1744 inn overlooking the Patapsco River; it offers "excellent", ever-changing menus and "wonderful service", so "pretend you're genteel for a night, then eat tuna fish for the rest of the year", because prices reflect its "special-occasion" status; N.B. the more casual McCubbin's Tavern now offers a small-plates menu.

El Trovador *Mexican/Salvadoran*

`23` `15` `20` `$20`

Fells Point | 318 S. Broadway (bet. Bank & Gough Sts.) | 410-276-6200 | www.eltrovadorrestaurant.com

"This is a real diamond in a rough area" say "south-of-the-border food lovers" about "the king of Baltimore's growing Latino section" just above Fells Point; "a great mix" of Mexican and Salvadoran dishes is served in a "homey but dressy" setting that's "so much nicer than you'd think" – in sum, it's a "real taste of the old country" that's "like eating with your family if they were friendly and mom could cook."

Faidley's Seafood Ⓢ *Seafood*

`25` `8` `14` `$16`

Downtown West | Lexington Mkt. | 203 N. Paca St. (Lexington St.) | 410-727-4898 | www.faidleyscrabcakes.com

"It ain't fine dinin', but it's mighty fine eatin'" as you savor "amazing" "softball-sized ur-crab cakes" "expertly prepared just for you" and eaten "standing up" at this "must when visiting Lexington Market"; "if you can handle a little grittiness" – "it's a market, for crying out loud" – you'll get nothing but "fresh seafood", "lively characters" and "a front row seat on real Baltimore"; N.B. they'll ship their specialty to anywhere in the country.

Finnerteas ☑ *Tearoom*

20 | 22 | 22 | $20

Hampden | 3547 Chestnut Ave. (36th St.) | 410-235-8327 | www.finnerteas.com

"Those without two X chromosomes may feel out of place" in this Hampden "high-estrogen zone" where "little girls and their mothers sip tea with biscuits" and nibble on "pretty sandwiches"; it's "a lovely way to spend an afternoon" (it's open Thursday–Sunday only), "leisurely" enjoying "one tasty goodie after another" in a setting that's "elegant, soothing and civilizing"; N.B. the second floor has been remade into a whimsical space suitable for children's afternoon tea parties.

☑ Five Guys *Hamburgers*

24 | 8 | 15 | $9

Inner Harbor | Harborplace Pratt Street Pavilion | 201 E. Pratt St. (South St.) | 410-244-7175
Canton | Shoppes at Brewers Hill | 3600 Boston St. (S. Conkling St.) | 410-522-1580
Mt. Vernon | 111 W. Centre St. (Ploy St.) | 410-244-5234
White Marsh | Shops at Nottingham Sq. | 5272 Campbell Blvd. (Franklin Square Dr.) | 410-933-1017
Woodlawn | 7091 Security Blvd. (N. Rolling Rd.) | 410-265-9590
www.fiveguys.com
Additional locations throughout the Baltimore area
See review in the Washington, DC, Directory.

Fleming's Prime Steakhouse & Wine Bar *Steak*

24 | 22 | 23 | $54

Inner Harbor East | 720 Aliceanna St. (President St.) | 410-332-1666 | www.flemingssteakhouse.com
See review in the Washington, DC, Directory.

Friendly Farm *American*

21 | 11 | 21 | $22

Upperco | 17434 Foreston Rd. (Mount Carmel Rd.) | 410-239-7400 | www.friendlyfarm.net

"Roll up your sleeves and commit yourself" to "eating a lot" of "bargain", "all-American comfort food" "served family-style" with "bottomless sides" at this "old-fashioned" "dining hall" in Upperco; it's "not much on decor", but "expect long lines" nonetheless, because its "rustic charm" makes diners "feel like kids again" – especially when they "save a roll to feed the ducks in the pond" post-meal.

G&M *Seafood*

22 | 8 | 16 | $24

Linthicum | 804 N. Hammonds Ferry Rd. (Nursery Rd.) | 410-636-1777 | www.gandmcrabcakes.com

"It's a bit of a dive", "but who cares when the crab cakes are this good" aver admirers of this Linthicum seafooder where the "draw is the size and price" of its "legendary" "beauties" with "very little filler" – so "skip the rest" of the menu; still, a few crustacean mavens find the specialty "big on size, small on taste", and say a meal here may entail "long lines" and "inconsistent service."

Gardel's ⓜ *Eclectic* ▽ 17 | 25 | 16 | $38

Little Italy | Fava Bldg. | 29 S. Front St. (Baltimore St.) | 410-837-3737 | www.gardels.com

"Tango with your tilapia?" – "sexy" "salsa experts" are the "brilliant accompaniment" to pizzas, small plates and other Latin-inflected Eclectic eats (a post-Survey chef change may outdate the Food score) at this "unique" "experience" just north of Little Italy, where diners take the floor when the spot morphs into a dance club at 10 PM; meanwhile, a "dramatic, theatrical" space compensates for what some call "slow" service; N.B. closed Mondays and Tuesdays.

Germano's Trattoria *Italian* 21 | 17 | 20 | $35

Little Italy | 300 S. High St. (Fawn St.) | 410-752-4515 | www.germanostrattoria.com

"Linger and enjoy" the "friendly old-world atmosphere" at this "homey", "longtime" Little Italy "favorite" for "authentic" "Tuscan specialties" served up by an "attentive" staff that "treats you like a king", all at "prices that aren't stratospheric"; but a few feel the "comfort food has gotten too comfortable" and the decor could use some "sprucing up."

Gertrude's ⓜ *Chesapeake* 22 | 24 | 20 | $33

Homewood | Baltimore Museum of Art | 10 Art Museum Dr. (N. Charles St.) | 410-889-3399 | www.gertrudesbaltimore.com

Chef-owner "John Shields evokes the spirit of his Grandma Gertie" with seafood-centric Chesapeake Regional cuisine "fit for a museum", appropriate since this "jewel" is "beautifully situated in the BMA"; it's a "favorite spot" "for lunch" or for Sunday jazz brunch "in the sculpture garden", but while the "arterati" "appreciate the Wednesday half-price wines and Tuesday $10 entrees", they're less enthused by "service that's not always consistent."

G. Hunter's *American* – | – | – | E

Frederick | 5903 Old National Pike (Mt. Phillip Rd.) | 301-663-8845 | www.ghunters.com

Whether they're looking to snag a sunset view from the patio or catch some oysters from the raw bar, Frederick's SUV set welcomes this "happening" New American "overlooking a golf course" on the west side of town; the "subdued" modern setting plays host to a menu that runs the gamut from brick-oven pizzas to up-to-date fin fare, with a selection of burgers and steaks for water-weary locals.

Golden West Cafe *New Mexican* 21 | 17 | 14 | $18

Hampden | 1105 W. 36th St. (Hickory Ave.) | 410-889-8891 | www.goldenwestcafe.com

"Chile sauce tops just about everything" at this "funky" Hampden "mecca" for "all-day New Mexican–inspired breakfast" goodies; what detractors dub "the Golden Wait Cafe" ("service is something you'll get when they're ready to provide it") attracts an "earthy and patient" crowd that insists "all is forgiven" with the arrival of a "check that seems too small for such a gut-busting bounty of goodness."

Great Sage ⓜ *Vegetarian*

-	-	-	M

Clarksville | Clarksville Square Shopping Ctr. | 5809 Clarksville Square Dr. (Rte. 108) | 443-535-9400 | www.great-sage.com

In a Columbia-area locale "lacking in out-of-the-ordinary dining", this sunny Clarksville strip-maller serves "sublime", globally influenced fare that only "happens to be vegetarian and vegan" – "even die-hard carnivores will be satisfied" – along with 'little sage' selections for kids and a variety of veg-friendly wines and smoothies; it's from the owners of the adjacent organic market, so expect the mid-priced meals to "compete with any cuisine for flavor."

Green Leaf *Pan-Asian*

∇ 22	14	18	$27

Hunt Valley | Shawan Plaza | 11313 York Rd. (Shawan Rd.) | 410-771-0030 | www.greenleafcuisine.com

At this "delightful neighborhood place" in a Hunt Valley "strip center", the "concept of healthy Pan-Asian" produces "primo sushi" along with a selection of "creatively named" dishes that "aren't far behind"; it's a "quirky place" that "tries very hard" and has a BYO policy to "keep the cost reasonable", which helps to make up for "average decor" and service that can be "a bit slow."

Greystone Grill *American*

20	20	19	$41

Ellicott City | MDG Corporate Ctr. | 8850 Columbia 100 Pkwy. (Centre Park Rd.) | 410-715-4739

Hunt Valley | Hunt Valley Town Ctr. | 118 Shawan Rd. (bet. McCormick & York Rds.) | 410-527-0999
www.greystonegrill.com

Searching for its "niche in the steakhouse market", these "upscale" New Americans offer "well-prepared" beef, seafood and other "standards" in an "attractive" atmosphere; "sides are included", but some still feel the prices are "a shocker" and complain of an "inexperienced staff"; N.B. a Rockville location opened post-Survey and a branch is expected to debut in Annapolis in fall 2007.

Hard Times Cafe ◐ *American*

19	13	17	$15

Frederick | 1003 W. Patrick St. (bet. Hoke Pl. & Rte. 40) | 301-695-0099 | www.hardtimes.com

See review in the Washington, DC, Directory.

Harryman House *American*

20	21	20	$37

Reisterstown | 340 Main St. (1¼ mi. north of Franklin Blvd.) | 410-833-8850 | www.harrymanhouse.com

It may be set in a 1791 building with each dining area "quainter than the next" ("the log cabin" is especially "romantic"), but this Reisterstown "diamond in the rough" serves a New American menu from which you "can order small plates" and other contemporary dishes; there's "friendly service" too, but a few note that the "serene" rooms can be "so cozy you can reach over to your neighbor's table."

	FOOD	DECOR	SERVICE	COST

Helen's Garden ⓜ *American* | 23 | 21 | 21 | $30 |

Canton | 2908 O'Donnell St. (S. Linwood Ave.) | 410-276-2233 |
www.helensgarden.com

The "chatty" owner "remembers everyone's name" at this "laid-back wine bar" and restaurant, where the Canton crowd "can actually taste" the half-price happy-hour sips and "eccentric" New American entrees because it's "non-smoking – a rare find in Baltimore"; the "funky but tasteful decor" and an enclosed porch deck make it a "classic first-date place", but "get there early" on $12-entree Wednesdays, as "it can get a little hectic."

☒ Helmand *Afghan* | 26 | 20 | 23 | $28 |

Mt. Vernon | 806 N. Charles St. (bet. Madison & Read Sts.) |
410-752-0311 | www.helmand.com

At this dinner-only "institution" in Mt. Vernon, "your taste buds will dance" to the "delicious diplomacy" of "complex, eye-opening" Afghan dishes that "go far, far beyond the kebab" "without being off-putting" (don't miss the "bliss-on-a-plate pumpkin appetizer"); "vegetarians and meat eaters alike" "may fall in love with" its "exotic character" and "reasonable prices", and if "seating can be crowded", most feel "the food is worth the coziness."

Henninger's Tavern ☒ⓜ *American* | 25 | 21 | 23 | $35 |

Fells Point | 1812 Bank St. (bet. Ann & Wolfe Sts.) | 410-342-2172 |
www.henningerstavern.com

"Buried among the row houses of upper Fells Point" lies this "real pub" packed with "yuppies and locals" chowing down on "adventurous" New American fare in a "comfortable setting" adorned with "cool memorabilia"; the dining side is "very small" and "doesn't take reservations", so diehards are understandably "hesitant about word getting out", although "fun entrees like TV dinners" make the bar an "enjoyable" alternative; N.B. it opens at 5 PM daily.

Holy Frijoles ◗ *Mexican* | 20 | 13 | 16 | $16 |

Hampden | 908 W. 36th St. (bet. Elm & Roland Aves.) | 410-235-2326

This "no-frills" Hampden "dive" dishing up "Mexican-like" eats may be "a victim of its own success": since "they expanded and added a bar", a few feel it's morphed from "hole-in-the-wall" "hangout" to "smoky" "madhouse"; its "ample portions", "wonderful margaritas" and "rock-bottom prices" have remained the same, however, but so has a "tattooed staff" with what some snipe is a "bit of an attitude."

Hull St. Blues *American* | 20 | 15 | 20 | $25 |

Locust Point | 1222 Hull St. (Fort Ave.) | 410-727-7476 |
www.hullstreetblues.com

"Come as you are" to this "casual" "neighborhood pub" set in a "homey" Locust Point row house for "hearty American staples" that are "not particularly highbrow" but are "decent" nonetheless – especially the "excellent Sunday brunch"; whether you opt for "the fancy side or the bar side", you'll get "friendly and responsive service" and, "if you're lucky, costumed reenactors from Fort McHenry will drop by for a post-revolutionary beer."

	FOOD	DECOR	SERVICE	COST

Hunan Manor *Chinese*   22 | 18 | 21 | $23

Columbia | 7091 Deepage Dr. (Snowden River Pkwy.) |
410-381-1134

"Raising suburban Chinese to a fine art", this "huge" but "always crowded" Columbia stand-alone proffers "plentiful portions" of "authentic", "not-too-Americanized" fare; "kids love it" for the "fascinating fish tank", while "great lunch specials" lure in local businessmen; still, some fear "it's going downhill", with a setting that "needs refurbishing."

Iggies 🖪 Ⓜ *Pizza*   ▽ 23 | 13 | 16 | $17

Downtown North | 818 N. Calvert St. (Read St.) | 410-528-0818 |
www.iggiespizza.com

With a "hip Italian Greyhound-themed decor" that pays homage to the owner's pet canines, this "welcome" option on "otherwise forgettable Calvert Street" northeast of the business district dishes up "pricey, gourmet" Neapolitan-inspired pies; "fresh ingredients" and "unique toppings" make for "delicious" pizzas, but the space is "tight", so it may be "better to carry out" at peak hours; P.S. "all tips go to charity – good food and good karma!"

Ikaros *Greek*   22 | 15 | 21 | $26

Greektown | 4805 Eastern Ave. (Ponca St.) | 410-633-3750

You get "so much, and so good, for so little" at this "Greektown classic", "you'll feel like dancing", even after you "overeat" the "hearty portions" of "delicious", "homestyle" Hellenic fare; most "go for the food, not the surroundings" – an "old-fashioned" "'50s setting" – but either way, you'll receive a "warm welcome" from the "friendly staff" and the "owners who are on top of everything"; N.B. it's closed on Tuesdays.

Iron Bridge Wine Company *American*   25 | 22 | 21 | $35

Columbia | 10435 Rte. 108 (¼ mi. west of Centennial Ln.) |
410-997-3456 | www.ironbridgewines.com

"Stay away and leave it for us locals!" cry Columbia's oenophiles about this "wine lovers' paradise" where you can "buy a bottle for $5 above retail and drink it there"; it's "been discovered", however, for its "delicious" New American small plates that are "to die for" – and "you could die before being seated" sniff impatient patrons, since "it's too small" with a "daunting no-reservations policy"; N.B. a Warrenton, VA, location is expected to open soon.

Isabella's Ⓜ *Spanish*   24 | 20 | 22 | $29

Frederick | 44 N. Market St. (Rte. 144) | 301-698-8922 |
www.isabellas-tavern.com

This "lively", "noisy" Spaniard "in historic Downtown Frederick" makes it "fun to try new and different" flavors as you "share several small plates" of "totally tasty tapas" off of an "extensive" "list of real winners"; since "it's hard to limit yourself to just a few" of the tiny tastes, this "great value" "can get expensive", leading some cost-conscious customers to opt for one of the entrees instead; N.B. they've added a tequila bar featuring 30-plus varieties.

Ixia 🗑 Ⓜ *American*

24 | 26 | 21 | $43

Mt. Vernon | 518 N. Charles St. (Centre St.) | 410-727-1800 |
www.ixia-online.com

At "one of the more gorgeous settings in Baltimore", the "picture of
Jackie Kennedy" dominates this "converted" Mt. Vernon bookstore
whose "blue walls and sheer draperies" are "a dreamy background"
to "inventive" New American small and large plates that "look like
they should be in a food magazine"; "you'll be shocked by the
taste" – but perhaps also "by the bill", which leads some to conclude
this "edgy restaurant" is "overwrought for our simple town."

NEW Jack's Bistro ◑Ⓜ *Eclectic*

- | - | - | M

Canton | 3123 Elliott St. (S. Robinson St.) | 410-878-6542 |
www.jacksbistro.net

Situated in a corner row house near Canton Square, this contemporary addition is hopping with gentrifiers who dig the Eclectic dinner
and Sunday brunch fare (think mac 'n' cheese with Belgian chocolate chunks) as well as monthly prix fixe meals, each of which is focused on a different region of the world; N.B. a late-night menu is
served until 1 AM, and the bar (with cozy, raised booths) is open
until 2 AM.

Jennings Cafe ◑🗑 *Pub Food*

▽ 19 | 10 | 23 | $18

Catonsville | 808 Frederick Rd. (Mellor Ave.) | 410-744-3824

"Join the regulars" at this "local place that's been there forever", "a
Catonsville must" for "meeting friends, talking and eating" "down-
to-earth cooking" off of a Traditional American pub food menu that
boasts a "great burger"; the "town-center air" "seems time-traveled
from 1954" – most of the "fun waitresses" "know most of the
customers" – but it comes with an era-appropriate "downside":
"the cigarette smoke."

Jesse Wong's Asean Bistro Ⓜ *Pan-Asian*

24 | 20 | 21 | $30

Columbia | 8775 Centre Park Dr. (Rte. 108) | 410-772-5300 |
www.aseanbistro.com

"Supper club meets suburbia" at this "instantly addictive", "upscale
Pan-Asian" in Columbia, where the "intimate setting and live piano"
nightly makes "for a romantic dinner with a difference"; the "unusual offerings" – just "beware the chile soy sauce won tons" – are
"beautifully presented" using "sculptured" "vegetable flowers"
and are served by an "attentive" staff; P.S. be sure not to miss the
"fabulous Sunday brunch."

Jesse Wong's Hong Kong Ⓜ *Chinese*

22 | 17 | 18 | $27

Columbia | 10215 Wincopin Circle (Little Patuxent Pkwy.) |
410-964-9193

"Quench your dim sum" thirst "without a long plane ride" at this
Columbia Chinese that's for "safe eaters and risk-takers" alike with
its mix of "well-prepared", traditional "Hong Kong–style" dumplings
and "pioneering" "inventions"; "the view of Lake Kittamaqundi makes
it easy to relax", unless you're going for weekend brunch pushcart
service – "get there early or plan to wait."

	FOOD	DECOR	SERVICE	COST

Jesse Wong's Kitchen *Pan-Asian*   ▽ 17 | 25 | 14 | $35

Hunt Valley | Hunt Valley Town Ctr. | 118 Shawan Rd. (Marble Hill) | 410-329-1088

"Don't go expecting traditional Chinese" at Jesse Wong's "attempt at fine" Pan-Asian dining in Hunt Valley, where "lunch is a steal compared to" what some warn are "pricey" dinner prix fixes; the "modern", multilevel setup features "a curving sushi bar" and "glass-paneled" exhibition kitchen, but foes who feel the "gorgeous room" isn't matched by the food and service hope "it improves with age."

Jimmy's *Diner*   18 | 9 | 17 | $12

Fells Point | 801 S. Broadway (Lancaster St.) | 410-327-3273

For "traditional breakfasts" "morning, noon and night" (until 9 PM), head to this waterfront diner "institution", where "characters galore" converge – from young folks "after a night in the Fells Point bars" to "see-and-be-seen politicians" to the "TV sports guy sopping up his eggs with toast"; this "no-frills joint" has "been around forever", but you won't be – the "lines out the door" "move fast."

JJ's Everyday Café *American*   19 | 10 | 20 | $24

Timonium | 2141 York Rd. (Timonium Rd.) | 410-308-2700

"It is what it says it is – a place to eat everyday", and this "hardworking family business" across from the Timonium fairgrounds "seems genuinely interested in serving nice meals" of "standard American" fare at "reasonable prices"; there's "no real interior design to speak of", but the "homey feel" and "attentive service" compensate.

John Steven, Ltd. *Seafood*   20 | 16 | 18 | $28

Fells Point | 1800 Thames St. (Ann St.) | 410-327-5561 | www.johnstevenltd.com

This seafood "staple" in Fells Point has been "fancying itself up" for the gentrifying area, which may outdate the above Decor score; it has "removed the sushi", freshened up the "other pub grub" and retained the same "delicious" fin fare, so "kick back with a pound of steamed shrimp" at the bar, head to the "pleasant dining area" or "be casual on the covered patio", because it's still "heaven on a cobblestone street."

Jordan's *Steak*   23 | 22 | 20 | $59

Ellicott City | 8085 Main St. (Old Columbia Pike) | 410-461-9776 | www.jordanssteakhouse.com

At Jordan and Ivette Naftal's "sure bet for a good steak", you can "sit at the window" and "dine at a leisurely pace" on "amazing" beef and other traditional dishes; a "staff that wants to help", plus "New York–quality" ambiance and nightly live jazz make it "nice for a date", but some warn it's "a little pricey for anywhere, but especially Ellicott City"; N.B. dinner-only with a Sunday jazz brunch.

Josef's Country Inn *Continental*   ▽ 25 | 21 | 25 | $45

Fallston | 2410 Pleasantville Rd. (Fallston Rd.) | 410-877-7800 | www.josefscountry.com

Set in "a converted house" "out in the country" near Fallston, this "touch of elegance" is a "reliable", "special-occasion" destination that's "catered to locals" for over 20 years with "manly" (read: "heavy"), "German-influenced" Continental fare brought around by "warm, friendly" servers; N.B. there are now a few New American plates on the menu.

Kali's Court *Mediterranean/Seafood* | 24 | 24 | 19 | $49

Fells Point | 1606 Thames St. (bet. Bond St. & B'way) | 410-276-4700 | www.kaliscourt.com

"For a fancy night out" or "a romantic dinner", this Fells Point "favorite with the boomers", "beautiful" ones and "suburban upper crust" offers "pricey but delicious" "Mediterranean fish prepared to taste"; however, some say the "upscale" setting and "great people-watching" come "with an attitude", from a dress code to "aloof" servers to "reservations that don't really matter"; P.S. a "brick-walled courtyard" and Sunday brunch are pluses.

Kings Contrivance, The *Continental* | 23 | 23 | 23 | $46

Columbia | 10150 Shaker Dr. (Rtes. 29 & 32) | 410-995-0500 | www.thekingscontrivance.com

"Everybody's special-occasion restaurant" is a "Columbia fixture" that's considered "just the place" for family gatherings with a "wonderful" Continental menu bearing "no unpleasant surprises"; the "old manor house" setting may have been "starting to fray", but a series of renovations (including new carpeting and flooring) is breathing "life" into the "standby"; P.S. the early-bird "prix fixe is a great bargain."

La Madeleine Bakery | 17 | 16 | 11 | $17
Café & Bistro *French*

Columbia | 6211 Columbia Crossing Dr. (Dobbin Rd.) | 410-872-4900 | www.lamadeleine.com

See review in the Washington, DC, Directory.

La Scala *Italian* | 24 | 19 | 24 | $34

Little Italy | 1012 Eastern Ave. (Central Ave.) | 410-783-9209 | www.lascaladining.com

"The atmosphere is the thing" ("you expect to see Frank Sinatra at the bar") at this "old-school", dinner-only "jewel in Little Italy" that's also known for an "outstanding grilled Caesar salad" so big you'll need to "share with someone else"; this "top-notch" Italian has a "personable, friendly feel", from its "well-seasoned" staff to a chef-owner who "swings through" to "make sure you're happy."

La Tasca *Spanish* | 16 | 20 | 16 | $30

NEW **Inner Harbor** | Harborplace Pratt Street Pavilion | 201 E. Pratt St. (Light St.) | 410-209-2562 | www.latascausa.com

See review in the Washington, DC, Directory.

La Tavola ⓜ *Italian* | 25 | 21 | 22 | $33

Little Italy | 248 Albemarle St. (bet. Fawn & Stiles Sts.) | 410-685-1859 | www.la-tavola.com

A "spectacular aroma draws you in" to this "slightly more inventive" Little Italy "secret" serving "a varied menu" of "pasta, homemade every day" and "as fresh as advertised"; the "low-key" space is "more understated than some of the competition" – "neither stuffy nor loud" – and overall it's "trying hard" to fulfill expectations with "attentive" service and "reasonable prices."

Laurrapin Grille ⓈⒹ American | - | - | - | M |

Havre de Grace | 209 N. Washington St. (Pennington Ave.) | 410-939-4956 | www.laurrapin.com

Residents of "rejuvenated" Havre de Grace are flocking to this "cozy", copper-colored New American where chef-owner Bruce Clarke turns out "fresh", "well-prepared" dishes like lobster cakes and vegetarian muffaletta; though still located between the "old merchants" and the "new art galleries", it's no longer "easy to miss" courtesy of an expansion that's added a large bar area offering the full menu until 10 PM and fancy pizzas until midnight.

ⓩ Lebanese Taverna   Lebanese | 22 | 17 | 18 | $26 |

NEW **Inner Harbor East** | 719 S. President St. (Aliceanna St.) | 410-244-5533 | www.lebanesetaverna.com

See review in the Washington, DC, Directory.

ⓩ Legal Sea Foods   Seafood | 20 | 16 | 18 | $36 |

Inner Harbor | 100 E. Pratt St. (Calvert St.) | 410-332-7360 | www.legalseafoods.com

See review in the Washington, DC, Directory.

Liberatore's   Italian | 20 | 18 | 20 | $37 |

Eldersburg | Freedom Village Shopping Ctr. | 6300 Georgetown Blvd. (Liberty Rd.) | 410-781-4114

Timonium | Timonium Corporate Ctr. | 9515 Deereco Rd. (Padonia Rd.) | 410-561-3300

Perry Hall | Honeygo Village Ctr. | 5005 Honeygo Center Dr. (Honeygo Blvd.) | 410-529-4567

Owings Mills | New Town Village Ctr. | 9712 Groffs Mill Dr. (Lakeside Blvd.) | 410-356-3100

Westminster | 140 Village Shopping Ctr. | 521 Jermor Ln. (Rte. 97) | 410-876-2121 Ⓜ

www.liberatores.com

"The convenience of staying Uptown" draws diners to these separately managed "classic Italians" that are nestled in office parks and strip malls north of the city; they're "not breaking any culinary barriers", but they're "pleasant and dependable" choices for "Southern-style" fare that's "good" if perhaps a little "pricey for Baltimore's suburbs"; P.S. come evening, they boast a "busy bar" "scene for the 40+ crowd."

ⓩ Linwoods   American | 26 | 25 | 25 | $49 |

Owings Mills | 25 Crossroads Dr. (bet. McDonogh & Reisterstown Rds.) | 410-356-3030 | www.linwoods.com

After nearly 20 years, surveyors can still "count on" this "upscale" Owings Mills "gold standard" "blessed with many" "consistently delicious" "spins on New American fare"; "owner Linwood Dame knows his business well", and his "clubby" restaurant "is all class" "without pretense", with an open kitchen and "professional service" to boot; some note, however, that a meal here can "put a dent in your wallet."

Little Spice *Thai*

- | - | - | I

Hanover | 1350 Dorsey Rd. (Ridge Rd.) | 410-859-0100 |
www.littlespice.org

Located halfway between Arundel Mills and BWI in Hanover, this teensy Thai is the brainchild of two young sisters who are cooking up some very old-country flavors; airport-bound travelers can tempt their taste buds with inexpensive dishes that go beyond the usual standards, as well as whole fish and a lengthy list of vegetarian options; one of the siblings spent time as a graphic designer, so expect an aesthetically pleasing setup.

Louisiana Ⓜ *Creole*

24 | 25 | 23 | $48

Fells Point | 1708 Aliceanna St. (B'way) | 410-327-2610

At this "N'Awlins"-style, "fancy Creole" fixture in "funky Fells Point", the "Southern touch is evident in everything", from the "decadent", "lick-your-plate" dishes to the "elegant but not stuffy setting"; "this is the place if you're trying to impress business associates", but "dim lighting", "pleasant service" and live piano on Saturdays also make it "lovely" for a "romantic date"; N.B. dinner-only.

L.P. Steamers *Seafood*

21 | 7 | 19 | $26

Locust Point | 1100 E. Fort Ave. (Woodall St.) | 410-576-9294 |
www.lpsteamers.com

If you're "on your way to Fort McHenry", then drop into this "no-frills" "corner tavern", a "casual" Locust Point seafooder where "you can be as messy as you want" as you "pick crabs and make friends with the locals" and the "colorful staff"; "if it's nice out", "avoid the smoky" interior and sit on the "comfortable rooftop deck" – it has a skyline "view that would make stale mac 'n' cheese taste like ambrosia."

Maggie Moore's ◗ *American/Irish*

19 | 23 | 19 | $25

Downtown West | 21 N. Eutaw St. (Fayette St.) | 410-837-2100 |
www.maggiemoores.com

"Set in a renovated bank across from the Hippodrome" Theatre, this bit of "good Irish fun" "from a real Irish couple" (owners John and Maggie Moore) serves "more than just pub food", with New American and Green Isle fare, weekend live music and a Monday evening poker night; set in a "gorgeous", "dark-wood" setting, it's a "great" option on Baltimore's "revived west side", albeit one with "friendly (but slow)" service.

Mama's on the Half Shell *Seafood*

21 | 20 | 19 | $29

Canton | 2901 O'Donnell St. (S. Linwood Ave.) | 410-276-3160

"Get your fix of reliably fresh" shellfish at this "warm" Canton Square "re-creation of a traditional oyster house", "the go-to place" for "seafood the way locals like it", including the signature bivalves "served any way you can imagine"; "arrive early" on weekends counsel quiet types, because a "young" first-floor bar crowd "makes for long waits" and "piercing decibel levels"; N.B. they serve a late-night raw bar menu until 2 AM.

Mamma Lucia *Italian*

| 19 | 12 | 17 | $22 |

Frederick | Shops of Monocacy | 1700 Kingfisher Dr. (Rte. 26) | 301-694-2600 | www.mammaluciarestaurants.com
See review in the Washington, DC, Directory.

M & S Grill *Seafood/Steak*

| 18 | 18 | 17 | $34 |

Inner Harbor | Harborplace Pratt Street Pavilion | 201 E. Pratt St. (Light St.) | 410-547-9333 | www.mandsgrill.com
See review in the Washington, DC, Directory.

Manor Tavern *American*

| 16 | 18 | 18 | $35 |

Monkton | 15819 Old York Rd. (Manor Rd.) | 410-771-8155 | www.themanortavern.com

"Be certain you have directions (or GPS)" before you head to this Traditional American "staple of the Monkton horse-riding set" decked out in equine-themed "paraphernalia"; "its beautiful location should make it worth driving to", but "inconsistent food" and "service that could be improved" give some patrons pause; P.S. the "informal dining section" is perfect for that "after-fox-hunt toddy."

☒ Mari Luna Mexican Grill Ⓜ *Mexican*

| 27 | 13 | 20 | $18 |

Pikesville | 102 Reisterstown Rd. (Seven Mile Ln.) | 410-486-9910 | www.mariluna.com

"Located in a converted Carvel store", this Pikesville "gem" "may not have a ton of curb appeal", but it does have "authentic" "Mexican (not Tex-Mex)" fare that's "divine"; locals say it's "easy to get hooked on" this "friendly, family-owned" "find" that's both "small" and "popular as all get-out", so be "prepared to fight for a table"; P.S. a BYO policy makes it even more of a "value."

Martick's ☒Ⓜ *French*

| 24 | 15 | 17 | $38 |

Downtown West | 214 W. Mulberry St. (bet. Howard St. & Park Ave.) | 410-752-5155

Just "when you think you're hopelessly lost" in an iffy neighborhood, you've arrived at this "institution" set in a "dark" "hole-in-the-wall former speakeasy" west of Downtown; "ring the bell to get in" and let the octogenarian "whiz of a French chef"-owner, Morris Martick, "lovingly prepare" you "divine bouillabaisse" and "profiteroles to melt your diet"; it's "not to be missed", "but you better hurry" – "Morris ain't getting any younger"; N.B. open Tuesday–Saturday.

Matsuri *Japanese*

| 24 | 15 | 21 | $28 |

South Baltimore | 1105 S. Charles St. (Cross St.) | 410-752-8561 | www.matsuri.us

"Right in the middle of everything" next to the Cross Street Market is this "real-deal" "standout" for "über-tasty" and "very fresh" sushi, plus "a good variety" of other Japanese dishes; "quick", "friendly service" helps many to overlook a "tight", "no-decor" setting, although if you elect "to be seated upstairs", you'll find an "adorable" room accented with Asian art that "transports you to Japan."

Matthew's Pizzeria *Pizza*

25 | 10 | 19 | $15

Highlandtown | 3131 Eastern Ave. (East Ave.) | 410-276-8755 | www.matthewspizza.com

For "addictive pizza" "Baltimore-style" – "not NY or NJ" – drop by this "casual" Highlandtown eatery that's "lasted since 1943 for a reason": "thick", "blow-you-away" pies made with "top-notch ingredients"; they're "huge" in taste but "small" in size, so "get the large" for "twice the acreage" of "unending bliss", and "get there early", as the "amazingly friendly staff" is sometimes "overwhelmed"; P.S. "their crab pie might be the best ever."

McCabe's Ⓜ *Pub Food*

20 | 11 | 18 | $25

Hampden | 3845 Falls Rd. (41st St.) | 410-467-1000

Located "in an area better known for its body shops", this Hampden "sleeper" may "look like a hole-in-the-wall from the outside", but inside it's "what chains dream of being": a "friendly, dependable", "non-corporate neighborhood bar" serving "sophisticated" American pub grub like "fine burgers" and "fabulous" "no-filler crab cakes"; it's "smoky" and "small" with patrons "packed in like sardines", but fans note that "doesn't mean we don't all love it!"

Ⓩ McCormick & Schmick's *Seafood*

21 | 20 | 20 | $41

Inner Harbor | Pier 5 Hotel | 711 Eastern Ave. (S. President St.) | 410-234-1300 | www.mccormickandschmicks.com

See review in the Washington, DC, Directory.

Mealey's Ⓜ *American*

21 | 19 | 22 | $34

New Market | 8 Main St./Old National Pike (I-70, exit 62) | 301-865-5488 | www.mealeysrestaurant.com

"It's hard to match the 18th-century setting" of this "cozy" New Market American nestled in a "charming" former inn and serving "traditional Maryland" meals, including "don't-miss crab cakes" and a Sunday brunch; "antiques-hunters" will find it a "relaxing" post-search "treat", while those looking for a "romantic experience" will relish its "wonderful" antebellum ambiance and occasional "wine tastings."

Mezze ❶ *Mediterranean*

24 | 21 | 20 | $30

Fells Point | 1606 Thames St. (Bond St.) | 410-563-7600 | www.kalismezze.com

"Linger over a bottle of wine" and an "endless stream" of "zesty" "Med tapas" at this "more casual" Fells Point alternative to sibling Kali's Court that's "cute, chic and comforting" (sit outside on a pleasant day) and "where all the beautiful people are", so "be ready for a wait"; it's "worth trying everything", but "your eyes might be bigger than your stomach" – and your wallet, since some say the "small plates have not-so-small prices."

NEW Michos *American/Mediterranean*

– | – | – | E

Reisterstown | 31 Main St. (Westminster Pike) | 410-517-3939 | www.michosrestaurant.com

Located at Reisterstown's main crossroads, this clubby, grown-up destination features a string of dining rooms, all serving a something-for-everyone mix of Mediterranean meze and modern, globally inflected New American surf 'n' turf; there's also a boisterous ground-level bar blaring live music and, on the second floor, a calmer, smoke-free lounge.

Milton Inn *American/Continental*

| 25 | 26 | 24 | $56 |

Sparks | 14833 York Rd. (3 mi. north of Shawan Rd.) | 410-771-4366 | www.miltoninn.com

For that "romantic celebration", gas up "your Range Rover" and "take your gold card" to this "charming" 1740 Sparks inn, a "cozy" "place to be pampered" with "gracious, attentive service" and Traditional American–Continental cuisine; it's "like dining at your millionaire uncle's house", with "fireplaces in winter and a garden in summer", but a few find it "a little stuffy" and quite "pricey", so "definitely try the $36 chef's tasting menu."

NEW Milton's Grill *American/BBQ*

| - | - | - | M |

Downtown North | 336 N. Charles St. (Mulberry St.) | 443-220-0180 | www.miltonsbaltimore.com

Set on a stretch of Downtown North that's growing into a dining destination, this urbane yet relaxed newcomer offers up an American menu specializing in barbecued meats; the grilled shrimp, smoked ribs and filling sides draw a diverse crowd – from business-lunchers to stroller moms – that appreciates the narrow setting's free WiFi and large front window opening up onto Charles Street.

Minato ☒ *Japanese*

| - | - | - | M |

Downtown North | 1013 N. Charles St. (Eager St.) | 410-332-0332 | www.minatorestaurant.com

Now that this sushi veteran has moved from a subterranean setting in Mt. Vernon to above-ground digs in Downtown North, its movers-and-shakers clientele can savor raw fin fare and other Japanese items in a townhouse space that actually has a window to the outside world; the room's tall ceiling features mod lighting, and there's a large seating area that can be made private for groups or special occasions.

Miss Shirley's *American*

| 23 | - | 19 | $17 |

Roland Park | 513 W. Cold Spring Ln. (Keswick Rd.) | 410-889-5272 | www.missshirleys.com

"They don't serve dinner", "but what a breakfast and lunch!" rave Roland Parkers about this "cheery" spot dishing out "scrumptious", "inventive takes" on "Southern-influenced comfort food" (the "crab-and-fried-green-tomato eggs Benedict is pure heaven"); plus, a recent move across the street to roomier digs is making the "wow" eats even more "worth it"; N.B. no reservations.

Monocacy Crossing Ⓜ *American*

| - | - | - | E |

Frederick | 4424A Urbana Pike (bet. Araby Church & Ball Rds.) | 301-846-4204 | www.monocacycrossing.com

A "pleasant" country drive leads you to this "charming" New American set "in an old house just south of the [namesake] battlefield" below Frederick; it looks "deceptively small" "but is larger than it appears", with a "nicely appointed" interior and patio seating outside; a "polished staff" and contemporary "comfort food with a little extra" pack in hungry Civil War wanderers, so reserve ahead.

Z Morton's, The Steakhouse *Steak*   25 | 20 | 23 | $63
Inner Harbor | Sheraton Inner Harbor Hotel | 300 S. Charles St. (Conway St.) | 410-547-8255 | www.mortons.com
See review in the Washington, DC, Directory.

Mr. Bill's Terrace Inn M *Crab House*   ▽ 24 | 11 | 18 | $30
Essex | 200 Eastern Blvd. (Helena Ave.) | 410-687-5996
"It's all about the crabs" at this Essex joint where there's "no terrace" and "beer and linoleum are de rigueur"; the "noisy, crowded" house of hardshells is considered the "best place" to "crack claws" according to "cops and carpenters" who claim that "any bad point" – like the "unbearable waits" – "is forgotten once you taste" the crustaceans.

Mughal Garden *Indian*   22 | 14 | 18 | $22
Mt. Vernon | 920 N. Charles St. (bet. Eager & Read Sts.) | 410-547-0001
"If you crave a curry", "get ready for spice" and head to this Mt. Vernon Indian that "hits all the staples" with its "tangy" "traditional meals"; it's "worth getting past the look of the place" because "the food's what earns it honors", including "awesome lunch buffets" that will "fill you for a week" – though if the "ticky-tacky" decor does prove overwhelming, they "deliver in record speeds too."

NEW Nasu Blanca Z M *Japanese/Spanish*   – | – | – | VE
Locust Point | 1036 E. Fort Ave. (Woodall St.) | 410-962-9890 | www.nasublanca.com
Incongruously located in blue-collar Locust Point, this sophisticated spot set in a nicely renovated row house whips up refreshingly modern renditions of traditional Japanese and Spanish fare, from paella to tempura to Kobe beef; the pricey food is served in a warm upstairs dining room featuring subtle nods to the cuisine's origins, and there's also a sleek ground-floor bar that's likely to suit the dressy suburban crowd just fine.

Neo Viccino *American*   20 | 18 | 18 | $31
Mt. Vernon | 1317 N. Charles St. (Mt. Royal Ave.) | 410-347-0349 | www.viccino.com
The "creative menu" of "well-prepared New American" fare matches the "upscale" decor at this Mt. Vernon "standby" that's a "pleasant" "place for a bite before a show" at the nearby Meyerhoff or Lyric (the restaurant runs a free shuttle service to the venues); meanwhile, "a captive U of B audience" drops by during the day for pizzas, sandwiches, pastas and salads.

Obrycki's *Crab House*   22 | 14 | 19 | $40
East Baltimore | 1727 E. Pratt St. (bet. B'way & Regester St.) | 410-732-6399 | www.obryckis.com
"You work for your food" at this seasonal East Baltimore "institution", a "casual" seafood house where "you crack crabs" "dumped on paper-covered tables", then "eat them with your hands"; it's a "must for tourists", who won't notice "the rest of the menu's a crapshoot", but some

locals take issue with the "tasty" "trademark seasoning": "how can you eat peppered crabs if you're a native? – pass the Old Bay, please."

☒ Oceanaire Seafood Room *Seafood*   24 | 22 | 23 | $54

Inner Harbor East | 801 Aliceanna St. (President St.) | 443-872-0000 | www.theoceanaire.com
See review in the Washington, DC, Directory.

Olive & Sesame *Chinese/Japanese*   22 | 14 | 17 | $24

Pikesville | 1500 Reisterstown Rd. (McHenry Ave.) | 410-484-7787
Towson | 2 W. Pennsylvania Ave. (York Rd.) | 410-494-4944
Sharing the same "usual and unusual" menu suspects, these Chinese-Japanese siblings in Pikesville and Towson emphasize "light, clean" preparations "with a bit of healthy flair" (including "decent sushi"); they'll "satisfy a craving", but given "packed tables", surveyors say they're "not places where you'd want to linger."

NEW Open Door Café *American*   – | – | – | M

Bel Air | 528 Baltimore Pike/Rte. 1 (Rte. 24) | 410-838-4393 | www.open-door-cafe.com
At this Bel Air coffeehouse-cum-restaurant, a mix of American classics (salads, burgers, mac 'n' cheese) and more contemporary dishes (made with locally sourced ingredients) is served in a quaint dining room done up to resemble an outdoor courtyard; it's owned by two families that are part of a local Lutheran ministry, but given the eatery's name, it's clear that everyone is welcome here.

Orchard Market & Café Ⓜ *Persian*   25 | 17 | 24 | $28

Towson | Orchard Plaza | 8815 Orchard Tree Ln. (Joppa Rd.) | 410-339-7700 | www.orchardmarketandcafe.com
You'll need to "bring your GPS to find" this BYO "strip-mall treasure" east of Towson, but it's "worth the search" for "spectacular", "homey Persian food in a quiet setting" that's "small" but "inviting"; the "friendly staff and owners" "work hard" to ensure you "get a terrific meal for minimal $$$" – a feat made easier by a "$12.95 Sunday brunch"; N.B. there's belly dancing on Wednesday nights.

Oregon Grille *Seafood/Steak*   25 | 25 | 24 | $58

Hunt Valley | 1201 Shawan Rd. (Beaver Dam Rd.) | 410-771-0505 | www.theoregongrille.com
Be sure to "hold on to your wallet" at this Hunt Valley "place for special occasions", but "if you have the bucks, they have the steaks": "excellent" dry-aged cuts as well as serious seafood; some surveyors find it "stuffy" – "what do you expect in horse country?" – but most admit the service is "top-notch" and the atmosphere is "stunning" (they now have a spacious patio too); still, casual customers wish they'd "get rid of" the "archaic" jacket-required evening dress code.

Oriental Manor ◐ *Chinese*   ▽ 20 | 16 | 20 | $20

Ellicott City | Chatham Station | 9180 Baltimore National Pike (Rte. 29) | 410-461-2714
It's "not fancy", but admirers agree this restaurant near Routes 29 and 40 in Howard County is "the area place for dim sum", a "taste of

home for the non-Western crowd" featuring "excellent", "no-nonsense" "weekend pushcart" action; it's also "the real thing" for "authentic", "traditional Chinese food", including some "exotic" "finds" – "who knew jellyfish tasted good?"

NEW oZ Chophouse *Steak* — | — | — | E

Fulton | 8191 Maple Lawn Blvd. (Rte. 216) | 301-490-4003 | www.ozchophouse.com

Set in a fledgling community west of Laurel, this office-park addition in Fulton may look corporate on the outside, but its dimly lit interior is an intimate setting for splurging on chophouse fare that ranges from seafood and poultry to steaks that can be cut to size; a tree in the center of the room adds a touch of whimsy, while a circular bar makes for a convivial meeting place.

Paolo's *Californian/Italian* 18 | 17 | 18 | $32

Towson | 1 W. Pennsylvania Ave. (York Rd.) | 410-321-7000 | www.paolosristorante.com

See review in the Washington, DC, Directory.

Papermoon Diner ◐ *Diner* 17 | 20 | 14 | $16

Hampden | 227 W. 29th St. (Remington Ave.) | 410-889-4444 | www.papermoondiner24.com

"If you've ever wondered what it would be like inside of Tim Burton's head", check out this 24/7 Hampden "diner on acid" with "wacky", "whimsical" ("and in some cases scary") "everything-but-the-kitchen-sink decor"; it "attracts students and townies alike" for a menu of "dressed-up" "comfort food" that will sate "late-night cravings", but "standard" eats and "cranky" service cause critics to quip "they rely on kitsch, not kitchen skills."

Paradiso *Italian* ▽ 22 | 15 | 20 | $33

Westminster | 20 Distillery Rd. (Railroad Ave.) | 410-876-1421 | www.paradiso-westminster.com

"Somewhat hidden" in a "rehabbed factory" behind Westminster's main retail strip is this Italian "date-night destination" that "doubles as a special-occasion spot" and family standby – it's big enough for that rehearsal dinner but casual enough for "when you don't want to cook and the kids are hungry"; though the "large menu" has "great variety", savvy diners say "always order the chef's specials – you won't be disappointed."

☑ Pazo *Mediterranean* 23 | 28 | 22 | $40

Inner Harbor East | 1425 Aliceanna St. (bet. S. Caroline St. & S. Central Ave.) | 410-534-7296 | www.pazorestaurant.com

"Are we still in Baltimore?" wonder denizens who've dined at this "sumptuous" "Harbor East hangout" from Charleston's Tony Foreman, where a "vast" "revamped warehouse" that "feels like an old Spanish cathedral" sets the stage for a tapas-oriented menu (new chef Michael Costa has added Mediterranean entrees); plus, there's a mezzanine level where "the young and beautiful" can "survey the scene", which gets increasingly "loud" and "clublike" as the night goes on.

Pazza Luna *Italian*

- | - | - | E

Locust Point | 1401 E. Clement St. (Decatur St.) | 410-962-1212 | www.pazzaluna.us

Recently reopened under new ownership (Riccardo Bosio of the stylish Sotto Sopra), this veteran Italian ensconced in a Locust Point row house is luring locals with its authentic, non-Americanized cuisine; gone is the Sinatra- and celestial-themed decor, replaced by a sleek, sophisticated aesthetic that includes an open kitchen, a bar area and a harlequin-esque upstairs dining room.

Peppermill *American*

18 | 13 | 20 | $29

Lutherville | Heaver Bldg. | 1301 York Rd. (bet. I-695 & Seminary Ave.) | 410-583-1107

"Old-fashioned, down-home" American cooking and a "caring staff" are hallmarks of this "nothing-fancy" Lutherville "standby"; a "senior citizens' hangout" ("talk about *A Wrinkle in Time*"), it's the perfect place to "take grandmother to for her birthday", and "her descendants" may just "dig it and come back" because even if the fare is "standard", it's also a "great bang for the buck."

Z Peter's Inn 🅂🅼 *American*

27 | 15 | 20 | $28

Fells Point | 504 S. Ann St. (Eastern Ave.) | 410-675-7313 | www.petersinn.com

"Defining Baltimore quirkiness" with its "strange collision" of "leather-clad biker" and "gourmet", this "teeny-tiny" Fells Point "hangout" may "look like a dive" but it's "as culinary as places twice as fancy and four times as dull" with a "limited" but "surprisingly ambitious" New American menu that "rotates weekly"; "get there early" since "it can get crowded" and "noisy", though regulars reveal "it's much more pleasant" "now that it's nonsmoking"; N.B. dinner-only.

Pete's Grille 🍴 *Diner*

- | - | - | I

York Road Corridor | 3130 Greenmount Ave. (E. 32nd St.) | 410-467-7698

The "owners work hard" behind the counter of this classic diner east of Charles Village and Homewood, a utilitarian but homey septuagenarian that continues to be "ideal for carbo-loading" on American breakfast items after produce-loading at the nearby Saturday farmer's market; though every stool in the narrow space is generally taken, turnover is quick; N.B. they close up just after lunch.

Z Petit Louis Bistro *French*

24 | 22 | 23 | $40

Roland Park | 4800 Roland Ave. (Upland Rd.) | 410-366-9393 | www.petitlouis.com

For "a slice of the Left Bank" "in staid Roland Park", try this "authentic bistro" serving Gallic "classics" in a "bustling" setting that a few sensitive sorts claim can be "loud even when it's quiet"; the "elegant meals" are "not for the budget-conscious", but savvy surveyors settle in for Sunday brunch or during the "less-rushed daytime" for a $20 prix fixe lunch "deal"; N.B. the kitchen remains steady after a post-Survey chef change.

☑ P.F. Chang's China Bistro *Chinese*

| 19 | 19 | 18 | $27 |

NEW **Inner Harbor** | Market Pl. | 600 E. Pratt St. (S. Gay St.) |
410-649-2750

Columbia | Mall in Columbia | 10300 Little Patuxent Pkwy.
(Wincopin Circle) | 410-730-5344
www.pfchangs.com
See review in the Washington, DC, Directory.

Phillips *Seafood*

| 15 | 15 | 16 | $33 |

Inner Harbor | Harborplace Light Street Pavilion | 301 Light St. (Pratt St.) |
410-685-6600 | www.phillipsseafood.com

If "you need to bring your out-of-town guests to that required
Baltimore meal", some say this "touristy chain" of seafooders with
"stunning" "waterfront locations" in the Inner Harbor and Annapolis
(plus a third in DC) is a "good value" and "nice for a stroll" after-
wards; although it draws "busloads" of visitors, some natives feel
it's "hanging on to a fading reputation", offering "factory-style" fare
and "crab cakes that don't do justice to a Maryland classic."

Pho Dat Thanh *Vietnamese*

| 23 | 12 | 20 | $17 |

Columbia | 9400 Snowden River Pkwy. (Broken Land Pkwy.) |
410-381-3839

Admirers look beyond the "lack of ambiance" at this "plain", unpretentious Columbia strip-maller to focus on its "intensely flavorful"
and "inexpensive" Vietnamese menu featuring "fine bowls of pho",
"great noodle dishes" and a few Chinese and Thai selections too;
"delightful servers" and a "warm" vibe ensure that "once you try it,
you'll keep going back."

Pierpoint Ⓜ *American*

| 25 | 16 | 22 | $44 |

Fells Point | 1822 Aliceanna St. (bet. Ann & Wolfe Sts.) | 410-675-2080 |
www.pierpointrestaurant.com

Fells Point fine-dining pioneer "Nancy Longo knows how to cook",
turning out an "adventurous" menu of Maryland-inspired New
American cuisine (try the "must-get smoked crab cake") that now
includes half-plates; still, some say it "needs to be updated" –
"please redo the interior!"; N.B. it also serves a Sunday brunch.

Pisces Ⓜ *Seafood*

| 22 | 23 | 21 | $46 |

Inner Harbor | Hyatt Regency | 300 Light St. (bet. Conway & Pratt Sts.) |
410-605-2835 | www.baltimore.hyatt.com

"The view beats the food, but the bar's been set quite high" since
"every table in the tiered dining room" of this "expense-account"
seafooder located atop the Hyatt Regency hotel has a "spectacular"
vista of Baltimore's Inner Harbor; the "romantic setting" and weekend jazz music provide "atmosphere for an important date", while
the "scrumptious" Sunday "champagne brunch" is "like dying and
going to heaven."

☑ Prime Rib ● *Steak*

| 27 | 24 | 26 | $62 |

Downtown North | 1101 N. Calvert St. (Chase St.) | 410-539-1804 |
www.theprimerib.com
See review in the Washington, DC, Directory.

	FOOD	DECOR	SERVICE	COST

Red Fish *American*
- | **-** | **-** | **E**

Canton | 2350 Boston St. (Chester St.) | 443-524-1454 |
www.redfishusa.com

At this "not-so-rowdy alternative" to the "Canton Square scene", a
"cool" modern dining room and outdoor tables "attract people of all
ages" for "consistent" New American fare that's priced for adults; "the
20- to 30-year-old crowd", however, is much more enamored with the
adjacent bar's "can't-be-beat appetizers" and live entertainment.

Red Maple ◑Ⓜ *Asian Fusion*
19 | **25** | **16** | **$34**

Mt. Vernon | 930 N. Charles St. (bet. Eager & Read Sts.) | 410-547-0149 |
www.930redmaple.com

"If you're not young and gorgeous, don't bother" is one take on this
Mt. Vernon "hot spot" with "pricey" "Asian fusion tapas", "deadly",
"high-end drinks" and a setting that's "visually stunning"; with DJs
spinning nightly, "it gets crowded", "so go early for food and stay
late for cocktails"; N.B. the lounge is open on Mondays.

Red Star *American*
19 | **21** | **19** | **$25**

Fells Point | 906 S. Wolfe St. (Thames St.) | 410-675-0212 |
www.redstarbar.us

"Underappreciated" in east Fells Point, this "modern pub" set in a
"beautiful old building" with "high ceilings and exposed brick" draws
an "active crowd" for New American bites that are "a step up from
the usual bar food" – think "crunchy pizzas" and crab hash; its logo was
once the symbol for the area's brothels, but this joint's just a "reliable", "laid-back" "place to grab drinks with friends" or "a casual
bite after work"; P.S. they have "free parking" and a Sunday brunch.

Regi's *American*
19 | **18** | **19** | **$27**

Federal Hill | 1002 Light St. (E. Hamburg St.) | 410-539-7344 |
www.regisamericanbistro.com

"Running a tight ship", the "hands-on" owners at this "Federal Hill
anchor" have made it a "solid" "neighborhood" New American with
a "friendly bistro feel" suitable "for a date or catching up with
friends"; it's also "great for brunch" on weekends, when you can sit
out on the sidewalk "over a second, third and fourth cup of coffee
(they'll keep pouring)" and down "fabulous homemade muffins."

🆕 Robert Oliver *Seafood*
- | **-** | **-** | **E**

Downtown | 1225 Cathedral St. (W. Preston St.) | 410-528-5950 |
www.robertoliverseafood.com

A pre-theater option by the Lyric and Meyerhoff, this Downtown
seafooder serves up a menu of Med-accented small plates and entrees
in a sleek space; there's also a bar backed with a colorful, bubbling
waterwall, and a streetside patio with plenty of people-watching;
N.B. reservations may be easier to come by on non-show nights.

Rocco's Capriccio *Italian*
24 | **18** | **22** | **$37**

Little Italy | 846 Fawn St. (bet. Albemarle & High Sts.) | 410-685-2710
The sounds of "Dean Martin singing" usher diners in to this "cozy"
Little Italy veteran where "good Italian" fare is served by a "charming"

staff that "makes you feel like family"; maybe it can be a "tad expensive", but most consider it an enjoyable "time warp to the '50s."

NEW Rocket to Venus *Eclectic* — | — | — | M

Hampden | 3360 Chestnut Ave. (W. 34th St.) | 410-235-7887 | www.rockettovenus.com

Just like the mock spaceship attached to this Hampden eatery's facade, its wide-ranging Eclectic menu travels at warp speed from cornmeal-fried oysters and grilled cheeses to fried pickles and jerk chicken; hipsters are drawn to the futuristic decor featuring concave ceiling tiles and custom-made metal accents, including a bar top constructed from copper tubing; N.B. it offers free WiFi and is nonsmoking until 9 PM.

Z Roy's *Hawaiian* 26 | 24 | 24 | $47

Inner Harbor East | 720B Aliceanna St. (President St.) | 410-659-0099 | www.roysrestaurant.com

"If you can't get to Hawaii, then at least your taste buds can" at this Harbor East link in Roy Yamaguchi's chain, appreciated for its "artful", "assertively flavored" fusion fare featuring "funky twists" on "super-fresh seafood"; it "breaks the mold", from "polished" service and an "exciting ambiance" to a "splash of Baltimore" "attitude", making some "wish they were open for lunch" too; P.S. order the "gooey" chocolate soufflé "as soon as you sit down."

NEW Rub *BBQ* — | — | — | M

South Baltimore | 1843 Light St. (Wells St.) | 410-244-5667 | www.rubbbq.com

Baltimore-area restaurateur Michael Marx (ex Blue Agave) and Texas native David Long have teamed up to bring Longhorn State–style BBQ – heavy on the smoke, light on the sauce, with rubs and marinades paramount – to South Baltimore; the boisterous first-floor bar allows smoking, so head to the more spartan upstairs dining room if you want to fully concentrate on the 'cue; N.B. closed Tuesdays.

NEW Rumor Mill 🗷 *Asian Fusion* — | — | — | M

Ellicott City | 8069 Tiber Alley (Main St.) | 410-461-0041 | www.therumormillrestaurant.com

Nestled in an alley behind Main Street's antique shops, this two-story Ellicott City addition offers Asian fusion fare – including exotic starters like tuna tartare with guacamole dip – to denizens relieved to have a local date-night destination priced somewhere between casual and stratospheric; the modern tastes are complemented by a calm, civilized setting dressed up with Asian murals and artwork.

Z Ruth's Chris Steak House *Steak* 24 | 21 | 23 | $57

Inner Harbor | 600 Water St. (bet. Gay St. & Market Pl.) | 410-783-0033

Inner Harbor | Pier 5 Hotel | 711 Eastern Ave. (S. President St.) | 410-230-0033

Pikesville | 1777 Reisterstown Rd. (Hooks Ln.) | 410-837-0033 www.ruthschris.com

See review in the Washington, DC, Directory.

	FOOD	DECOR	SERVICE	COST

Sabatino's ● *Italian*

18 | 14 | 19 | $31

Little Italy | 901 Fawn St. (High St.) | 410-727-9414 | www.sabatinos.com

This 52-year-old "landmark" is "the granddaddy" of Little Italy's "red-sauce stalwarts", proffering "big plates of pasta" and an "oh-mamma-mia 'Bookmaker' salad"; like a "comfortable old shoe", it "doesn't just have character, it is a character", so "who cares" if critics say it's "tired" – when "you're starving" for your "after-bar" "Sab's fix", "it's always there and always open" (until midnight Sunday–Thursday and 3 AM on weekends).

Saffron Ⓜ *Eclectic*

- | 25 | 21 | $38

Mt. Vernon | 802 N. Charles St. (Madison St.) | 410-528-1616 | www.saffronbaltimore.com

At this "chic" Mt. Vernon venue, a fusion-y Eclectic menu is served by a "warm, friendly" staff in a "sumptuous" setting; it's a "romantic", "special-occasion" destination that's truly a "lovely place to eat", but surveyors can expect big changes in the kitchen with the June 2007 departure of local star chef Edward Kim.

Salt Ⓢ *American*

- | - | - | E

East Baltimore | 2127 E. Pratt St. (Collington St.) | 410-276-5480 | www.salttavern.com

Area foodies have found this swanked-up corner bistro moderne on the Butchers Hill side of Patterson Park, where exposed brick and colorful touches complement complex, cutting-edge New American fare and upscale pub food; but while locals meet and greet their neighbors at the buzzing granite bar, their far-flung counterparts circle the block looking for parking; N.B. dinner-only.

Sammy's Trattoria Ⓜ *Italian*

- | - | - | M

Mt. Vernon | 1200 N. Charles St. (Biddle St.) | 410-837-9999 | www.sammystrattoria.com

Sam Curreri (ex Chiapparelli's) is the talent behind this high-ceilinged trattoria near the Lyric and Meyerhoff in Mt. Vernon; it offers giant, shareable plates of pastas, neo-Southern Italian mains and lunchtime pizzas for the business crowd, plus a $35 per person, traditional family-style dinner option that's enough to sate any appetite.

🄩 Samos Ⓢ🄵 *Greek*

27 | 12 | 20 | $18

Greektown | 600 S. Oldham St. (Fleet St.) | 410-675-5292 | www.samosrestaurant.com

Meet the "Greektown family you never knew you had": chef-owner Nick Georgalas, "there every day" with "capable son Michael at his side", along with "hometown waitresses" who "call you 'hon' and mean it" as they bring around "huge portions" of "divinely zesty" "delights"; it's "no-frills" and "doesn't take reservations", but diners have determined it's "far and away" "Baltimore's top Greek", with a "BYO that makes it easy on the wallet" too; N.B. cash-only.

San Sushi *Japanese*

21 | 14 | 20 | $25

Timonium | 9832 York Rd. (Padonia Rd.) | 410-453-0140

(continued)

(continued)

San Sushi Too/Thai One On *Japanese/Thai*

Towson | 10 W. Pennsylvania Ave. (York Rd.) | 410-825-0908

These "fun, local" siblings continue to "wow" even as they express their unique identities: "the more expensive" Timonium original serves raw fin fare that "ain't New York, but is above average" to the suburban set, while the "Downtown Towson location" lures a spice-seeking "high-Scoville following" to its newly expanded sushi bar and fills up at night with "trendy" scenesters "in the club side"; P.S. the Towson branch also offers "tasty Thai."

Sascha's 527 🄢 *American*   21 | 23 | 20 | $29

Mt. Vernon | 527 N. Charles St. (Baltimore St.) | 410-539-8880 | www.saschas.com

The "decorators did a nice job" on this airy Mt. Vernon townhouse, giving it "the perfect feel" for a "split-personality" venue that's as "delightful" "for a business lunch" as it is "elegant" and "electric" come evening; the "adventurous" New American "small-plates fare" "with flair" "pleases many different palates", while rotating "artwork on the walls" and "great jazz" on Thursdays push it "beyond expectations."

Shin Chon *Korean*   - | - | - | M

Ellicott City | Lotte Plaza Ctr. | 8801 Baltimore National Pike (Rte. 29) | 410-461-3280

A growing, Ellicott City–area Korean-American population heads to this cheerful strip-mall barbecue specialist to enjoy a "traditional" taste of home and celebrate multigenerational special occasions; it's also "welcoming to newcomers", offering a "good variety" of simmering hot pots, grill-it-yourself marinated meats and zippy sides to satisfy even the most curious convert.

Shula's Steak House 🄢 *Steak*   18 | 17 | 18 | $54

Downtown | Sheraton Baltimore City Center Hotel | 101 W. Fayette St. (bet. Charles & Liberty Sts.) | 410-385-6601 | www.donshula.com

See review in the Washington, DC, Directory.

SoBo Cafe *American*   24 | 17 | 15 | $22

South Baltimore | 6 W. Cross St. (S. Charles St.) | 410-752-1518

"Leave mom at home, but bring your art school pals" to this "laid-back", "bohemian" "bargain" in SoBo that "gets packed" with "effervescent diners" downing "slightly reinvented" New American "comfort food done right", including mac 'n' cheese that's "worth the weight"; the "funky waitresses" can be "slower than a turtle crawling through cement", but fans nevertheless plead "please keep this slice of heaven to yourself, or I may never get a seat."

Sonny Lee's Hunan Taste 🄜 *Chinese/Japanese*   24 | 18 | 23 | $24

Reisterstown | 750 Main St. (bet. Bosley Ln. & Caraway Rd.) | 410-833-7288 | www.thehunantaste.com

At this "high-energy, high-volume" Reisterstown Chinese, a "gracious" owner compensates for what some call a "standard" strip-mall

	FOOD	DECOR	SERVICE	COST

setup "with a smile and a welcome", giving diners his "constant attention" as they dig into "dependable, occasionally inspired" dishes; it's "now an 'in' spot – and it should be" – so "make a reservation" and BYOB to "keep the bill under control"; P.S. "if you like Japanese", a second menu has "some of that as well."

Sotto Sopra *Italian*
24 | 23 | 22 | $43

Mt. Vernon | 405 N. Charles St. (bet. Franklin & Mulberry Sts.) | 410-625-0534 | www.sottosoprainc.com

"Travel to Italy by way of" this "opulent", "high-ceilinged" Mt. Vernonite where the "big-city feel" matches a "hip", "ambitious menu" of Northern Italian fare (with a few New American touches) and its "attentive but unobtrusive service"; a few dissenters "don't understand the fuss about this place", but they're in the minority; P.S. a "can't-miss opera night" with a six-course prix fixe and "top-notch performers" is held on the third Sunday of every month.

Stone Mill Bakery & Cafe *Bakery*
22 | 11 | 15 | $16

Brooklandville | Greenspring Station | 10751 Falls Rd. (Greenspring Valley Rd.) | 410-821-1358 | www.stonemillbakery.com

For a "healthy" bite from a "uniformly marvelous" menu of "creative sandwiches" and "fabulous soups", plus artisanal breads, this "bustling" Brooklandville "bakery-cum-lunch destination" (dinner service is planned) is "where it's at", although it's also "pricey" for what it is; if you can't handle "mobbed" midday conditions, try the "great patio seating" instead; N.B. a 2007 expansion added multiple counters serving everything from Italian food to ice cream.

Sushi Hana Ⓜ *Japanese*
23 | 15 | 19 | $27

Towson | 6 E. Pennsylvania Ave. (York Rd.) | 410-823-0372

This "reliable" Towson sushi bar spins out "the usual rolls and dishes", including "fresh", "high-quality" fin fare and a "nice variety" of cooked items; the decor "could use an overhaul" assert aesthetes, but "prompt", "homey service" and "great-deal quantities" mean its loyal following is "always forming a line" at mealtimes.

Sushi King Ⓢ *Japanese*
24 | 16 | 22 | $31

Columbia | 6490 Dobbin Rd. (Rte. 175) | 410-997-1269 | www.sushikingmd.com

"Your taste buds will kneel before the king" at this Japanese restaurant "hidden" in a Columbia strip mall; the setting is "sparse", but the "melt-in-your-mouth sushi" and a "wide selection" of "imaginative", "original specialty rolls" "make up for it"; "personal service and relative affordability" are more reasons why it's "getting harder to get a table."

◪ Sushi Sono Ⓢ *Japanese*
28 | 19 | 24 | $34

Columbia | 10215 Wincopin Circle (Little Patuxent Pkwy.) | 410-997-6131 | www.sushisonomd.com

"Lovely views" "overlooking serene Lake Kittamaqundi" "add to the Zen ambiance" at "Columbia's pristine Japanese haven", rated No. 1 for Food in the Baltimore Survey; "unmatched sushi and sashimi" and a "mouthwatering" "selection of specialty rolls" are "served with grace and charm" by a "kimono-clad" staff that has "a way of making you feel welcome"; "it's like being in another world" (especially after a few cups of sake), but be advised that it can be "quite pricey" and "packed."

Suzie's Soba *Korean*   20 | 17 | 16 | $21

Downtown | Munsey Bldg. | 7 N. Calvert St. (Fayette St.) | 410-528-8883 ⓩ

Hampden | 1009 W. 36th St. (Roland Ave.) | 410-243-0051

When you're "looking for something different", this Hampden noodle house "hits the spot" for "a hot bowl" of "the ultimate" Korean "comfort food", plus "a range of other Asian" dishes; a "pretty back patio" makes it a "reprieve" from the 36th Street "bustle", but nitpickers find the interior "borderline cramped" and say service can be "surly"; N.B. the Downtown outpost is lunch-only.

Szechuan House *Chinese*   24 | 13 | 24 | $18

Lutherville | 1427 York Rd. (Seminary Ave.) | 410-825-8181

At this "authentic Chinese" in Lutherville, the "food doesn't take orders from General Tso", which means this "local favorite" attracts even "picky transplanted New Yorkers"; it's "always full", but the "quick" kitchen keeps up, pumping out "fresh", "enormous portions" at "fast-food prices"; so overlook the "pistachio shells on the floor" – the nuts are free while you wait – but be sure to notice the "excellent", underappreciated sushi bar; N.B. it also delivers.

Tapas Teatro Ⓜ *Eclectic/Mediterranean*   22 | 20 | 19 | $29

Downtown North | 1711 N. Charles St. (bet. Lafayette Ave. & Lanvale St.) | 410-332-0110 | www.tapasteatro.net

Nosh on "big flavor combinations" at this "hip little" Eclectic-Med serving "delightful bites" of "gourmet" tapas in an "ultraconvenient" space "attached to the independent Charles Theatre" – it draws a "massive pre- and post-movie crowd", so try to "time your arrival" to avoid "long waits" and "chaotic service"; P.S. it's also nice to "sit outside during the summer" and savor pitchers of "killer sangria."

Taste Ⓜ *American*   20 | 23 | 19 | $41

North Baltimore | Belvedere Sq. | 510 E. Belvedere Ave. (York Rd.) | 443-278-9001 | www.tasterestaurant.biz

Set in a "stunning" tri-level renovation of an "Old Baltimore shoe store", this "classy" Belvedere Square spot offers an "innovative" New American menu that "reaches for the stars" but occasionally "only makes it into a low orbit"; "it has a lot of potential", but a few are "disappointed" by the "uneven" food and "still-struggling service", especially given the price point; N.B. it's now dinner-only.

Tasting Room ⓩ *American*   25 | 20 | 22 | $40

Frederick | 101 N. Market St. (Church St.) | 240-379-7772

"'Taste' is the operative word" at this "trendy" New American that's "more than just a wine bar", serving "superbly prepared dishes" to go with its "impeccable" vino list; it might be "a little pretentious for lil' ol' Frederick", but it's "where the hip sip", with an "eye on the Market Street action" via "huge plate-glass windows"; just "don't go looking for intimate dining" advise quiet types, since "tight quarters" make this "fishbowl" "frantic" and "loud."

☑ Tersiguel's *French*   27 | 23 | 26 | $51

Ellicott City | 8293 Main St. (Old Columbia Pike) | 410-465-4004 | www.tersiguels.com

"Allow chef/co-owner Michel Tersiguel to take you on a tour" of "fine French country cuisine" at this "first-rate", family-run Gallic "in the heart of Ellicott City"; it "has a following" for its "rich", "fabulous food" (they even "grow their own vegetables"), and the "extensive wine" list and "wonderful service" help to ensure it's "perfect for a special occasion"; a "whopping bill" doesn't deter fans who note they've "paid three times as much for offerings that don't compare."

Thai Ⓜ *Thai*   23 | 13 | 22 | $20

York Road Corridor | 3316-18 Greenmount Ave. (bet. 33rd & 34th Sts.) | 410-889-6002

"Looks can be deceiving" at this "underappreciated" Thai just east of Homewood that's "small and sketchy on the outside", but "big and friendly on the inside"; just "like in the 'Land of Smiles'", the staff is "bend-over-backwards" "gracious" as they deliver "richly flavored curries" and "can't-be-beat pad Thai" at "bargain" prices, but be sure you mean it "when you ask them to turn up the spice" – you'll find "the kitchen listens."

Thai Arroy Ⓜ *Thai*   23 | 14 | 20 | $21

South Baltimore | 1019 Light St. (Cross St.) | 410-385-8587 | www.thaiarroy.com

"Go early" to this "unassuming" "neighborhood Thai" "as it's in a tiny", "cozy storefront" that gets "very busy" with South Baltimoreans "jonesing" for "fresh flavors at inexpensive prices" that are "made even better" by a BYO policy; the "charming" staff doles out dishes that are "spicy-as-you-want-'em" "on a scale of one–10" – so maybe it's a blessing in disguise that they serve what a few call the "smallest portions ever."

Thai Landing Ⓢ *Thai*   24 | 13 | 21 | $23

Mt. Vernon | 1207 N. Charles St. (bet. Biddle & Preston Sts.) | 410-727-1234

Though "nothing fancy", this "long-standing" Mt. Vernon Thai offers "first-rate", "authentic", "super-spicy food" that "will knock your socks off" *and* "makes your lips burn" – though "they can alter the heat for spice wimps too"; the "sweet and helpful staff" "is a kick", and it's "perfect pre-opera or -symphony", although big eaters may find the portions "small."

NEW Three... Ⓢ Ⓜ *American*   – | – | – | M

Highlandtown | 2901 E. Baltimore St. (Linwood Ave.) | 410-327-3333

Nestled in the former Parkside space on the corner of Patterson Park, this stylish newcomer dishes out New American small and large plates that are decidedly not pub food – the only burgers here are lamb sliders on foccacia; a warmly lit setting with exposed-brick walls and a long bar helps to attract a mix of local denizens and young creative types; N.B. dinner-only Tuesday–Saturday, with plans for a Sunday brunch.

Tiburzi's ⚹ Italian
| 19 | 12 | 20 | $25 |

Canton | 900 S. Kenwood Ave. (Hudson St.) | 410-327-8100
"Don't let the corner bar look fool you": this "very friendly, family-run" row house "off the beaten path in Canton" serves up "homey" "standard Italian" (think "mama's lasagna") that can run "hot and cold" but is always "made with love"; regulars admit the "cute" but "simple environment" can get "crowded and noisy" with "sometimes spotty service" – but say that's "just like eating at home!"

Timbuktu Seafood
| 19 | 10 | 16 | $27 |

Hanover | 1726 Dorsey Rd. (Coca-Cola Dr./Rte. 100) | 410-796-0733 | www.timbukturestaurant.com
It's in the middle of "nowhere", but "for hungry fliers" this "soooo Baltimore" seafooder is "perfectly located by BWI" in Hanover; the "huge menu has huger portions" ("doggy bags are common") of "Chesapeake Bay everything", but given the "gargantuan", "all-lump-meat", "no-filler crab cakes", crustacean-cravers cry "why order anything else?"; a redo has "classed it up", but some say the decor and service still "could use improvement."

Timothy Dean Bistro ⚹ American
| 23 | 21 | 19 | $49 |

Fells Point | 1717 Eastern Ave. (B'way) | 410-534-5650 | www.tdbistro.com
Fells Point foodies are "glad" that the namesake chef-owner "decided to settle here", because "this guy can cook", spinning out "thrillingly upscale", "pricey" New American fare that's "clearly a labor of love"; "filled with urbane yuppies and buppies", the space has a "cozy but stylish" "energy", although a "distracted" staff leads some to conclude this "rising star" "could be outstanding if Timothy would get the service to be as good as his food."

Tio Pepe Continental/Spanish
| 24 | 21 | 22 | $49 |

Mt. Vernon | 10 E. Franklin St. (bet. Charles & St. Paul Sts.) | 410-539-4675
At this "classic" Mt. Vernon "destination for generations", "the old guard" relishes "substantial portions" of "reliable", "upscale Spanish"-Continental fare like a "sublime shrimp in garlic sauce" and some "off-the-menu" treasures for "those in-the-know"; still, surveyors have conflicting views on the setting ("cozy" vs. a "dark" "warren of underground rooms") and service ("excellent" vs. "condescending"), and a few skeptics say this "standby" "is resting on its laurels."

Trapeze American/Seafood
| – | – | – | E |

Fulton | 8180 Maple Lawn Blvd. (Rte. 216 W.) | 301-498-4411 | www.trapezeonline.net
Located in a retail/housing development in Fulton, this New American restaurant features a seasonal, seafood-heavy menu that swings

from fried-green tomatoes to sea bass and back again; plus, the warm-toned, high-ceilinged setting has two dining rooms and a plush bar/lounge, all of which are nonsmoking; N.B. an outdoor patio adds appeal.

Trattoria Alberto ☒ *Italian* | 26 | 17 | 24 | $59 |

Glen Burnie | 1660 Crain Hwy. S. (bet. Hospital Dr. & Rte. 100 overpass) | 410-761-0922 | www.trattoriaalberto.com

Way out "in the 'burbs" near Glen Burnie is this "upscale" Northern Italian serving "exceptional" cuisine that's all the more "amazing" when you consider "the strip center it's in"; "from food to service, it's so old-world", but some note that specials can induce "sticker shock" and ask "for these prices, couldn't they hire a decorator?"

TRUE ☒Ⓜ *American* | ▽ 23 | 23 | 19 | $42 |

Fells Point | The Admiral Fell Inn | 888 S. Broadway (Thames St.) | 410-522-2195 | www.truedining.com

Those who are "into 'natural' food" should try this Fells Pointer located in the waterfront Admiral Fell Inn, where the healthy, "innovative" regional New American fare – think duck over cherry polenta with wild mushrooms – is made with mostly organic ingredients "from local suppliers"; perhaps due to its low-visibility basement setup, diners are still catching on to this "cozy, quiet" spot; N.B. open Wednesday–Saturday for dinner only.

Vin *American* | - | - | - | E |

Towson | 1 E. Joppa Rd. (Delaware Ave.) | 410-337-0797 | www.vinbaltimore.com

A grown-up destination amid Towson's chains and student pubs, this upscale, dinner-only New American is worthy of client outings with its sleek, dark-wood space; plus, a fireplace and tiered banquettes create a romantic setting ideal for sipping a glass of vino and relaxing to weekend live music; N.B. the same menu is served across the street at their outdoor patio, The Grove.

Windows *Seafood* | 19 | 22 | 19 | $42 |

Inner Harbor | Renaissance Harborplace Hotel | 202 E. Pratt St., 5th fl. (bet. Calvert & South Sts.) | 410-685-8439 | www.renaissanceharborplace.com

Out of sight on the fifth floor of the Renaissance Harborplace Hotel, this "little-known" seafooder has carved out a niche as a "breakfast meeting" and "power-lunch" destination; area office-dwellers impress their "out-of-town clients" with the "spectacular" Inner Harbor views, while less-business-minded munchers "sit back" and enjoy the "pleasant atmosphere" and "top-notch" Sunday brunch boasting choices "you don't normally see on a buffet."

Wine Market *American* | 23 | 21 | 22 | $36 |

Locust Point | 921 E. Fort Ave. (Lawrence St.) | 410-244-6166 | www.the-wine-market.com

"If you hadn't figured it out by the name, the best thing" about this Locust Point "nouveau American" is the "attached wine store", where "SoBo's gentrifiers" "pick their bottle off the shelf" "for a mere $9 corkage fee" (there's a "knowledgeable staff" to decipher the "huge list"); it's ideal "for a gossipy lunch or cozy dinner", though some say the "reclaimed industrial" space's "good buzz" is actually "high decibel levels", so opt for "the patio on nice days."

XS ● *Eclectic* | 19 | 20 | 13 | $22 |

Mt. Vernon | 1307 N. Charles St. (bet. Mount Royal Ave. & Preston St.) | 410-468-0002 | www.xsbaltimore.com

"There's no other place for sushi and pancakes at 1:30 AM", so surveyors think it's "a shame" this "edgy", four-story Mt. Vernonite near the U of B is "marred by tragically hip service"; still, fans have a "hard-to-kick relationship" with its WiFi-equipped space and its "brilliant" Eclectic mix of raw fish, "all-day breakfast" and "sublime desserts", though "takeout is recommended" by some; N.B. open till midnight daily and 2 AM on weekends.

Ze Mean Bean Café *E Euro.* | 22 | 20 | 19 | $25 |

Fells Point | 1739 Fleet St. (Ann St.) | 410-675-5999 | www.zemeanbean.com

Be sure not to let "the name make you underestimate" this "homey", "genuine" Fells Pointer serving "fancified Eastern European" "comfort food" that ranges into "adventurous" territory yet remains "deeply satisfying" to those who are homesick for "old-world charm"; plus, a "big fireplace", a "wonderful Sunday jazz brunch" and weekend live music make it a "cute date place"; N.B. it's adding a wine bar in summer 2007.

Zodiac ■ *Eclectic/Vegetarian* | 20 | 17 | 18 | $24 |

Downtown North | 1724 N. Charles St. (Lanvale St.) | 410-727-8815

"Don't be fooled by" its exterior – this "totally unique", "bohemian" "retro" spot "across from the Charles Theatre" is an "awesome" choice for "yummy" "vegan- and veggie-friendly" Eclectic eats that rotate with the Sun signs; you "need to be hip to grip" the "somewhat precious", astrologically themed decor and equally "spacey" service, but those who do dub it "true Baltimore"; P.S. "it's bedlam" at peak weekend hours.

Zorba's Bar & Grill ● *Greek* | 22 | 12 | 17 | $22 |

Greektown | 4710 Eastern Ave. (Oldham St.) | 410-276-4484

Upon entering you'll still find the same "dark", "worn-looking" bar lined with "men watching soccer", but this "old Baltimore" Greektowner has a secret: a "big upstairs dining room" that's "calm and smoke-free"; so head there to focus on "stellar" Greek food prepared on an "open grill" "over charcoal", like "juicy, zesty lamb chops" and as many as 20 varieties of "simple", "whole fish" – just "don't get carried away, as the plates are big"; N.B. dinner-only.

Annapolis

Aqua Terra *American*
21 | 18 | 20 | $44

Annapolis | 164 Main St. (Conduit St.) | 410-263-1985 |
www.aquaterraofannapolis.com

It "sometimes works, sometimes doesn't", but locals aver this "de-
lightfully eclectic" storefront on Main Street is "worth a try" for its
"innovative" New American fare and "creative" small plates; still,
some find it "overly trendy", with "close quarters", "sterile" decor
and "prices that are far too high"; N.B. now open for lunch.

Boatyard Bar & Grill ● *Pub Food*
16 | 20 | 18 | $25

Eastport | 400 Fourth St. (Severn Ave.) | 410-216-6206 |
www.boatyardbarandgrill.com

"Bring your deck shoes" and "swap a sea story" at this "raucous"
Eastport "place for sailors" and "well-heeled" "wannabes"; some salute "inspired" Eclectic pub grub, others say it's really "just a base
for beer", but Wednesday night "boat race videos" and occasional
live music help to make it "a port in stormy weather."

Café Normandie *French*
20 | 19 | 18 | $34

Annapolis | 185 Main St. (Conduit St.) | 410-263-3382

"Take the chill off" "on a cold winter's day" around the "wonderful
fireplace in the center" of this "cozy" "bit of France in Downtown
Annapolis"; its "French country" cuisine generally "meets expectations", but faultfinders point to "cramped tables" and service that
"runs the gamut" from "very helpful" to "painfully slow."

Cantler's Riverside Inn *Seafood*
22 | 13 | 17 | $32

Annapolis | 458 Forest Beach Rd. (Browns Woods Rd.) | 410-757-1311 |
www.cantlers.com

"If you can find" this "prototypical crab shack" "overlooking Mill
Creek" outside of Annapolis, join the "long line of cars" for your turn
to "dive into a pile" of "awesome" steamed "jumbos worth the cost";
the communal "brown paper-covered tables" on the deck have a
"great view" of "the watermen unloading their catch", so "swill
beer" "with hundreds of your new best friends" "and enjoy."

Carrol's Creek Cafe *Seafood*
22 | 23 | 21 | $41

Eastport | 410 Severn Ave. (4th St.) | 410-263-8102 |
www.carrolscreek.com

For arguably the "best sunset dining in town", "take the water taxi
from City Dock" to this Eastport "sure thing", a "picturesque" creek-
side seafooder with a "don't-miss" patio and views "of yachts you
can't afford"; the menu boasts "some winners", and if some feel the
"pricey" plates "don't quite live up to the setting", few seem to mind.

Chick & Ruth's Delly ●⇄ *Deli*
16 | 12 | 17 | $14

Annapolis | 165 Main St. (Conduit St.) | 410-269-6737 |
www.chickandruths.com

"Wacky, cluttered and cramped", this "politico-crammed" Main
Street deli brims with "local 'Naptown flavor" – "too much of it" for

some – as it serves up "uniquely named sandwiches" and "thick, rich" chocolate malts; it's "dining as theater" here, so "watch the floor show" as the "owner does magic tricks" and everyone "stands and says the Pledge of Allegiance" each morning; P.S. steer clear of the "table reserved for former and sitting governors."

Davis' Pub *Pub Food*   18 | 12 | 18 | $18

Eastport | 400 Chester Ave. (4th St.) | 410-268-7432

"Tucked away on a side street in Eastport", this "cramped", "smoky" spot is lauded as the "perfect neighborhood dive": it "excels at not raising your expectations", with "cheap beer that flows" and "average" American pub grub served by a "friendly" staff; plus, "if you want local color", this "old Annapolis sailing scene" "is the place" – as long as you "can get a seat" now that "the tourists have overridden it."

Domenica's ⊠ *Italian*   ▽ 25 | 23 | 26 | $54

Annapolis | 2444 Solomons Island Rd. (Forest Dr.) | 410-266-7595 | www.domenicasannapolis.com

It may be set "in a strip center" on Annapolis' western fringe, but this "amazing" dinner-only Italian is "top-notch with a price tag to match"; the "well-dressed dining room" is complemented by "polished service", and they've recently "expanded" to include a private dining area and a "looker" of a lounge with a "tapas and conversation" attitude; P.S. nightly live jazz makes for a "calm date night" away from the crowds.

❷ Five Guys *Hamburgers*   24 | 8 | 15 | $9

Annapolis | Village Greens | 509 S. Cherry Grove (4th Dr.) | 410-216-7971 | www.fiveguys.com

See review in the Washington, DC, Directory.

Galway Bay *Irish*   – | – | – | M

Annapolis | 63 Maryland Ave. (State Circle) | 410-263-8333 | www.galwaybayannapolis.com

"Hiding on an Annapolis side street", this unusually serious homage to "authentic Irish cooking" goes beyond the stereotypes, supplying expats with a "warm ambiance" and "substantial" dishes – think homemade soda bread and shepherd's pie – while giving a nod to the locals with crab cakes; the wood-beamed, high-ceilinged "dining room is separate from the bar" and hosts a Sunday jazz brunch buffet featuring Emerald Isle–inflected fare.

Harry Browne's *American*   22 | 22 | 22 | $47

Annapolis | 66 State Circle (bet. East St. & Maryland Ave.) | 410-263-4332 | www.harrybrownes.com

"Grab a window seat and watch the comings and goings at the State Capitol" from this Chesapeake-inspired New American, a "place to rub shoulders" with "Annapolis lobbyists" and "hungry politicos" "who don't pay for their own meals"; the opposing party claims "it relies on location" and "reputation", but the majority of voters agrees this "sophisticated" "classic" is "a tough reservation" for good reason, so try for a night "when the boys are out of session."

	FOOD	DECOR	SERVICE	COST

Jalapeños *Mexican/Spanish*   26 | 21 | 24 | $32

Annapolis | Forest Plaza | 85 Forest Dr. (Riva Rd.) | 410-266-7580 |
www.jalapenosonline.com

"Don't let the strip-mall exterior fool you" – this Annapolis "favorite" is "packed with locals" won over by "wonderful Mexican and Spanish food" and a "warm", "expanded and improved" "terracotta-influenced interior"; "diverse, flavorful" offerings from a "huge tapas menu" will "leave an indelible impression", as will "the most gracious owners in the area" and their "courteous staff"; P.S. the "well-kept secret" is out, so "avoid weekends."

☑ Joss Cafe & Sushi Bar *Japanese*   28 | 16 | 23 | $34

Annapolis | 195 Main St. (Church Circle) | 410-263-4688 |
www.josscafe-sushibar.com

"You'd have to catch it yourself to get fish any fresher" than at this "adventurous" "source of pride" in Annapolis, where sushi-philes savor "heaven-in-a-wrapper" rolls plus "yummy options that don't involve raw" fin fare; claustrophobes complain it's "cramped" and "crowded" and "doesn't take reservations", but once you're in, expect "efficient" service and "kitschy" if "sparse" decor.

NEW Kyma *Mediterranean*   - | - | - | E

Annapolis | 69 West St. (Calvert St.) | 410-268-0003 |
www.kymarestaurant.com

A partnership between the owners of DC's Mie N Yu and Annapolis native Dmitri Sfakiyanudis, this modern Med is set in a renovated 200-year-old building on West Street; the name is Greek for 'wave', so expect ocean-themed decor to go with a menu that focuses on meze and Spanish tapas but also includes complex paellas and grilled seafood; N.B. weekend DJs and exotic martinis heighten the edgy vibe.

☑ Lebanese Taverna *Lebanese*   22 | 17 | 18 | $26

Annapolis | Annapolis Harbour Ctr. | 2478 Solomons Island Rd.
(Aris T. Allen Blvd.) | 410-897-1111 | www.lebanesetaverna.com
See review in the Washington, DC, Directory.

☑ Lemongrass *Thai*   27 | 19 | 21 | $28

Annapolis | 167 West St. (Colonial Ave.) | 410-280-0086
NEW **Annapolis** | Gateway Village Shopping Ctr. | 2625A Housely Rd.
(bet. General Hwy. & Rte. 450) | 410-224-8424
www.lemongrassannapolis.com

"Annapolis rejoices!" – "finally, decent Thai" comes to wild West Street in the guise of this "hip" "oasis for absolutely top-notch" fare "beautifully served" by a "relaxed staff"; the "innovative" dishes are proffered in a setting that's "too damn small" but "lively, noisy and hot" – "both the spices and the clientele"; N.B. a second site (with a covered patio) opened post-Survey just west of 'Naptown.

Les Folies Brasserie *French*   26 | 23 | 24 | $46

Annapolis | 2552 Riva Rd. (Aris T. Allen Blvd.) | 410-573-0970 |
www.lesfoliesbrasserie.com

Set in an "off-the-beaten-path" location in western Annapolis, this "formal" brasserie "maintains a friendly charm", from fresh "flowers in abundance" to "owners who could not be more cordial"; it's "a real treat" "for that special night out" with "well-prepared French cuisine", "incredible shellfish arrays" at the raw bar and attentive "service that makes you feel like you're the only table in the room."

Lewnes' Steakhouse *Steak*

26 | 20 | 24 | $53

Eastport | 401 Fourth St. (Severn Ave.) | 410-263-1617 |
www.lewnessteakhouse.com

This "low-key", two-story Eastport chophouse "proves that a local, family-owned restaurant" can "trump" the national chains with "the real thing": "melt-in-your-mouth steaks", "sides without compare" and a "can-do" "staff that knows you by name"; carnivores also give "kudos" to an "intimate" setup with a "separate area where you can enjoy a cigar" and "meet the locals"; N.B. an expansion (to be completed in summer 2007) will double its capacity.

Luna Blu ⊠ *Italian*

- | - | - | M

Annapolis | 36 West St. (Calvert St.) | 410-267-9950 |
www.lunabluofannapolis.com

Nestled in a narrow storefront near the State House, this Annapolis veteran churns out lunchtime pizzas and pastas for government workers in a warm, blue-hued space spruced up with murals of the owners' native Naples; in the evenings, there's a more ambitious menu of Southern Italian fare, plus a $35 prix fixe option to make it an even more affordable choice.

Main Ingredient Café *American*

22 | 14 | 20 | $25

Annapolis | 914 Bay Ridge Rd. (Georgetown Rd.) | 410-626-0388 |
www.themainingredient.com

"Tucked in a strip mall" away from the tourist areas, this "casual" Annapolis bakery/cafe is "a place locals love to go" for New American "home cooking" from a seasonal menu with "something for every craving"; it earns special praise as "the spot for Sunday brunch" or an "oversized breakfast" in a "comfortable" setting.

Metropolitan Ⓜ *American*

23 | 24 | 22 | $51

Annapolis | 169 West St. (Murray Ave.) | 410-268-7733 |
www.metropolitanannapolis.com

"Finally, what we've been waiting for" – "conservative" 'Naptown gets "a taste of urban chic" via this "stunning" tri-level "hipster hangout" serving up "splurge"-worthy seasonal New American fare and "yummy" "tapaslike" "half-plates"; the dinner-only spot is "trying hard to be cool", but some say it's "the staff that needs to take a chill pill"; P.S. drinks at the "happening rooftop bar" may "have you calling an area realtor to relocate."

Northwoods Ⓜ *Continental*

23 | 20 | 24 | $45

Annapolis | 609 Melvin Ave. (Ridgely Ave.) | 410-268-2609 |
www.northwoodsrestaurant.com

"Reserved for special occasions", this "well-established" "neighborhood Continental" offers "the best deal going" for "upscale" "gourmet dining" in 'Naptown: the $34.95 "four-course prix fixe dinner" is a "run of the menu" ranging from filet mignon to rainbow trout;

FOOD DECOR SERVICE COST

"personal service and an intimate feel" ("tight" to some) have made it an "old favorite" for "romantic evenings", so "make your reservations early"; N.B. there's terrace seating in season.

O'Learys Seafood *Seafood*

| 26 | 21 | 23 | $50 |

Eastport | 310 Third St. (Severn Ave.) | 410-263-0884 | www.olearysseafood.com

Skip the Annapolis "circus" and head to Eastport for this "lovely", "white-linen" "fish palace" "proudly featuring the Chesapeake's bounty" on a "creative", "mouthwatering" menu served by a "knowledgeable, on-its-toes" staff; it's "very popular", but fans feel it's "worth the noise and crowding" – as well as the "pricey" bill; P.S. it's dinner-only and "reservations are a must."

NEW Osteria 177 *American/Italian*

| – | – | – | E |

Annapolis | 177 Main St. (Conduit St.) | 410-267-7700 | www.osteria177.com

Set in an ever-changing corner space on Main Street, this Annapolis addition draws a mixed crowd of locals and visitors for Italian appetizers and pastas and New American entrees; the owners once worked together at Glen Burnie's Trattoria Alberto, and they've created a sophisticated setting to complement the contemporary fare: sleek and dark, with white leather chairs and modern artwork; N.B. it also serves a Sunday brunch.

Paul's Homewood Café ⊠ *American/Greek*

| 22 | 14 | 21 | $26 |

Annapolis | 919 West St. (Taylor Ave.) | 410-267-7891

The "excellent spanakopita" and "can't-beat souvlaki" served at this "family-run" Annapolis Greek taste even better thanks to the "warm owners" and "smiley" "server-relatives" who dish it up (there's a selection of "wholesome" New American offerings too); eating here is "like having your best friend make dinner for you", with "size the only problem" – "cozy" equals "crowded" to some; N.B. an expansion began in early summer 2007.

Phillips *Seafood*

| 15 | 15 | 16 | $33 |

Annapolis | 12 Dock St. (Randall St.) | 410-990-9888 | www.phillipsseafood.com

See review in the Baltimore Directory.

Piccola Roma *Italian*

| 24 | 22 | 24 | $44 |

Annapolis | 200 Main St. (Church Circle) | 410-268-7898

A "what you want, how you want it" attitude augments "classic" "Italian comfort food" "you wish your mother could have made" at this "elegant" dinner-only "destination" in Downtown Annapolis; "all guests receive VIP treatment" via a "crisp, professional" staff and an owner who "visits every table", while "window seats right on Main Street" are "great for people-watching."

Red Hot & Blue *BBQ*

| 19 | 14 | 17 | $20 |

Annapolis | 200 Old Mill Bottom Rd. S. (Rte. 50, exit 28) | 410-626-7427 | www.redhotandblue.com

See review in the Washington, DC, Directory.

	FOOD	DECOR	SERVICE	COST

Reynolds Tavern *Eclectic*　　21 | 23 | 22 | $33

Annapolis | Reynolds Tavern | 7 Church Circle (West St.) | 410-295-9555 |
www.reynoldstavern.org

"Feel like you're going back in time" at "one of the oldest buildings in
Annapolis", this 1747 Georgian inn whose "period antiques" – and
"resident ghost" – lend a bit of "Colonial atmosphere" to a "quaint
parlor" that's "wonderful for lunch" or tea in the afternoon and casual Eclectic dinners Wednesday–Saturday; the lustier Sly Fox Pub
downstairs offers British pub grub, while the pet-friendly courtyard
patio is a "favorite of humans and canines" alike.

Rockfish, The *American*　　21 | 20 | 20 | $39

Eastport | 400 Sixth St. (Severn Ave.) | 410-267-1800 |
www.rockfishmd.com

At this Eastport destination just over the bridge from City Dock, a
"large, loud" dining room pumps out "straightforward" seafood-
centric New American fare, while a "bar with buzz" adds "pickup"
appeal; it's "popular with sailors" and has "plentiful parking", but
there's "no view" – unless you count the "cute staff" – and some say
it "hasn't found its groove yet."

☑ Ruth's Chris Steak House *Steak*　　24 | 21 | 23 | $57

Eastport | 301 Severn Ave. (3rd St.) | 410-990-0033 | www.ruthschris.com
See review in the Washington, DC, Directory.

Sam's on the Waterfront *American*　　– | – | – | E

Annapolis | 2020 Chesapeake Harbour Dr. E. (Edgewood Rd.) |
410-263-3600 | www.samswaterfrontcafe.net

It's "a pain to find" "tucked away" south of Annapolis, but this "hideaway" rewards your search with a "prime waterfront location" that's
perfect for "a romantic walk before a meal"; the view is paired with
a raw bar and a seasonal New American menu that hits heavily on
seafood and aged beef; outdoor seating, weekend jazz and "space to
dock your boat" add appeal.

Severn Inn, The *American*　　16 | 23 | 14 | $43

Annapolis | 1993 Baltimore Annapolis Blvd. (Redwood Ave.) |
410-349-4000 | www.severninn.com

With an "exceptional" "view of the Naval Academy across the
Severn River", this restaurant just north of Annapolis "has a lot of
promise", but some find its potential is left unfulfilled by an "average" New American surf 'n' turf menu, a "ho-hum" interior and
"spotty service"; locals who like its deckside vistas are "still hope-
ful" it might one day justify its "premium prices."

Sputnik Cafe ⓜ *Eclectic*　　23 | 18 | 20 | $36

Crownsville | 1397 Generals Hwy. (Crownsville Rd.) | 410-923-3775 |
www.sputnikcafe.com

"The Martians have landed" is one response to the orange-hued,
"retro *Austin Powers*" trappings at this Crownsville Eclectic that's
"hard to find" given its location a "few miles [west] of the usual
Annapolis orbit"; the "bizarre"-looking decor "may be a bit much for

	FOOD	DECOR	SERVICE	COST

some", but get past it and you'll find a "creative" menu "with Asian flair", "ultrahip" servers and a "great wine list"; P.S. the "unique experience" includes a Sunday dim sum brunch.

Treaty of Paris *American*

| 17 | 21 | 19 | $52 |

Annapolis | Maryland Inn | 16 Church Circle (Main St.) | 410-216-6340 | www.historicinnsofannapolis.com

Enjoying a "killer location" with great "potential" – the basement of a "romantic" 1773 inn near the Annapolis State House – this Traditional American dishes up "decent" if "generally uninspired" fare in a "history"-tinged setting; still, that doesn't pacify critics who feel it's "in need of an update" and "not worth the price."

Tsunami ● *Asian Fusion*

| 25 | 20 | 21 | $36 |

Annapolis | 51 West St. (bet. Calvert St. & Church Circle) | 410-990-9868 | www.tsunamiannapolis.com

Annapolis' "place to meet other good-looking people" is riding a wave of "popularity" with a "young crowd" downing "top-notch" Asian fusion entrees and items off of a "fabulous" late-night sushi menu (until 1 AM); it's "so cool, so hip" and so "loud" – with "close tables", "the din of diners drowns out any hope of conversation" – but "it's becoming legendary" for "great cocktails" and a "lively", clublike ambiance fueled by DJs.

Wild Orchid Café *American*

| 24 | 20 | 23 | $38 |

Eastport | 909 Bay Ridge Ave. (Chesapeake Ave.) | 410-268-8009 | www.thewildorchidcafe.com

You'll "work up an appetite" looking for this "hard-to-find" Eastport New American, but most agree it's "worth the drive"; set in a "redone" house with pictures of "beautiful orchids everywhere", it's a "serene", romantic "date spot" where "you can actually have a conversation" while enjoying "gourmet delights" delivered by "attentive but unfussy" servers; you "can't beat" the $39 prix fixe dinner, and there's a "nice, warm-weather" patio too.

Yellowfin *American*

| 21 | 21 | 19 | $42 |

Edgewater | 2840 Solomons Island Rd. (Old South River Rd.) | 410-573-1371 | www.yellowfinrestaurant.com

"Plan your meal around sunset" because this "busy" Edgewater New American serving "sassy seafood" and serious steaks has a "to-die-for" "view of the South River"; there are "excellent half-price happy-hour appetizers", but the trade-off is a "smoky, oh-so-noisy" "meat-market" buzz; N.B. dinner-only.

Yin Yankee *Asian Fusion*

| 24 | 18 | 21 | $33 |

Annapolis | 105 Main St. (Green St.) | 410-268-8703 | www.yinyankee.com

At this "weird place" "off City Dock", the "quirky decor complements the quirky" Chesapeake Bay–tinged Asian fusion fare and full sushi menu, both of which are served by a "charming staff"; those who say the Annapolis original is "cramped" may be pleased with the post-Survey opening of an expansive Bethesda offshoot featuring the same menu in a mod restaurant, lounge and sushi bar setting.

Eastern Shore

Bistro St. Michaels *American*

St. Michaels | 403 S. Talbot St. (Mulberry St.) | 410-745-9111 |
www.bistrostmichaels.com

"Reservations are important (even off-season)" at what diners deem "the best thing going" in "sleepy" St. Michaels: this "top-notch", family-run bistro featuring a New American menu with French and Eastern Shore accents – "don't miss the mussels" – served by a staff that "truly cares"; "the tables can be a bit close" for romance, so "request the glassed-in porch" for "a more private experience"; N.B. dinner-only and closed Tuesdays and Wednesdays.

Chesapeake Chicken & Rockin' Ribs *BBQ*

Grasonville | 101 Hissey Rd. (Rte. 50) | 410-827-0030 |
www.chesapeakechicken.com

A popular spot with Eastern Shore beachgoers, this Grasonville country kitchen dishes up old-fashioned BBQ eats, rotisseried birds, homey sides and diet-busting cookies, brownies and lemon bars; an Americana-filled cafe/market offshoot just opened in Bethesda, and both locations cater for picnics and lawn parties.

Crab Claw ⊅ *Crab House*

St. Michaels | 304 Mill St. (Talbot St.) | 410-745-2900 |
www.thecrabclaw.com

Though some locals label this St. Michaels "seafood joint" "a tourist trap", they admit it's "fun just the same", a "noisy, busy", "basic crab house" that's "perfect for drinking beer and eating" crustaceans "true Maryland-style" "on picnic tables by the water"; "if you want fancy, this isn't for you" – "casual is the key word" here – but there's also an upstairs dining room with "a view of the Maritime Museum."

Fisherman's Inn/Crab Deck *Seafood*

Grasonville | 3116 Main St. (Rte. 50) | 410-827-8807 |
www.fishermansinn.com

It's "not a destination", but it is a "welcome stop on the way to the Shore" say fans of this Grasonville "standby" for "family-style" munching on "reliably good" Traditional American seafood; the "civilized dining room" boasts a "treasure" of an "oyster plate collection" and "great Bay views", but a few find the adjacent "open-air" Crab Deck "the better bet" for "spending a Sunday afternoon" waterside with a "tasty crab claw."

Harris Crab House *Seafood*

Grasonville | 433 Kent Narrows Way N. (Rte. 50, exit 42) | 410-827-9500 |
www.harriscrabhouse.com

If you're "into crackin' crabs", "get down and dirty" and "dive right in" to crustaceans piled high "on paper-lined tables" at this "rustic", "unpretentious" Kent Narrows seafood house that's "all about sunny days on the deck with a cold beer" "watching the boats slide by"; it's a "popular spot for tourists" "headed to the beaches", so expect it to be "mobbed in summer"; P.S. be sure to "save room for their homemade Nutty Buddies."

Holly's *Diner* · 15 | 8 | 17 | $18

Grasonville | 108 Jackson Creek Rd. (Rte. 50) | 410-827-8711 | www.hollysrest.com

Showing there's "still some old Eastern Shore left in Grasonville", this "nothing-fancy" "classic '50s roadhouse" "is worth a detour" for "huge portions" of "real" American diner fare that's "a family tradition" for breakfast or "on the way back from the beach"; so "starve yourself", then hit this "throwback" for as much fried chicken and "chocolate malt as you can fit down your sunburned gullet."

Inn at Easton, The Ⓜ *American* · 26 | 24 | 24 | $64

Easton | Inn at Easton | 28 S. Harrison St. (South Ln.) | 410-822-4910 | www.theinnateaston.com

"Wonderful chef/co-owner Andrew Evans" shows off his Aussie training on an "unbelievable", ever-changing New American fusion menu that "always has something surprising" (and "expensive") in store – so "try the kangaroo filet"; the Colonial-style drawing room scene seems a "little stiff" to some, "delightful" to others, but few would deny that "staying the night" in the restored 1790 Easton inn is "the perfect dessert"; N.B. closed Mondays and Tuesdays.

Julia's ⓏⓂ *American* · ▽ 26 | 20 | 26 | $48

Centreville | 122 N. Commerce St. (bet. B'way & Rte. 304) | 410-758-0471

At this "rising star" set in an 1870 town square storefront in "sleepy Centreville", husband-and-wife-owners "David and Valerie Clark take great pride" in their "skillfully prepared" and "beautifully served" New American "creations", which "shine" with Asian tinges and "touches of Maryland seafood"; add a "charming, cozy" space and "well-trained staff that always impresses", and patrons proclaim it a "must-visit."

🆕 Local, Restaurant *American* · - | - | - | VE

Easton | Tidewater Inn | 101 E. Dover St. (Harrison St.) | 410-819-8088 | www.tidewaterinn.com

Highly visible on the first floor of Easton's Tidewater Inn, this sleek, tall-ceilinged newcomer hopes to capitalize on the town's sophisticated denizens and high-profile weekenders; the ambitious New American menu showcases regional, locally sourced ingredients and is complemented by a long vino list – so long, in fact, that the dining area features a glass-walled wine room with a private table; N.B. there's complimentary valet parking.

Mason's Ⓩ *American* · 23 | 22 | 21 | $47

Easton | 22 S. Harrison St. (South Ln.) | 410-822-3204 | www.masonsgourmet.com

"If you haven't been there in a while, go back", because this "charming" New American set in a renovated "old house" in Downtown Easton has a "talented chef" revving up the regularly rotating menu and a full bar offering lighter fare; meanwhile, the "friendly" staff, "elegant" dining room and "delightful" courtyard and porch add appeal; N.B. lunch-only on Mondays.

Narrows, The *Seafood*

23 | 19 | 21 | $39

Grasonville | 3023 Kent Narrows Way S. (Rte. 50, exit 41/42) | 410-827-8113 | www.thenarrowsrestaurant.com

For "a bit of elegance in an area filled with rustic restaurants", pay the bridge toll and go "way out of your way" to this Kent Narrows seafooder; grab "a seat on the porch" for a "fabulous waterfront view" as a "smooth" staff serves you the "simple" dishes that make this "a perennial favorite", including "phenomenal crab cakes" that may allow locals to "stop arguing – *these* are the best"; N.B. a post-Survey chef change may outdate the Food score.

Out of the Fire *American*

23 | 21 | 22 | $39

Easton | 22 Goldsborough St. (Washington St.) | 410-770-4777 | www.outofthefire.com

"Sit at the counter" facing the open kitchen and stone hearth oven at this "intimate" Easton option and "watch the chefs at work" as they prepare "excellent pizzas" and other "inventive", "regularly changing" New American fare; it's "always a good bet" "on the way to the Eastern Shore" with "friendly service", a "delightful atmosphere" and a wine bar, but it can get "crowded", so some savvy surveyors advise "call ahead"; N.B. it now serves Sunday brunch.

Pope's Tavern Ⓜ *American*

-| -| -| E

Oxford | Oxford Inn | 504 S. Morris St. (Oxford Rd.) | 410-226-5220 | www.oxfordinn.net

Located in non-touristy Oxford in a classy old inn with water views and Eastern Shore style, this unpretentious restaurant/tavern turns out contemporary, European-influenced takes on American cuisine; a bar menu features comfort fare like mac 'n' cheese and meatloaf, and there's outside seating on a timeworn front porch; N.B. open Wednesday–Sunday for dinner only.

Robert Morris Inn *Seafood*

21 | 22 | 21 | $42

Oxford | Robert Morris Inn | 314 N. Morris St. (E. Strand) | 410-226-5111 | www.robertmorrisinn.com

"Take the ferry" to this "historic" 1710 Oxford inn for "well-prepared" seafood – including "crab cakes made famous by James Michener" – served in a "magnificent setting" on the Tred Avon River; eating by the fireplace can be "cozy in winter", adding up to a "total experience" that's "like going back in time" for some, although for modernists that means the "outdated menu and decor" "could use an upgrade"; N.B. no dinner on Tuesdays or Wednesdays.

Scossa Ⓜ *Italian*

▽ 22 | 27 | 21 | $49

Easton | 8 N. Washington St. (Dover Rd.) | 410-822-2202 | www.scossarestaurant.com

This "impressive" spot in tiny, tony Easton is living up to its name (meaning 'surprise') with a "well-presented" Northern Italian menu from chef/co-owner Giancarlo Tondin (ex NYC's Cipriani empire);

the "beautiful" storefront space has a "very New York feel", from its "elegantly decorated" dining room with leather seating and a granite-topped bar to a "posh" "lounge in back", leading some to say this establishment "could be tops."

Sherwood's Landing *American* | 23 | 24 | 22 | $59 |

St. Michaels | Inn at Perry Cabin | 308 Watkins Ln. (Talbot St.) | 410-745-2200 | www.perrycabin.com

It's "not a destination restaurant" and some find it "just a little bit twee", with "Martha Stewart-y decor", but this St. Michaels New American "is a gem when combined with a stay at the wonderful" Inn at Perry Cabin; a "lovely" waterfront view overshadows the "polished presentations" of "decent" local seafood, so "hold out for a table overlooking the Chesapeake"; P.S. "you'll need $$$", as this "treat" is "very expensive."

Town Dock Restaurant *American/Seafood* | 21 | 16 | 20 | $37 |

St. Michaels | 125 Mulberry St. (Talbot St.) | 410-745-5577 | www.town-dock.com

"The view is the decor" at Michael Rork's "consistently good" New American seafooder "right at the marina" in St. Michaels; the local catch drives the menu, so expect "fried oystahs", bouillabaisse and "soft-shell crabs in season", plus a "very good" Friday night surf 'n' turf buffet; still, some among the "captive audience" claim it "could use an upgrade"; N.B. make sure to sit on the outside patio.

208 Talbot Ⓜ *American* | - | - | - | E |

St. Michaels | 208 N. Talbot St. (North St.) | 410-745-3838 | www.208talbot.com

Reopened in 2006, this St. Michaels stalwart now features a more casual wine bar that serves small-plate versions of the Southern- and Spanish-accented New American fare available in the more sophisticated dining room; with choices ranging from oysters with curried butternut puree to seared rockfish, Saturday evening's four-course, $55 prix fixe seems a fine way to assess the situation; N.B. closed Tuesdays in winter.

subscribe to zagat.com

BALTIMORE, ANNAPOLIS AND THE EASTERN SHORE INDEXES

All properties are in the Baltimore area unless otherwise noted
(Annap=Annapolis; E Shore=Eastern Shore).

vote at zagat.com   251

Cuisines

Includes restaurant names, neighborhoods and Food ratings. ☒ indicates places with the highest ratings, popularity and importance.

AFGHAN

☒ Helmand | **Mt. Vernon** — 26

AMERICAN (NEW)

Abacrombie | **Mt. Vernon** — 26
Acacia Fusion | **Frederick** — -
☒ Antrim 1844 | **Taneytown** — 27
Aqua Terra | **Annap** — 21
Baldwin's Station | **Sykesville** — 20
Birches | **Canton** — 24
Bistro St. Michaels | **E Shore** — 25
BlueStone | **Timonium** — 21
Brewer's Art | **Mt. Vernon** — 21
Bright. Orangerie | **Inner Harbor** — 23
Chameleon Cafe | **NE Balt** — 26
☒ Charleston | **Inner Harbor E** — 27
Christopher Daniel | **Timonium** — 22
City Cafe | **Mt. Vernon** — 18
Copra | **D'town N** — 22
Corks | **S Balt** — 25
Cosmopolitan B&G | **Canton** — 18
NEW Cynthia's | **Severna Pk** — -
NEW Dogwood | **Hampden** — -
Elkridge Furnace | **Elkridge** — 24
G. Hunter's | **Frederick** — -
Greystone Grill | **multi. loc.** — 20
Harry Browne's | **Annap** — 22
Harryman Hse. | **Reist'town** — 20
Helen's Garden | **Canton** — 23
Henninger's | **Fells Pt** — 25
Inn at Easton | **E Shore** — 26
Iron Bridge Wine | **Columbia** — 25
Ixia | **Mt. Vernon** — 24
Julia's | **E Shore** — -
Laurrapin | **Havre de Grace** — -
☒ Linwoods | **Owings Mills** — 26
NEW Local | **E Shore** — -
Main Ingredient | **Annap** — 22
Mason's | **E Shore** — 23
Metropolitan | **Annap** — 23
NEW Michos | **Reist'town** — -
Monocacy Cross. | **Frederick** — -
Neo Viccino | **Mt. Vernon** — 20
NEW Open Door | **Bel Air** — -
NEW Osteria 177 | **Annap** — -
Out of the Fire | **E Shore** — 23
Paul's Homewood | **Annap** — 22
☒ Peter's Inn | **Fells Pt** — 27
Pierpoint | **Fells Pt** — 25
Pope's Tav. | **E Shore** — -

Red Fish | **Canton** — -
Red Star | **Fells Pt** — 19
Regi's | **Fed Hill** — 19
Rockfish, The | **Annap** — 21
Salt | **E Balt** — -
Sam's/Waterfront | **Annap** — -
Sascha 527 | **Mt. Vernon** — 21
Severn Inn | **Annap** — 16
Sherwood's Land. | **E Shore** — 23
SoBo Cafe | **S Balt** — 24
Taste | **N Balt** — 20
Tasting Rm. | **Frederick** — 25
NEW Three... | **Hi'town** — -
Timothy Dean | **Fells Pt** — 23
Town Dock | **E Shore** — 21
Trapeze | **Fulton** — -
TRUE | **Fells Pt** — 23
208 Talbot | **E Shore** — -
Vin | **Towson** — -
Wild Orchid | **Annap** — 24
Wine Market | **Locust Pt** — 23
Yellowfin | **Annap** — 21

AMERICAN (TRADITIONAL)

Baugher's | **Westminster** — 18
Blue Moon Cafe | **Fells Pt** — 25
Brass Elephant | **Mt. Vernon** — 23
Cafe Hon | **Hampden** — 15
☒ Cheesecake Fact. | **Inner Harbor** — 18
☒ Clyde's | **Columbia** — 18
Coburn's | **Canton** — 20
Davis' Pub | **Annap** — 18
Dutch's Daughter | **Frederick** — 20
Fisherman's Inn | **E Shore** — 18
☒ Five Guys | **multi. loc.** — 24
Friendly Farm | **Upperco** — 21
Hard Times Cafe | **Frederick** — 19
Holly's | **E Shore** — 15
Hull St. Blues | **Locust Pt** — 20
Jennings | **Catonsville** — 19
JJ's Everyday | **Timonium** — 19
Maggie Moore's | **D'town W** — 19
M & S Grill | **Inner Harbor** — 18
Manor Tav. | **Monkton** — 16
McCabe's | **Hampden** — 20
Mealey's | **New Mkt** — 21
Milton Inn | **Sparks** — 25
NEW Milton's Grill | **D'town N** — -
Miss Shirley's | **Roland Pk** — 23

NEW Open Door | **Bel Air** —

Peppermill | **Lutherville** 18

Pete's Grille | **York Rd Corr** —

Treaty of Paris | **Annap** 17

ASIAN FUSION

Acacia Fusion | **Frederick** —

Jesse Wong's Kit. | **Hunt Valley** 17

Red Maple | **Mt. Vernon** 19

NEW Rumor Mill | **Ellicott City** —

Tsunami | **Annap** 25

Yin Yankee | **Annap** 24

BAKERIES

Atwater's | **multi. loc.** 25

Au Bon Pain | **multi. loc.** 16

La Madeleine | **Columbia** 17

Main Ingredient | **Annap** 22

Stone Mill | **Brook'ville** 22

BARBECUE

NEW Alabama BBQ | **NE Balt** —

Andy Nelson's BBQ | **Cockeysville** —

Big Bad Wolf BBQ | **NE Balt** 25

Ches. Chicken/Ribs | **E Shore** —

NEW Milton's Grill | **D'town N** —

Red Hot & Blue | **Annap** 19

NEW Rub | **S Balt** —

BRITISH

Reynolds Tav. | **Annap** 21

CALIFORNIAN

Paolo's | **Towson** 18

CHESAPEAKE

Gertrude's | **Homewood** 22

CHINESE

(* dim sum specialist)

Bamboo Hse. | **Cockeysville** 19

Cafe Zen | **N Balt** 22

Chinatown Café* | **D'town** 22

David Chu's | **Pikesville** 21

Hunan Manor | **Columbia** 22

Jesse Wong's HK* | **Columbia** 22

Olive & Sesame | **multi. loc.** 22

Oriental Manor* | **Ellicott City** 20

P.F. Chang's | **multi. loc.** 19

Sonny Lee's | **Reist'town** 24

Szechuan Hse. | **Lutherville** 24

COFFEEHOUSES

City Cafe | **Mt. Vernon** 18

COFFEE SHOPS/DINERS

Cafe Hon | **Hampden** 15

Holly's | **E Shore** 15

Jimmy's | **Fells Pt** 18

Papermoon | **Hampden** 17

Pete's Grille | **York Rd Corr** —

CONTINENTAL

Josef's Country | **Fallston** 25

Kings Contrivance | **Columbia** 23

Milton Inn | **Sparks** 25

Northwoods | **Annap** 23

Tio Pepe | **Mt. Vernon** 24

CRAB HOUSES

Bo Brooks | **Canton** 17

Cantler's Inn | **Annap** 22

Costas Inn | **Dundalk** 22

Crab Claw | **E Shore** 20

Faidley's | **D'town W** 25

Harris Crab | **E Shore** 19

Mr. Bill's Terr. Inn | **Essex** 24

Obrycki's | **E Balt** 22

CREOLE

Louisiana | **Fells Pt** 24

CUBAN

Babalu Grill | **Inner Harbor** 20

DELIS

Attman's Deli | **E Balt** 24

Chick & Ruth's | **Annap** 16

EASTERN EUROPEAN

Ze Mean Bean | **Fells Pt** 22

ECLECTIC

b | **D'town N** 24

Z Bicycle, The | **S Balt** —

Boatyard B&G | **Annap** 16

Gardel's | **Little Italy** 17

NEW Jack's Bistro | **Canton** —

Reynolds Tav. | **Annap** 21

NEW Rocket/Venus | **Hampden** —

Saffron | **Mt. Vernon** —

Sputnik Cafe | **Annap** 23

Tapas Teatro | **D'town N** 22

XS | **Mt. Vernon** 19

Zodiac | **D'town N** 20

ETHIOPIAN

Dukem | **Mt. Vernon** 23

FRENCH

Z Antrim 1844 | **Taneytown** 27

Elkridge Furnace | **Elkridge** 24

La Madeleine | **Columbia** 17

Martick's | **D'town W** 24

Z Tersiguel's | **Ellicott City** 27

FRENCH (BISTRO)

Café de Paris | **Columbia**	23
Café Normandie | **Annap**	20
Crêpe du Jour | **Mt. Wash**	21
☑ Petit Louis | **Roland Pk**	24

FRENCH (BRASSERIE)

Brass. Tatin | **Homewood**	23
Les Folies | **Annap**	26

GREEK

Black Olive | **Fells Pt**	26
Ikaros | **Gr'town**	22
Paul's Homewood | **Annap**	22
☑ Samos | **Gr'town**	27
Zorba's B&G | **Gr'town**	22

HAMBURGERS

☑ Clyde's | **Columbia**	18
☑ Five Guys | **multi. loc.**	24
Jennings | **Catonsville**	19
McCabe's | **Hampden**	20

HAWAIIAN

☑ Roy's | **Inner Harbor E**	26

ICE CREAM PARLORS

Broom's Bloom Dairy | **Bel Air**	23
Stone Mill | **Brook'ville**	22

INDIAN

Akbar | **multi. loc.**	22
☑ Ambass. Din. Rm. | **Homewood**	25
Banjara | **S Balt**	21
Mughal Garden | **Mt. Vernon**	22

IRISH

An Poitín Stil | **Timonium**	17
Galway Bay | **Annap**	–
Maggie Moore's | **D'town W**	19

ITALIAN

(N=Northern; S=Southern)

AIDA Bistro | **Columbia**	23
Aldo's | S | **Little Italy**	26
Amicci's | **Little Italy**	22
Boccaccio | N | **Little Italy**	25
Caesar's Den | S | **Little Italy**	22
Café Troia | **Towson**	22
Chiapparelli's | **Little Italy**	19
Ciao Bella | **Little Italy**	23
Da Mimmo | **Little Italy**	22
Della Notte | **Little Italy**	21
Domenica's | **Annap**	25
Germano's | N | **Little Italy**	21
La Scala | **Little Italy**	24
La Tavola | **Little Italy**	25
Liberatore's | S | **multi. loc.**	20
Luna Blu | S | **Annap**	–
Mamma Lucia | **Frederick**	19
🆕 Osteria 177 | **Annap**	–
Paolo's | **Towson**	18
Paradiso/Pizzeria | **Westminster**	22
Pazza Luna | N | **Locust Pt**	–
Piccola Roma | **Annap**	24
Rocco's Capriccio | **Little Italy**	24
Sabatino's | **Little Italy**	18
Sammy's Tratt. | S | **Mt. Vernon**	–
Scossa | N | **E Shore**	22
Sotto Sopra | N | **Mt. Vernon**	24
Tiburzi's | **Canton**	19
Tratt. Alberto | N | **Glen Burnie**	26

JAPANESE

(* sushi specialist)

Chiu's Sushi* | **Inner Harbor E**	21
Edo Sushi* | **multi. loc.**	25
Green Leaf* | **Hunt Valley**	22
☑ Joss Cafe/Sushi* | **Annap**	28
Matsuri* | **S Balt**	24
Minato* | **D'town N**	–
🆕 Nasu Blanca | **Locust Pt**	–
Olive & Sesame* | **multi. loc.**	22
San Sushi/Thai* | **multi. loc.**	21
Sonny Lee's | **Reist'town**	24
Sushi Hana* | **Towson**	23
Sushi King* | **Columbia**	24
☑ Sushi Sono* | **Columbia**	28
Szechuan Hse.* | **Lutherville**	24
Tsunami* | **Annap**	25
XS* | **Mt. Vernon**	19

KOREAN

(* barbecue specialist)

An Loi | **Columbia**	25
Shin Chon* | **Ellicott City**	–
Suzie's Soba | **multi. loc.**	20

KOSHER

David Chu's | **Pikesville**	21

LEBANESE

Carlyle Club | **Homewood**	24
☑ Lebanese Tav. | **multi. loc.**	22

MEDITERRANEAN

Kali's Court | **Fells Pt**	24
🆕 Kyma | **Annap**	–
Mezze | **Fells Pt**	24
🆕 Michos | **Reist'town**	–
☑ Pazo | **Inner Harbor E**	23
Tapas Teatro | **D'town N**	22

subscribe to zagat.com

MEXICAN

Arcos | **E Balt**	19
Blue Agave | **Fed Hill**	22
Cacique | **Frederick**	22
El Trovador | **Fells Pt**	23
Holy Frijoles | **Hampden**	20
Jalapeños | **Annap**	26
☑ Mari Luna | **Pikesville**	27

NEW MEXICAN

Golden West | **Hampden**	21

NOODLE SHOPS

An Loi | **Columbia**	25
Pho Dat Thanh | **Columbia**	23
Suzie's Soba | **multi. loc.**	20

PAN-ASIAN

Green Leaf | **Hunt Valley**	22
Jesse Wong's Asean | **Columbia**	24
Jesse Wong's Kit. | **Hunt Valley**	17

PERSIAN

Orchard Mkt. | **Towson**	25

PERUVIAN

Chicken Rico | **Hi'town**	20

PIZZA

Gardel's | **Little Italy**	17
Iggies | **D'town N**	23
Mamma Lucia | **Frederick**	19
Matthew's Pizzeria | **Hi'town**	25
Out of the Fire | **E Shore**	23
Sammy's Tratt. | **Mt. Vernon**	-

PUB FOOD

An Poitín Stil | **Timonium**	17
Boatyard B&G | **Annap**	16
Brewer's Alley | **Frederick**	17
☑ Clyde's | **Columbia**	18
Coburn's | **Canton**	20
Davis' Pub | **Annap**	18
Jennings | **Catonsville**	19
John Steven | **Fells Pt**	20
McCabe's | **Hampden**	20

SALVADORAN

El Trovador | **Fells Pt**	23

SANDWICHES

Attman's Deli | **E Balt**	24
Atwater's | **multi. loc.**	25
Au Bon Pain | **multi. loc.**	16
Chick & Ruth's | **Annap**	16
Stone Mill | **Brook'ville**	22

SEAFOOD

Aquatica | **Havre de Grace**	24
Bertha's | **Fells Pt**	19
Black Olive | **Fells Pt**	26
Blue Sea Grill | **D'town**	24
BlueStone | **Timonium**	21
Bo Brooks | **Canton**	17
Cantler's Inn | **Annap**	22
Carrol's Creek | **Annap**	22
Crab Claw | **E Shore**	20
Dutch's Daughter | **Frederick**	20
Faidley's | **D'town W**	25
Fisherman's Inn | **E Shore**	18
G&M | **Linthicum**	22
Harris Crab | **E Shore**	19
John Steven | **Fells Pt**	20
Kali's Court | **Fells Pt**	24
☑ Legal Sea Foods | **Inner Harbor**	20
L.P. Steamers | **Locust Pt**	21
Mama's/Half Shell | **Canton**	21
M & S Grill | **Inner Harbor**	18
☑ McCormick/Schmick | **Inner Harbor**	21
Mr. Bill's Terr. Inn | **Essex**	24
Narrows, The | **E Shore**	23
Obrycki's | **E Balt**	22
☑ Oceanaire | **Inner Harbor E**	24
O'Learys | **Annap**	26
Oregon Grille | **Hunt Valley**	25
Phillips | **multi. loc.**	15
Pisces | **Inner Harbor**	22
Robert Morris Inn | **E Shore**	21
NEW Robert Oliver | **D'town**	-
Rockfish, The | **Annap**	21
Severn Inn | **Annap**	16
Timbuktu | **Hanover**	19
Town Dock | **E Shore**	21
Trapeze | **Fulton**	-
Windows | **Inner Harbor**	19
Yellowfin | **Annap**	21
Zorba's B&G | **Gr'town**	22

SMALL PLATES

(See also Spanish tapas specialist)

AIDA Bistro | Italian | **Columbia**	23
Aqua Terra | Amer. | **Annap**	21
Brass Elephant | Amer. | **Mt. Vernon**	23
☑ Charleston | Amer. | **Inner Harbor E**	27
Gardel's | Eclectic | **Little Italy**	17
Harryman Hse. | Amer. | **Reist'town**	20
Iron Bridge Wine | Amer. | **Columbia**	25
Ixia | Amer. | **Mt. Vernon**	24

Jalapeños | Mex. | **Annap** 26

NEW Kyma | Med. | **Annap** -

Metropolitan | Amer. | **Annap** 23

Mezze | Med. | **Fells Pt** 24

Z Pazo | Med. | **Inner Harbor E** 23

Red Maple | Asian Fusion | **Mt. Vernon** 19

Sascha's 527 | Amer. | **Mt. Vernon** 21

Tapas Teatro | Eclectic | **D'town N** 22

NEW Three... | Amer. | **Hi'town** -

SOUP

Atwater's | **multi. loc.** 25

SPANISH

(* tapas specialist)

Cacique | **Frederick** 22

Isabella's* | **Frederick** 24

Jalapeños* | **Annap** 26

La Tasca* | **Inner Harbor** 16

NEW Nasu Blanca | **Locust Pt** -

Tio Pepe | **Mt. Vernon** 24

STEAKHOUSES

Z Capital Grille | **Inner Harbor** 25

Fleming's Steak | **Inner Harbor E** 24

Greystone Grill | **multi. loc.** 20

Jordan's | **Ellicott City** 23

Lewnes' Steak | **Annap** 26

M & S Grill | **Inner Harbor** 18

Z Morton's | **Inner Harbor** 25

Oregon Grille | **Hunt Valley** 25

NEW oZ Chophse. | **Fulton** -

Z Prime Rib | **D'town N** 27

Z Ruth's Chris | **multi. loc.** 24

Shula's | **D'town** 18

TEAROOMS

Finnerteas | **Hampden** 20

TEX-MEX

Austin Grill | **Canton** 16

THAI

Bân Thai | **D'town N** 21

Z Lemongrass | **Annap** 27

Little Spice | **Hanover** -

San Sushi/Thai | **Towson** 21

Thai | **York Rd Corr** 23

Thai Arroy | **S Balt** 23

Thai Landing | **Mt. Vernon** 24

TURKISH

NEW Cazbar | **D'town N** -

VEGETARIAN

(* vegan)

Great Sage* | **Clarksville** -

Zodiac* | **D'town N** 20

VIETNAMESE

An Loi | **Columbia** 25

Pho Dat Thanh | **Columbia** 23

subscribe to zagat.com

Locations

Includes restaurant names, cuisines and Food ratings. ⓩ indicates places with the highest ratings, popularity and importance.

Baltimore

BUSINESS DISTRICT/ CAMDEN YARDS/ CONVENTION CENTER/ DOWNTOWN/ INNER HARBOR

Au Bon Pain	*Bakery*	16
Babalu Grill	*Cuban*	20
Blue Sea Grill	*Seafood*	24
Bright. Orangerie	*Amer.*	23
ⓩ Capital Grille	*Steak*	25
ⓩ Cheesecake Fact.	*Amer.*	18
Chinatown Café	*Chinese*	22
Edo Sushi	*Jap.*	25
ⓩ Five Guys	*Hamburgers*	24
La Tasca	*Spanish*	16
ⓩ Legal Sea Foods	*Seafood*	20
M & S Grill	*Seafood/Steak*	18
ⓩ McCormick/Schmick	*Seafood*	21
ⓩ Morton's	*Steak*	25
ⓩ P.F. Chang's	*Chinese*	19
Phillips	*Seafood*	15
Pisces	*Seafood*	22
NEW Robert Oliver	*Seafood*	-
ⓩ Ruth's Chris	*Steak*	24
Shula's	*Steak*	18
Suzie's Soba	*Korean*	20
Windows	*Seafood*	19

CANTON

Austin Grill	*Tex-Mex*	16
Birches	*Amer.*	24
Bo Brooks	*Crab*	17
Coburn's	*Amer.*	20
Cosmopolitan B&G	*Amer.*	18
ⓩ Five Guys	*Hamburgers*	24
Helen's Garden	*Amer.*	23
NEW Jack's Bistro	*Eclectic*	-
Mama's/Half Shell	*Seafood*	21
Red Fish	*Amer.*	-
Tiburzi's	*Italian*	19

DOWNTOWN NORTH/ CHARLES ST./ MT. VERNON

Abacrombie	*Amer.*	26
Akbar	*Indian*	22
b	*Eclectic*	24
Bân Thai	*Thai*	21
Brass Elephant	*Amer.*	23
Brewer's Art	*Amer.*	21
NEW Cazbar	*Turkish*	-
City Cafe	*Amer.*	18
Copra	*Amer.*	22
Dukem	*Ethiopian*	23
ⓩ Five Guys	*Hamburgers*	24
ⓩ Helmand	*Afghan*	26
Iggies	*Pizza*	23
Ixia	*Amer.*	24
NEW Milton's Grill	*Amer./BBQ*	-
Minato	*Jap.*	-
Mughal Garden	*Indian*	22
Neo Viccino	*Amer.*	20
ⓩ Prime Rib	*Steak*	27
Red Maple	*Asian Fusion*	19
Saffron	*Eclectic*	-
Sammy's Tratt.	*Italian*	-
Sascha's 527	*Amer.*	21
Sotto Sopra	*Italian*	24
Tapas Teatro	*Eclectic/Med.*	22
Thai Landing	*Thai*	24
Tio Pepe	*Continental/Spanish*	24
XS	*Eclectic*	19
Zodiac	*Eclectic/Veg.*	20

DOWNTOWN WEST

Faidley's	*Seafood*	25
Maggie Moore's	*Amer./Irish*	19
Martick's	*French*	24

EAST BALTIMORE

Arcos	*Mex.*	19
Attman's Deli	*Deli*	24
Obrycki's	*Crab*	22
Salt	*Amer.*	-

FELLS POINT

Bertha's	*Seafood*	19
Black Olive	*Greek/Seafood*	26
Blue Moon Cafe	*Amer.*	25
El Trovador	*Mex./Salvadoran*	23
Henninger's	*Amer.*	25
Jimmy's	*Diner*	18
John Steven	*Seafood*	20
Kali's Court	*Med./Seafood*	24
Louisiana	*Creole*	24
Mezze	*Med.*	24
ⓩ Peter's Inn	*Amer.*	27
Pierpoint	*Amer.*	25
Red Star	*Amer.*	19
Timothy Dean	*Amer.*	23

TRUE	*Amer.*	23
Ze Mean Bean	*E Euro.*	22

HAMPDEN/ ROLAND PARK

Cafe Hon	*Diner*	15
NEW Dogwood	*Amer.*	–
Finnerteas	*Tea*	20
Golden West	*New Mex.*	21
Holy Frijoles	*Mex.*	20
McCabe's	*Pub*	20
Miss Shirley's	*Amer.*	23
Papermoon	*Diner*	17
☑ Petit Louis	*French*	24
NEW Rocket/Venus	*Eclectic*	–
Suzie's Soba	*Korean*	20

HIGHLANDTOWN/ GREEKTOWN

Chicken Rico	*Peruvian*	20
Ikaros	*Greek*	22
Matthew's Pizzeria	*Pizza*	25
☑ Samos	*Greek*	27
NEW Three...	*Amer.*	–
Zorba's B&G	*Greek*	22

HOMEWOOD

☑ Ambass. Din. Rm.	*Indian*	25
Brass. Tatin	*French*	23
Carlyle Club	*Lebanese*	24
Gertrude's	*Chesapeake*	22

INNER HARBOR EAST/ LITTLE ITALY

Aldo's	*Italian*	26
Amicci's	*Italian*	22
Boccaccio	*Italian*	25
Caesar's Den	*Italian*	22
☑ Charleston	*Amer.*	27
Chiapparelli's	*Italian*	19
Chiu's Sushi	*Jap.*	21
Ciao Bella	*Italian*	23
Da Mimmo	*Italian*	22
Della Notte	*Italian*	21
Fleming's Steak	*Steak*	24
Gardel's	*Eclectic*	17
Germano's	*Italian*	21
La Scala	*Italian*	24
La Tavola	*Italian*	25
☑ Lebanese Tav.	*Lebanese*	22
☑ Oceanaire	*Seafood*	24
☑ Pazo	*Med.*	23
Rocco's Capriccio	*Italian*	24
☑ Roy's	*Hawaiian*	26
Sabatino's	*Italian*	18

LOCUST POINT

Hull St. Blues	*Amer.*	20
L.P. Steamers	*Seafood*	21
NEW Nasu Blanca	*Jap./Spanish*	–
Pazza Luna	*Italian*	–
Wine Market	*Amer.*	23

MT. WASHINGTON

Crêpe du Jour	*French*	21

NORTH BALTIMORE/ YORK ROAD CORRIDOR

Atwater's	*Bakery/Soup*	25
Cafe Zen	*Chinese*	22
Pete's Grille	*Diner*	–
Taste	*Amer.*	20
Thai	*Thai*	23

SOUTH BALTIMORE

(Including Federal Hill)

Banjara	*Indian*	21
☑ Bicycle, The	*Eclectic*	–
Blue Agave	*Mex.*	22
Corks	*Amer.*	25
Matsuri	*Jap.*	24
Regi's	*Amer.*	19
NEW Rub	*BBQ*	–
SoBo Cafe	*Amer.*	24
Thai Arroy	*Thai*	23

Outer Baltimore

BROOKLANDVILLE

Stone Mill	*Bakery*	22

BWI/ELKRIDGE/ HANOVER/LINTHICUM

Elkridge Furnace	*Amer./French*	24
G&M	*Seafood*	22
Little Spice	*Thai*	–
Timbuktu	*Seafood*	19

CATONSVILLE

Jennings	*Pub Food*	19

CLARKSVILLE

Great Sage	*Veg.*	–

COLUMBIA

AIDA Bistro	*Italian*	23
Akbar	*Indian*	22
An Loi	*Viet.*	25
Café de Paris	*French*	23
☑ Clyde's	*Amer.*	18
Hunan Manor	*Chinese*	22

Iron Bridge Wine | *Amer.* 25
Jesse Wong's Asean | *Pan-Asian* 24
Jesse Wong's HK | *Chinese* 22
Kings Contrivance | *Continental* 23
La Madeleine | *French* 17
🅩 P.F. Chang's | *Chinese* 19
Pho Dat Thanh | *Viet.* 23
Sushi King | *Jap.* 24
🅩 Sushi Sono | *Jap.* 28

ELDERSBURG/ SYKESVILLE

Baldwin's Station | *Amer.* 20
Liberatore's | *Italian* 20

ELLICOTT CITY

Greystone Grill | *Amer.* 20
Jordan's | *Steak* 23
Oriental Manor | *Chinese* 20
🆕 Rumor Mill | *Asian Fusion* -
Shin Chon | *Korean* -
🅩 Tersiguel's | *French* 27

ESSEX/DUNDALK

Costas Inn | *Crab* 22
Mr. Bill's Terr. Inn | *Crab* 24

FULTON

🆕 oZ Chophse. | *Steak* -
Trapeze | *Amer./Seafood* -

GLEN BURNIE/ SEVERNA PARK

🆕 Cynthia's | *Amer.* -
Tratt. Alberto | *Italian* 26

HARFORD COUNTY

(Including White Marsh)
Broom's Bloom Dairy | *Ice Cream* 23
🅩 Five Guys | *Hamburgers* 24
Josef's Country | *Continental* 25
🆕 Open Door | *Amer.* -

HAVRE DE GRACE

Aquatica | *Seafood* 24
Laurrapin | *Amer.* -

HUNT VALLEY/NORTH BALTIMORE COUNTY

Friendly Farm | *Amer.* 21
Green Leaf | *Pan-Asian* 22
Greystone Grill | *Amer.* 20
Jesse Wong's Kit. | *Pan-Asian* 17
Manor Tav. | *Amer.* 16
Milton Inn | *Amer./Continental* 25
Oregon Grille | *Seafood/Steak* 25

LUTHERVILLE/ COCKEYSVILLE/ TIMONIUM

Andy Nelson's BBQ | *BBQ* -
An Poitín Stil | *Pub* 17
Bamboo Hse. | *Chinese* 19
BlueStone | *Seafood* 21
Christopher Daniel | *Amer.* 22
Edo Sushi | *Jap.* 25
JJ's Everyday | *Amer.* 19
Liberatore's | *Italian* 20
Peppermill | *Amer.* 18
San Sushi/Thai | *Jap.* 21
Szechuan Hse. | *Chinese* 24

NORTHEAST BALTIMORE/ PERRY HALL

🆕 Alabama BBQ | *BBQ* -
Big Bad Wolf BBQ | *BBQ* 25
Chameleon Cafe | *Amer.* 26
Liberatore's | *Italian* 20

OWINGS MILLS/ PIKESVILLE

David Chu's | *Chinese* 21
Edo Sushi | *Jap.* 25
Liberatore's | *Italian* 20
🅩 Linwoods | *Amer.* 26
🅩 Mari Luna | *Mex.* 27
Olive & Sesame | *Chinese/Jap.* 22
🅩 Ruth's Chris | *Steak* 24

REISTERSTOWN/ FINKSBURG

Harryman Hse. | *Amer.* 20
🆕 Michos | *Amer./Med.* -
Sonny Lee's | *Chinese/Jap.* 24

TOWSON

Atwater's | *Bakery/Soup* 25
Café Troia | *Italian* 22
Olive & Sesame | *Chinese/Jap.* 22
Orchard Mkt. | *Persian* 25
Paolo's | *Calif./Italian* 18
San Sushi/Thai | *Jap./Thai* 21
Sushi Hana | *Jap.* 23
Vin | *Amer.* -

WESTMINSTER

Baugher's | *Amer.* 18
Liberatore's | *Italian* 20
Paradiso/Pizzeria | *Italian* 22

WOODLAWN

🅩 Five Guys | *Hamburgers* 24

Frederick/Central Maryland

Restaurant	Cuisine	
Acacia Fusion	*Asian Fusion*	–
☑ Antrim 1844	*Amer./French*	27
Brewer's Alley	*Pub*	17
Cacique	*Mex./Spanish*	22
Dutch's Daughter	*Amer.*	20
G. Hunter's	*Amer.*	–
Hard Times Cafe	*Amer.*	19
Isabella's	*Spanish*	24
Mamma Lucia	*Italian*	19
Mealey's	*Amer.*	21
Monocacy Cross.	*Amer.*	–
Tasting Rm.	*Amer.*	25

Annapolis/Anne Arundel

Restaurant	Cuisine	
Aqua Terra	*Amer.*	21
Boatyard B&G	*Pub*	16
Café Normandie	*French*	20
Cantler's Inn	*Seafood*	22
Carrol's Creek	*Seafood*	22
Chick & Ruth's	*Deli*	16
Davis' Pub	*Pub*	18
Domenica's	*Italian*	25
☑ Five Guys	*Hamburgers*	24
Galway Bay	*Irish*	–
Harry Browne's	*Amer.*	22
Jalapeños	*Mex./Spanish*	26
☑ Joss Cafe/Sushi	*Jap.*	28
NEW Kyma	*Med.*	–
☑ Lebanese Tav.	*Lebanese*	22
☑ Lemongrass	*Thai*	27
Les Folies	*French*	26
Lewnes' Steak	*Steak*	26
Luna Blu	*Italian*	–
Main Ingredient	*Amer.*	22
Metropolitan	*Amer.*	23

Restaurant	Cuisine	
Northwoods	*Continental*	23
O'Learys	*Seafood*	26
NEW Osteria 177	*Amer./Italian*	–
Paul's Homewood	*Amer./Greek*	22
Phillips	*Seafood*	15
Piccola Roma	*Italian*	24
Red Hot & Blue	*BBQ*	19
Reynolds Tav.	*Eclectic*	21
Rockfish, The	*Amer.*	21
☑ Ruth's Chris	*Steak*	24
Sam's/Waterfront	*Amer.*	–
Severn Inn	*Amer.*	16
Sputnik Cafe	*Eclectic*	23
Treaty of Paris	*Amer.*	17
Tsunami	*Asian Fusion*	25
Wild Orchid	*Amer.*	24
Yellowfin	*Amer.*	21
Yin Yankee	*Asian Fusion*	24

Eastern Shore

Restaurant	Cuisine	
Bistro St. Michaels	*Amer.*	25
Ches. Chicken/Ribs	*BBQ*	–
Crab Claw	*Crab*	20
Fisherman's Inn	*Seafood*	18
Harris Crab	*Seafood*	19
Holly's	*Diner*	15
Inn at Easton	*Amer.*	26
Julia's	*Amer.*	26
NEW Local	*Amer.*	–
Mason's	*Amer.*	23
Narrows, The	*Seafood*	23
Out of the Fire	*Amer.*	23
Pope's Tav.	*Amer.*	–
Robert Morris Inn	*Seafood*	21
Scossa	*Italian*	22
Sherwood's Land.	*Amer.*	23
Town Dock	*Amer./Seafood*	21
208 Talbot	*Amer.*	–

Special Features

Listings cover the best in each category and include restaurant names, locations and Food ratings. Multi-location restaurants' features may vary by branch. ☑ indicates places with the highest ratings, popularity and importance.

BALTIMORE AREA

ADDITIONS

(Properties added since the last edition of the book)

Alabama BBQ | **NE Balt**	-
Cazbar | **D'town N**	-
Cynthia's | **Severna Pk**	-
Dogwood | **Hampden**	-
Jack's Bistro | **Canton**	-
Local | **E Shore**	-
Luna Blu | **Annap**	-
Michos | **Reist'town**	-
Milton's Grill | **D'town N**	-
Minato | **D'town N**	-
Nasu Blanca | **Locust Pt**	-
Open Door | **Bel Air**	-
Osteria 177 | **Annap**	-
oZ Chophse. | **Fulton**	-
Pope's Tav. | **E Shore**	-
Robert Oliver | **D'town**	-
Rocket/Venus | **Hampden**	-
Rub | **S Balt**	-
Rumor Mill | **Ellicott City**	-
Three... | **Hi'town**	-

BOAT DOCKING FACILITIES

Bo Brooks | **Canton**	17
Cantler's Inn | **Annap**	22
Crab Claw | **E Shore**	20
Fisherman's Inn | **E Shore**	18
Harris Crab | **E Shore**	19
Narrows, The | **E Shore**	23
Sam's/Waterfront | **Annap**	-
Severn Inn | **Annap**	16
Town Dock | **E Shore**	21
Yellowfin | **Annap**	21

BREAKFAST

(See also Hotel Dining)

Baugher's | **Westminster**	18
Blue Moon Cafe | **Fells Pt**	25
Cafe Hon | **Hampden**	15
Chick & Ruth's | **Annap**	16
City Cafe | **Mt. Vernon**	18
Coburn's | **Canton**	20
Golden West | **Hampden**	21
Holly's | **E Shore**	15
Jimmy's | **Fells Pt**	18
La Madeleine | **Columbia**	17
Main Ingredient | **Annap**	22

Miss Shirley's | **Roland Pk**	23
Papermoon | **Hampden**	17
Pete's Grille | **York Rd Corr**	-
Stone Mill | **Brook'ville**	22
XS | **Mt. Vernon**	19

BRUNCH

Abacrombie | **Mt. Vernon**	26
Acacia Fusion | **Frederick**	-
☑ Ambass. Din. Rm. | **Homewood**	25
b | **D'town N**	24
Bertha's | **Fells Pt**	19
Carrol's Creek | **Annap**	22
City Cafe | **Mt. Vernon**	18
☑ Clyde's | **Columbia**	18
Dutch's Daughter | **Frederick**	20
Gertrude's | **Homewood**	22
Harryman Hse. | **Reist'town**	20
Helen's Garden | **Canton**	23
Hull St. Blues | **Locust Pt**	20
Jesse Wong's Asean | **Columbia**	24
Main Ingredient | **Annap**	22
Orchard Mkt. | **Towson**	25
Pisces | **Inner Harbor**	22
Regi's | **Fed Hill**	19
Reynolds Tav. | **Annap**	21
Windows | **Inner Harbor**	19
Ze Mean Bean | **Fells Pt**	22

BUSINESS DINING

Boccaccio | **Little Italy**	25
Bright. Orangerie | **Inner Harbor**	23
☑ Capital Grille | **Inner Harbor**	25
☑ Charleston | **Inner Harbor E**	27
Dutch's Daughter | **Frederick**	20
Fleming's Steak | **Inner Harbor E**	24
Greystone Grill | **multi. loc.**	20
Harry Browne's | **Annap**	22
Lewnes' Steak | **Annap**	26
☑ Linwoods | **Owings Mills**	26
☑ Morton's | **Inner Harbor**	25
☑ Oceanaire | **Inner Harbor E**	24
NEW oZ Chophse. | **Fulton**	-
☑ Roy's | **Inner Harbor E**	26
☑ Ruth's Chris | **Inner Harbor**	24
Timbuktu | **Hanover**	19
Vin | **Towson**	-
Windows | **Inner Harbor**	19

SPECIAL FEATURES

BYO

Abacrombie	**Mt. Vernon**	26
Andy Nelson's BBQ	**Cockeysville**	-
Big Bad Wolf BBQ	**NE Balt**	25
NEW Dogwood	**Hampden**	-
Edo Sushi	**multi. loc.**	25
Green Leaf	**Hunt Valley**	22
Iggies	**D'town N**	23
Z Mari Luna	**Pikesville**	27
NEW Open Door	**Bel Air**	-
Orchard Mkt.	**Towson**	25
Z Samos	**Gr'town**	27
Sonny Lee's	**Reist'town**	24
Szechuan Hse.	**Lutherville**	24
Thai Arroy	**S Balt**	23

CATERING

NEW Alabama BBQ	**NE Balt**	-
Andy Nelson's BBQ	**Cockeysville**	-
Attman's Deli	**E Balt**	24
Big Bad Wolf BBQ	**NE Balt**	25
Brass Elephant	**Mt. Vernon**	23
Cafe Hon	**Hampden**	15
Main Ingredient	**Annap**	22
Paul's Homewood	**Annap**	22
Z Samos	**Gr'town**	27
Sascha's 527	**Mt. Vernon**	21
Wild Orchid	**Annap**	24

CHILD-FRIENDLY

(Alternatives to the usual fast-food places; * children's menu available)

b*	**D'town N**	24
Baugher's*	**Westminster**	18
Cafe Hon*	**Hampden**	15
Chick & Ruth's*	**Annap**	16
Friendly Farm*	**Upperco**	21
Great Sage	**Clarksville**	-
Holly's*	**E Shore**	15
NEW Milton's Grill	**D'town N**	-
Z P.F. Chang's	**Columbia**	19
Z Samos	**Gr'town**	27

DESSERT

b	**D'town N**	24
Baugher's	**Westminster**	18
Cafe Hon	**Hampden**	15
Z Cheesecake Fact.	**Inner Harbor**	18
Chick & Ruth's	**Annap**	16
City Cafe	**Mt. Vernon**	18
Crêpe du Jour	**Mt. Wash**	21
Holly's	**E Shore**	15
McCabe's	**Hampden**	20
Paul's Homewood	**Annap**	22
Stone Mill	**Brook'ville**	22

ENTERTAINMENT

(Call for days and times of performances)

AIDA Bistro	jazz	**Columbia**	23
An Poitín Stil	bands	**Timonium**	17
Bamboo Hse.	dancing	**Cockeysville**	19
Bertha's	blues/jazz	**Fells Pt**	19
Boatyard B&G	acoustic	**Annap**	16
Coburn's	DJ	**Canton**	20
Domenica's	varies	**Annap**	25
Gardel's	salsa/tango	**Little Italy**	17
Gertrude's	jazz	**Homewood**	22
Jesse Wong's Asean	jazz/piano	**Columbia**	24
Maggie Moore's	Irish	**D'town W**	19
Z Prime Rib	jazz	**D'town N**	27
Red Fish	varies	**Canton**	-
Red Maple	DJ	**Mt. Vernon**	19
Reynolds Tav.	bands	**Annap**	21
Sotto Sopra	opera	**Mt. Vernon**	24
Ze Mean Bean	jazz	**Fells Pt**	22

FIREPLACES

Z Ambass. Din. Rm.	**Homewood**	25
Z Antrim 1844	**Taneytown**	27
Brass. Tatin	**Homewood**	23
Brewer's Art	**Mt. Vernon**	21
Café Normandie	**Annap**	20
Dutch's Daughter	**Frederick**	20
Elkridge Furnace	**Elkridge**	24
Fisherman's Inn	**E Shore**	18
Harry Browne's	**Annap**	22
Harryman Hse.	**Reist'town**	20
Hull St. Blues	**Locust Pt**	20
Inn at Easton	**E Shore**	26
Manor Tav.	**Monkton**	16
Milton Inn	**Sparks**	25
NEW Milton's Grill	**D'town N**	-
Oregon Grille	**Hunt Valley**	25
Paradiso/Pizzeria	**Westminster**	22
Z Petit Louis	**Roland Pk**	24
Regi's	**Fed Hill**	19
Robert Morris Inn	**E Shore**	21
Rockfish, The	**Annap**	21
Z Ruth's Chris	**multi. loc.**	24
Sherwood's Land.	**E Shore**	23
Treaty of Paris	**Annap**	17
Vin	**Towson**	-
Wild Orchid	**Annap**	24
Ze Mean Bean	**Fells Pt**	22

HISTORIC PLACES

(Year opened; * building)

1710	Robert Morris Inn*	**E Shore**	21
1740	Milton Inn*	**Sparks**	25

1744 | Elkridge Furnace* | **Elkridge** 24
1747 | Reynolds Tav.* | **Annap** 21
1772 | Faidley's* | **D'town W** 25
1773 | Treaty of Paris* | **Annap** 17
1790 | Inn at Easton* | **E Shore** 26
1793 | Mealey's* | **New Mkt** 21
1806 | TRUE* | **Fells Pt** 23
1816 | Sherwood's Land.* | **E Shore** 23
1836 | Rumor Mill* | **Ellicott City** -
1844 | Antrim 1844* | **Taneytown** 27
1847 | Maggie Moore's* | **D'town W** 19
1850 | Martick's* | **D'town W** 24
1864 | Louisiana* | **Fells Pt** 24
1869 | Gardel's* | **Little Italy** 17
1870 | Julia's* | **E Shore** 26
1872 | Brewer's Alley* | **Frederick** 17
1874 | Coburn's* | **Canton** 20
1883 | Baldwin's Station* | **Sykesville** 20
1889 | Hull St. Blues* | **Locust Pt** 20
1890 | Lewnes' Steak* | **Annap** 26
1890 | Mason's* | **E Shore** 23
1890 | Metropolitan* | **Annap** 23
1890 | Petit Louis* | **Roland Pk** 24
1900 | Kings Contrivance* | **Columbia** 23
1900 | Luna Blu* | **Annap** -
1906 | Brewer's Art* | **Mt. Vernon** 21
1906 | Wild Orchid* | **Annap** 24
1920 | Josef's Country* | **Fallston** 25
1925 | Attman's Deli | **E Balt** 24
1930 | Fisherman's Inn | **E Shore** 18
1935 | Pete's Grille | **York Rd Corr** -
1940 | Chiapparelli's | **Little Italy** 19
1943 | Matthew's Pizzeria | **Hi'town** 25
1944 | Obrycki's | **E Balt** 22
1947 | Jimmy's | **Fells Pt** 18
1948 | Baugher's | **Westminster** 18
1949 | Paul's Homewood | **Annap** 22
1955 | Holly's | **E Shore** 15
1955 | Sabatino's | **Little Italy** 18

HOTEL DINING

Abacrombie
  Abacrombie | **Mt. Vernon** 26
Admiral Fell Inn
  TRUE | **Fells Pt** 23
Carlyle Inn & Suites
  Carlyle Club | **Homewood** 24
Hyatt Regency
  Pisces | **Inner Harbor** 22
Inn at Easton
  Inn at Easton | **E Shore** 26

Inn at Perry Cabin
  Sherwood's Land. | **E Shore** 23
InterContinental Harbor Court
  Bright. Orangerie | **Inner Harbor** 23
Maryland Inn
  Treaty of Paris | **Annap** 17
Oxford Inn
  Pope's Tav. | **E Shore** -
Pier 5 Hotel
  Z McCormick/Schmick | **Inner Harbor** 21
  Z Ruth's Chris | **Inner Harbor** 24
Renaissance Harborplace
  Windows | **Inner Harbor** 19
Sheraton Baltimore
  Shula's | **D'town** 18
Sheraton Inner Harbor
  Z Morton's | **Inner Harbor** 25
Tidewater Inn
  NEW Local | **E Shore** -

LATE DINING

(Weekday closing hour)
Amicci's | 12 AM | **Little Italy** 22
An Poitín Stil | 12 AM | **Timonium** 17
Bamboo Hse. | 12 AM | **Cockeysville** 19
Boatyard B&G | 12 AM | **Annap** 16
Brewer's Art | 2 AM | **Mt. Vernon** 21
NEW Cazbar | 12 AM | **D'town N** -
Costas Inn | 1 AM | **Dundalk** 22
Hard Times Cafe | varies | **Frederick** 19
Holy Frijoles | 1 AM | **Hampden** 20
NEW Jack's Bistro | 1 AM | **Canton** -
Jennings | 12:30 AM | **Catonsville** 19
Maggie Moore's | 12 AM | **D'town W** 19
Mezze | 12 AM | **Fells Pt** 24
Oriental Manor | 12 AM | **Ellicott City** 20
Papermoon | 24 hrs. | **Hampden** 17
Red Maple | 12 AM | **Mt. Vernon** 19
Sabatino's | 12 AM | **Little Italy** 18
Tsunami | 1 AM | **Annap** 25
XS | varies | **Mt. Vernon** 19
Zorba's B&G | 2 AM | **Gr'town** 22

LOCAL FAVORITES

Cafe Hon | **Hampden** 15
Chameleon Cafe | **NE Balt** 26
City Cafe | **Mt. Vernon** 18
Costas Inn | **Dundalk** 22
Faidley's | **D'town W** 25
Helen's Garden | **Canton** 23
Z Helmand | **Mt. Vernon** 26
Jennings | **Catonsville** 19
Miss Shirley's | **Roland Pk** 23

Mr. Bill's Terr. Inn | **Essex**	24
Narrows, The | **E Shore**	23
Paul's Homewood | **Annap**	22
Peppermill | **Lutherville**	18
☑ Samos | **Gr'town**	27
Szechuan Hse. | **Lutherville**	24
Wine Market | **Locust Pt**	23

MEET FOR A DRINK

Acacia Fusion | **Frederick**	-
AIDA Bistro | **Columbia**	23
Brass Elephant | **Mt. Vernon**	23
Brewer's Art | **Mt. Vernon**	21
Café de Paris | **Columbia**	23
Cafe Hon | **Hampden**	15
City Cafe | **Mt. Vernon**	18
Galway Bay | **Annap**	-
Helen's Garden | **Canton**	23
Henninger's | **Fells Pt**	25
Iron Bridge Wine | **Columbia**	25
John Steven | **Fells Pt**	20
Lewnes' Steak | **Annap**	26
Manor Tav. | **Monkton**	16
Out of the Fire | **E Shore**	23
☑ Pazo | **Inner Harbor E**	23
Pazza Luna | **Locust Pt**	-
Red Maple | **Mt. Vernon**	19
NEW Rocket/Venus | **Hampden**	-
Tasting Rm. | **Frederick**	25
NEW Three... | **Hi'town**	-
Vin | **Towson**	-
Wine Market | **Locust Pt**	23

OFFBEAT

Bertha's | **Fells Pt**	19
Blue Moon Cafe | **Fells Pt**	25
Brewer's Art | **Mt. Vernon**	21
Cafe Hon | **Hampden**	15
Chick & Ruth's | **Annap**	16
City Cafe | **Mt. Vernon**	18
Golden West | **Hampden**	21
Martick's | **D'town W**	24
Papermoon | **Hampden**	17
☑ Peter's Inn | **Fells Pt**	27
SoBo Cafe | **S Balt**	24
Sputnik Cafe | **Annap**	23
Yin Yankee | **Annap**	24
Zodiac | **D'town N**	20

OUTDOOR DINING

(G=garden; P=patio; S=sidewalk; T=terrace)

☑ Ambass. Din. Rm. | G | **Homewood**	25
Arcos | P | **E Balt**	19
Austin Grill | S | **Canton**	16

b | S | **D'town N**	24
Baldwin's Station | T | **Sykesville**	20
Birches | S | **Canton**	24
Bo Brooks | T | **Canton**	17
Cantler's Inn | T | **Annap**	22
Carlyle Club | P | **Homewood**	24
Carrol's Creek | P | **Annap**	22
Chameleon Cafe | S | **NE Balt**	26
City Cafe | S | **Mt. Vernon**	18
Crab Claw | P | **E Shore**	20
Crêpe du Jour | P, S | **Mt. Wash**	21
Gertrude's | G | **Homewood**	22
G. Hunter's | P | **Frederick**	-
Harris Crab | T | **E Shore**	19
Helen's Garden | P | **Canton**	23
Jesse Wong's HK | S | **Columbia**	22
John Steven | P, S | **Fells Pt**	20
Mason's | G | **E Shore**	23
Monocacy Cross. | P | **Frederick**	-
Narrows, The | T | **E Shore**	23
Paolo's | S | **Towson**	18
☑ Peter's Inn | S | **Fells Pt**	27
Red Fish | S | **Canton**	-
Reynolds Tav. | P | **Annap**	21
Sam's/Waterfront | P | **Annap**	-
Sherwood's Land. | P | **E Shore**	23
Stone Mill | P | **Brook'ville**	22
Suzie's Soba | P | **Hampden**	20
Tapas Teatro | S | **D'town N**	22
Town Dock | P | **E Shore**	21
Wild Orchid | P | **Annap**	24
Wine Market | P | **Locust Pt**	23
Yin Yankee | S | **Annap**	24

PEOPLE-WATCHING

Cafe Hon | **Hampden**	15
City Cafe | **Mt. Vernon**	18
Faidley's | **D'town W**	25
Gardel's | **Little Italy**	17
Harry Browne's | **Annap**	22
Jimmy's | **Fells Pt**	18
Kali's Court | **Fells Pt**	24
Mezze | **Fells Pt**	24
Mr. Bill's Terr. Inn | **Essex**	24
Papermoon | **Hampden**	17
☑ Pazo | **Inner Harbor E**	23
Red Maple | **Mt. Vernon**	19
Sabatino's | **Little Italy**	18
Tsunami | **Annap**	25

POWER SCENES

Boccaccio | **Little Italy**	25
☑ Capital Grille | **Inner Harbor**	25
☑ Charleston | **Inner Harbor E**	27
Harry Browne's | **Annap**	22
Lewnes' Steak | **Annap**	26

⧉ Linwoods | **Owings Mills**	26
⧉ Prime Rib | **D'town N**	27
Windows | **Inner Harbor**	19

PRIVATE ROOMS

(Restaurants charge less at off times; call for capacity)

⧉ Antrim 1844 | **Taneytown**	27
Bamboo Hse. | **Cockeysville**	19
Cafe Hon | **Hampden**	15
⧉ Charleston | **Inner Harbor E**	27
⧉ Clyde's | **Columbia**	18
Copra | **D'town N**	22
Dutch's Daughter | **Frederick**	20
Elkridge Furnace | **Elkridge**	24
Fleming's Steak | **Inner Harbor E**	24
Harry Browne's | **Annap**	22
Harryman Hse. | **Reist'town**	20
Kings Contrivance | **Columbia**	23
Lewnes' Steak | **Annap**	26
NEW Local | **E Shore**	-
Milton Inn | **Sparks**	25
⧉ Morton's | **Inner Harbor**	25
O'Learys | **Annap**	26
Oregon Grille | **Hunt Valley**	25
⧉ Pazo | **Inner Harbor E**	23
Sabatino's | **Little Italy**	18
⧉ Tersiguel's | **Ellicott City**	27
Trapeze | **Fulton**	-
Vin | **Towson**	-

PRIX FIXE MENUS

(Call for prices and times)

⧉ Antrim 1844 | **Taneytown**	27
Café de Paris | **Columbia**	23
Café Troia | **Towson**	22
Jesse Wong's Kit. | **Hunt Valley**	17
Luna Blu | **Annap**	-
Milton Inn | **Sparks**	25
Northwoods | **Annap**	23
⧉ Petit Louis | **Roland Pk**	24
⧉ Tersiguel's | **Ellicott City**	27
Wild Orchid | **Annap**	24

QUIET CONVERSATION

Abacrombie | **Mt. Vernon**	26
Acacia Fusion | **Frederick**	-
⧉ Ambass. Din. Rm. | **Homewood**	25
Bân Thai | **D'town N**	21
NEW Cynthia's | **Severna Pk**	-
Great Sage | **Clarksville**	-
Jordan's | **Ellicott City**	23
⧉ Linwoods | **Owings Mills**	26
Little Spice | **Hanover**	-
Paul's Homewood | **Annap**	22

Thai Arroy | **S Balt**	23
Wild Orchid | **Annap**	24

ROMANTIC PLACES

Acacia Fusion | **Frederick**	-
⧉ Ambass. Din. Rm. | **Homewood**	25
Amicci's | **Little Italy**	22
⧉ Antrim 1844 | **Taneytown**	27
⧉ Charleston | **Inner Harbor E**	27
Corks | **S Balt**	25
Da Mimmo | **Little Italy**	22
Helen's Garden | **Canton**	23
Jordan's | **Ellicott City**	23
⧉ Linwoods | **Owings Mills**	26
Milton Inn | **Sparks**	25
Paul's Homewood | **Annap**	22
⧉ Pazo | **Inner Harbor E**	23
Pazza Luna | **Locust Pt**	-
⧉ Petit Louis | **Roland Pk**	24
⧉ Samos | **Gr'town**	27
⧉ Tersiguel's | **Ellicott City**	27
Thai Arroy | **S Balt**	23

SENIOR APPEAL

Café Hon | **Hampden**	15
⧉ Capital Grille | **Inner Harbor**	25
Josef's Country | **Fallston**	25
Liberatore's | **multi. loc.**	20
Peppermill | **Lutherville**	18
⧉ Prime Rib | **D'town N**	27
Tio Pepe | **Mt. Vernon**	24

SINGLES SCENES

Brewer's Art | **Mt. Vernon**	21
Cosmopolitan B&G | **Canton**	18
Gardel's | **Little Italy**	17
Liberatore's | **multi. loc.**	20
⧉ Pazo | **Inner Harbor E**	23
Red Maple | **Mt. Vernon**	19
Tasting Rm. | **Frederick**	25
Tsunami | **Annap**	25

SLEEPERS

(Good to excellent food, but little known)

Aquatica | **Havre de Grace**	24
Broom's Bloom Dairy | **Bel Air**	23
Domenica's | **Annap**	25
Green Leaf | **Hunt Valley**	22
Iggies | **D'town N**	23
Josef's Country | **Fallston**	25
Julia's | **E Shore**	26
Mr. Bill's Terr. Inn | **Essex**	24
Paradiso/Pizzeria | **Westminster**	22
Scossa | **E Shore**	22
TRUE | **Fells Pt**	23

BALTIMORE AREA

SPECIAL FEATURES

TEA SERVICE

Bertha's | **Fells Pt**	19
Bright. Orangerie | **Inner Harbor**	23
Finnerteas | **Hampden**	20
Reynolds Tav. | **Annap**	21
Sherwood's Land. | **E Shore**	23

TRENDY

Arcos | **E Balt**	19
Brewer's Art | **Mt. Vernon**	21
NEW Dogwood | **Hampden**	-
NEW Jack's Bistro | **Canton**	-
☑ Lemongrass | **Annap**	27
☑ Mari Luna | **Pikesville**	27
Minato | **D'town N**	-
☑ Pazo | **Inner Harbor E**	23
Red Maple | **Mt. Vernon**	19
NEW Rocket/Venus | **Hampden**	-
Salt | **E Balt**	-
Tasting Rm. | **Frederick**	25
Tsunami | **Annap**	25
Wine Market | **Locust Pt**	23

VALET PARKING

Aldo's | **Little Italy**	26
☑ Ambass. Din. Rm. | **Homewood**	25
Babalu Grill | **Inner Harbor**	20
☑ Bicycle, The | **S Balt**	-
Black Olive | **Fells Pt**	26
Blue Sea Grill | **D'town**	24
Bo Brooks | **Canton**	17
Boccaccio | **Little Italy**	25
Brass Elephant | **Mt. Vernon**	23
Bright. Orangerie | **Inner Harbor**	23
Caesar's Den | **Little Italy**	22
Café Troia | **Towson**	22
☑ Capital Grille | **Inner Harbor**	25
Carlyle Club | **Homewood**	24
☑ Charleston | **Inner Harbor E**	27
☑ Cheesecake Fact. | **Inner Harbor**	18
Chiapparelli's | **Little Italy**	19
Ciao Bella | **Little Italy**	23
Da Mimmo | **Little Italy**	22
Edo Sushi | **Inner Harbor**	25
Fleming's Steak | **Inner Harbor E**	24
Gardel's | **Little Italy**	17
Germano's | **Little Italy**	21
Kali's Court | **Fells Pt**	24
La Scala | **Little Italy**	24
La Tavola | **Little Italy**	25
Louisiana | **Fells Pt**	24
☑ McCormick/Schmick | **Inner Harbor**	21
Mezze | **Fells Pt**	24

☑ Morton's | **Inner Harbor**	25
Neo Viccino | **Mt. Vernon**	20
☑ Oceanaire | **Inner Harbor E**	24
☑ Pazo | **Inner Harbor E**	23
Pisces | **Inner Harbor**	22
☑ Prime Rib | **D'town N**	27
Rocco's Capriccio | **Little Italy**	24
☑ Roy's | **Inner Harbor E**	26
☑ Ruth's Chris | **multi. loc.**	24
Sabatino's | **Little Italy**	18
Shula's | **D'town**	18
Sotto Sopra | **Mt. Vernon**	24
Taste | **N Balt**	20
TRUE | **Fells Pt**	23
Vin | **Towson**	-
Windows | **Inner Harbor**	19
XS | **Mt. Vernon**	19
Yellowfin | **Annap**	21

VIEWS

(See also Waterside)

☑ Antrim 1844 | **Taneytown**	27
Bright. Orangerie | **Inner Harbor**	23
Broom's Bloom Dairy | **Bel Air**	23
Della Notte | **Little Italy**	21
Friendly Farm | **Upperco**	21
Gertrude's | **Homewood**	22
G. Hunter's | **Frederick**	-
Harry Browne's | **Annap**	22
Iron Bridge Wine | **Columbia**	25
L.P. Steamers | **Locust Pt**	21
Pisces | **Inner Harbor**	22
Pope's Tav. | **E Shore**	-
Windows | **Inner Harbor**	19

VISITORS ON EXPENSE ACCOUNT

☑ Bicycle, The | **S Balt**	-
Black Olive | **Fells Pt**	26
Boccaccio | **Little Italy**	25
☑ Capital Grille | **Inner Harbor**	25
☑ Charleston | **Inner Harbor E**	27
Corks | **S Balt**	25
NEW Cynthia's | **Severna Pk**	-
Da Mimmo | **Little Italy**	22
Domenica's | **Annap**	25
Fleming's Steak | **Inner Harbor E**	24
G. Hunter's | **Frederick**	-
Greystone Grill | **multi. loc.**	20
Harry Browne's | **Annap**	22
Inn at Easton | **E Shore**	26
Jordan's | **Ellicott City**	23
Les Folies | **Annap**	26
Lewnes' Steak | **Annap**	26
☑ Linwoods | **Owings Mills**	26
Milton Inn | **Sparks**	25

☑ Morton's | **Inner Harbor**	25
☑ Oceanaire | **Inner Harbor** E	24
O'Learys | **Annap**	26
Oregon Grille | **Hunt Valley**	25
NEW oZ Chophse. | **Fulton**	-
☑ Petit Louis | **Roland Pk**	24
Pisces | **Inner Harbor**	22
☑ Prime Rib | **D'town N**	27
☑ Roy's | **Inner Harbor** E	26
☑ Ruth's Chris | **Inner Harbor**	24
Sherwood's Land. | **E Shore**	23
Shula's | **D'town**	18
☑ Tersiguel's | **Ellicott City**	27

WATERSIDE

Baldwin's Station | **Sykesville**	20
Bo Brooks | **Canton**	17
Cantler's Inn | **Annap**	22
Carrol's Creek | **Annap**	22
☑ Charleston | **Inner Harbor** E	27
☑ Cheesecake Fact. | **Inner Harbor**	18
☑ Clyde's | **Columbia**	18
Crab Claw | **E Shore**	20
Davis' Pub | **Annap**	18
Fisherman's Inn | **E Shore**	18
Harris Crab | **E Shore**	19
Jesse Wong's HK | **Columbia**	22
M & S Grill | **Inner Harbor**	18
☑ McCormick/Schmick | **Inner Harbor**	21
Narrows, The | **E Shore**	23
Phillips | **multi. loc.**	15
Robert Morris Inn | **E Shore**	21
Sam's/Waterfront | **Annap**	-
Severn Inn | **Annap**	16
Sherwood's Land. | **E Shore**	23
Town Dock | **E Shore**	21
Yellowfin | **Annap**	21
Yin Yankee | **Annap**	24

WINNING WINE LISTS

☑ Antrim 1844 | **Taneytown**	27
Café de Paris | **Columbia**	23
☑ Capital Grille | **Inner Harbor**	25
☑ Charleston | **Inner Harbor** E	27
Corks | **S Balt**	25
Della Notte | **Little Italy**	21
Fleming's Steak | **Inner Harbor** E	24
Helen's Garden | **Canton**	23
Iron Bridge Wine | **Columbia**	25
Oregon Grille | **Hunt Valley**	25
Out of the Fire | **E Shore**	23
☑ Pazo | **Inner Harbor** E	23
☑ Petit Louis | **Roland Pk**	24
Tasting Rm. | **Frederick**	25
☑ Tersiguel's | **Ellicott City**	27
208 Talbot | **E Shore**	-
Vin | **Towson**	-
Wine Market | **Locust Pt**	23

WORTH A TRIP

Annapolis	
Cantler's Inn	22
☑ Joss Cafe/Sushi	28
Bel Air	
Broom's Bloom Dairy	23
Centreville	
Julia's	26
Dundalk	
Costas Inn	22
Essex	
Mr. Bill's Terr. Inn	24
Grasonville	
Harris Crab	19
Narrows, The	23
Oxford	
Pope's Tav.	-
Taneytown	
☑ Antrim 1844	27
Westminster	
Baugher's	18

Wine Vintage Chart

This chart, based on our 0 to 30 scale, is designed to help you select wine. The ratings (by **Howard Stravitz,** a law professor at the University of South Carolina) reflect the vintage quality and the wine's readiness to drink. We exclude the 1987, 1991–1993 vintages because they are not that good. A dash indicates the wine is either past its peak or too young to rate.

Whites	86	88	89	90	94	95	96	97	98	99	00	01	02	03	04	05
French:																
Alsace	–	–	26	26	25	24	24	23	26	24	26	27	25	22	24	25
Burgundy	25	–	23	22	–	28	27	24	23	26	25	24	27	23	25	26
Loire Valley	–	–	–	–	–	–	–	–	–	–	24	25	26	23	24	25
Champagne	25	24	26	29	–	26	27	24	23	24	24	22	26	–	–	–
Sauternes	28	29	25	28	–	21	23	25	23	24	24	28	25	26	21	26
California:																
Chardonnay	–	–	–	–	–	–	–	–	–	24	23	26	26	27	28	29
Sauvignon Blanc	–	–	–	–	–	–	–	–	–	–	–	27	28	26	27	26
Austrian:																
Grüner Velt./ Riesling	–	–	–	–	25	21	28	28	27	22	23	24	26	26	26	
German:	–	25	26	27	24	23	26	25	26	23	21	29	27	25	26	26

Reds	86	88	89	90	94	95	96	97	98	99	00	01	02	03	04	05
French:																
Bordeaux	25	23	25	29	22	26	25	23	25	24	29	26	24	25	23	27
Burgundy	–	–	24	26	–	26	27	26	22	27	22	24	27	24	24	25
Rhône	–	26	28	28	24	26	22	24	27	26	27	26	–	25	24	–
Beaujolais	–	–	–	–	–	–	–	–	–	–	24	–	23	27	23	28
California:																
Cab./Merlot	–	–	–	28	29	27	25	28	23	26	22	27	26	25	24	24
Pinot Noir	–	–	–	–	–	–	–	24	23	24	23	27	28	26	23	–
Zinfandel	–	–	–	–	–	–	–	–	–	–	–	25	23	27	22	–
Oregon:																
Pinot Noir	–	–	–	–	–	–	–	–	–	–	–	26	27	24	25	–
Italian:																
Tuscany	–	–	–	25	22	24	20	29	24	27	24	26	20	–	–	–
Piedmont	–	–	27	27	–	23	26	27	26	25	28	27	20	–	–	–
Spanish:																
Rioja	–	–	–	–	26	26	24	25	22	25	24	27	20	24	25	–
Ribera del Duero/Priorat	–	–	–	–	26	26	27	25	24	25	24	27	20	24	26	–
Australian:																
Shiraz/Cab.	–	–	–	–	24	26	23	26	28	24	24	27	27	25	26	–

subscribe to zagat.com

ON THE GO.
IN THE KNOW.

ZAGAT TO GO℠

Unlimited access
to Zagat dining &
travel content
in 65 major cities.

Search and browse
by ratings, cuisines,
special features
and Top Lists.

For BlackBerry,® Palm,®
Windows Mobile®
and mobile phones.

Get it now at **mobile.zagat.com**
or text* **ZAGAT** to **78247**

*Standard text rates apply. Check with your carrier or terms of your wireless
plan for details.